Twentieth Century Weekly Community Newspapers in the United States

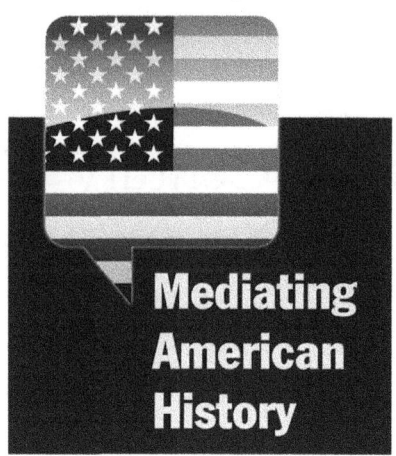

Kimberly Wilmot Voss
Series Editor

Vol. 22

Beth Garfrerick

Twentieth Century Weekly Community Newspapers in the United States

PETER LANG
New York · Berlin · Bruxelles · Chennai · Lausanne · Oxford

Library of Congress Cataloging-in-Publication Data

Names: Garfrerick, Beth, author.
Title: Twentieth century weekly community newspapers in the United States /
Beth Garfrerick.
Description: New York: Peter Lang, 2024. |
Series: Mediating American history; vol. 22
ISSN 2331-0588 (print) | ISSN 2166-6474 (online)
Includes bibliographical references and index.
Identifiers: LCCN 2023040575 (print) | LCCN 2023040576 (ebook) |
ISBN 9781433197659 (paperback) | ISBN 9781433197642 (epub) |
ISBN 9781433197635 (pdf)
Subjects: LCSH: Community newspapers—United States—History—20th century. |
Newspaper publishing—United States—History—20th century. |
Publishers and publishing—United States—History—20th century.
Classification: LCC PN4888.C594 G37 2024 (print) | LCC PN4888.C594
(ebook) | DDC 071/.3—dc23/eng/20220511
LC record available at https://lccn.loc.gov/2023040575
LC ebook record available at https://lccn.loc.gov/2023040576
DOI 10.3726/b21315

Bibliographic information published by the Deutsche Nationalbibliothek.
The German National Library lists this publication in the German
National Bibliography; detailed bibliographic data is available
on the Internet at http://dnb.d-nb.de.

Cover design by Peter Lang Group AG

ISSN 2331-0588 (print)
ISSN 2166-6474 (online)
ISBN 9781433197659 (paperback)
ISBN 9781433197635 (ebook)
ISBN 9781433197642 (epub)
DOI 10.3726/b21315

Readers are advised that this book contains quotations from historical primary sources that use language that may be considered offensive.

© 2024 Peter Lang Group AG, Lausanne
Published by Peter Lang Publishing Inc., New York, USA
info@peterlang.com - www.peterlang.com

All rights reserved.
All parts of this publication are protected by copyright.
Any utilization outside the strict limits of the copyright law, without the permission of the publisher, is forbidden and liable to prosecution.
This applies in particular to reproductions, translations, microfilming, and storage and processing in electronic retrieval systems.

This publication has been peer reviewed.

To Bob, Andrew, Adam, and Aaron

CONTENTS

Abstract		ix
Acknowledgments		xi
Introduction		1
Chapter 1	The Early 1900s: Consistency in Content, Appearance, and Style	17
Chapter 2	The 1910s: Propaganda, Publicity, Paper and Postal Rates, and Patriotism	43
Chapter 3	The 1920s: New Competition, Influence, and Commercial Success	73
Chapter 4	The 1930s: Boosterism and Business Survival	99

Chapter 5 The 1940s: Patriotism, Production, Professionalism, and the Postwar Period	127
Chapter 6 The 1950s: Becoming Localized in News, Centralized in Operations	163
Chapter 7 The 1960s: A Time to Rethink, Redefine, Recruit, and Regionalize	199
Chapter 8 The 1970s: Careers, Content, Consumers, Consolidations, and Computerization	239
Chapter 9 The 1980s: Technology vs. Technique; Corporate-owned vs. Community-owned; and Economics vs. Enterprise	277
Chapter 10 The 1990s: Localism in Ownership and Content; the Wal-Mart Factor; Weekly/Worker Competition; and a 24-Hour News Cycle	309
Chapter 11 A Century of Changes and Challenges: Community Weeklies Come Full Circle	337
Index	347

ABSTRACT

This study is an examination of community weekly newspapers in the United States during the twentieth century. In this work, the weekly "community" newspaper is defined as a newspaper operating in small towns and rural areas that placed an emphasis on local news. This study analyzes the nature of the weekly community newspaper and how it reflected American society throughout the twentieth century.

Despite all of the problems that faced the weekly newspaper industry throughout its long and proud history, the constants that remained were survival tactics in terms of reactive versus proactive responses to content, commercial, and professional concerns. Several times throughout the decades an obituary had been written for community weeklies. But they always found a way to fight back and happen upon a means, a method, or a message that resonated with audiences and advertisers enough so as to allow them to keep their doors open for another business day.

Community weeklies told the story of average American daily lives more thoroughly and in a more personal manner than the big-city dailies. In essence, the weekly publisher-editor served as author of his community's life story.

ACKNOWLEDGMENTS

I am extremely grateful to Butler Cain, Ph.D., and the late Jim Martin, Ph.D., for reviewing my book and offering helpful suggestions and edits. The publication of this work would not have come to fruition without the assistance of Madeleine Liseblad, Ph.D., who ushered me through the book proposal process. And finally, a special note of gratitude to my academic adviser and mentor, Wm. David Sloan, Ph.D., for instilling in me a love and appreciation for media history.

INTRODUCTION

Historical works on American journalism have given little attention to weekly community newspapers after the period when most newspapers in this country fell into that publication category. Despite the rapid rise of the daily metropolitan newspaper in the early twentieth century, weekly community newspapers continued, although many historians viewed them as insignificant and hard to label. Critics considered weekly newspapers, also referred to as "grassroots journalism," the "country press," the "rural press," or the "community press," as nothing more than smaller, low-quality versions of their larger daily counterparts. The terms "weekly," "community," "country," "rural," and "grassroots" are used interchangeably throughout this work to describe the small-town community weekly newspapers referred to in this study.

Perhaps the problem comes in defining a weekly community newspaper. An obvious category would be newspapers that published only once a week. But the term "community" separates those into further categories, because some weeklies served a small geographic area, while others, such as labor and religious publications, reached out to a special-interest audience. These special-interest weeklies served readers who shared an interest or a cause but not a geographical community concern. Some weeklies were published in suburban communities and urban neighborhoods, so they would not qualify for the designation of "country" or "rural" press. For this study, attention will be given to weekly "community" newspapers in small towns and rural areas that placed an emphasis on local news, exploring the nature of the weekly community newspaper and how it reflected American society throughout the twentieth century. Community weeklies told the story of average American daily lives more thoroughly and in a more personal manner than the big-city dailies. The tonal writing of most of these weeklies was that of a family member or friend, providing encouragement and support to their community family. Sensationalism was largely avoided; and a community's life story was told through birth, marriage, and death announcements, the comings and goings of the social elite, the accomplishments of local students, and the gatherings of community clubs, business and professional organizations, and church groups.

The period under consideration in this study begins in the year 1900, when a clear separation began between the daily and non-daily publishing communities. By the 1970s, offset printing and the advent of computerized, desktop publishing changed the face of the publication industry and made it possible for the explosion of specialized and issue-oriented non-dailies, such as "shoppers," that took on some characteristics of the community weekly. A "shopper" was usually tabloid in size, designed specifically to display classified and retail advertising. Some newspaper operations printed their own separate shopper, but most shoppers were in direct competition with general-news weeklies for advertising revenue. A majority of the shoppers were circulated free of charge, relying heavily on advertising revenue for profits.

The twentieth-century community weekly encompasses the cultural, political, and technological changes taking place in other aspects of American life. This work incorporates the business, technological, and governmental considerations of owning a small business and operating a weekly community press. It explores politics and the important role of the crusading editor. Throughout this work, references to a weekly publisher and/or editor are most often referred to in terms of "he" or "him" to reflect a large majority of the articles written by or about weekly publishers and editors during a period in which males held a high percentage of those positions.

As some community weeklies grew in circulation and advertising revenue, they merged with other weeklies to become daily newspapers. But others, despite expensive and problem-prone equipment, small staffs, and revenue shortcomings, continued publishing as community weeklies. From a business standpoint, profit appeared to become the dividing line between dailies and community weeklies, as dailies entered the world of big business and profit motive while community weeklies focused on public service and idealism in the face of financial uncertainty. However, new business practices introduced in the latter half of the century allowed more community weeklies to become profitable enterprises.

During the twentieth century, small-town weekly newspapers connected with more small towns and villages on a regular basis than did the country's metropolitan newspapers. For example, in large sectors of the country the nearest metropolitan newspaper was located hundreds of miles away. A decade into the twentieth century, only 51 percent of Americans lived in metropolitan areas. The weekly newspapers of small communities played an important role in keeping the citizenry informed on local and national news. While a growing number of rural residents subscribed to both metropolitan dailies and their community newspaper, it was the weekly community paper that contained the news most relevant to those in the immediate geographic area. The introduction of radio, television, and mega-merged metropolitan dailies with "community news" inserts did not supplant the weekly community newspaper as the main source for local news.

Because of the inherently "localized" tone of the community weekly, the accepted standards of "professional" practices in journalism do not apply in full to community weeklies. They differ in content, context, and purpose from daily newspapers, responding to the specific needs of residents in sparsely populated regions. Their tone could often be described as "optimistic" and "informal," easily dismissed by critics as unprofessional and inconsequential. But despite the fact that most journalism historical works have considered weeklies and dailies together when referring to newspapers, this study separates weekly community newspapers into a category of their own, emphasizing the importance of attention rather than avoidance when it comes to explaining the role of newspapers in everyday lives.

As privately owned businesses, weeklies and dailies shared similar day-to-day operations and duties, although the differing size and scope of their readership, business relationships, and operational concerns dictated differing responses and problem-solving measures. There were many commonalities among weeklies and dailies in terms of general standards of practice in newsgathering and revenue-generating models. However, small and large newspapers differed extensively in their tonal approaches to editorial content and community activism. Weekly publishers and editors were often under the threat of government intervention in such areas as postal, pricing, advertising, antitrust, and censorship regulations. But they also served as a valuable government partner to distribute war propaganda and to support various elected officials and their partisan politics.

Despite numerous threats to its existence, the weekly community newspaper survived and continued to play a prominent role in a community's quality of life, growth, and development.

Community Weekly Newspapers as Reflected in Journalism Historical Works

Only a select number of journalism historians devoted entire works to the subject of community weekly newspapers in the United States. Comprehensive works in journalism history tend to mention the weekly field only briefly, perhaps in a chapter, but mostly in occasional paragraphs within topical chapters. However, two 1948 works by Thomas D. Clark stand out in the literature of the community weekly press because they emphasized the rural press of the South. *The Southern Country Editor* focused on the region's sectional problems, such as race, a one-party political system, and one-crop agriculture that were prominent in both news and editorializing in the region's community newspapers.[1] In *The Rural Press and the New South*, he asserted that the southern country press served as a guide to the common man's thinking because its readers could easily understand the writing style in which community, state, and national problems were presented.[2]

Two decades later, former weekly newspaper editor-publisher and University of Minnesota journalism professor John Cameron Sim published *The Grass Roots Press: America's Community Newspapers*. He explored the viability of the community newspaper press and considered its long-range prospects in terms of chances for survivability in the future. Early chapters discussed the beginnings of the weekly press to its heyday in the first two decades of the twentieth century. Later chapters considered the perception of the weekly's role, the rise of weekly suburban newspapers, the impact of new technology, and the role community newspapers would have in the future.[3]

Considering perceptions of the weekly's role, Sim pointed out that many community newspapers followed the guidelines set by Houston Waring, who retired in 1966 as editor of Colorado's *Littleton Independent* and was a recognized leader in the community newspaper field. He outlined these functions of the community newspaper: (1) community newspapers make a community's economy work by advertising; (2) all sides of a question can be debated by permitting expression of public opinion through interviews and "letters to the editor"; (3) the press has a decision-forcing function with massive publicity requiring citizens to take a stand and no longer ignore an issue that has become a topic of conversation; (4) the press has a status-conferring function because those picked for mention are recognized as standing out from the crowd; (5) the press acquaints community leaders with the activities of other leaders; (6) the newspaper helps the reader understand his environment, i.e., when to pay taxes, where to register a child for school, etc.; (7) newspapers can assist citizens in crusading for improvement; (8) the press is a sounding board for policy; (9) the press strengthens moral resolution because tempted men fear newspaper publicity and thus are better able to resist temptation, making the press unwittingly a community chaperone; (10) the press is a medium of entertainment; (11) by devoting so much space to sports, the press encourages readers to think more about sports than war, focusing on the glories of basketball and horse racing instead of victories in combat; (12) the press attends to small and basic needs of readers through classified advertisements; and (13) the press gives Americans a sense of identity and belonging to a certain community.[4]

The important tie between the residents of a small town or agricultural region and their local community weekly was chronicled in Robert F. Karolevitz's *From Quill to Computer: The Story of America's Community Newspapers*. His 1985 work was published in recognition of the 100th anniversary of the National Newspaper Association (also known for 80 years as the National Editorial Association). The association was founded to serve America's community press and continues to do so from its headquarters in Pensacola, Florida. Karolevitz noted that during the period just prior to the heyday of the Penny Press before the Civil War, gazettes were generally short-run editions, limited by the printing process and populations. But with the emergence of metropolitan areas and the improvement of power presses, a marked division began to occur in the size and target of newspapers. It was also during the latter half of the nineteenth century that an emphasis in the writing and teaching of journalism history shifted heavily to the big names and the big dailies and away from the hometown press. Big-name editors and publishers of large-circulation newspapers from that period on dominated the story of American journalism.[5]

John Tebbel gave more attention to country weeklies in his general history of U.S. journalism than previous works. Published in 1963, *The Compact*

History of the American Newspapers included a chapter titled "The Rise and Fall of Country Newspapers." He went into much detail on the earliest traditions of the small-town paper, with special attention given to technological challenges. He stressed that in the 1900s, the country press was still operating as if it were in the colonial stage, if viewed from a technological standpoint. By the 1940s, influences in big-city publishing permeated the country press as well. As metropolitan newspapers became big business, country papers became small business. A decline in the number of country newspapers began in the 1920s with mergers and suspensions, which accelerated during the depression years.[6]

Other journalism histories make only brief mention of the weekly press and incorporate it in general discussions of technological and developmental changes and innovations, including mergers and consolidations that affected both the daily and weekly press. They also discuss, in some detail, the evolution from weekly or non-daily to daily publication of the country's major metropolitan dailies. Also mentioned is the advent of ready-print and its utilization by papers of all sizes throughout the country.[7] Ready-printed pages, a system introduced in this country by Wisconsin weekly publisher Ansel Nash Kellogg, were usually two, inside, preprinted pages sent to smaller newspapers to help fill a four-page newspaper. The material on these preprinted pages contained general news and features of a regional interest. The other sides of these preprinted pages were left blank to be filled with local content. Ready-print was also referred to as "patent insides" or "printed service pages."

The controversy surrounding the use of patent medicine advertisements in newspapers and magazines, and particularly in weekly newspapers, was addressed fully in Frank Presbrey's *The History and Development of Advertising*.[8] These topics were also covered in James Playsted Wood's *The Story of Advertising*.[9]

Because of a heavier involvement in their respective state press associations, the historical accounts of these associations tend to provide more details about small-town and rural newspapers than the larger, comprehensive journalism histories. State press association historical works included dates and frequency of publication of the states' member newspapers, providing a chronological record of the numerous weekly startups, consolidations, sell-offs, and closures. Some of these works are no more than collections of minutes of the associations' annual conferences and meetings of governing officials, but they reflect changes in the newspaper field, from a financial, technological, and ethical viewpoint.[10]

The Georgia Press Association, the University of Georgia Press and the Henry W. Grady School of Journalism and Graduate School at the University of Georgia collaborated on the 1950 publication of an expansive history of journalism in the state—from its beginnings in 1763 to the mid-twentieth century. Authors and University of Georgia professors Louis Turner Griffith and John Erwin Talmadge divided their work, *Georgia Journalism 1763–1950*, into three parts. The first part examines the influence of state newspapers throughout the period of study on political, social, economic, and everyday occurrences. The second part is based on the official minutes from gatherings of the Georgia Press Association. Part three features individual Georgia weekly and daily newspaper histories, arranged alphabetically by city and town.[11]

J. Cecil Alter's *Early Utah Journalism*—published in 1938 by the Utah State Historical Society—is subtitled: A half century of forensic warfare, waged by the West's most militant press. The Introduction begins: "The pioneer editor usually considered himself a weakling if he did not stand positively and aggressively for or against something, monitoring the thoughts and actions of the community with the dignity and severity of a Dictator—even if at the same time he was guilty of neglecting to print news items in his columns, or to meet his creditor's bills when due!" He lamented that despite their efforts and intellectual power that should have set them up as successful merchants and professional men, those editors that tirelessly sought to mold public opinion soon found themselves "manning his ship alone." As a result, he wrote that seven or eight country newspapers in Utah "perished" to each one that remained on operation at the time of the book's printing. The work covers Utah's first newspaper—the *Deseret* (UT) *News*, first published in 1850—to those published in the early 1930s. The Introduction also mentions the combative actions of these crusading editors, referencing "gunshot wounds, broken bones, coats of tar and feathers, blazing night-time duels, imprisonments, and conflicts and quarrels... all in the name of a free press and a free speech, too freely interpreted!"[12]

The *Story of Oklahoma Newspapers 1844 to 1984* by former newspaperman and University of Oklahoma School of Journalism professor L. Edward Carter was published in 1984, the result of a cooperative effort between the Oklahoma Newspaper Foundation, the Oklahoma Press Association, and the Oklahoma Heritage Association. It features chapters on such Oklahoma newspaper topics as early newspaper chains, the black press, college journalism programs, smaller dailies, and the metropolitan press. Individual chapters are devoted to the area's earliest Native American newspaper—the *Cherokee Advocate*, first published in 1844 long before Oklahoma statehood in 1907—and renowned editors with descriptors such as "pioneer woman" and "gun-slinging." A chapter devoted to the weekly press offers historical profiles of several types of weeklies and their editors/publishers, from dozens of country weeklies scattered across the state and suburban weeklies in the larger metropolitan areas, to a suburban "society" weekly and an Oklahoma City-based weekly chain.[13]

Historical works of state newspaper dynasties are also prevalent, among them Daniel Webster Hollis, III's *An Alabama Newspaper Tradition: Grover C. Hall and the Hall Family*.[14]

Several sociological works have explored the role and influence of a newspaper in its community. Although they include some historical detail, their focus has been on contemporary conditions rather than history. Among them is *Middletown: A Study in American Culture* by Robert S. Lynd and Helen M. Lynd.[15] Another such study is *Small Town in Mass Society* by Arthur J. Vidich and Joseph Bensman, which addressed the overall tone of the small-town press and how its writing styles and selections impacted readers. The community newspaper, according to this study, "always emphasized the positive side of life, never reporting local arrests, shotgun weddings, mortgage foreclosures, lawsuits, bitter exchanges in public meetings, suicides or any other 'unpleasant happening.'" By constantly focusing on warm and human qualities in all public situations, the authors observed, the public character of the community took on those qualities, which was very different from city life.[16] Although Morris Janowitz's *The Community Press in an Urban Setting* focused on suburban weeklies, it is considered a prominent sociological work in the study of community media.[17]

In their 1980 study, *Community Conflict and the Press*, Phillip J. Tichenor, George Donohue, and Clarice N. Olien explored how information was generated and communicated to various publics in a community and the relationships between communication processes and community structure and conflict. Data for the study was collected from field studies in 19 Minnesota communities. Referring to various agenda-setting studies, they emphasized that selective attention by the media to select topics tended to reinforce certain values and norms in society. In addition, the study considered control of information to the public and the "community editor" role, which is concerned with maintaining spirit, harmony, and consensus by printing only information relating to a community's good points.[18]

Within the newspaper industry, a number of professional publications, including *Editor & Publisher, Editor & Publisher International Yearbook, National Publisher, National Printer-Journalist, The Publishers' Auxiliary, Grassroots Editor, N.W. Ayer & Son's Directory of Newspapers and Periodicals*, and *The American Press*, have provided extensive information on the weekly newspaper field. *Editor & Publisher* for many years ran a regular feature, "The Weekly Editor," which profiled weekly publishers and editors from across the country. *The Publishers' Auxiliary*, which was written specifically for the weekly newspaper industry, featured articles on individual weeklies, their editors, and staff members. In support of small business within the weekly newspaper field, trade publications addressed the weekly's distinctive features, such as ownership (mostly family-owned through the first half of the twentieth century), small staff sizes of family members and friends with a publisher who often also served as printer and/or editor, the importance of ready-print for content and financial purposes, and encouragement for strong local news coverage and a "homegrown" editorial voice.[19]

Although scholarly articles related to community weekly newspapers were limited in number, *Journalism Quarterly* and several social science journals, such as *Public Opinion Quarterly* and Malcolm Willey's 1926 study of weeklies published in the book, *The Country Newspaper*, addressed topics of interest in the weekly field.[20]

First-person accounts of practicing rural journalism were re-told in a number of works, including those of Sherwood Anderson, Alexander Brook, Hodding Carter, Earl V. Chapin, John H. Cutler, P.D. East, Henry Beetle Hough, Clayton Rand, and William Allen White.[21] Famed publisher-editor White, of the *Emporia (KS) Gazette*, was the rare small-town weekly editor who gained national attention for serving as an unofficial presidential adviser and national political activist. He is more often linked with his fellow muckraking journalists at the New York City-based *McClure's* magazine and as a close friend and adviser to President Theodore Roosevelt than for spending his days in the compositing room generating articles on local Sunday school picnics and garden club meetings, according to historian Doris Kearns Goodwin in her 2013 work, *The Bully Pulpit*.[22] An extensive look at White's life and career can be found in Sally Foreman Griffith's *Home Town News: William Allen White and the Emporia Gazette*.[23]

In addition, "how-to" manuals, handbooks, resource material, and textbooks on rural or community journalism were authored by Charles L. Allen, Millard V. Atwood, Thomas F. Barnhart, Phil C. Bing, Kenneth Byerly,

Emerson P. Harris and Florence Harris Hooke, Grant M. Hyde, Bruce M. Kennedy, John McKinney, C.M. Meredith, Jr., Norman J. Radder, Walter Rae, James Clifford Safley, Malcolm Willey, Edward Miller, Kathleen Cushman, and Larry Anderson, to name a few.[24]

A Look at Community Weeklies across the Country throughout the Twentieth Century

For this work, weekly newspaper samples were selected from each of the major geographical regions in the United States and at least one sample from each of the years of study. Newspapers were selected that displayed evidence of a pattern of weekly publication (every seven days) or through content within the pages of an edition to verify that a newspaper was published on a weekly basis. Newspapers in communities with smaller populations were selected to avoid suburban weeklies. Within each 10-year period, newspaper samples were selected from different months, years, and geographic regions. No specific dates were deliberately selected based on major historical events (such as the assassination of President John F. Kennedy). The availability of newspapers was more limited in the earlier years under study. Several states have an extensive list of weeklies to choose from (particularly Iowa and Texas) while other states have fewer weeklies accessible for certain decades or the entire period under study. Thus, more samples were included from specific states and regions. Library microfilm, personal files, and in-person interviews provided information on most Alabama weeklies included in this work.

Notes

1 Thomas D. Clark, *The Southern Country Editor*, 1st ed. (Indianapolis: The Bobbs-Merrill Company, 1948).
2 Thomas D. Clark, *The New Rural Press and the New South* (Baton Rouge, LA: Louisiana State University Press, 1948).
3 John Cameron Sim, *The Grass Roots Press: America's Community Newspapers*, 1st ed. (Ames, IA: The Iowa State University Press, 1969; reprint, 1970).
4 Ibid., 87–88.
5 Robert F. Karolevitz, *From Quill to Computer: The Story of America's Community Newspapers* (Freeman, SD: Pine Hill Press for National Newspaper Foundation, 1985), 36.
6 John Tebbel, *The Compact History of the American Newspaper* (New York: Hawthorn Books, 1963), 258.

7 Tracy Lucht, Erika Pribanic-Smith, and Wm. David Sloan, eds., *The Media in America: A History*, 11th ed. (Northport, AL: Vision Press, 2020); Willard Grosvenor Bleyer, *Main Currents in the History of American Journalism* (Boston: Houghton Mifflin, 1927); Edwin Emery and Michael Emery, *The Press and America: An Interpretive History of the Mass Media*, 8th ed. (Englewood Cliffs, NJ: Prentice-Hall, 1996); Jean Folkerts and Dwight L. Teeter, Jr., *Voices of a Nation: A History of the Media in the United States* (New York: Macmillan, 1989); Sidney Kobre, *Development of American Journalism* (Dubuque, IA: Wm. C. Brown Company, 1969); Alfred McClung Lee, *The Daily Newspaper in America: The Evolution of a Social Instrument* (New York: Macmillan, 1937); James Melvin Lee, *History of American Journalism* (Garden City, NY: The Garden City Publishing Co., 1923); Frank Luther Mott, *American Journalism* (New York: Macmillan, 1941); Michael Schudson, *Discovering the News: A Social History of American Newspapers* (New York: Basic Books, 1978).
8 Frank Presbrey, *The History and Development of Advertising* (Garden City, NY: Doubleday, Doran & Company, 1929).
9 James Playsted Wood, *The Story of Advertising* (Garden City, NY: Ronald Press, 1958).
10 Among state newspaper histories or collections that include twentieth-century publications are: Fred W. Allsopp, *History of the Arkansas Press for a Hundred Years and More* (Little Rock: Parke-Harper Publishing Co., 1922); J. Cecil Alter, *Early Utah Journalism* (Salt Lake City: Utah State Historical Society, 1938); Lester J. Cappon, *Virginia Newspapers, 1821–1935* (New York: D. Appleton-Century Co., 1936); L. Edward Carter, *The Story of Oklahoma Newspapers 1844 to 1984* (Muskogee, OK: Western Heritage Books, 1984); Rhoda C. Ellison, *Early Alabama Publications* (Tuscaloosa, AL: University of Alabama Press, 1947); Herndon J. Evans, *The Newspaper Press in Kentucky* (Lexington, KY: The University Press of Kentucky, 1976); Louis T. Griffith and John E. Talmadge, *Georgia Journalism, 1763–1950* (Athens, GA: University of Georgia Press, 1951); Osman Castle Hooper, *History of Ohio Journalism, 1793–1933* (Columbus, OH: The Spahr & Glenn Co., 1933); Walter C. Johnson and Arthur T. Robb, *The South and Its Newspapers, 1903–1953* (Chattanooga, TN: The Southern Newspaper Publishers Association, 1954); Eugene Jones, "A Decade of the Country Editor: 1954–1964," *West Texas Historical Association Year Book* 62 (1968): 52–68; Douglas C. McMurtrie, *Early Printing in Tennessee* (Chicago: Chicago Club of Printing House Craftsmen, 1933); Douglas C. McMurtrie, *Early Printing in Wisconsin* (Seattle: Dogwood Press, 1931); Nyle H. Miller, et al., *Kansas in Newspapers* (Topeka: Kansas State Historical Society, 1963); Ira A. Nichols, *Forty Years of Rural Journalism in Iowa* (Fort Dodge: Messenger Press, 1938); Thad Stem, Jr., *The Tar Heel Press* (Charlotte, NC: North Carolina Press Association, 1973); George S. Turnbull, *History of Oregon Newspapers* (Portland: Binfords & Mort, Publishers, 1939); H.L. Williamson, *History of the Illinois Press Association* (Springfield: Hartman-Jefferson Printing Co., 1934).
11 Griffith and Talmadge, *Georgia Journalism, 1763–1950*, x.
12 Alter, *Early Utah Journalism*, 9–10.
13 Carter, *The Story of Oklahoma Newspapers 1844 to 1984*, vii, 218–229.
14 Daniel Webster Hollis, III, *An Alabama Newspaper Tradition: Grover C. Hall and the Hall Family* (Tuscaloosa, AL: The University of Alabama Press, 1983).

15 Robert S. Lynd and Helen M. Lynd, *Middletown: A Study in American Culture* (New York: Harcourt, Brace & Co., 1929).
16 Arthur J. Vidich and Joseph Bensman, *Small Town in Mass Society* (Princeton, NJ: Princeton University Press, 1968), 31.
17 Morris Janowitz, *The Community Press in an Urban Setting* (Glencoe, IL: The Free Press, 1952).
18 Phillip J. Tichenor, George Donohue, and Clarice N. Olien, *Community Conflict and the Press* (Beverly Hills, CA: Sage, 1980), 19, 87.
19 *N.W. Ayer & Son's American Newspaper Annual and Directory* (Philadelphia: N.W. Ayer & Sons, 1924).
20 Malcolm M. Willey, *The Country Newspaper* (Chapel Hill, NC: There University of North Carolina Press, 1926).
21 Sherwood Anderson, *Nearer the Grass Roots (and a Journey to Elizabethton)* (San Francisco: Westgate Press, 1929); Alexander B. Brook, *The Hard Way: The Odyssey of a Weekly Newspaper Editor* (Bridgehampton, NY: Bridge Works Publishing Co., 1993); Hodding Carter, *Where Main Street Meets the River* (New York: Rinehart & Company, 1953); Hodding Carter, *First Person Rural* (Garden City, NY: Doubleday & Company, 1963); Earl V. Chapin, *Long Wednesdays* (New York: Abelard Press, 1953); John Henry Cutler, *Put It on the Front Page, Please!* (New York: Ives Washburn, 1960); P.D. East, *The Magnolia Jungle: The Life, Times, and Education of a Southern Editor* (New York: Simon and Schuster, 1960); Emerson P. Harris and Elizabeth H. Hooke, *The Community Newspaper* (New York: D. Appleton and Company, 1923); Henry Beetle Hough, *Country Editor* (New York: Doubleday, Doran & Company, 1940); Clayton Rand, *Ink on My Hands* New York: Carrick & Evans, 1940); William A. White, *The Autobiography of William Allen White* (New York: Macmillan, 1946).
22 Doris Kearns Goodwin, *The Bully Pulpit* (New York: Simon & Schuster, 2013).
23 Sally Foreman Griffith, *Home Town News: William Allen White and the Emporia Gazette* (New York: Oxford University Press, 1989).
24 Charles L. Allen, *Country Journalism* (New York: Thomas Nelson and Sons, 1928); Millard V. Atwood, *The Country Newspaper*, The National Social Science Series (Chicago: A.C. McClurg & Co., 1923); Thomas F. Barnhart, *Weekly Newspaper: A Bibliography, 1925–1941* (Minneapolis, MN: Burgess Publishing Co., 1941); Thomas F. Barnhart, *Weekly Newspaper Management* (New York: D. Appleton-Century, 1936); Thomas F. Barnhart, *Weekly Newspaper Writing and Editing* (New York: The Dryden Press, 1949); Phil C. Bing, *The Country Weekly: A Manual for the Rural Journalist and for Students of the Country Field* (New York: D. Appleton & Co., 1917); Kenneth R. Byerly, *Community Journalism* (New York: Chilton Company, 1961); Grant M. Hyde, *Newspaper Reporting and Correspondence* (New York: D. Appleton and Company, 1912); Bruce M. Kennedy, *Community Journalism, A Way of Life* (Ames, IA: Iowa State University Press, 1974); John McKinney, *How to Start Your Own Community Newspaper*, 3rd ed. (Port Jefferson, NY: Meadow Press, 1977); C.M. Meredith, Jr., *The Country Weekly* (Boston: Bruce Humphries, 1937); Edward Miller, Kathleen Cushman, and Larry Anderson, *How to Produce a Small Newspaper* (Harvard, MA: The Harvard Common Press, 1978); Clement Moore and Herman Roe, *The First National Survey of the Weekly Newspaper Publishing Business in the U.S.* (St. Paul: National

INTRODUCTION 13

Editorial Assn., 1929); Norman J. Radder, *Newspapers in Community Service* (New York: McGraw-Hill Book Co., 1926); Norman J. Radder, *The Small-City Daily and the Country Weekly* (Bloomington: Indiana University Department of Journalism, 1927); James Clifford Safley, *The Country Newspaper and Its Operation* (New York: D. Appleton and Company, 1930); Elmo Scott Watson, *A History of Newspaper Syndicates in the United States, 1865–1935* (Chicago: The Publishers' Auxiliary, 1936).

References

Allen, Charles L. *Country Journalism.* New York: Thomas Nelson and Sons, 1928.
Allsopp, Fred W. *History of the Arkansas Press for a Hundred Years and More.* Little Rock: Parke-Harper Publishing Co., 1922.
Alter, J. Cecil. *Early Utah Journalism.* Salt Lake City: Utah State Historical Society, 1938.
American Press Association et al v. United States et al. (1917).
Anderson, Sherwood. *Nearer the Grass Roots (and a Journey to Elizabethton).* San Francisco: Westgate Press, 1929.
Atwood, Millard V. *The Country Newspaper*, The National Social Science Series. Chicago: A.C. McClurg & Co., 1923.
Barnhart, Thomas F. *Weekly Newspaper: A Bibliography, 1925–1941.* Minneapolis, MN.: Burgess Publishing Co., 1941.
Barnhart, Thomas F. *Weekly Newspaper Management.* New York: D. Appleton-Century, 1936.
Barnhart, Thomas F. *Weekly Newspaper Writing and Editing.* New York: The Dryden Press, 1949.
Bing, Phil C. *The Country Weekly: A Manual for the Rural Journalist and for Students of the Country Field.* New York: D. Appleton & Co., 1917.
Bleyer, Willard Grosvenor. *Main Currents in the History of American Journalism.* Boston: Houghton Mifflin, 1927.
Brook, Alexander B. *The Hard Way: The Odyssey of a Weekly Newspaper Editor.* Bridgehampton, NY: Bridge Works Publishing Co., 1993.
Byerly, Kenneth R. *Community Journalism.* New York: Chilton Company, 1961.
Cappon, Lester J. *Virginia Newspapers, 1821–1935.* New York: D. Appleton-Century Co., 1936.
Carter, Hodding. *First Person Rural.* Garden City, NY: Doubleday & Company, 1963.
Carter, Hodding. *Where Main Street Meets the River.* New York: Rinehart & Company, 1953.
Carter, L. Edward. *The Story of Oklahoma Newspapers 1844 to 1984.* Muskogee, OK.: Western Heritage Books, 1984.
Chapin, Earl V. *Long Wednesdays.* New York: Abelard Press, 1953.
Clark, Thomas D. *The Southern Country Editor.* 1st ed. Indianapolis: The Bobbs-Merrill Company, 1948.
Clark, Thomas D. *The New Rural Press and the New South.* Baton Rouge, La.: Louisiana State University Press, 1948.
Cutler, John Henry. *Put It On The Front Page, Please!* New York: Ives Washburn, 1960.
East, P.D. *The Magnolia Jungle: The Life, Times, and Education of a Southern Editor.* New York: Simon and Schuster, 1960.

Ellison, Rhoda C. *Early Alabama Publications*. Tuscaloosa, AL: University of Alabama Press, 1947.

Emery, Edwin, and Michael Emery. *The Press and America: An Interpretive History of the Mass Media*. 8th ed. Englewood Cliffs, NJ: Prentice-Hall, 1996.

Evans, Herndon J. *The Newspaper Press in Kentucky*. Lexington, KY: The University Press of Kentucky, 1976.

Folkerts, Jean, and Dwight L. Teeter, Jr. *Voices of a Nation: A History of the Media in the United States*. New York: Macmillan, 1989.

Goodwin, Doris Kearns. *The Bully Pulpit*. New York: Simon & Schuster, 2013.

Griffith, Louis T., and Talmadge, John E. *Georgia Journalism, 1763–1950*. Athens, GA: University of Georgia Press, 1951.

Harris, Emerson P., and Elizabeth H. Hooke. *The Community Newspaper*. New York: D. Appleton and Company, 1923.

Hollis, Daniel Webster, III. *An Alabama Newspaper Tradition: Grover C. Hall and the Hall Family*. Tuscaloosa, AL: The University of Alabama Press, 1983.

Hooper, Osman Castle. *History of Ohio Journalism, 1793–1933*. Columbus, OH: The Spahr & Glenn Co., 1933.

Hough, Henry Beetle. *Country Editor*. New York: Doubleday, Doran & Company, 1940.

Hyde, Grant M. *Newspaper Reporting and Correspondence*. New York: D. Appleton and Company, 1912.

Janowitz, Morris. *The Community Press in an Urban Setting*. Glencoe, IL: The Free Press, 1952.

Johnson, Walter C., and Robb, Arthur T. *The South and its Newspapers, 1903–1953*. Chattanooga, TN: The Southern Newspaper Publishers Association, 1954.

Jones, Eugene. "A Decade of the Country Editor: 1954–1964." *West Texas Historical Association Year Book* 62 (1968): 52–68.

Karolevitz, Robert F. *From Quill to Computer: The Story of America's Community Newspapers*. Freeman, SD: Pine Hill Press for National Newspaper Foundation, 1985.

Kennedy, Bruce M. *Community Journalism, A Way of Life*. Ames, IA: Iowa State University Press, 1974.

Kobre, Sidney. *Development of American Journalism*. Dubuque, IA: Wm. C. Brown Company, 1969.

Lee, Alfred McClung. *The Daily Newspaper in America: The Evolution of a Social Instrument*. New York: Macmillan, 1937.

Lee, James Melvin. *History of American Journalism*. Garden City, NY: The Garden City Publishing Co., 1923.

Lucht, Tracy, Pribanic-Smith, Erika, and, Sloan, Wm. David, eds. *The Media in America: A History*. 11th ed. Northport, AL: Vision Press, 2020.

Lynd, Robert S., and Helen M. Lynd. *Middletown: A Study in American Culture*. New York: Harcourt, Brace & Co., 1929.

McKinney, John. *How to Start Your Own Community Newspaper*. 3rd ed. Port Jefferson, NY: Meadow Press, 1977.

McMurtrie, Douglas C. *Early Printing in Tennessee*. Chicago: Chicago Club of Printing House Craftsmen, 1933.

McMurtrie, Douglas C. *Early Printing in Wisconsin*. Seattle: Dogwood Press, 1931.
Meredith, C.M., Jr. *The Country Weekly*. Boston: Bruce Humphries, 1937.
Miller, Edward, Kathleen Cushman, and Larry Anderson. *How to Produce a Small Newspaper*. Harvard, MA: The Harvard Common Press, 1978.
Miller, Nyle H., et al. *Kansas in Newspapers*. Topeka: Kansas State Historical Society, 1963.
Moore, Clement and Roe, Herman. *The First National Survey of the Weekly Newspaper Publishing Business in the U.S.* St. Paul: National Editorial Assn., 1929.
Mott, Frank Luther. *American Journalism*. New York: Macmillan, 1941.
Nichols, Ira A. *Forty Years of Rural Journalism in Iowa*. Fort Dodge: Messenger Press, 1938.
N.W. Ayer & Son's American Newspaper Annual and Directory. Philadelphia: N.W. Ayer & Sons, 1924.
Presbrey, Frank. *The History and Development of Advertising*. Garden City, NY: Doubleday, Doran & Company, 1929.
Radder, Norman J. *Newspapers in Community Service*. New York: McGraw-Hill Book Co., 1926.
Radder, Norman J. *The Small-City Daily and the Country Weekly*. Bloomington: Indiana University Department of Journalism, 1927.
Rand, Clayton. *Ink on My Hands*. New York: Carrick & Evans, 1940.
Safley, James Clifford. *The Country Newspaper and Its Operation*. New York: D. Appleton and Company, 1930.
Schudson, Michael. *Discovering the News: A Social History of American Newspapers*. New York: Basic Books, 1978.
Sim, John Cameron. *The Grass Roots Press: America's Community Newspapers*. 1st ed. Ames, IA: The Iowa State University Press, 1969. Reprint, 1970.
Stem, Thad, Jr. *The Tar Heel Press*. Charlotte, NC: North Carolina Press Association, 1973.
Tebbel, John. *The Compact History of the American Newspaper*. New York: Hawthorn Books, 1963.
Tichenor, Phillip J., George Donohue, and Clarice N. Olien. *Community Conflict and the Press*. Beverly Hills, CA: Sage, 1980.
Turnbull, George S. *History of Oregon Newspapers*. Portland: Binfords & Mort, Publishers, 1939.
Vidich, Arthur J., and Joseph Bensman. *Small Town in Mass Society*. Princeton, NJ: Princeton University Press, 1968.
Watson, Elmo Scott. *A History of Newspaper Syndicates in the United States, 1865–1935*. Chicago: The Publishers' Auxiliary, 1936.
White, William A. *The Autobiography of William Allen White*. New York: Macmillan, 1946.
Willey, Malcolm M. *The Country Newspaper*. Chapel Hill, NC: The University of North Carolina Press, 1926.
Williamson, H.L. *History of the Illinois Press Association*. Springfield: Hartman-Jefferson Printing Co., 1934.
Wood, James Playsted. *The Story of Advertising*. Garden City, NY: Ronald Press, 1958.

· 1 ·

THE EARLY 1900S: CONSISTENCY IN CONTENT, APPEARANCE, AND STYLE

Community weekly newspapers in early-twentieth-century America were similar to their predecessors in terms of content, appearance, and style. This was due largely to business practices and financial constraints that limited the size of their newsgathering staffs and their ability to purchase more efficient technology. Their business practices were established by newspapers in Colonial America, while their newsgathering methods were largely reflective of techniques and technologies introduced in the last half of the nineteenth century.

However, unlike their predecessors, weeklies in the early twentieth century faced more direct competition from nearby metropolitan dailies that attempted to lure away subscribers, advertising dollars, and staff. Some newspaper industry insiders even predicted the death of the weekly because of direct competition with the metropolitan and small-town dailies. But as some weeklies struggled to survive, the more financially successful operations were faced with deciding whether or not to convert to a daily or multi-weekly publication schedule. The move to a multi-week publication schedule was usually the result of increased circulation and advertising revenue.

From its earliest days, the weekly newspaper business depended heavily upon commercial and government job printing or bookselling to stay afloat.

For example, the first newspaper printed in Colonial America, the single issue *Publick Occurrences Both Forreign and Domestick*, was published in 1690 by Boston bookstore and coffee house owner, Benjamin Harris. Boston postmaster John Campbell began publishing the country's first continuous newspaper, the *Boston News-Letter*, on April 24, 1704. It was his position as postmaster that enabled him to print government documents, the profits of which propped up his newspaper operation. Thus, printer-publisher, or postmaster-publisher, became a common job title in the community newspaper field.

Newsgathering for the weekly in the early 1900s continued to rely heavily on newspaper syndication services despite the efforts of a small, but vocal group of weekly publishers who resisted the use of syndicate material, also referred to as "ready-print," "canned copy" or "boilerplate." They argued that quality was more important than quantity, and they preferred the use of strictly locally generated news, although it cost more time and money. Their arguments were backed by the growing recognition that formal journalism training would better equip newspapermen to gather facts, write stories and editorials, solicit advertisers and subscribers, and design their pages for the most efficient use of space.

During the early twentieth century, a number of college journalism programs were developed, especially in the Midwest, which was home to the largest number of weeklies. Weekly publishers and editors of the numerous small-town Midwest weeklies found welcome partnerships with regional universities that produced a growing number of skilled journalists. But for most weeklies, it was simply a matter of finances that dictated their extensive use of syndicate material. Examples of syndicate material are generously apportioned throughout the pages of many weeklies during the decade. But whether locally generated copy commanded a large portion of the weekly, or only a few sections, local editorial comment, opinion letters, and columns were closely watched by state and national politicians because they were representative of the thinking among "grassroots" community residents.

The Business of Community Weekly Newspapers

It did not take long for a novice country editor-publisher to learn that what mattered most in his profession was not the ability to write beautiful prose or compose sharp-witted commentary, but rather the ability to balance the books to keep presses rolling, supplies in stock, and equipment in workable shape. Ever present on his mind was how to increase local advertising revenue, how to attract national advertising, and how to increase circulation, as well as collect overdue subscription payments.

But ultimately, he discovered that advertising and subscription revenues simply were inadequate to keep most small-town newspapers in business. The problem for many rural publishers was that they knew how to produce a printed product, but they lacked management skills to run their operations in an efficient manner. To this end, the concept of a college degree in journalism became more readily acceptable as veteran pressmen began to realize the benefits that could come with a journalist trained in writing, sales, and management.

The lifeblood of most rural newspaper operations was commercial printing, although low rates did impact profit margins. For example, a 1902 issue of *The Hendricks* (MN) *Pioneer* contained a three-line advertisement in the lower right corner of page one marked, "Job Printing." The self-promotion advertisement boasted that *The Hendricks Pioneer* was equipped with all necessary presses for job printing—"the kind you want." *The Hendricks Pioneer* was established in 1900. It boasted of being "A newspaper for conveying intelligence of passing events, etc."[1]

Often the biggest money maker for small-town printers was the county government's printing contract, as evidenced in an October 1900 classified listing for the sale of a community newspaper in *The Publishers' Auxiliary*, a trade publication provided free of charge to subscribing members of the A.N. Kellogg (later Western Newspaper Union) newspaper syndication service. The publication featured tips on workplace efficiency and updates on legislative issues related to the publication industry. Incorporated extensively throughout the issue were articles promoting the benefits of using syndicate-supplied materials, which was of obvious financial benefit to the Kellogg company.

> The advertisement read in part,
> A Special Snap-A DEMOCRATIC NEWSPAPER and job office in a democratic town and democratic county. Only one other democratic paper in the county. By agreement the county printing is equally divided between the two papers and all the county officers are warm friends to the paper ....[2]

Serving as the county's official government printer also proved lucrative to *The Rio Grande Republican* of Las Cruces, New Mexico, which boasted on its nameplate of being the official paper of Dona Ana County. As the official "recorder" of county business, the paper's March 3, 1905 edition included a detailed report on a county commission meeting.[3] Likewise, *The Hendricks Pioneer's* masthead on page four included the phrase "Official Paper of Village of Hendricks."

Even though government printing contracts usually went to the low bidder, they were still highly sought by small newspaper publishers for status and business connections. But sometimes even a heavy schedule of commercial jobs meant a losing financial endeavor for the printer who charged his customers too little. In the early 1900s, Kansas legislators considered establishing certain rates for all types of official printing business. This fixed-rate proposal was in conflict with the practice of the day of awarding the printing contract to the lowest bidder. A January 1903 column in *The Publishers' Auxiliary* called on the support of the country newspaper "fraternity" to support fixed rates for government printing services. The column raised the question, "Why should the county printing be let to the lower bidder any more than the recording of deeds or the work of any other county officer?" Such practice often resulted "in forcing the price down to a figure that imposes an actual loss upon the man who does it."[4]

Publishers had to commit a larger investment in a printing operation that supported both revenue-generating commercial jobs and a weekly newspaper because of the need for more personnel and supplies, and better-equipped and maintained press machinery. While some weeklies could be purchased in the $1,000-plus range, the asking price for a better-equipped and more profitable community newspaper-printing operation could be double or triple that price. For example, a January 1900 classified listing in *The Publishers' Auxiliary* read in part: "Wanted. Will pay $1,000 to $1,200[5] down on Republican county seat weekly in eastern or central Kansas. Must be making money."[6]

In his 1907 presidential address to the Twenty-Second Annual Convention of the National Editorial Association in Norfolk, Virginia, John E. Junkin called upon the members to become more active in promoting improvement in the newspaper business. For example, he implored the membership to publicly voice its disapproval of paper stock being "in the hands of a great trust," resulting in "extortion" prices.[7] He also referred to price controls on lead type and the availability of only one typesetting machine "that can only be purchased at an exorbitant price."[8] Type refers to a metal casting of all the letters of the alphabet, both capitals and lowercase, punctuation marks, and numbers, set in different styles, fonts, and sizes, measured in points. The Monotype was the trade name for a machine that made and cast type. It was invented by

Tolbert Lanston and put into commercial use around 1899. By the early twentieth century, many printers were moving from hand-set type to Linotype, the trade name of a typesetting machine, invented by Ottmar Mergenthaler in 1886, which used a keyboard to compose type. Thus, the quality of a weekly in terms of content and appearance was largely determined by the level of financial investment in equipment and personnel.

The phrase "all home print" was viewed by many publishers as bragging rights, because they believed that a community newspaper containing solely locally generated articles assured its readers of a higher quality publication. However, for many publishers, it simply was not financially feasible to handle such a printing load at their local offices. To do so would have required the hiring of more pressmen and typesetters, as well as the maintenance and replacement of expensive printing equipment and supplies. Type wore out or pieces were lost, which made it more difficult to fill pages with local copy and replace the expensive lead type.

Other business concerns of the weekly press were the threat of increased second-class postal rates, a lack of revenue from low subscription rates, and too many requests for free publicity from community organizations and publicity agents. An August 1901 column in *The Publishers' Auxiliary* referred to proposed federal legislation to require weekly newspapers using the carrier delivery system to stamp every copy sent to local subscribers with one or two-cent stamps, according to weight. The editorial stated, "The proposed change would be mostly felt by the country weekly publisher, and would mean the extinction of many, as they would not be able to bear the increased expenses."[9] Given that an average subscription rate for weeklies was one dollar per year, much of the subscription revenue would have been absorbed in circulation costs. The proposed legislation was not approved. Even though the cost of delivering newspapers was out of the publisher's control, he did determine his newspaper's subscription rate. Commenting on both rising printing costs and low subscription rates, a Missouri publisher wrote in *The Publishers' Auxiliary*, "Many experienced publishers assert that one dollar a year is too little for a good country weekly, and there is justice in their claim. Would it not be a good time to increase your subscription price?"[10]

Compounding the problem of low subscription rates was a high demand for free publicity space. Country editors were constantly bombarded with requests for free publicity for community fundraising events. In an article about publishing a country weekly, longtime *Abilene (KS) Reflector* editor Charles Moreau Harger wrote that editors were criticized for charging for certain items that no city editor would have printed free, such as church and lodge notices about fundraising events, and free advertising for semi-public entertainment events sought by travel promoters.[11]

The publishers of *Shenandoah Valley* in New Market, Virginia, were very specific in identifying items that would not be published free of charge in their weekly. A page three notice in its January 15, 1903 edition proclaimed that the paper would not publish free "notices of shows, entertainments, festivals, cards of thanks, in memoriums, resolutions of respect by churches, Sunday-schools [sic], and orders; advertising and advertising puffs by correspondents, etc." The paper would accept one insertion, free of charge, for a religious or charitable notice of general community interest "if it does not exceed 40 words ...."[12]

However, one publicity practice welcomed by country editors, especially those who attended the annual conferences of the National Editorial Association, was the exchange of courtesies with railroads, which Congress outlawed by its passage of the Hepburn Act prior to the group's 1907 annual gathering. The Interstate Commerce Act of 1887 created the Interstate Commerce Commission, which was responsible for oversight of railroads. A major controversy included attempts by railroads to obtain influence over opinion leaders by offering free passes. For newspaper editors, this practice entailed an "exchange" of a railroad pass for free newspaper advertising and favorable editorials. The Hepburn Act of 1906 strengthened existing railroad regulations, including the restriction of the use of free passes.

As a result, for the first time in more than 20 years, conference attendees were not given free railroad transportation to the conference, nor did they benefit from a conference entertainment excursion, which previously had been provided by the railroads. The law put an end to complimentary newspaper write-ups as a fair return for a railroad trip, and trading advertising space for transportation. In his address to the 1907 National Editorial Association annual convention, Kansas publisher and organization president John E. Junkin observed that the railroad rate bill had "disturbed relations" of newspapers and railroads that had existed since the earliest days of railroading. But, he added, "We will even in time take pride in our independence of the trade patronage of the railroads."[13]

An example of favorable railway publicity appeared in the form of an open letter, unsigned, from Southern Railway that occupied three-fifths of a page in the February 1, 1907 edition of *The Laurel* (MS) *Ledger*. The open letter addressed "To the Public Served by the Southern Railway Company" explained operating increases for the railway but assured readers that there would be no resulting passage rate increases. The letter concluded with the announcement that more information would be forthcoming in the following week's issue.[14]

Syndication Services Impact Production and Personnel Costs

While the printer-publisher or postmaster-publisher had to focus much of his time and effort on revenue-generating operations, he still had to produce a weekly newspaper. An important source for keeping his production and personnel costs down was the newspaper syndicate service, which distributed feature and news articles, commentary, illustrations, and advertisements from a centralized, non-local source. The first newspaper syndicate was a business born from a newspaper publisher's desperation to stay in business during the Civil War. It was established in 1865 by Baraboo, Wisconsin, weekly publisher Ansel Nash Kellogg after his printer joined the Union army. He had difficulty filling his pages, so he ordered half-sheet supplements containing war news from the Madison, Wisconsin, *State Journal* that were folded into his newspaper. His first issue with these preprinted pages was published July 12, 1861. Other weekly publishers soon realized the benefit of ready-printed pages and started syndicate services of their own, but Kellogg took the lead in the burgeoning industry and eventually bought out smaller companies.

Another syndication pioneer was Wisconsin publisher Andrew Jackson Aikens. His service differed from Kellogg's in that he sold advertising space to Milwaukee businesses to reduce his cost to produce ready-prints and to provide a wider audience for the Milwaukee-based companies. He eventually bought out other Madison syndicate services, but his operation never reached the level of success of the Kellogg Company.

In October 1871, Kellogg's business was destroyed in the great Chicago fire that damaged much of the city. Because of the company's temporary shutdown, many small-town newspapers had to suspend their publications, or readers received their newspapers with some blank pages inside. *Scientific American* magazine wrote of the incident, "The fire in Chicago had the curious effect of spoiling the 'outsides' of nearly two hundred weekly newspapers which are published, hundreds of miles from that city, in Illinois, Iowa, Wisconsin, and Minnesota. One of the leading printers of Chicago did a large business in printing these 'outsides' in duplicate and sending them to different places, where the local publishers printed the news on the other side. The farmers who depended upon these sheets for their weekly supply of news must have been puzzled to know how the Chicago fire could have deprived them of their village newspaper while the home office remained intact."[15]

Kellogg quickly re-established his Chicago business and expanded his syndication service to include such "boilerplate" materials as literary serials, illustrated stories, and stereotype plates. Stereotype plates required squeezing a sheet of damp cardboard over the type. The cardboard sheet was then dried, lifted, and turned over and molten metal was poured onto the cardboard, making a cast. Stereotype plates were more expensive to use than ready-print because they required a press run, but some editors preferred the stereotype plates because they could move the syndicated material around on the pages. The term "boilerplate" was popularized to refer to any syndicated material.[16] In 1886, Kellogg died in Thomasville, Georgia, having seen his company grow to 1,400 subscribers.

Soft News from a Silent Partner

Soft news can be described as news focusing on entertainment or information that is personally useful. The syndicate material of general interest often fell into the categories of humor or interesting facts, while special series were related to such varied topics as religion, homemaking, and movie and stage celebrities. An example of a humorous syndicate-supplied item that appeared in *The Hendricks* (MN) *Pioneer* was headlined "Didn't Know Ping-Pong." The article originated in the *Chicago Chronicle* and relayed the story of a father who became upset after his daughter declared she was "in love" with ping-pong. He was unfamiliar with the game and thought she was smitten with a "Chinaman."[17]

The local content, printed on the blank sides of the ready-print newspapers, was usually designed to promote good will in the community. A "names make news" approach was popular in determining newsworthy local articles. Weekly subscribers looked to correspondents from small, rural communities within the newspaper's service area to provide detailed accounts of local weddings, baptisms, and funerals. Agriculture, illness, and religious revivals were also topics in high demand among rural newspaper readers.

By 1900, there were nearly 12,000 newspapers published in the United States, roughly 9,000 of which were community weeklies located mostly in towns with a population of 10,000 or less.[18] For national and world event coverage, most rural subscribers relied on ready-print and boilerplate to provide that type of information. However, the question of whether or not readers enjoyed the national and world reports was not always as much of a concern to the publisher as was filling his pages. Without syndicate materials he would have to hire more staff, order more supplies, or purchase new press equipment. In fact, newspaper syndicates were always quick to point out the cost benefits of using their services. A March 1901 article in the Kellogg Company trade publication, *The Publishers' Auxiliary*, gave examples of editors who left ready-print, only to come back, mostly for economic reasons. Thus, newspaper syndicates became the "silent partner" of the country press, writing and influencing the opinion of thousands of rural newspaper readers who were unaware of the source of much of their news.[19]

The Power and Influence of Newspaper Syndicates

Aside from providing newspaper publishers a means to cut production and personnel costs, the syndicates also heavily influenced the content and style of weeklies and, subsequently, the lifestyles of small-town and rural residents. The most influential of these syndicates was the Western Newspaper Union. Since its establishment in Des Moines, Iowa, in 1880, the syndicate had more subscribers and geographic spread than any other weekly news service. A large majority of its customers were located in the Midwest region of the country where there was an abundance of small communities, in which it was not uncommon to have more than one weekly newspaper. By the early 1900s, W.N.U. subscriber newspapers represented more than half of the country's total newspaper circulation, with an estimated audience numbering 25 million.

George Joslyn, a successful patent medicine salesman who moved into the ready-print business, became the W.N.U. president in 1890. To build a subscriber base, the W.N.U. and other syndicates worked out franchise agreements with their subscriber newspapers in which editors agreed to purchase a specified number of preprinted newspapers, paid for by cash on delivery. In return, the syndicate provided the subscriber the newsprint and half of the editorial, typesetting, and printing costs. The syndicate could afford to provide the newsprint and production costs because of revenue generated from the national advertising sold on the ready-print pages. W.N.U. was aggressive in its expansion tactics, enabling the company to purchase Kellogg's Chicago-based company and two other leading ready-print companies in 1906.

Readers of W.N.U.-subscribing newspapers read material edited by Wright A. "Pat" Patterson, a former Iowa publisher and Kellogg Company news editor who was hired as editor-in-chief when the Kellogg syndicate was purchased by W.N.U. in 1906. Few knew of his enormous contributions and influence in the country press, starting in the late 1880s. A hint of the influential role Patterson had among the nation's rural newspaper readers was reflected in the headline of an article written about him in the October 1927 issue of *The American Magazine*. The headline read: "Patterson Helps to Edit Twelve Thousand Newspapers." The article, written by Neil M. Clark, began with an account of a meeting between President Theodore Roosevelt and the W.N.U. editor-in-chief, although the specific date of the meeting was not indicated. The article stated that Roosevelt was apparently unaware of the number of readers represented by the newspaperman, who was requesting that the administration play an even-handed role with the country press and the metropolitan press when it came to releasing important information. According to the article, veteran newspaperman Edward B. Clark, who was also in the room, asked the president, "I wonder if you know exactly who this is you are talking to?" When the president replied, "yes," Clark allegedly responded, "Do you realize that Patterson helps to edit twelve thousand newspapers; that the biggest paper in the country has nowhere near so many readers as he has?" The article reported that Roosevelt then asked Patterson for a meeting so he could explain his syndicate's operation to the president.[20]

After 30 years with W.N.U., Patterson, who also served on the faculty of the Medill School of Journalism at Northwestern University in Chicago, relinquished his editor's position in 1940. He then moved to Orange County, California, but continued to write his "Grassroots" column in the W.N.U. trade publication, *The Publishers' Auxiliary*, until 1953. When he died in 1954, few knew of his enormous contributions to the country press, but small-town editors throughout the country knew him to be the man behind numerous stories and advice-filled columns for more than 60 years.

Patterson and other syndicate editors and writers heavily influenced the lifestyles of small-town and rural residents. The "soft-news" material they wrote, edited, and selected for distribution served as a valuable tool for education, entertainment, and even spiritual uplifting. Boilerplate material was as varied as the thousands of community newspapers that subscribed to the syndicate services. There were "women's" columns on housekeeping, fashion, and celebrities, although it was unclear whether women wrote them because no authors' names were provided. Columns geared to men touched on politics, agriculture, world affairs, and business. Page seven of a 1904 edition of *The Indiana* (PA) *Democrat* contained syndicate-supplied material geared to the homemaker. The section title for the page was "Of Interest to Women." It contained tips "For the Dark-Haired Damsel," and instructions on "How to Gain a Correct Poise." A "Household Affairs" column provided recipes for curried lobster and frizzled oysters, while "Household Hints" offered tips on mildew and ink stain removal.[21]

In the early 1900s, many smaller communities lacked a public library and their residents could not afford lavish book collections, so often the community newspaper, a few agricultural journals, and the Bible were the few types of reading material found in a rural home.[22] Housewives clipped the serial novels and short stories of noted authors that were published in weeklies and saved them in scrapbooks for reading material. News items of interest and social commentaries were also collected and served as lessons on government, politics, and current affairs.

One popular feature of the Kellogg plate service was "American History Puzzles." The goal, according to the Kellogg Company, was to develop the puzzles along school lessons so schoolchildren would make use of them. The company wrote in its trade publication, "From innumerable letters which we have received we know that these puzzle pictures have been decided helps in the study of history in the schools, some teachers going so far as to make them a feature of each day's history lesson."[23]

As for educating readers on political issues, the syndicates provided columns written by various political commentators, Patterson among them. Many of the columns were not attributed to the syndicate writer and so were presumed to have been written by the local newspaper editor. *The Troy* (IL) *Weekly Call* ran a regular column titled "Washington Letter" that proclaimed to contain "National and International Affairs of Interest." A sub-headline described the column as "A Budget of News Notes from our regular Correspondent" although no writer was identified by name.[24]

Aware of the opportunity provided through the syndicates to distribute political propaganda anonymously, some politicians tried to exploit the country press. Country editors were forewarned of this practice by the Kellogg syndicate, which proclaimed to its subscribers that, unlike its competitors, it would not distribute such propaganda. A column, titled "Free of Isms," observed in part that a publisher "wants a service he can trust with full confidence that he will not be misrepresented. He does not want to examine the columns of his own paper to discover whether he is advocating a political faith counter to his own ideas or that of his party or readers."[25] Advisories of this sort were printed in The Publishers' Auxiliary, a publication provided free of charge to syndicate subscribers of the A.N. Kellogg newspaper syndicate service (later the Western Newspaper Union). The publication featured tips on workplace efficiency and updates on legislative issues related to the publication industry. Incorporated extensively throughout the issue were articles promoting the benefits of using syndicate-supplied materials, which was of obvious financial benefit to the Kellogg Company.

The Chillicothe (MO) Constitution was one weekly that did not shy away from strong endorsements or condemnations of local political candidates. A 1906 editorial in the weekly accused an incumbent official of political corruption and tainted ties to liquor and railroad interests. The paper strongly encouraged that the official be denied a third term. The endorsed challenger was described as honest, untainted by railroad influence, and in no need of a "whitewashing" of his record. The Chillicothe Constitution had consolidated with the Chillicothe Mail and the Chillicothe Star on Sept. 1, 1900. It was later designated the official county paper.[26]

In contrast, the Laurel (MS) Ledger only went so far as to publish positive biographical sketches of all those seeking county and city offices. Endorsements were not given and commentary was not provided as to the qualifications or lack of qualifications among the office seekers. The Laurel Ledger proclaimed itself to be "The Official Organ of All who Till the Soil." The Cotton Growers' Association and Farmers' Educational Union were listed as sponsors of a page dedicated to agricultural news.[27]

Thus, careful editing at the syndicate offices to eliminate politically partisan material resulted in the local editor rarely having to "choose sides" in relation to ready-print material contained in his newspaper. Since ready-print was designed to be non-controversial, Wright A. Patterson explained in Neil M. Clark's 1927 article in The American Magazine that the syndicate dealt with straight news by summarizing the most significant state, national or international happenings. He added that controversial subjects were "handled as if we didn't have a single opinion of our own."[28]

For entertainment purposes, literary serials were among the most popular ready-print and boilerplate materials. A January 1903 article in *The Publishers' Auxiliary* urged publishers to purchase literary serials, especially following the Christmas holiday season, since their subscribers would have more time for reading following the busy Christmas holiday season. It was suggested, of course, that they run serials provided by the Kellogg Company. "Get a reader interested in a good serial and he will count the days until the next issue of the paper is due," the article stated. "This feeling carries him past the time for cutting off the subscription, if it is the end of his year, and should he be so minded, and insures his continuing on your list."

Publishers were encouraged to print the first chapters of a new serial before concluding another, to hold their readers' interest "so they'll never want to leave you." They were also advised to run an extra printing of the first few chapters of a serial and send it out as a way to attract more subscribers. Betterman Lindsey was the author of a series titled "A Nez Perce Lochinvar" that took up three columns of an eight-columned front page in the September 7, 1901 issue of *The Denton* (MD) *Journal*. An identifying line stated, "Supplied Syndicate Literary Series."[29] Western-themed series were also popular, including "Langford of the Three Bars," which was authored by Kate and Virgil D. Boyles.[30] Other popular serials being published at the time were "The Kidnapped Millionaires," by Frederick Upham Adams, and "A Knave of Conscience" and "The Trouble on the Torolito," both by Francis Lynde.[31]

And finally, on the issue of religious matters, ready-print and boilerplate materials served as a supplement to the Bible. Despite efforts to remain unbiased on religious matters, the ready-print industry did show partiality to its larger Protestant audience, with many of its editorial stances focusing on religious and temperance issues. *The Troy* (IL) *Weekly Call* ran a column titled "Heroes of Faith" that featured weekly Sunday School lessons "specially arranged for this paper."[32]

A New Century, an Old Problem: Local News vs. Syndicated Material

The twentieth century introduced an ever-increasing dividing line between community newspapers devoted to locally generated news and editorials, and those that were content to fill a majority of their pages with nationally syndicated material. "All home print" became the mantra of small-town editors who believed their newspapers were of a higher quality because their news and editorials were written locally. They relied on the curiosity of townspeople to subscribe to their newspapers, which featured lively accounts of local occurrences. Strong, locally oriented editorials were also a common feature of the "all-home-print" publications. In fact, the ranks of "all home print" advocates grew as more rural publishers became graduates of college journalism programs that multiplied, especially across the Midwest and numbered 32 by the year 1912.[33]

College journalism programs in the Midwest had a large potential enrollment population given the high number of community weeklies throughout that region and recognition of the importance of small-town weeklies among its college-age residents. The University of Missouri, which began offering a journalism course in 1878, was the country's first college or university to establish a journalism degree program in 1908. In the late 1800s, journalism courses were offered at University of Missouri (1878), Denver University (1882), Cornell University (1888), State University of Iowa and Ohio State University (1892), University of Pennsylvania and University of Indiana (1893), University of Kansas (1894), University of Michigan (1895), Bessie Tift College of Atlanta (1898), and University of Chicago (1899). At the turn of the century, journalism courses were offered at University of Oregon (1902), University of North Dakota, Iowa State College, and Wharton School of Business at University of Pennsylvania (1903), University of Illinois (1904), and University of Wisconsin (1906).[34]

One of the most outspoken leaders among the "all home print" editors was William Allen White, publisher of the *Emporia* (KS) *Gazette*, who earned a national reputation for his well-crafted editorials on state and national issues. In 1895, at age 27, he purchased the *Emporia Gazette*, which reflected his devotion to locally generated news. He recalled, "We stressed local news and printed a number of items that ordinarily would not have been printed in a strictly conventional newspaper. We were chatty, colloquial, incisive, impertinent, ribald, and enterprising in our treatment of local events ..."[35]

Other publishers in the "all home print" movement joined him to encourage small-town editors to incorporate more local news and features so that their publications were a reflection of their distinctive communities rather than a hodgepodge collection of general interest items. White's strategy paid off as local subscriptions and advertising revenue increased for his newspaper, along with a national appreciation for his editorial opinions that were admired as examples of common sense and honesty originating from small-town America. Small-town weekly editors across the country exchanged newspapers with White and reprinted his editorials in their publications. His writings became so well known that the *Emporia Gazette* attracted subscribers nationwide, especially in the nation's capital. He is best known for his now-famous 1896 campaign editorial, "What's the Matter with Kansas?" which pointed out that while other neighboring states had increased in population and wealth, Kansas had not. He threw pointed criticisms at state officials and the electorate for returning them to office. As a result, he received letters, some angry, most complimentary, from across the nation. Reprints were sent out, and newspapers throughout the country asked for exchanges, or copies, to reproduce in their publications. Despite his growing celebrity, and continued pleas to join the staffs of the nation's leading newspapers and magazines, he remained in Kansas to do the work he loved most, publishing a community newspaper. He remained, however, a regular contributor to such national magazines as *McClure's*, *Scribner's*, *Saturday Evening Post*, and *Collier's*.

The syndicate services aggressively sought ways to downplay the "all home print" movement among weeklies. The syndicates had a way of disguising their ready-print and boilerplate material so as to appear as if it were locally written. Because there were so many neighboring newspapers subscribing to the same ready-print syndicate, there was concern that readers would discover the duplication of pages and determine that their local newspaper was not "all home print." W.N.U.'s Wright Patterson observed, "The service is so organized that papers in the same town, or nearby towns, never are embarrassed by both getting the same material." To prevent neighboring newspapers from receiving the same ready-print pages, different preprinted stories were sent for same-date issues. In addition to avoiding duplication of articles, the W.N.U. editorial office was careful in sending out material without bias. The editorial office was ever mindful that the same articles were read in Protestant and Catholic homes, by blacks and whites, and Republicans and Democrats. Patterson explained, "A man's bringing-up and education have a great deal to do with what he will read and how he takes it …. The great majority are not, consciously, very critical; and yet, subconsciously, they are the keenest of critics—they know what they like, what is helpful to them, what rings true."[36]

As a result of the extensive use of ready-print and boilerplate in weeklies and a decrease in locally written editorials and opinion columns, the image of the crusading editor of the nineteenth century was giving way to the newspaper businessman. The businessman-editor was seen as being more concerned about advertising revenue and not offending the business community than stirring up controversy and increasing subscriptions. By the early twentieth century, fewer community newspapers were identified as "political organs." In 1907, the 1,500-circulation *Indiana* (PA) *Democrat* professed to be "the only Democratic newspaper published in Indiana County."[37]

But beyond identifiable affiliation with a particular political party, editors of weeklies had to be careful even in deciding whether or not to choose sides in a local controversy, because in doing so, they would certainly lose some advertisers or subscribers, not to mention good friends. In a 1907 article about the challenges facing local newspaper editors, Charles Harger pointed out these types of local struggles, such as where to locate a school, whether or not to build a bridge, or even, who should be appointed justice of the peace. He related how activists on opposing sides of local issues sought the newspaper's support. "One leader is, perhaps, a liberal advertiser; to offend him means loss of business. Another is a personal friend; to anger him means the loss of friendship. The editor of the only paper in the town must be a diplomat if he is to guide safely through the channel," he wrote.[38] The inclusion of more local coverage invited more controversy and criticism of the community newspapers. Thus, it made the task of "all home print" advocates to convince their professional peers to abandon syndicate materials seem much more difficult.

But it was not so much a difference in opinion on syndicate content that kept many publishers away from an "all-home-print" edition as it was a matter of money. Being an "all-home-print" publication meant being able to afford more personnel, including trained journalists, and better equipment and supplies to support a 100 percent locally produced and printed publication. Weekly editors who ran "canned" editorials and filled half of their pages with syndicate material did not believe that their publications were any less a "community" newspaper. They simply recognized that without the financial, advertising, and content support of the syndicates, there would be no community newspaper. And a majority of weekly editors, though admittedly there were steadfast holdouts, did aspire to eventually release the shackles of syndication and have their newspapers join the ranks of "all-home-print" publications.

Formal Journalism Education Impacts Weekly Newspaper Content, Personnel

Was a college degree required to efficiently operate a weekly newspaper in the twentieth century? Veteran journalists largely supported the belief that "office" or "shop" training was the only legitimate means to learn the newspaper business. In a 1904 issue of *North American Review*, Horace White, editor of *The Chicago Tribune*, argued strongly against a proposal by renowned newspaperman Joseph Pulitzer to establish a graduate school of journalism at Columbia University. White observed, "Every experienced journalist will agree that a nose for news cannot be cultivated at college."[39] However, more newspapermen realized the advantages of journalism education and their professional organizations began endorsing the concept. Early endorsements for formal journalism education came from Walter Williams, a respected country editor and leader among Missouri's state press association, and other Missouri editors who called for a program at their state university. In fact, the University of Missouri established the country's first college or university degree program in journalism and named Williams as its dean. At the University of Wisconsin, professor Willard Bleyer first taught journalism courses in 1906 as part of a two-year program, which was later expanded to create a department of journalism in 1912. Journalism textbooks were not available in the early years of these programs; so, professors had only their experience and notes to rely on.

Previously, some journalism courses were offered at a handful of universities beginning in the 1870s. The first course was established by former Civil War hero Robert E. Lee, who, after the war, accepted a position as president of Washington University (later Washington and Lee University). He wanted to boost the economic opportunities for young men in the devastated South by offering scholarships in journalism and printing. Within the next few years, more journalism courses appeared among colleges, many in the Midwest, before the degree-offering programs began in the early 1900s. Other professional journalists that early on supported the idea of college journalism courses were prominent New York editor R.R. Bowker, Missouri Press Association president William Switzler, and *The Philadelphia Times* editor Eugene Camp.[40]

As college-educated journalists sought jobs in the field, many were drawn to the allure of a big city and its metropolitan dailies. However, others were attracted to the idea of guiding a community's voice through its hometown newspaper and becoming a community leader. The college-educated country editor was more likely to write a personal column or editorial and replace syndicate material with locally written copy. Another attraction of small-town newspapers was that the publisher-editor reached an elevated status, alongside the local lawyer, doctor, and merchant. In his 1907 article in *The Atlantic Monthly* titled "The Country Editor of To-Day," Charles Harger observed that more country editors were operating like businessmen and that the role of a small-town publisher had become more attractive to the trained journalist. He referred to the number of country papers that operated typesetting machines, ran presses with an electric motor, and gave the editor an income of $3,000 or more and vacation days.[41] "The country editor gets a good deal out of life. He lives well; he travels much; he meets the best people of his state; and, if he be inclined, he can accomplish much for his own improvement," he wrote. Thus, colleges began turning out more graduates who aspired to take on the community leadership role bestowed upon the small-town newspaper editor.

So, while the trained journalist became more of a fixture at metropolitan dailies and small-town newspapers, the commonly held assumption that most journalists aspired to work at the large dailies did not always hold true. Harger observed, "It is often remarked that the ambition of the country editor is to secure a position on a city paper. I have had many city newspapermen confide to me that their fondest hope was to save enough money to buy a country weekly in a thriving town."[42]

Competition between Daily and Weekly Newspapers for Advertisers and Subscribers

As the early twentieth century introduced more competition between dailies and weeklies for college-trained journalists and national advertising contracts, it also ushered in more aggressive actions by dailies to attract rural subscribers, which seemingly would have threatened the very existence of many weeklies. It was also during this period that the more successful weeklies, those that expanded quickly in circulation and advertising revenue, had to decide whether or not to move to a multi-weekly or even daily publication, thus changing the "rural press" image of their publications.

The metropolitan newspapers introduced a new strategy to lure subscribers away from their community weekly by publishing their own weekly editions aimed at rural readers. These weekly editions were mostly compilations of the week's news and contained little or no news from the rural communities. The metropolitan newspapers also sought more rural customers for their daily editions. However, only those farmers who lived close to a post office would bother to pick up their mail more than once a week. It was not unusual for those farmers who subscribed to a metropolitan daily to come in once a week to pick up their sack full of that week's newspapers. To many of these farmers, it just seemed more sensible to subscribe to a weekly.[43] In response to its metropolitan competitors, the community press advertised itself as the best source for local news, though many papers continued to include world and national news from ready-print and boilerplate.

Aside from the dailies attempting to lure away their subscribers, a bigger concern for weekly publishers was that they were being overlooked by national advertisers who opted for the larger audiences guaranteed at a daily newspaper. Charles Allen, in his 1928 textbook on community journalism, observed that small-town publishers had themselves to blame for a lack of national advertising contracts because they did not adhere to fair rates and rules governing national advertising placements. Also, there was no standard column measure among weeklies. National advertisers were, therefore, required to work with individual newspapers instead of sending out a standard-sized advertisement for multiple placements.[44] If weeklies were to continue to grow and thrive in the new century, they would have to adopt better business practices and attract not only subscribers but advertisers, both local and national. In fact, concerns about competition with the metropolitan dailies for subscribers and advertisers, voiced by country editors since the late nineteenth century, had been addressed when Minnesota weekly publisher Benjamin Briggs Herbert led a group of publishers from across the nation to New Orleans in late 1885 to organize the National Editorial Association, a professional organization for the country press. From its Chicago base, the association began publishing a trade magazine, the *National Editorial Journalist and Printer and Publisher* (later renamed the *National Printer-Journalist*) in 1893.

Readership, advertising, and competition from other newspapers were the usual factors that determined whether or not a weekly would convert to a daily publication. However, a 1903 article in *The Publishers' Auxiliary* referred to another community characteristic important in determining if the citizens would support a daily newspaper. The article described the types of communities most accommodating to daily newspapers, as compared to those deemed less accepting. Non-daily towns, according to the article, were those whose people were unprogressive, whose merchants bought and sold in small quantities with no interest in expanding their business volume, and whose town leaders were not interested in securing new industries or holding old ones. But towns more accepting of a daily newspaper, according to the article, were usually located next to railroad connections and were surrounded by potentially profitable territory. The article continued, "If the publishers of some of the local weeklies do not take up the work of giving such towns a daily, some outsider will do so." The article was self-serving for the Kellogg Company because it promoted its ready-prints as a much less expensive means to publish a daily newspaper by providing "everything of a general nature that is supplied by the metropolitan press to its readers."[45]

Despite the aforementioned concerns by weekly publishers that competition from city dailies would put an end to their papers, those concerns were largely dismissed in the latter part of the decade as weeklies continued to thrive. The small-town publications attracted newly trained journalists and, for the most part, hung on to their subscribers despite the best efforts of metropolitan newspapers to pull them away. Charles Harger predicted that an effort by the dailies to include rural community news would not attract enough new subscribers to put the weeklies out of business. In his 1907 article on the country editor, he observed, "The life of a forceful paper is long. One such paper was sold and its name changed eighteen years ago; yet letters and subscriptions still are addressed to the old publication. A hold like that on a community's life cannot be broken by competition."[46]

Frank Gwin, publisher of the *New Albany* (IN) *Public Press* told a 1903 gathering of the Southern Indiana Press Association that every well-established newspaper, whether daily or weekly, had a "clientele peculiarly its own." Gwin advised country editors that the best way to overcome competition from metropolitan newspapers was "to represent people's views in the current events of the day in the news columns. Spicy comments out of the ordinary create talk for the paper, and keep the publication in the public mind."[47]

Harger argued that there were sentimental, even psychological, attachments one had for his hometown newspaper that could not be matched by readers of a metropolitan daily. He observed that a city businessman would throw away financial papers and sensational tabloids but would eagerly open the pencil-addressed home papers "that bring to him memories of new-mown hay and fallow fields and boyhood. Regardless of its style, its grammar, or its politics, it holds its reader with a grip that the city editor may well envy." He said the time had not yet come for the country paper to "assume city airs," nor would it be for many years to come. He explained, "The city journal is the paper of the masses; the country weekly or small daily is the paper of the neighborhood. One is general and impersonal; the other, direct and intimate. One is the marketplace; the other, the home."[48]

Community Weeklies Seek a Stronger Political Voice and Profit Margin

In addition to competing with the dailies for subscribers and advertising revenue, weeklies vied against their metropolitan counterparts to get the ear of their state and national legislators as a means to influence legislation, particularly bills that related to rural residents. Harger argued that small-town weeklies and dailies were more effective at lobbying their congressmen because of the readership they represented. He referred to the remarks of a Midwest congressman who said that he had seen many stacks of community newspapers on the desks of fellow congressmen. According to an unnamed congressman, much attention was given to any country editor who offered a rational idea about a national issue in an editorial because the idea came "from the grass-roots."

The end of the first decade of the twentieth century marked the beginning of a period of phenomenal growth in small-town journalism. The number of newspapers grew at a rapid pace, and country newspaper operations became more sophisticated in their technology and profit-oriented in their business practices. As their metropolitan daily counterparts turned up their noses at these so-called "boilerplate" operations, country editors turned the heads of politicians and businessmen alike who recognized fully the benefit of advertising in their papers and winning the political backing of their readers. In his article about the rural press Harger concluded, "The country editor is doing very well, and the trend of his business affairs is in the direction of better financial returns and wider influence.... Closest to the people, nearest to their home life, its hopes and its aspirations, the country editor is at the foundation of journalism."[49]

Notes

1 "Job Printing," *The Hendricks* (MN) *Pioneer*, October 2, 1902, 1. Hendricks, in Lincoln County, is located in southwest Minnesota. Hendricks had a population of 757 in 1900. *Twelfth Census of the United States*, "Population," volume 1, part 1, section 6, 221, Table 5. http://newspaperarchive.com/, http://www.census.gov/.

2 "A Special Snap," *The Publishers' Auxiliary*, October 1900, 66.

3 *The Rio Grande Republican*, March 3, 1905, 1, 4. Las Cruces, in Dona Ana County, is located in southwest New Mexico. Las Cruces had a population of 1,221 in 1900. *Twelfth Census of the United States*, "Population," volume 1, part 1, section 6, 272, Table 5. http://newspaperarchive.com/, http://www.census.gov/.

4 "For County Printers: Are Entitled to Fair Remuneration," *The Publishers' Auxiliary*, January 15, 1903, 1.

5 In 2022, according to the latest government figures based on the Consumer Price Index, $1,000 from 1900 was worth $35,908 and $1,200 from 1900 was worth $43,090. http://www.measuringworth.com/.

6 "Classified-I Want to Buy," *The Publishers' Auxiliary*, January 1900, 8.

7 John E. Junkin, "President's Annual Address" (paper presented at the Twenty-Second Annual Convention of the National Editorial Association, Norfolk, VA, 1907), 66.

8 Ibid., 66.

9 "A Dangerous Bill," *The Publishers' Auxiliary*, August 1901, 1.

10 "Increased Cost of Stock," *The Publishers' Auxiliary*, February 1900, 1.

11 Charles M. Harger, "The Editor of To-day," *The Atlantic Monthly*, January 1907, 90.

12 "Notices Not Published Free," *Shenandoah Valley*, January 15, 1903, 3. New Market is located in Shenandoah County, in northwest Virginia. New Market had a population of 684 in 1900. *Twelfth Census of the United States*, "Population," volume 1, part 1, section 6, 401, Table 5. http://newspaperarchive.com/, http://www.census.gov/.

13 Junkin, "President's Annual Address," 67.

14 "To the Public Served by the Southern Railway Company," *The Laurel* (MS) *Ledger*, February 1, 1907, 6. Laurel, in Jones County, is located in southeast Mississippi. Laurel had a population of 8,193 in 1900. *Twelfth Census of the United States*, "Population," volume 1, part 1, section 8, 459, Table 8. http://newspaperarchive.com/, http://www.census.gov/.

15 "Our Chicago Exchanges," *Scientific American* 25:20 (November 11, 1871): 313.

16 Eugene C. Harter, *Boilerplating America: The Hidden Newspaper* (Lanham, MD: University Press of America, 1991), 33.

17 "Didn't Know Ping-Pong," *The Hendricks* (MN) *Pioneer*, September 7, 1902, 7.

18 N.W. Ayer & Son's American Newspaper Annual (Philadelphia: N.W. Ayer & Son, 1900), 8.

19 "Ready Print vs. Home Print," *The Publishers' Auxiliary*, March 1901, 1.

20 Neil M. Clark, "Patterson Helps to Edit Twelve Thousand Newspapers," *The American Magazine*, October 1927, 37, 158.

21 "Of Interest to Women," *The Indiana* (PA) *Democrat*, December 7, 1904, 7. Indiana is a borough in the county seat of Indiana County, with a population of 4,142 in 1900. *Twelfth Census of the United States*, "Population," volume 1, part 1, section 6, 340, Table 5. http://newspaperarchive.com/, http://www.census.gov/.

22 William E. Garnett, "Rural Organizations in Relation to Rural Life in Virginia," *Virginia Agricultural Experiment Station Bulletin* 256 (1927): 110.

23 "Talks About Plates," *The Publishers' Auxiliary*, February 15, 1903, 4.

24 "Washington Letter," *The Troy* (IL) *Weekly Call*, June 5, 1909, 4. Troy in Madison County, is located in southwest Illinois, just east of St. Louis. Troy had a population of 1,080 in 1900. *Twelfth Census of the United States*, "Population," volume 1, part 1, section 8, 446, Table 8. http://newspaperarchive.com/, http://www.census.gov/.

25 "Free of Isms," *The Publishers' Auxiliary*, July 1900, 1.
26 "Get to the Polls," *The Chillicothe* (MO) *Constitution*, April 26, 1906, 2. Chillicothe, in Livingston County, is located in north-central Missouri. Chillicothe had a population of 6,905 in 1900. *Twelfth Census of the United States*, "Population," volume 1, part 1, section 8, 459, Table 8. http://newspaperarchive.com/, http://www.census.gov/.
27 *The Laurel* (MS) *Ledger*, February 1, 1907, 2.
28 Clark, "Patterson Helps to Edit Twelve Thousand Newspapers," 163.
29 Batterman Lindsay, "A Nez Perce Lochinvar," *The Denton* (MD) *Journal*, September 7, 1901, 1. Denton, in Caroline County, is located in east-central Maryland. Denton had a population of 900 in 1900. *Twelfth Census of the United States*, "Population," volume 1, part 1, section 8, 454, Table 8. http://newspaperarchive.com/, http://www.census.gov/.
30 Kate Boyles and Virgil Boyles, "Langford of the Three Bars," *Marshall* (MI) *Expounder*, May 1, 1908, 6. Marshall in Calhoun County, is located in south-central Michigan, just east of Battle Creek. Marshall had a population of 4,370 in 1900. *Twelfth Census of the United States*, "Population," volume 1, part 1, section 8, 456, Table 8. http://newspaperarchive.com/, http://www.census.gov/.
31 "Secure New Subscribers—Hold Old Ones," *The Publishers' Auxiliary*, January 1, 1903, 8.
32 "Heroes of Faith," *The Troy* (IL) *Weekly Call*, June 5, 1908, 7.
33 Walter Wilcox, "Historical Trends in Journalism Education," *Journalism Educator* 14:3 (1959): 5.
34 Tom Dickson, *Mass Media Education in Transition: Preparing for the 21st Century* (Mahwah, NJ: Lawrence Erlbaum Associates, 2000), 15.
35 William A. White, *The Autobiography of William Allen White* (New York: Macmillan, 1946), 269.
36 Clark, "Patterson Helps to Edit Twelve Thousand Newspapers," 158, 160.
37 *The Indiana* (PA) *Democrat*, December 7, 1904, 5.
38 Harger, "The Editor of To-day," 90.
39 Horace White, "The School of Journalism," *North American Review* 178 (January 1904): 26.
40 The facts and occurrences of the development of college and university journalism education programs are reported in several journalism history works, among them Richard T. Baker, *A History of the Graduate School of Journalism, Columbia University* (New York: Columbia University Press, 1954); Tom Dickson, *Mass Media Education in Transition: Preparing for the 21st Century* (Mahwah, NJ: Lawrence Erlbaum Associates, Publishers, 2000); Wm. David Sloan, *Makers of the Media Mind: Journalism Educators and Their Ideas* (Hillsdale, NJ: Lawrence Erlbaum Associates, 1990); and Albert Alton Sutton, *Education for Journalism in the United States from Its Beginning to 1940* (Menasha, WI: George Banta Publishing Company, 1945).
41 In 2022, according to the latest government figures based on the Consumer Price Index, $3,000 from 1907 was worth $96,255. http://www.measuringworth.com/.
42 Harger, "The Editor of To-day," 94–96.
43 Wayne E. Fuller, *RFD: The Changing Face of Rural America* (Bloomington, IN: Indiana University Press, 1966), 291.
44 Charles L. Allen, *Country Journalism* (New York: Thomas Nelson and Sons, 1928), 250.

45 "The Value of Newspaper Fields: There Is Danger of Underdoing Quite as Much as Overdoing in the Publishing Business," *The Publishers' Auxiliary*, January 15, 1903, 1.
46 Harger, "The Editor of To-day," 95.
47 Frank Gwin, "The Competition of City Papers," *The Publishers' Auxiliary*, August 15, 1903, 1.
48 Harger, "The Editor of To-day," 92, 94.
49 Ibid., 96.

References

Allen, Charles L. *Country Journalism*. New York: Thomas Nelson and Sons, 1928.
Baker, Richard T. *A History of the Graduate School of Journalism, Columbia University*. New York: Columbia University Press, 1954.
Boyles, Kate, and Virgil Boyles. "Langford of the Three Bars." *Marshall* (MI) *Expounder*, May 1, 1908, 6.
Clark, Neil M. "Patterson Helps to Edit Twelve Thousand Newspapers." *The American Magazine*, October 1927, 36–37, 158, 160–164.
"Classified-I Want to Buy." *The Publishers' Auxiliary*, January 1900, 8.
"A Dangerous Bill." *The Publishers' Auxiliary*, August 1901, 1.
Dickson, Tom. *Mass Media Education in Transition: Preparing for the 21st Century*. Mahwah, NJ: Lawrence Erlbaum Associates, 2000.
"Didn't Know Ping-Pong." *The Hendricks* (MN) *Pioneer*, September 7, 1902, 7.
"For County Printers: Are Entitled to Fair Remuneration." *The Publishers' Auxiliary*, January 15, 1903, 1.
"Free of Isms." *The Publishers' Auxiliary*, July 1900, 1.
Fuller, Wayne E. *RFD: The Changing Face of Rural America*. Bloomington, IN: Indiana University Press, 1966.
Garnett, William E. "Rural Organizations in Relation to Rural Life in Virginia." *Virginia Agricultural Experiment Station Bulletin*, no. 256 (1927): 59, 110.
"Get to the Polls." *The Chillicothe* (MO) *Constitution*, April 26, 1906, 2.
Gwin, Frank. "The Competition of City Papers." *The Publishers' Auxiliary*, August 15, 1903, 1.
Harger, Charles M. "The Country Editor of To-day." *The Atlantic Monthly*, January, 1907, 89–96.
Harter, Eugene C. *Boilerplating America: The Hidden Newspaper*. Lanham, MD: University Press of America, 1991.
"Heroes of Faith." *The Troy* (IL) *Weekly Call*, June 5, 1908, 7.
"Increased Cost of Stock." *The Publishers' Auxiliary*, February 1900, 1.
"Job Printing." *The Hendricks* (MN) *Pioneer*, October 2, 1902, 1.
Junkin, John E. "President's Annual Address." Speech presented at the 22nd Annual Convention of the National Editorial Association, Norfolk, VA. 1907.
The Laurel (MS) *Ledger*, February 1, 1907, 2.
Lindsay, Batterman. "A Nez Perce Lochinvar." *The Denton* (MD) *Journal*, September 7, 1901, 1.
"Notices Not Published Free." *Shenandoah Valley*, January 15, 1903, 3.

N.W. Ayer & Son's American Newspaper Annual. Philadelphia: N.W. Ayer & Son, 1900.
"Of Interest to Women." *The Indiana (PA) Democrat*, December 7, 1904, 7.
"Our Chicago Exchanges." *Scientific American* 25:20 (November 11, 1871): 313.
"Ready Print vs. Home Print." *The Publishers' Auxiliary*, March 1901, 1.
The Rio Grande Republican, March 3, 1905, 1, 4.
"Secure New Subscribers—Hold Old Ones." *The Publishers' Auxiliary*, January 1, 1903, 8.
Sloan, Wm. David. *Makers of the Media Mind: Journalism Educators and Their Ideas*. Hillsdale, NJ: Lawrence Erlbaum Associates, 1990.
"A Special Snap." *The Publishers' Auxiliary*, October 1900, 5.
Sutton, Albert Alton. *Education for Journalism in the United States from Its Beginning to 1940*. Menasha, WI: George Banta Publishing Company, 1945.
"Talks About Plates." *The Publishers' Auxiliary*, February 15, 1903, 4.
"To the Public Served by the Southern Railway Company." *The Laurel (MS) Ledger*, February 1, 1907, 6.
Twelfth Census of the United States. Population. 1900. Edited by United States Census Office. Washington, DC: United States Census Office, 1901.
"The Value of Newspaper Fields: There Is Danger of Underdoing Quite as Much as Overdoing in the Publishing Business." *The Publishers' Auxiliary*, January 15, 1903, 1.
"Washington Letter." *The Troy (IL) Weekly Call*, June 5, 1909, 4.
White, Horace. "The School of Journalism." *North American Review* 178 (January 1904): 26.
White, William A. *The Autobiography of William Allen White*. New York: Macmillan, 1946.
Wilcox, Walter. "Historical Trends in Journalism Education." *Journalism Educator* 14:3 (1959): 5.
www.measuringworth.com.

· 2 ·

THE 1910S: PROPAGANDA, PUBLICITY, PAPER AND POSTAL RATES, AND PATRIOTISM

Weekly newspapers of the second decade of the twentieth century were marked by four main concerns: propaganda, publicity, paper and postal rates, and patriotism. Syndicate services had a diverse audience nationwide but a sameness in content that made it easier for them to promote a political, economic, or social agenda. Press agents, representing public and private concerns, inundated the weekly press with news from any place other than home, which prompted an "all-home-print" backlash movement within the weekly field. But syndicate-heavy and all-home-print weeklies eventually came together in a cooperative effort to bring paper and postal rates down and support the country's war effort, under the watchful eye of a censor-minded government oversight committee.

A vast majority of the roughly 15,000 weeklies across the country subscribed to syndicated ready-print and boilerplate services. Thus, syndicate services had a wide audience for various types of propaganda material, particularly the unsigned editorials and opinion pieces distributed by politicians, political parties, and publicity agencies representing corporate and political interests.

Publicity bureaus became well established in the largest metropolitan areas. They began churning out "free publicity" targeted to weeklies in an effort to promote their clients' products and issues without having to pay advertising space for their messages. "Free publicity" was a derogatory phrase uttered by community weekly publishers embittered by the practice of advertising agencies to place most of their national advertisements in dailies and seek placement of publicity releases in the non-daily newspapers at no charge. The weekly industry fought back, encouraging its members to refuse the material and opt instead for locally generated copy. But ready-print and boilerplate proved too beneficial to smaller news operations, particularly those with three or fewer employees, because they relied on the syndicate material to fill their pages.

Affording the paper on which the syndicate material was printed and mailing costs to distribute their newspapers became major concerns for publishers during this decade. Governmental intervention both helped and hurt the small newspaper industry in terms of paper costs and postal rates. Fortunately, price-fixing among paper manufacturers was brought to an end and proposed higher postal rates for second-class mailings were rescinded.

Resentment on the part of the community weekly establishment toward free publicity turned to patriotic zeal with the outbreak of the Great War, which lasted from 1914 until 1918 and was presumed to be the final multinational military engagement of modern times. However, it was renamed World War I after another multi-national war broke out several decades later that became known as World War II. Weeklies became a vital partner with the federal government to promote patriotism and community support of the war effort. But in the postwar period, the patriotic zeal of a large number of weeklies was carried to the extreme in the form of selective censorship because these newspapers refused to report on growing labor unrest and a surge in the Socialist movement. Many rural editors viewed these issues as a threat to the patriotic principles that their readers overwhelmingly supported.

Community Weeklies: Propaganda Tools?

Country journalism reached a peak in the United States by 1914–1915 as 14,500 weeklies were in operation throughout the country. Though the total for all types of weeklies is listed at 16,277 for 1915, the number of general-circulation community weeklies is considered to be about 14,500.[1] Powerful business and government lobbyists recognized the influence of community newspapers over public opinion because of the vast distribution of ready-print and boilerplate material to an estimated audience of 60 million. There was continued growth in the "all-home-print" movement, but the weeklies that opted for locally typeset news pages were far outnumbered by the small-town newspapers that subscribed to newspaper syndicates. Some weeklies moved away from ready-print, but continued to purchase stereotype plates that could be spread throughout the publication, giving the appearance of an "all-home-print" edition.

Congressmen and other elected officials took notice of the power of persuasive messages emanating from the editorial offices of the country's leading ready-print and boilerplate syndicates and recognized the potential for both influencing public opinion and distributing their campaign material. Lobbyists for big business, foreign governments, and societal concerns also saw the potential to disseminate their carefully crafted messages through syndicate services and used the weeklies to full advantage.

As weeklies became recognized for their use as propaganda tools, government officials grew more concerned about the potential for a single company to monopolize the ready-print and boilerplate industry, thereby monopolizing propaganda messages. By the second decade of the twentieth century, the leading sources for propaganda distribution were the Chicago-based Western Newspaper Union and the New York-based American Press Association. The two companies made a failed attempt at consolidation in 1909 and were embroiled in a bitter trade war in 1911. The federal government intervened in 1912 with a decree in a civil antitrust suit against the news agencies. A *New York Times* article reported that the defendants were restrained from combining or continuing alleged unfair methods in competition. Otherwise, the decree stated, the agencies would destroy one or the other, leaving the other as a monopoly to influence the readers of 16,000 small newspapers, which represented roughly two-thirds of the country's population.

The government did not seek dissolution of either company. It reasoned that news gathering and dissemination could best be performed for the general public through the larger agencies if there remained "fair, genuine and substantial competition." The decree referred to the agencies' failed effort to consolidate that resulted in a 1911 campaign of destructive competition. The decree enjoined the W.N.U. and the A.P.A. syndicates from underselling competitors or issuing false reports that would influence the customers of competitors. The decree forbade such business practices to continue. Otherwise, it stated, a monopoly would have resulted, most likely W.N.U. with its assets of $6.5 million as compared to the A.P.A.'s $1.6 million. It should be noted that estimates on the number of weekly newspapers differed because some totals included special-interest weekly publications, such as labor, immigrant, and minority newspapers, while others referred only to "general circulation" small-town weeklies.[2]

Just three years later, a government petition was filed against the W.N.U. and three of its officials, George Joslyn, H.H. Fish, and M.H. McMillan. The officials were held in contempt of court for failing to comply with the court decree in the 1912 antitrust suit. According to an article in *The New York Times*, the petition was based on affidavits that indicated the W.N.U. circulated unfair reports about competitors in Toledo, Ohio, and Grand Rapids, Michigan, and sold its services to newspapers in Ohio and Michigan for a lower price than its published rates.[3]

The American Press Association syndicate had only 5 percent of the ready-print business in 1912 but by 1917 had fallen to one percent because its chief competitor, the W.N.U., was able to sell ready-print at lower rates. In 1912, the A.P.A. had a large part of the stereotype plate business, but W.N.U. was able to reduce its price on miscellaneous plate matter by one-fourth and on serials by one-third, pulling more A.P.A. customers away. By 1917, A.P.A. decided to close its plate business and petitioned the federal government to see if it had to dispose of its plate plant as junk, or whether it could be sold to W.N.U., its only likely bidder. The court overturned the original decree of 1912, thus allowing W.N.U. to be a bidder and purchaser of A.P.A.'s plate plant. But the outbreak of the Great War turned the government's attention away from the once-warring syndicate factions, which by this time began working more closely together as the increased scarcity of newsprint and mounting prices reduced the size of many country newspapers and caused quite a number to close down.

Aside from protecting competitors in the newspaper syndicate industry from the threat of a monopoly, the federal government also intervened in the affairs of the syndicates on behalf of its readers who were alleged to be unwilling participants in various propaganda campaigns. A 1913 hearing of the U.S. Senate Subcommittee of the Committee on the Judiciary addressed the use of syndicate plate matter for propaganda purposes. Senator Albert Cummins, a Republican from Iowa, asked a lobbyist for the beet sugar manufacturers about the use of syndicated material to affect public opinion, or, in his words, "giving to the public as news, arguments or statements that are intended to promote or sustain a particular propaganda and where the public has no way of knowing that the matter was collected by a person in the employ of a particular interest?" The lobbyist referred to President Woodrow Wilson and Senator Oscar Underwood of Alabama as having used syndicated material from the A.P.A. in their nominating campaigns. Cummins also questioned the lobbyist about the use of syndicated material to affect public opinion "which in turn is intended to influence legislation." Asked to identify all of the men employed by large corporations "to create a public opinion" through use of ready-print and plate matter, the lobbyist responded, "I do not think you would have enough space in this room for them all." The lobbyist mentioned the W.N.U. as being the largest of these syndication services.[4]

The Senate committee's investigation of syndicate material continued into the next year, when it explored the use of ready-print in country newspapers to lure nearly one million Americans to Canada through the use of advertising that was disguised as news. H.D. Cheshire, an immigration agent of one of the large railroads in the Northwest, said in an April 1913 article in *The Washington Post* that close to one million Americans moved to Canada after the turn of the century. He said that despite the efforts of Canadian immigration agents and government officials to lure U.S. farmers, "there are cheap lands in Canada, but they require years of cultivation and many hundreds of dollars' worth of improvements before they can be classed with the farming lands of the United States."[5] A few months later, however, House Speaker James "Champ" Clark of Missouri said that the United States should loosen restrictions on homesteading and promote irrigation to deter the number of American farmers moving to Canada. He estimated that the mass emigration was costing the country roughly $1.23 million a year. For example, Clark reported on a one-week period in 1913 during which 1,845 American farmers, worth $388,500 in cash and $145,000 in personal property, crossed into western Canada to settle permanently in British North America.[6] A New York-based columnist attributed Canada's immigration success to a $2.5 million publicity campaign.[7]

Newspaper syndicate officials and a Canadian interior department official backed up the columnist's claim that advertisements presented as news in small country newspapers were a factor in luring hundreds of thousands of American farmers into Canada. A January 18, 1914 article in *The New York Times* reported that Courtland Smith, president of the A.P.A., testified to the Senate committee investigating syndicate material that the Canadian government paid more than $100,000 a year to the W.N.U., his company's major competitor, for the distribution of ready-print that contained alleged interviews with supposed financially successful settlers in northwest Canada.[8]

He also asserted that the W.N.U. Canadian contract called for the publication of a specified number of the interviews in a specified number of papers. Smith claimed that he had been approached several times by Canadian agents seeking a similar contract but that he always refused the offers.[9] Smith said the press association supplied "plate insides" to small country papers. He submitted a copy of a country paper in the West, with an example of the alleged propaganda. The story was about an Iowa farmer who allegedly nearly starved trying to make a living. He then sold out and moved to Canada, and subsequently became rich and prosperous.[10] An interior department official of the Canadian government testified voluntarily before the Senate committee that his country spent $70,000 a year on publicity to draw American farmers to Canada's northwest region.[11] His testimony was followed by that of H.E. Washington of Chicago, advertising manager for the W.N.U., who testified that the Canadian government paid his organization $42,000 a year to print in 4,800 "ready print" papers statements "portraying in the brightest colors the possibilities of agriculture in Canada."[12]

An unsigned commentary appeared in *The Washington Post* in late January advising the politicians who complained about Canada's publicity campaign to take a closer look at U.S. policies related to homesteading and irrigation. It asked, "Was it merely because they [American farmers] saw an ad or an article in the newspapers that the Americans sold their land in this country and took all their possessions with them into Canada?" It noted that advertising was a potent force, but that it must be supported by solid foundations of truth in order to be successful. Unlike the United States, it observed, "encouragement of the farmer and business man is the gospel of the [Canadian] government."[13]

A June *Collier's* magazine article reported on later testimony by George Joslyn, president of the W.N.U., before the same Senate committee. The article included the following brief extract from his testimony:

> Chairman (Senator Lee S. Overman of North Carolina)-I understand that any company, person, corporation, association, or firm who desire to exploit themselves or exploit their business, and to create public opinion, could come to you and pay you a certain sum... and you would send out the matter they wanted you to send the different papers, which would print it?
>
> Mr. Joslyn-Yes, sir.
>
> The Chairman-And for that sum of money you would send it out to these papers without marking it "Advertisement"?
>
> Mr. Joslyn-Yes, sir.

Cummins blamed the emigration of some 800,000 American farmers to Canada during the previous 12 years on "paid propaganda in the guise of honest news." While the investigation revealed only that the Canadian government was a W.N.U. customer, the article concluded, "It would be interesting to know something about the other 'persons, corporations, associations, or firms' who exploit themselves through the Western Newspaper Union."[14]

Prior to Senate investigations on syndicate material, weekly publishers and editors made no attempt to identify boilerplate and ready-print as coming from a central source rather than the local newsroom. Ready-print pages did not attach author bylines to articles except for some regularly featured columns, such as a popular W.N.U.-syndicated religious column, "Sunday School Lessons," written by the Rev. P.B. Fitzwater of the Moody Bible Institute in Chicago. The July 7, 1918 lesson was titled "Beginning the Christian Life."[15] The column lasted until the ready-print service died in 1953. Therefore, the impression was that their publications were "all-home-print" editions without such a claim ever being made. Homogeneous news items were sent to a majority of the country's newspaper readers without their even knowing it. Thus, weekly publishers and editors were just as misleading in not providing attribution for syndicate articles as syndicate officials were in failing to identify paid publicity or paid advertisements displayed in news-column format as news.

Despite the propaganda assertions made against ready-print and boilerplate, weeklies relied heavily on syndicate material for commercial success. As more local advertisements were sold, more syndicate material was needed to fill additional pages. However, because of the Senate investigations into propaganda and the powerful newspaper syndicates, boilerplate and ready-print were more readily marked in newspapers as advertisements, or small-font letters representing the syndicate, such as "W.N.U." were placed at the bottom of the article, as readers of weeklies were viewing the same articles on a wide assortment of topics. For example, the July 3, 1918 edition of the *Manchester* (IA) *Democrat* published chapters 23 and 24 of "Over the Top," a syndicated newspaper series based on the book of the same title authored by Arthur Guy Empey.[16] He was an American who was frustrated with his country's hesitation to enter the Great War and thus joined the British Army in 1915, serving as a machine gunner in France. Empey described himself in his byline as "An American Soldier Who Went." The series recounted experiences during Empey's military service during the Great War.[17] Ninety miles north and west, in Cresco, Iowa, the *Cresco Plain Dealer* ran the same Empey series and chapters in its July 5, 1918 edition.[18]

In addition to the Bourne Newspaper Publicity law, passed by Congress in 1912 requiring newspapers to make public its owners and circulation figures, and the Audit Bureau of Circulations, established in 1913 by advertisers, advertising agents, and publishers to furnish reliable information on the size and character of the circulation of newspapers and magazines that belonged to the Bureau, other steps were taken during this time to promote honesty in advertising and to protect all newspaper readers.[19] For example, the Standards of Newspaper Practice was adopted in June 1914 by the Newspaper Division of the Associated Advertising Clubs of the World at its annual convention in Toronto. The standards outlined the following duties of a newspaper: to protect the honest advertiser and newspaper readers from deceptive or offensive advertising; to sell advertising as a commodity on the basis of proven circulation; to maintain uniform rates according to classifications; to reject advertising deemed antagonistic to the public welfare; and to cooperate with other newspapers in maintaining the standards.[20]

Western Newspaper Union bought out the American Press Association's boilerplate and ready-print business in 1917, at which time the A.P.A. converted into an advertising agency. Wealthy Omaha, Nebraska, businessman George Joslyn died in 1916, having served as W.N.U.'s president since 1890. In addition to W.N.U. stock, he built his fortune on patent medicine manufacturing and sales.

Free Publicity for Politics, Product Persuasion, and Promotional Purposes

While bitter competition between the dominant ready-print and boilerplate syndicates played out in a courtroom, syndicate material heavily influenced the court of public opinion in the 1912 presidential race, according to George Kibbe Turner who wrote about the election in a *McClure's* article. The 1912 presidential race not only brought a new face to the White House when Woodrow Wilson defeated incumbent President William H. Taft, but it also brought a new means of manufacturing public opinion. Suddenly press bureaus and the placement of free publicity became all important in the election of a national candidate. Turner observed that "direct popular choice of candidates had arrived; the presidential preference primary was here; and candidates, not parties, must introduce themselves directly to the voters--and incidentally finance the machinery for doing so."[21] Democratic nominee Wilson was the first of the candidates to get his press bureau going. Three main outlets for presidential publicity campaigns were daily newspapers, weekly newspapers, and direct-appeal pamphlets and letters. The September 24, 1912 issue of the *Centralia* (WA) *Weekly Chronicle* contained these Wilson-related headlines: "Bryan Will Help Wilson," "Wilson Takes Issue with Roosevelt," and "Wilson Gets Enthusiastic Reception." The articles were released through the United Press Leased Wire.[22] The last name "Bryan" in the first headline referred to William Jennings Bryan, the Democratic presidential candidate in 1896, 1900, and 1908. Twelve years earlier, Luther B. Little had written an article, "The Printing Press in Politics," in *Munsey's Magazine* 23 (1900) about the flood of campaign literature sent out by rival parties in a presidential election. He noted that in the 1896 election, the Republicans distributed, from their National Committee headquarters, roughly 2,000 tons of campaign literature.

What made the 1912 election even more interesting was that former President Theodore Roosevelt ran as a Progressive Party candidate. His campaign representative, Chicago newsman Medill McCormick, sent out queries asking country editors if they wanted a full news service on the Roosevelt campaign. Return postal cards were sent out to 1,500 dailies and 6,000 weeklies. Three-fourths of the newspapers solicited for the campaign news service signed up to receive it. A September 1912 issue of the *Centralia* (WA) *Weekly Chronicle* reflected the political posturing of the candidates in a headline that announced: "Roosevelt Makes Reply to Wilson." The only article related to then-President Taft in that Centralia issue was headlined, "Taft Says He Will Be Re-Elected," and there was no article referring to Socialist Party of America presidential candidate Eugene V. Debs. Democrat Woodrow Wilson won the election.

The *McClure's* article also pointed out that for years, country editors had been receiving plate matter from their syndicates, headquartered in New York or Chicago, for all types of political campaigns. In receiving syndicate campaign material, the editor also received news and composition free, while the politician was the beneficiary of free advertising.[23] Soon followed the passage of the Seventeenth Amendment in 1913 which allowed for the popular election of U.S. senators instead of by state legislatures.

Novelist, muckraking journalist, Socialist, and labor activist Upton Sinclair was a harsh critic of country newspapers because of their use of boilerplate campaign material. His scathing attack on journalism in a 1920 self-published book, *The Brass Check*, pointed out that campaign literature was printed in small-town newspaper offices because so many of them operated as both a printing job and newspaper operation. He noted that much of the campaign publicity also appeared as news in country weeklies. He described the practice of presenting campaign publicity as news as "a graft which is found in every state and county of the Union, and is a means by which hundreds of millions of dollars are paid as a disguised subsidy by the interests which run our two-party political system."[24]

While individual politicians benefited from publicity campaigns waged in weeklies, certain political issues were also the focus of intense propaganda efforts. Pressure from Protestant churches discouraged beer and liquor advertisements from appearing on ready-print pages as national Prohibition became one of ready-print's campaigns. The W.N.U. worked closely with fundamentalist churches for the eventual 1919 passage of the Eighteenth Amendment, which prohibited the production and distribution of alcohol. Numerous anti-liquor and pro-Prohibition editorials and other publicity items were distributed through the syndicate's ready-print and boilerplate services. Among the pro-Prohibition matter was the "Temperance Notes" column that began appearing regularly at the turn of the century.

In fact, W.N.U. Editor-in-Chief Wright Patterson recalled in a magazine article that Prohibition was a subject not to be joked about with the syndicate's readers. He said that a vast majority of humor in the Prohibition era seemed built around bootleggers and illicit liquor, but, he added, "Any joke on the subject offends a good many people, for the simple reason that they do not feel that good citizenship is promoted by ridiculing the law of the land."[25]

By 1920, it was estimated that 95 percent of small-town newspapers used either the W.N.U.'s ready-print or stereotype plate services. A list of W.N.U. ready-print newspapers in 1915, totaled 5,866. The largest subscribing states were in the Midwest, including Illinois, Iowa, Kansas, Minnesota, Missouri, Nebraska, Ohio, Oklahoma, South Dakota, and Wisconsin. W.N.U. Distribution centers were located in Atlanta, Baltimore, Birmingham, Boston, Charlotte, Chicago, Cincinnati, Cleveland, Dallas, Denver, Des Moines, Detroit, Fargo, Ft. Wayne, Houston, Indianapolis, Kansas City, Lincoln, Little Rock, Memphis, Milwaukee, Minneapolis, New York, Oklahoma City, Omaha, Pittsburgh, St. Louis, Salt Lake City, Sioux City, Sioux Falls, and Wichita.[26]

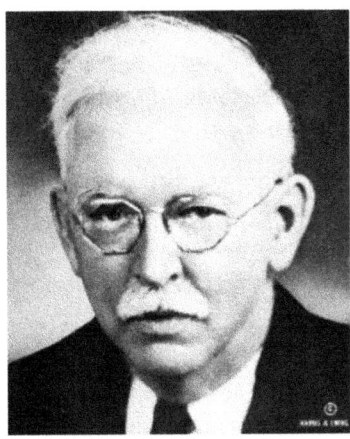

Figure 3.1 Wright A. Patterson, longtime Western Newspaper Union editor. Copyright claimant, Elmo Scott Watson, *A History of Newspaper Syndicates in the United States, 1865–1935*. Chicago, 1936.

In addition to political and governmental affairs publicity, businesses that wanted to promote their products and services looked to the country newspapers for free publicity. Weeklies were filled with publicity items for pharmaceutical products masquerading as legitimate news stories. The appearance of these publicity pieces even resembled regular news stories, both in type style and size and headline writing. For example, an article appeared at the top of page two in the May 6, 1914 issue of the *Stevens Point* (WI) *Gazette* under the headline, "Stevens Point's Reply." A sub-headline, "Stevens Point Accepts the Evidence and Many Stevens Point Readers Will Profit by It," implied a topic of much importance. The article was a testimonial from Mrs. O.E. Smith who wrote to the paper about a backache, headaches, and inflamed kidneys she endured the previous summer. According to Mrs. Smith, a family member suggested she try Doan's Kidney Pills and she was soon able to do her own housework. The "article" concluded, "Don't simply ask for a kidney remedy--get Doan's Kidney Pills--the same that Mrs. Smith had."[27]

Publicity agents for vaudeville and circus troupes and religious revival organizations also sought publicity without having to pay for it. Grant M. Hyde, who wrote one of the earliest handbooks for country editors and journalism students, made the observation that "almost everybody is looking for publicity in these days …" He referred to advertising pamphlets and pointed out that newspaper articles could be derived from the pamphlets that contained some legitimate news of interest.[28]

A Los Angeles brewing company did receive publicity from one of its advertising pamphlets, but certainly not the kind it hoped for. The company sent an advertising pamphlet to residents in nearby Covina, California, promoting its beer. An unsigned editorial, "Bottled Beer and Resurrection" in the March 22, 1913 edition of *The Covina Argus*, derided the company for comparing drinking its beer to the Resurrection of Christ. The pamphlet was sent out during Eastertide when, according to the brewer, people were filled with thoughts of "coming to life and the Resurrection." The company claimed that its beer would "put new life into your veins, a species of resurrection, so to speak." The editorial speculated that the advertiser would not be bothered by criticisms about the "ill-association of subjects." It continued, "The only and the subtlest suggestion that would be entertained by this brewing company advertising genius would probably be a swift kick in the southern exposure of his jeans."[29]

Business Opportunities and Losses: Government Printing Contracts and Rural Free Delivery

Of course, free promotional publicity meant the loss of advertising revenue for country newspapers, prompting printer-publishers to improve revenue-generating services that largely supported the newspaper operation through government printing contracts. North Dakota small-town editor Roy T. Porte found a workable solution to the problem of printers losing money when they bid on government and private printing jobs. Not long after he moved to Salt Lake City in 1916 to become secretary of the Ben Franklin Club, an organization of commercial printers, he published the first edition of the Franklin Printing Price List, which contained suggested charges for a wide range of printing jobs. Commercial printers, newspaper offices, type foundries, paper houses, and syndicates quickly adopted the uniform pricing list nationwide. The following decade, Roy T. Porte established the Porte Publishing Company to continue printing the pricing catalog. The Porte system, as it was known by many printers, included a cost-accounting system with forms designed to gather accurate information to determine individual printing job costs.

The impact of Rural Free Delivery has also been associated with a downturn in weekly advertising in the early 1900s because it brought the closing of thousands of smaller post offices around the country, many of which were located within general stores. Also, Sears and Roebuck expanded its mail-order company, greatly increasing catalog sales, which also hurt small-town businesses. Both of these factors hurt local businesses, which in turn, hurt potential advertising revenues for weeklies.

Cutting into Profits: Paper Costs and Postal Rates

During the period of international conflict leading up to the eventual entry of the United States into the Great War, many small newspapers were on the brink of closing because of supply shortages and rising operation costs. But government officials quickly realized their potential as a mouthpiece for the war effort and provided relief through investigations and legislation to keep costs down. War also brought personnel shortages in the print shops, so wives, daughters, and younger sons were called upon to keep their family newspaper operations running.

A greater number of newspaper consolidations began during the war because of high operation and supply costs; thus, the number of smaller towns supporting two or more newspapers declined steadily. For example, price-fixing among newsprint manufacturers made it difficult for weekly newspapers to stay in business. In 1916, the Federal Trade Commission invoked antitrust laws against the paper industry, which was considering a price hike for sheet newsprint used by weeklies. The F.T.C. found that during the first half of 1916, contract prices for large quantities of paper went as high as $3 per pound, and after July 1, were as high as $3.50. Most metropolitan dailies fell into this category of customer. Before January 1916, market prices for paper ranged generally between $2 and $3 per 100 pounds. However, after January, prices steadily climbed, reaching as much as $6 or $7 per 100 pounds. Prices were even higher for smaller orders, such as those placed among weekly operations. A tentative agreement was reached in which the F.T.C. would administer a distribution plan for paper manufacturers to sell to smaller publishers at contract prices equal to those of larger companies.[30] Effective April 1, 1918, the F.T.C. worked out an agreement with paper manufacturers and set fixed prices ranging from $3.22 ½ per 100 pounds for roll print and $3.62 ½ per 100 pounds for sheet print.[31] Through their national and state press associations, many weeklies joined together for cooperative purchases at more reasonable prices for newsprint, which, as in previous war times, was in short supply.

Proposed postal rate increases also threatened the ability for a country newspaper to stay in operation during this period. In May 1917, a delegation of 150 newspaper and periodical publishers appeared before the Senate Finance Committee to voice their disapproval of a provision in the War Revenue bill to increase second-class postal rates on periodicals and newspapers. The publishers asserted that the rate increases would put two-thirds of the nation's publications out of business. Arthur Dunn of the American Press Association, representing thousands of small newspapers, said country newspapers would suffer most. "Their resources are smaller and they cannot stand much of a strain," he said. "To double the postage rates would drive half of them out of business at once."[32]

An editorial the following month in *The New York Times* described the proposed postage increase as "practically prohibitory upon newspaper circulation in parts of the country remote from the seat of publication." It was pointed out that the government justified the proposed increases by claiming that second-class rates did not adequately cover transportation costs. The editorial concluded that the country's newspapers were willing to "give freely of their profits and their substance to enable the Government to pay the costs of war, but they see no justice in the attempt to single them out for special burdens, heavier by far than those imposed upon the majority of other industries."[33] In September 1917, the Senate turned down a House-proposed system of zones to increase second-class postage. The zone system meant that publications mailed to destinations that were closer to the place of publication would have endured only slight postage rate increases. Thus, mailings to locations in outer zones would have been cost-prohibitive for most country weeklies and publications with circulation beyond a 200-mile radius.[34]

But postal concerns continued to plague small newspapers as Congress approved zone rates for second-class mailings in 1918. Despite general disapproval of the increased mail rates among the publishing community, a North Dakota weekly publisher claimed in an April 1918 issue of *The Publishers' Auxiliary* that the postal zone system would be the "salvation of the country press." J.H. Bloom, editor-publisher of the *Devils Lake* (ND) *Journal*, responded to efforts by the Authors' League, representing the country's national magazines, to repeal the second-class postal zone system.[35] In an open letter to Authors' League president Rex Beach, Bloom argued that country editors and magazine publishers had different purposes: providing news in newspapers as opposed to stories and information in magazines. Thus, Bloom said he could understand the government allowing lower newspaper mail rates because newspapers served a quasi-governmental role in disseminating important news to citizens. But the same argument did not apply to magazines, according to Bloom.

Bloom further argued that postal rates should cover distribution costs, and that newspapers and magazines should increase their subscription rates to meet delivery expenses. He asserted that loyal subscribers would pay higher rates and the distribution of "junk" mail would lessen. For example, he said that farmers in his community would be relieved of the "junk" mail "masquerading as farm journals" that cluttered their mailboxes. According to Bloom, too many magazines "sponged" their transportation from the government, which enabled them to boost circulation and advertising dollars. He opposed the classification of newspapers with magazines because of their differing purposes and delivery distances. He observed that national magazines were circulated over thousands of miles while country newspapers were generally delivered within a 50-mile radius. Bloom concluded that country editors should oppose efforts of the Authors' League to repeal the new second-class postal rates. But, he admitted, his colleagues would more than likely follow big-city newspaper and magazine publishers in denouncing the postal increases, "blissfully unconscious of the fact that by so doing they are assisting the chief agents of the mail-order houses in stealing away their trade."[36]

During this period, it was also common practice for country editors to rely on the "free-in-county" circulation privilege to reduce their overall operating costs. A July 1918 article in *The Publishers' Auxiliary* on a House Ways and Means Committee hearing indicated that the free-in-county privilege for country newspapers would likely not be changed. The article pointed out that "… in every measure proposed to increase second class rates during the past ten years, there has always been a provision excepting the free-in-county circulation of the present law."[37] After the war ended in November 1918, the postwar economy eventually settled, and paper supplies and costs returned to more reasonable rates.

The National Editorial Association went through some significant changes in the latter part of the decade following the 1917 death of N.E.A.'s founder and first president, Ben Herbert, who served in that position for 29 years. In 1919, N.E.A. hired Minnesotan Herbert Cleveland Hotaling, as its first field secretary. The headquarters was moved from Mapleton, Minnesota, to St. Paul, at which time an engraving department was established to provide halftone and line cuts at a reduced cost for member papers.

Patriotism: Country Weeklies and the Great War

President Woodrow Wilson was re-elected in 1916 when the national conversation was dominated by talk of war preparedness. Newspapers, both weeklies and dailies, were filled with pro-Allied forces editorials. After signing a declaration of war, Wilson appointed newspaperman George Creel to spearhead a war propaganda effort. Creel headed the Committee on Public Information, which was established to disseminate facts about the war, coordinate the government's propaganda efforts, and serve as the government's liaison with newspapers.[38]

The Committee drew up a voluntary censorship code; and in May 1917 it began publishing an *Official Bulletin*, which was reprinted in newspaper form. It contained a compilation of war-related pronouncements, announcements, and regulations from all government agencies and departments, including casualty and prisoner lists. Dailies for the most part subscribed to the *Official Bulletin*, but a special free weekly edition was sent to community weeklies in recognition that cooperation was more likely to come from the smaller publications. An article in *The New York Times* announcing the *Official Bulletin's* arrival pointed out that weekly editors in particular were encouraged by the Committee to "copy as many items as possible" from the government-issued newspaper.[39]

In his book *How We Advertised America*, Creel said he initially did not endorse the concept of the *Official Bulletin*, but that Wilson was insistent on it. Creel said of the proposed publication, "I knew in my heart that it would be misrepresented, possibly to a degree that would destroy its usefulness." However, he acknowledged that the *Official Bulletin* proved to be beneficial to the administration in its war-promotion campaign.[40]

In their examination of Creel and the Committee, authors James Mock and Cedric Larson pointed to the impact that the country's war-related propaganda effort had on the typical farm family, which they described as having no phone, living dozens of miles from any railroad, telegraph, or post office, and previously paying little attention to public affairs. But because of C.P.I. propaganda, they asserted, rural residents became more conscious of the war than more "literate" people had been of any previous war. Every item of war news they saw, from their county weekly, agricultural magazines, or the city daily occasionally picked up at the general store, was information of "precisely the same kind that millions of their fellow citizens were getting at the same moment."[41]

New censorship regulations were approved in April 1918. The updated regulations outlined four conditions for articles: maintain accuracy in statement and implication; avoid supplying information to the enemy; avoid injuring the morale of soldiers; and avoid embarrassing the United States or her allies.[42] Concerns were raised at the American Newspaper Publisher Association's April 1918 convention in New York concerning enforcement of the code, so A.N.P.A. representatives called for a gathering of select newspaper publishers to investigate the Committee and issue a report to Creel. Frank Glass, publisher of *The Birmingham* (AL) *News* and president of the A.N.P.A., wrote Creel stating that the Committee review would be beneficial to the country and its newspapers, but would also strengthen the Committee's "power for good."[43] However, an effort to establish the A.N.P.A. committee failed, and criticism of the Committee waned.

The Committee asked major advertisers and newspapers to donate space for war-related campaigns such as soldier recruitment drives. *The Logansport* (IN) *Chronicle* prominently displayed a 1917 front page call to arms that urged young men to "Join the U.S. Army or Navy Now—Your Country Needs You!"[44] A front-page article in the Monticello, Iowa, weekly described how the selective service draft would operate; and how local youths of military age would be "called to the colors."[45]

Red Cross advertisements were particularly rousing in their call for aid on the home front. For example, the back page of a 1917 issue of *The Logansport* (IN) *Chronicle* was headlined "Join the Red Cross." Citizens were encouraged to pay the one dollar fee to join the Red Cross and proudly wear its membership "badge of honor." The promotional stated, "Not only will the Red Cross care for the captive wounded of the enemy as well as our own American Boys, but all measures for local relief, such as caring for needy dependents of the Logansport boys who heed the call of duty, will be centered in the Red Cross Chapter." And finally, Logansport residents were reminded, "The Boys will be fighting your battle. They deserve every ounce of your Moral Support and Your Dollar, too."[46]

A local bank-sponsored advertisement encouraging Monticello, Iowa, residents to join the Red Cross was equally as patriotic as the Logansport message, but much more serious in tone. It stated, "If you give cheerfully and fairly your full share, you are a right minded, patriotic American citizen. If you don't, you are an enemy of this United States of ours and will be known, recorded and treated."[47] A March 1918 article in *The Publishers' Auxiliary* was indicative of the wide-ranging cooperation of weeklies to publish Committee-sponsored articles and advertisements in support of government war fund drives and volunteer campaigns. It reported that country newspapers made it possible for the federal government to raise $100 million for the war fund and increase Red Cross membership to 23 million.[48]

Another war propaganda effort that relied heavily on the support of country newspapers for its success was the Liberty Loan Drive, a war-supported program encouraging citizens to buy war bonds in support of the war effort. Page one of the May 26, 1917 issue of *The Logansport* (IN) *Chronicle* contained three brief articles related to the Liberty Loan Drive. The headlines posed questions such as "What Is a Liberty Loan Bond?" and "What Is the Security for a Liberty Loan Bond?" The third headline asked, "What Is the Nature of a Liberty Loan Bond?" Each article was designed to answer the basic questions about the drive and encourage residents to buy into the war-support program.[49]

An April 1918 article in *The Publishers' Auxiliary* reported that one million dollars would be spent with country daily and weekly newspapers to advertise the third Liberty Loan Drive. According to the article, newspapers secured advertising either from the W.N.U. or from the Liberty Loan committee of one of several Federal Reserve districts.[50] A week later, a report on results of the first week of the loan drive emphasized the importance of publicizing the drive through country newspapers. The article estimated that the third Liberty Loan drive would show greater sales than the first or second "because of the greatly increased publicity given to this loan through the country press."[51]

In his 1927 *American Magazine* interview, W.N.U. Editor-in-Chief Wright A. Patterson talked about the successful relationship of the U.S. Treasury Department and his newspaper syndicate, which placed numerous advertisements supporting the Liberty Loan in its ready-print and boilerplate matter. "The copy was free; it was up to the editor to get the space paid for by patriotic organizations or individuals. In a sense, this was pure propaganda. But the cause was legitimate," he stressed.[52]

Some syndicated war news was informational in nature, such as describing the effort behind providing 210,000 soldier meals while on vessel transport. This article, "Feeding Soldiers on the Transports: Mess Officer of the Vessel Must Provide 210,000 Meals at Sea," was published July 5, 1918 in the *Cresco* (IA) *Plain Dealer*.[53] It was also published in the July 4, 1918 edition of the *Missouri Valley* (IA) *Times*, located more than 300 miles southwest of Cresco.[54] Other syndicated war-related material included a bylined column supporting the war effort, written by Clarence L. Speed, secretary of the War Committee of the Union League Club of Chicago. Column No. 4 in his "Why We Fight" series described Germany's long-fought efforts to undermine the United States government and its ideals, which was published in the July 5, 1918 issue of *The Bystander* in Des Moines, Iowa.[55] That same week, *The Leon (IA) Reporter*, situated 70 miles south of the state capital in south-central Iowa, published column No. 2 in the "Why We Fight" series in its July 4, 1918 edition. The No. 2 column focused on Germany's laws and doctrine.[56]

A similar observation was recorded in a commentary published in April 1918 in *The Publishers' Auxiliary* on the vast amount of publicity opportunities that were available, and the growing number of publicity agents who took advantage of those opportunities. The article pointed out that while some newspaper publishers had pledged a ban on free advertising, a large number gave away more space in news and advertising columns than ever before, but for a good cause: the war effort. The commentary stated, "Simmered down, this free space is being given to the government as a war aid. Thousands of columns of newspaper space are being contributed by the patriotic newspaper publishers throughout the country every week to the cause of winning the war."[57]

While the Committee on Public Information found the country press to be a valuable partner in its campaign to build and maintain support of the country's war effort, the Committee also acted to suppress information considered to be disloyal to the American and Allied war cause. The Espionage Act of 1917 outlined crimes that were punishable by heavy fines and imprisonment for willfully issuing false reports or making false statements that interfered with the country's war effort, or promoted disloyalty in the armed forces, especially as it pertained to military recruitment. The Trading-with-the-Enemy Act of 1917 authorized censorship of all communications moving in or out of the United States. The Sedition Act of 1918 amended and broadened the Espionage Act, allowing the U.S. Post Office to ban publications from the mails. Roughly 75 newspapers, mostly special-interest and German-language, lost their mailing privileges or were pressured to self-censor news about the war. Among the newspapers that were censored were two daily Socialist publications, the *New York Call* and *The Milwaukee Leader*. Also, a Censorship Board, which President Woodrow Wilson established in October 1917, censored foreign cable, telephone, or telegraph communications. *The Publishers' Auxiliary* printed a copy of the only photograph ever made of the Censorship Board. Appearing in the page-one photograph were: Capt.

David W. Todd, U.S. Navy, chief cable censor and director of naval communications; Maj. Gen. Frank McIntyre, chief military censor and chief of the Bureau of Insular Affairs; Robert L. Maddox, chairman of the board and chief postal censor; Paul Fuller, Jr., director of the Bureau of War Trade Intelligence; George Creel, chairman of the Committee on Public Information; Genevieve Chapin, assistant to the secretary of the board; Frederick Blakely Hyde, secretary; and Eugene Russell White, deputy chief postal censor.[58]

It was not uncommon to find C.P.I.-provided and locally written newspaper articles that condemned German military actions or questioned the loyalty of German-American citizens. For example, a 1918 edition of the *Monticello* (IA) *Express* included a page-one article, re-published from *The New York Times*, on German threats to imprison French citizens and inflict injuries on American prisoners in retaliation for German prisoners not being released.[59] A news brief on the front page asserted that German propaganda was "throttled" in attempting to influence congressional representatives following a no-dissent vote in Congress to approve a substantial war bond issue.[60] A brief article on page six of that same issue reported that Russian printers who were prisoners in Germany were forced to print books in Russian "to popularize the Kaiser and everything German."[61] On the back page of the July 4, 1918 edition, an article reported on rumors that a Monticello man of German ancestry was a German spy. According to the article, H.F. Kettlitz, of Monticello, assisted a German-born friend from a nearby community who was arrested on sedition charges. The article explained that Kettlitz was a naturalized American citizen who "is in harmony with the spirit of our institutions and loyal to the country of his adoption." It continued, "He [Kettlitz] says that he is chagrined that someone should do him the injury of circulating untrue reports that reflect on his honor. He lives an open life, and says anyone disposed to believe the slanders has full liberty to follow his movements, during all of his waking hours."[62]

The tone of reporting war news in many weekly newspapers was that of a more personal approach, mainly because of the weekly's inability to hire overseas correspondents. This resulted in readership loyalty to community newspapers, asserted Kansas weekly publisher, Mrs. Thomas E. Thompson, co-publisher with her husband of *The Courant* in Howard, Kansas. She addressed a 1918 gathering of the Kansas Editorial Association at which she talked about competition from metropolitan dailies and the inability of weeklies to compete with the aggressive reporting practices of the better-financed dailies.[63] She asserted that despite warnings that "the days of the country newspaper are numbered" she believed that the country newspaper was "capable of a still greater work than ever it has performed, because of close personal ties to its readers."[64]

Addressing Personnel Problems during a War-Torn Economy

In addition to competing against daily newspapers for war news, small-town newspaper operations also had to compete against the metropolitan dailies for printers and trained journalists with a solid business sense to keep their newspaper operations afloat in a war-torn economy. As in previous wars, the Great War brought personnel shortages to community newspapers, but apprentice programs were not as common as in decades past. However, despite a decline in apprenticeship programs, there was a dramatic increase in college journalism courses and degree offerings. During the decade, 74 colleges initiated journalism instruction, which brought the total to 131 schools in 1920. The American Association of Teachers of Journalism convened at Chicago on November 25, 1912, a year in which 32 colleges were offering journalism courses. In 1917, the American Association of Schools and Departments of Journalism was organized as a sister body to A.A.T.J.

A few college journalism textbooks were published during this period as well, including Grant Milnor Hyde's 1912 publication of *Newspaper Reporting and Correspondence* and Phil C. Bing's 1917 work, *The Country Weekly*. Hyde, a journalism professor at the University of Wisconsin, designed his book to serve as a general guide for all journalists on how to write different types of news stories.[65] Bing, a University of Minnesota journalism professor, directed his manual to students and practitioners of rural journalism. He wrote that despite ridicule from metropolitan dailies and "city folk in general," the country newspaper was the best paper printed.[66]

As during wars past, wives and daughters took over largely family-owned operations, including newspapers. However, by this decade the woman's suffrage movement was in full swing and women who were sole proprietors, or those who assisted their husbands in the publishing business, recognized their important civic role and the need to stay abreast of political issues. Mrs. Thomas E. Thompson, of *The Courant* in Howard, Kansas, was quoted in a 1918 article in *The Publishers' Auxiliary* concerning the importance for the country newspaper woman to be as aware of current political affairs as her husband. "It is now up to her to know something of politics--with which newspapers are so much concerned--of statecraft, of current world history and present-day progress," Thompson said.[67]

Beyond the Battlefields and on to the Business of Boosterism

The pro-war effort of the country's weeklies ended with the signing of the Versailles Treaty in June 1919, followed by a period during which community readers were largely left out of the national discussion on the spread of labor unrest and the Socialist Party, unless they also read a metropolitan daily. The W.N.U.'s Wright A. Patterson readily admitted that controversial subjects in ready-print and boilerplate matter were avoided or "handled as if we didn't have a single opinion of our own" because controversial topics aroused animosity among the syndicate's subscribers.[68] So, even though boilerplate allowed weekly editors to "pick and choose" among syndicate material provided rather than run entire ready-print pages, their choices were limited because controversial topics had already been censored by Patterson, in his role as editor-in-chief, at the centralized syndicate office.

Upton Sinclair, who was a regular contributor to the Socialist *New York Call*, had harsh words for the country editors he claimed were more concerned with "boosterism" and advertising revenues than the terrible working conditions of the American laborer. He wrote in his self-published 1920 work *The Brass Check* that the average country editor was an "ignorant" man whose idea of what was good for his readers included "optimism and boost," "cheer-up" stuff, "mother, home and heaven" stuff, "sob" stuff, and "slush for the women." He criticized country editors for their use of ready-print and boilerplate. He also pointed out that sandwiched between this "filler" material was the "poison propaganda" of the Merchants' and Manufacturers' Association, tariff lobbyists, railroad lobbyists, liquor lobbyists, and "the whole machine of capitalist graft and greed."[69]

In Bing's manual for the rural journalist, the author argued that country newspapers should focus on local matters rather than national or international events that had no local repercussions. He acknowledged that although there was a tendency among metropolitan dailies and their readers to ridicule the country newspaper, the criticism should be overlooked. However, *The Butts County* (GA) *Progress* could not overlook the fact that *The Atlanta*

Constitution applauded a 1911 *Progress* editorial on the evolution of agriculture in the state. The editorial stated in part: "The one-horse farmer is no longer a term of derision. Time was when the one-horse farmer belonged to the poor trash class. Not so now. The one-horse farmer is the best investment any county can have, same as the one-horse merchant." The editorial supported small farmers who worked their own land, as opposed to the thousands of acres held in "cold storage" by large plantations that promoted the "undesirable condition of tenancy."[70]

The *Butts County Progress* editorial brought attention and acclaim to the state's rural residents, which certainly would have been considered a worthwhile endeavor to Bing, who argued that the country weekly's role was to promote the interests of the common man. Comparing metropolitan dailies and country weeklies, Bing asserted that the small-town weekly was the better newspaper than the metropolitan daily because "it comes nearer to fulfilling the purpose for which it was established–that of telling the news about its own community and of neighboring communities—than any other kind of paper can possibly come."[71]

Notes

1 N.W. Ayer & Son's *American Newspaper Annual and Directory* (Philadelphia: N.W. Ayer & Sons, 1916), 11.

2 "News Trust Checked by Government Suit: Western Newspaper Union and American Press Association Restrained by Court, Affects 60,000,000 Readers: Government Saw Possibility of a Combination Which Would Be Used to Sway Public Opinion," *The New York Times*, August 4, 1912, 8. In 2022, according to the latest government figures based on the Consumer Price Index, $6.5 million from 1912 was worth $202 million and $1.6 million from 1912 was worth $439.7 million. http://www.measuringworth.com/.

3 "Accuse Newspaper Union: Western Syndicate Charged with Violating Federal Court's Order," *The New York Times*, June 8, 1915, 9.

4 Subcommittee of the Committee on the Judiciary, *Maintenance of a Lobby to Influence Legislation*, Sixty-Third Congress, First Session, August 1913, 1,113.

5 "Come Back from Canada," *The Washington Post*, April 8, 1913, 6.

6 "Millions Lost to U.S.," *The Washington Post*, June 23, 1913, 4. In 2022, according to the latest government figures based on the Consumer Price Index, $1.23 million from 1913 was worth $38.545 million, $388,500 was worth $12.174 million and $145,000 was worth $4.543 million. http://www.measuringworth.com/.

7 Holland, "Holland Says Publicity Aids in Canada's Vast Industrial Growth," *The Washington Post*, August 18, 1913, 7. In 2022, according to the latest government figures

8 based on the Consumer Price Index, $2.5 million from 1913 was worth $78.343 million. http://www.measuringworth.com/.
 8 In 2022, according to the latest government figures based on the Consumer Price Index, $100,000 from 1913 was worth $3,044,750. http://www.measuringworth.com/.
 9 "Canada Accused of Luring Farmers," *The New York Times*, January 18, 1914, 1.
10 "'Misled by Canada'" *The Washington Post*, January 18, 1914, 4.
11 In 2022, according to the latest government figures based on the Consumer Price Index, $70,000 from 1913 was worth $2,131,325. http://www.measuringworth.com/.
12 "Against Canadian Lure," *The Washington Post*, January 29, 1914, 2. In 2022, according to the latest government figures based on the Consumer Price Index, $42,000 from 1913 was worth $1,278,795. http://www.measuringworth.com/.
13 "Canada's Advertising," *The Washington Post*, January 30, 1914, 6.
14 "A Real Case of Tainted News," *Collier's*, June 6, 1914, 16.
15 Rev. P.D. Fitzwater, "Sunday School Lesson: Beginning the Christian Life," *Audubon County* (IA) *Journal*, July 4, 1918, 7. Audubon is in Audubon County, which is located in southwest Iowa. The county had a total population of 12,671 in 1910. *Thirteenth Census of the United States*, "Population," volume 1, section 2, 107, Table 64. http://newspaperarchive.com/, http://www.census.gov/.
16 Arthur Guy Empey, *Over the Top* (New York: Putnam's/The Knickerbocker Press, 1917).
17 Empey, "Over the Top," *The Manchester* (IA) *Democrat*, July 3, 1918, 7. Manchester in Delaware County, is located in northeast Iowa. It had a population of 2,758 in 1910. *Thirteenth Census of the United States*, "Population," volume 1, section 2, 90, Table 59. http://newspaperarchive.com/, http://www.census.gov/.
18 Empey, "Over the Top," *The Cresco* (IA) *Plain Dealer*, July 5, 1918, 3. Cresco is a town in Howard County, Iowa. In 1910, it had a population of 2,658. *Thirteenth Census of the United States*, "Population," volume 1, section 2, 90, Table 59. http://newspaperarchive.com/, http://www.census.gov/.
19 Bleyer, *Main Currents in the History of American Journalism*, 418–420.
20 "Advertising Ethics Are Now Codified," *The New York Times*, June 24, 1914, 4.
21 George Kibbe Turner, "Manufacturing Public Opinion: The New Art of Making Presidents by Press Bureau," *McClure's* July 1912, 318.
22 *Centralia* (WA) *Weekly Chronicle*, September 24, 1912, 2, 4, 7. Centralia in Lewis County, is located in southwest Washington, south of Olympia. Centralia had a population of 7,311 in 1910. *Thirteenth Census of the United States*, "Population," volume 1, section 2, 97, Table 59. http://newspaperarchive.com/, http://www.census.gov/.
23 Turner, "Manufacturing Public Opinion: The New Art of Making Presidents by Press Bureau," 323–324.
24 Upton Sinclair, *The Brass Check* (Pasadena, CA: Upton Sinclair, 1920): 238.
25 Neil M. Clark, "Patterson Helps to Edit Twelve Thousand Newspapers," *The American Magazine*, October 1927, 163.
26 Eugene C. Harter, *Boilerplating America: The Hidden Newspaper* (Lanham, MD: University Press of America, 1991), 54, 225.
27 "Stevens Point's Reply," *The Stevens Point Gazette*, May 6, 1914, 2. Stevens Point, in Portage County, is located in central Wisconsin. Stevens Point had a population of 8,692

in 1910. *Thirteenth Census of the United States*, "Population," volume 1, section 2, 97, Table 59. http://newspaperarchive.com/, http://www.census.gov/.
28 Grant M. Hyde, *Newspaper Reporting and Correspondence* (New York: D. Appleton and Company, 1912), 10, 121.
29 "Bottled Beer and Resurrection," *The Covina* (CA) *Argus*, March 22, 1913, 4. Covina is located in Los Angeles County, 22 miles east of Los Angeles. The population of Covina in 1910 was 3,476. *Thirteenth Census of the United States*, "Population," volume 1, section 2, Table 2. http://newspaperarchive.com/, http://www.census.gov/.
30 "Trade Board Wants to Divide Up Paper," *The New York Times*, December 13, 1916, 17. In 2022, according to the latest government figures based on the Consumer Price Index, $2 to $7 from 1916 was worth $54.94 to $192.30. http://www.measuringworth.com/.
31 "Federal Trade Commission Fixes Prices," *The Publishers' Auxiliary*, June 22, 1918, 1.
32 "Publishers Attack Postal Increase," *The New York Times*, May 15, 1917, 4.
33 "Taxing Newspapers," *The New York Times*, June 20, 1917, 10.
34 "The Postage Tax," *The New York Times*, September 17, 1917, 12.
35 Devils Lake, in North Dakota's Ramsey County, had a population of 5,157 in 1910. *Thirteenth Census of the United States*, "Population," volume 1, section 2, 583, Table 1. http://newspaperarchive.com/, http://www.census.gov/.
36 "Zone System Is Salvation of Country Newspapers," *The Publishers' Auxiliary*, April 27, 1918, 1.
37 "Free County Circulation Will Remain: No Likelihood of Change in Law as It Now Affects Many Country Publishers," *The Publishers' Auxiliary*, July 20, 1918, 1.
38 "Creel to Direct Nation's Publicity," *The New York Times*, April 15, 1917, 1.
39 "A Government Newspaper," *The New York Times*, May 10, 1917, 9.
40 George Creel, *How We Advertised America: The First Telling of the Amazing Story of the Committee on Public Information that Carried the Gospel of Americanism to Every Corner of the Globe* (New York: Harper & Brothers, 1920), 208.
41 James R. Mock and Cedric Larson, *Words that Won the War: The Story of the Committee on Public Information, 1917–1919* (Princeton, NJ: Princeton University Press, 1939), 6.
42 "Provisions of New Censorship Regulations Are Made Public," *The Publishers' Auxiliary* 53:15 (April 13, 1918), 1.
43 "Creel Promised Quick Inquiry by Publishers," *The Publishers' Auxiliary*, May 11, 1918, 1.
44 "Join the U.S. Army or Navy Now—Your Country Needs You!" *The Logansport* (IN) *Chronicle*, May 26, 1917, 1. Logansport in Cass County, is located in north-central Indiana. Logansport had a population of 19,050 in 1910. *Thirteenth Census of the United States*, "Population," volume 1, section 2, 89, Table 59. http://newspaperarchive.com/, http://www.census.gov/.
45 "Draft Numbers Are All Drawn at Washington," *The Monticello* (IA) *Express*, July 4, 1918, 6. Monticello, in Jones County, is located in east-central Iowa. Monticello had a population of 2,043 in 1910. *Thirteenth Census of the United States*, "Population," volume 2, section 5, 595, Table 1. Population of Minor Civil Divisions: 1910, 1900, and 1890. http://newspaperarchive.com/, http://www.census.gov/.
46 "Join the Red Cross," *The Logansport* (IN) *Chronicle*, May 26, 1917, 8.
47 "Remember the Red Cross," *The Monticello* (IA) *Express*, July 4, 1918, 1.

48 Henry P. Davison, "Publishers of America Deserve Credit for Greatness of Red Cross," *The Publishers' Auxiliary*, March 23, 1918, 1. In 2022, according to the latest government figures based on the Consumer Price Index, $100,000,000 from 1918 was worth $1,940,876,494. http://www.measuringworth.com/.
49 "What Is a Liberty Loan Bond?" *The Logansport* (IN) *Chronicle*, May 26, 1917, 1.
50 "Big Sum to Be Spent for Liberty Loan Ads," *The Publishers' Auxiliary*, April 6, 1918, 1.
51 "Country Newspapers Deserve Credit for Loan Drive Success," *The Publishers' Auxiliary*, April 13, 1918, 1.
52 Clark, "Patterson Helps to Edit Twelve Thousand Newspapers," 164.
53 "Feeding Soldiers on the Transports: Mess Officer of the Vessel Must Provide 210,000 Meals at Sea," *Cresco* (IA) *Plain Dealer*, July 5, 1918, 7.
54 "Feeding Soldiers on the Transports: Mess Officer of the Vessel Must Provide 210,000 Meals at Sea," *Missouri Valley* (IA) *Times*, July 4, 1918, 3. Missouri Valley is a town in Harrison County in west-central Iowa. Missouri Valley had a population of 3,187 in 1910. *Thirteenth Census of the United States*, "Population," volume 2, section 5, 90, Table 59. Population of Minor Civil Divisions: 1910, 1900, and 1890. http://newspaperarchive.com/, http://www.census.gov/.
55 Clarence L. Speed, "Why We Fight: No. 4," *The* (Des Moines, IA) *Bystander*, July 5, 1918, 2. Des Moines had a population of 86,368 in 1910. *Thirteenth Census of the United States*, "Population," volume 1, section 2, 84, Table 58. http://newspaperarchive.com/, http://www.census.gov/.
56 Clarence L. Speed, "Why We Fight: No. 2," *The Leon* (IA) *Reporter*, July 4, 1918, 6. Leon is in Decatur County, Iowa, and had a population of 1,991 in 1910. *Thirteenth Census of the United States*, "Population," volume 2, section 5, 578, Table 1. Population of Minor Civil Divisions: 1910, 1900, and 1890. http://newspaperarchive.com/, http://www.census.gov/.
57 "… This Paper has Enlisted with the Government in the Cause of America for the Period of the War …: Publicity," *The Publishers' Auxiliary*, April 6, 1918, 4.
58 "Government Board of Censorship Which Says What Newspapers May Print on War," *The Publishers' Auxiliary*, May 11, 1918, 1.
59 "More Atrocities Are Threatened," *The Monticello* (IA) *Express*, July 4, 1918, 1.
60 "A Brief," *The Monticello* (IA) *Express*, July 4, 1918, 1.
61 "Worth Knowing," *The Monticello* (IA) *Express*, July 4, 1918, 6.
62 Ibid., 8.
63 Howard Kansas, in Elk County, is located in southeast Kansas. The town had a population of 1,165 in 1910. *Thirteenth Census of the United States*, "Population," volume 2, section 5, 576, Table 1. Population of Minor Civil Divisions: 1910, 1900, and 1890. http://newspaperarchive.com/, http://www.census.gov/.
64 "Newspaper Woman Has Own Place: There Is Distinct Field in Which She Can be of Service, Says an Editor's Wife," *The Publishers' Auxiliary*, June 8, 1918, 5.
65 Grant M. Hyde, *Newspaper Reporting and Correspondence* (New York: D. Appleton and Company, 1912).
66 Phil C. Bing, *The Country Weekly: A Manual for the Rural Journalist and for Students of the Country Field* (New York: D. Appleton & Co., 1917), 7.
67 "Newspaper Woman Has Own Place," 5.

68 Clark, "Patterson Helps to Edit Twelve Thousand Newspapers," 163.
69 Sinclair, *The Brass Check* (Pasadena, CA: Upton Sinclair, 1920), 239.
70 "Constitution Endorses the Progress Editorial," *The Butts County* (GA) *Progress*, February 10, 1911, 1. Jackson in Butts County, is located in north-central Georgia, southeast of Atlanta. Jackson had a population of 1,862 in 1910. *Thirteenth Census of the United States*, "Population," volume 2, section 3, 343, Table 1. Population of Minor Civil Divisions: 1910, 1900, and 1890. http://newspaperarchive.com/, http://www.census.gov/.
71 Bing, *The Country Weekly: A Manual for the Rural Journalist and for Students of the Country Field*, 7.

References

"Accuse Newspaper Union: Western Syndicate Charged with Violating Federal Court's Order." *The New York Times*, June 8, 1915, 9.
"Advertising Ethics Are Now Codified." *The New York Times*, June 24, 1914, 4.
"Against Canadian Lure." *The Washington Post*, January 29, 1914, 2.
"Big Sum to Be Spent for Liberty Loan Ads." *The Publishers' Auxiliary*, April 6, 1918, 1.
Bing, Phil C. *The Country Weekly: A Manual for the Rural Journalist and for Students of the Country Field*. New York: D. Appleton & Co., 1917.
Bleyer, Willard Grosvenor. *Main Currents in the History of American Journalism*. Boston: Houghton Mifflin, 1927.
"Bottled Beer and Resurrection." *The Covina* (CA) *Argus*, March 22, 1913, 4.
"A Brief." *The Monticello* (IA) *Express*, July 4, 1918, 1.
"Canada Accused of Luring Farmers." *The New York Times*, January 18, 1914, 1.
"Canada's Advertising." *The Washington Post*, January 30, 1914, 6.
Centralia (WA) *Weekly Chronicle*, September 24, 1912, 2, 4, 7.
Clark, Neil M. "Patterson Helps to Edit Twelve Thousand Newspapers." *The American Magazine*, October 1927, 36–37, 158, 160–164.
"Come Back from Canada." *The Washington Post*, April 8, 1913, 6.
"Constitution Endorses The Progress Editorial." *The Butts County* (GA) *Progress*, February 10, 1911, 1.
"Country Newspapers Deserve Credit for Loan Drive Success." *The Publishers' Auxiliary*, April 13, 1918, 1.
Creel, George. *How We Advertised America: The First Telling of the Amazing Story of the Committee on Public Information that Carried the Gospel of Americanism to Every Corner of the Globe*. New York: Harper & Brothers, 1920.
"Creel Promised Quick Inquiry by Publishers." *The Publishers' Auxiliary*, May 11, 1918, 1.
"Creel to Direct Nation's Publicity." *The New York Times*, April 15, 1917, 1.
Davison, Henry P. "Publishers of America Deserve Credit for Greatness of Red Cross." *The Publishers' Auxiliary*, March 23, 1918.
"Draft Numbers Are All Drawn at Washington." *The Monticello* (IA) *Express*, July 4, 1918, 6.
Empey, Arthur Guy. *Over the Top*. New York: Putnam's/The Knickerbocker Press, 1917.

Empey, "Over the Top." *The Manchester* (IA) *Democrat*, July 3, 1918, 7.

Empey, "Over the Top." *The Cresco* (IA) *Plain Dealer*, July 5, 1918, 3.

"Federal Trade Commission Fixes Prices." *The Publishers' Auxiliary*, June 22, 1918, 1.

"Feeding Soldiers on the Transports: Mess Officer of the Vessel Must Provide 210,000 Meals at Sea." *Cresco* (IA) *Plain Dealer*, July 5, 1918, 7.

"Feeding Soldiers on the Transports: Mess Officer of the Vessel Must Provide 210,000 Meals at Sea." *Missouri Valley* (IA) *Times*, July 4, 1918, 3.

Fitzwater, Rev. P.D. "Sunday School Lesson: Beginning the Christian Life." *Audubon County* (IA) *Journal*, July 4, 1918, 7.

"Free County Circulation will Remain: No Likelihood of Change in Law as it Now Affects Many Country Publishers." *The Publishers' Auxiliary*, July 20, 1918, 1.

"Government Board of Censorship Which Says What Newspapers May Print on War." *The Publishers' Auxiliary*, May 11, 1918, 1.

"A Government Newspaper." *The New York Times*, May 10, 1917, 9.

Holland. "'Holland' Says Publicity Aids in Canada's Vast Industrial Growth." *The Washington Post*, August 18, 1913, 7.

Hyde, Grant M. *Newspaper Reporting and Correspondence*. New York: D. Appleton and Company, 1912.

"Join the Red Cross." *The Logansport* (IN) *Chronicle*, May 26, 1917, 8.

"Join the U.S. Army or Navy Now—Your Country Needs You!" *The Logansport* (IN) *Chronicle*, May 26, 1917, 1.

"Millions Lost to U.S." *The Washington Post*, June 23, 1913, 4.

"'Misled by Canada.'" *The Washington Post*, January 18, 1914, 4.

Mock, James R., and Cedric Larson. *Words that Won the War: The Story of the Committee on Public Information, 1917–1919*. Princeton, NJ: Princeton University Press, 1939.

"More Atrocities are Threatened." *The Monticello* (IA) *Express*, July 4, 1918, 1.

"News Trust Checked by Government Suit: Western Newspapers Union and American Press Association Restrained by Court, Affects 60,000,000 Readers: Government Saw Possibility of a Combination Which Would Be Used to Sway Public Opinion." *The New York Times*, August 4, 1912, 8.

"Newspaper Woman Has Own Place: There Is Distinct Field in Which She Can be of Service, Says an Editor's Wife." *The Publishers' Auxiliary*, June 8, 1918, 5.

N.W. Ayer & Son's American Newspaper Annual and Directory. Philadelphia: N.W. Ayer & Sons, 1916.

"The Postage Tax." *The New York Times*, September 17, 1917, 12.

"Provisions of New Censorship Regulations Are Made Public." *The Publishers' Auxiliary* 53:15 (April 13, 1918), 1.

"Publishers Attack Postal Increase." *The New York Times*, May 15, 1917, 4.

"A Real Case of Tainted News." *Collier's*, June 6, 1914, 16.

"Remember the Red Cross." *The Monticello* (IA) *Express*, July 4, 1918, 1.

Sinclair, Upton. *The Brass Check*. Pasadena, Calif.: Upton Sinclair, 1920.

Speed, Clarence L. "Why We Fight: No. 4." *The* (Des Moines, IA) *Bystander*, July 5, 1918, 2.

Speed, Clarence L. "Why We Fight: No. 2," *The Leon* (IA) *Reporter*, July 4, 1918, 6.

"Stevens Point's Reply." *The Stevens Point* (WI) *Gazette*, May 6, 1914, 2.

Subcommittee of the Committee on the Judiciary. *Maintenance of a Lobby to Influence Legislation*, Sixty-Third Congress, First Session, August 1913.

"Taxing Newspapers." *The New York Times*, June 20, 1917, 10.

Thirteenth Census of the United States. Population. 1910. edited by United States Bureau of the Census: Washington, DC: Government Printing Office, 1913.

"… This Paper has Enlisted with the Government in the Cause of America for the Period of the War…: Publicity." *The Publishers' Auxiliary*, April 6, 1918, 4.

"Trade Board Wants to Divide Up Paper." *The New York Times*, December 13, 1916, 17.

Turner, George Kibbe. "Manufacturing Public Opinion: The New Art of Making Presidents by Press Bureau." *McClure's*, July, 1912, 316–327.

"What Is a Liberty Loan Bond?" *The Logansport* (IN) *Chronicle*, May 26, 1917, 1.

"Worth Knowing." *The Monticello* (IA) *Express*, July 4, 1918, 6.

www.measuringworth.com.

"Zone System is Salvation of Country Newspapers." *The Publishers' Auxiliary*, April 27, 1918, 1.

· 3 ·

THE 1920S: NEW COMPETITION, INFLUENCE, AND COMMERCIAL SUCCESS

During the 1920s, a period often referred to as the Roaring Twenties, advanced technologies such as automobiles and radio, new forms of artistic expression such as jazz music and art deco design styles, and business risk-taking brought a new era of modernity and optimism to the United States. The community newspaper field became a part of the business boom-or-bust cycle in the midst of expanded competition, community influence, and commercial success. Radio became a financial threat to weeklies as the medium moved from single-sponsor programs to individual advertising messages placed between and during scheduled programs. During the decade, academic studies, particularly in the area of sociology, began to consider not only the content of a community's newspaper, but its influence on local decision-making as well. And finally, weeklies declined in number but increased in financial well-being as consolidations and mergers closed down the weeklies that were unable to remain as stand-alone operations.

Competition with metropolitan dailies for local and national advertising dollars grew as did aggressive advertising-seeking tactics of billboard, sign-painting, and handbill (a precursor to the weekly "shopper" newspaper) businesses. But the biggest advertising threat for weeklies to emerge in the 1920s was radio. A growing number of retailers and companies transferred portions, large and small, of their advertising budgets from weeklies to radio. The advertisers were drawn to large listening audiences and the novelty of "hearing" their paid messages as opposed to just "seeing" them.

Despite financial uncertainties in the fight for advertising dollars, the status of the small-town newspaper and its social influence on the community remained firm. Some sociologists recognized the key role of the community newspaper as well, and began studying the political and social influences of weeklies and their editors. Interestingly, some of the media-influence studies occurred at the same time that elitist metropolitan journalists and literary writers criticized small-town editors for avoiding controversy in editorial columns or abandoning editorial writing altogether.

Newspaper consolidations, mergers, and chain ownership in the 1920s dramatically decreased the number of weeklies but resulted in newspapers that were more commercially viable. Commercial success came to the weekly publishers who improved their business skills, modernized their printing operations, and attracted national advertisers. The stock market crash of 1929, however, brought a devastating financial blow to the surviving newspaper groups and chains, leaving many more publications to fight for survival into the next decade.

Small-Town Press vs. Radio for Advertising in the Rapidly Expanding Spend-Credit Economy

The potential to increase advertising revenue grew enormously for weeklies in the early 1920s as new products and services flooded the marketplace. But the economic resurgence in the weekly field was short-lived after radio was introduced to the general public. National advertisers were especially drawn to the new communications medium, and many transferred their advertising dollars away from print and into radio. However, a healthy consumer appetite and growing credit market proved to be enough to ensure a steady flow of advertising revenue to the majority of small-town newspapers.

In the early 1920s, the weekly served as a valuable advertising medium to facilitate "efficient merchandising" and support a community's economic health.[1] A common-folk phrasing of the same message was delivered in 1922 in a page-one plea in *The Brookshire* (TX) *Times* to the merchants of Brookshire and Waller County, Texas. It read as follows:

When someone stops advertising, someone stops buying.
   When someone stops buying, someone stops selling.
   When someone stops selling, someone stops making.
   When someone stops making, someone stops earning.
   When someone stops earning, everybody stops buying.
KEEP GOING.[2]

Fortunately for small-town newspaper owners, advertising in the 1920s grew enormously as new businesses were developed or expanded and new products were introduced into the marketplace. Some of the newer products were directly tied to "discovered diseases," such as athlete's foot, that were developed by advertising copywriters to create a need for certain products to fight illnesses or conditions. According to James Playsted Wood in his work, *The Story of Advertising*, companies made up names for various bodily discomforts, odors, and conditions for which the companies claimed their product(s) would provide comfort, relief, and even cures. The most successful of these "discovered diseases" in terms of advertising success was athlete's foot. The newly named illnesses and conditions were instrumental in increasing advertising revenues for weeklies.[3]

For example, a one-column advertisement on the ready-print insides of *The Rocky Mount* (NC) *Weekly News* promoted the use of Cardui: The Woman's Tonic, to help women who felt "weak, dizzy and worn out."[4] All sorts of personal hygiene products were developed and advertised in national campaigns, among them deodorizing soaps, mouthwash, and toothpaste. The twenties became a spend, spend, spend economy as high-pressured salesmanship introduced new terms such as "no money down," "credit terms," "nothing to pay until ___," and "liberal trade-ins."[5] For example, Burger's furniture store in Newburgh, New York, advertised "Liberal Credit Terms in Effect" in a 1927 edition of the *Highland Mills* (NY) *Star*, which served the towns of Middletown and Highland Mills in Orange County, New York.[6]

However, the historical problem of businesses wanting to circumvent advertising purchases to promote their products and services through free publicity continued into the 1920s. In a 1927 article about the country press, published in *The American Journal of Sociology*, Tulane professor Jesse Frederick Steiner wrote that publicity agents for business interests furnished syndicate material "designed to mold public opinion in their favor." He added that newspaper syndicates had not sold out to these special interests, but rather had found it convenient to use the already-prepared material. In doing so, the syndicates foisted upon the country press "propaganda of this kind to a larger extent than is ordinarily realized." The article also pointed out that advertisements by monopolistic corporations, such as the Standard Oil Corporation and railroads, were used to gain "goodwill." But, he added, "If the facts were known, it is likely that the rural press is no more hampered in its editorial policy by advertising interests than are the large city dailies."[7]

University of Illinois journalism professor Charles L. Allen, who wrote one of the earliest handbooks for country editors and journalism students, said of publicity men that "... as long as they succeed in getting copy printed as news, which is really advertising, they will never use paid advertising space. Most of the concerns which put out such material never took an inch of advertising in any country paper, and never will." Of the various types of free publicity, Allen expressed special concern about the use of product publicity. He questioned the fairness to readers of country newspapers who "expect to read fair news when they look in the news columns and if they find there a mass of propaganda talking up some certain product, they are disappointed and tricked." He explained that because publicity material, referred to as mail copy, was so well written it was difficult for the country editor to tell what part of it was legitimate news and what was "pure advertising."[8]

The bright outlook for small-town newspaper advertising in the 1920s dimmed when a new mass communicator and advertising competitor was introduced to the general public. In 1920, the Westinghouse Company launched radio station KDKA in Pittsburgh; by the end of 1922, the number of radio stations had grown from fewer than 20 to nearly 600, according to an excerpt from the 1922 Annual Report of the Radio Corporation of America's Board of Directors. The Federal Communications Commission was formed in 1927 by Congress to issue operating licenses and decide on the amount of power allocated per station.[9]

By 1927, radios were in 6.5 million homes. Much of the radio programming was entertainment oriented. So, to service its readers who were also radio listeners, weeklies ran radio programming schedules as an unpaid-for public service. For example, the *Highland Mills Star* in New York ran a listing of radio programs for Thursday through Sunday that filled three of a page's eight-column format.[10] The feature was titled "Radio Programs for Week-End" and was organized alphabetically by a radio station's location. Radio stations were listed from cities such as Atlanta, Baltimore, Boston, Buffalo, Chicago, Cincinnati, Cleveland, Dallas, Detroit, Kansas City, Los Angeles, Memphis, Miami Beach, New York, Omaha, Philadelphia, Pittsburgh, and smaller Midwest cities such as Davenport and Des Moines, Iowa, and Hot Springs,

Arkansas. Programs were labeled with headings such as band concert, dinner music, lecture, orchestra, organ recital, and basketball game. Sunday programming was largely devoted to church music, sermons, lectures, and classical music performances.[11] Weeklies discontinued the practice when radio was perceived as a direct competitor for national and local advertising dollars. But, in a competitive twist, radio management found that a "consistent and intelligent paid newspaper advertising campaign must back up a commercial radio program to make such programs successful," as stated in a National Editorial Association newsletter article.[12]

Although many national advertisers and some local merchants transferred advertising dollars away from newspapers and into radio, new products and services and a growing credit market for automobiles and high-end home appliances found willing customers among community newspaper readers.

Community Influence of a Local Newspaper

The 1920s introduced a period of study of the weekly during which sociologists began to recognize the importance of a community newspaper to conduct social investigation, particularly in the area of politics. A 1925 article in *The American Political Science Review* reported on discussions about research methods at a 1924 gathering of political scientists. Conference attendees were told that it would be useful to study the effects of various types of newspaper publicity upon elections in relation to the "amount of newspaper space for and against, number of papers for and against, as well as their circulation, amount of logical and emotional writing, and other factors." But they were warned that studies using newspaper editorials could be complicated by the fact that candidates and particular issues were sometimes supported editorially to enhance the prestige of the newspaper and its publisher.[13]

For example, Robert and Helen Lynd conducted a sociological study of Muncie, Indiana, in the mid-1920s and found evidence of local political patronage. They observed that the city's leading daily newspaper rarely said anything editorially calculated to offend local businessmen, while the city's weaker daily occasionally took an editorial stand on issues such as child labor. In fact, neither of the city's daily newspapers was personally edited by its owner, both of whom lived out of town. Also, the leading daily was a member of a national syndicate of papers so most of its editorials were written by a central board located in another city. It was the city's independently owned weekly, however, that regularly commented freely on local affairs. For example, the weekly's editor denounced the city's daily newspapers for ignoring the arrests of several youths from prominent local families on liquor law violations. The editorial stated, "We hope the day will come when it will be a criminal offense for newspapers to protect higher-ups and ruin the reputations of those without influence."[14]

North Carolina State College professor Carl C. Taylor conducted the first study of the content of country newspapers. He reported his findings at the Fourth National Country Life Conference held in 1921 in New Orleans, which was sponsored by the American Country Life Association. The purpose of his study was to examine the sources of content for country weeklies and to determine if the newspapers were agents of service. The news articles in his study, taken from 243 Missouri weekly newspapers, were classified according to local, town, and county. The published conference proceedings included his report in the chapter titled "The Country Newspapers as a Town-Country Agency." He argued that country newspapers should not compete with metropolitan dailies to serve as a community's primary source for national news, commentary, or advertising. According to Taylor, country newspapers should strive instead to become a community institution with a mission and a future. He suggested that weeklies avoid local and national partisan political issues. He also recommended that weeklies reflect all of the communities that they serve and not just report news from the immediate vicinity. The report also included a brief analysis of survey results from 73 North Carolina weeklies that found the same general tendencies as those represented in the Missouri study.[15]

Cornell University assistant professor Millard V. Atwood asserted in his 1923 work *The Country Newspaper* that the small-town newspaper was indeed a "community institution" like the church, school, public library, and farm and home bureaus. He said many failed to recognize the country newspaper as such because, unlike traditional institutions, it was an enterprise in which the publisher had money invested. According to Atwood, the country newspaper met the definition of an institution as being "anything forming a characteristic and persistent feature in social or national life or habits." For example, he said there was no more characteristic habit of small-town life than "waiting at the local post office for the weekly to be distributed."[16]

Professor Atwood had also served as managing editor of the *Utica* (NY) *Observer-Dispatch* and the *Rochester* (NY) *Times-Union*. He later became associate editor for all Gannett papers and served as secretary of the New York

State Society of Newspaper Editors and of the American Society of Newspaper Editors. While working for the extension service at Cornell University, he served as president of the Association for Communication Excellence in Agriculture, Natural Resources and Life, and Human Sciences.

In 1926, Malcolm M. Willey—assistant professor of sociology at Dartmouth College—conducted a study of Connecticut weeklies. He found, however, that they fell short of their potential as a social influence because much of their content was boilerplate material. His 1926 study of the country newspaper looked at 35 newspapers published in Connecticut. Issues from four months in a one-year period were included in the content analysis that found three-fourths of the newspapers devoted less than one-half of their reading space to local news.[17] He argued that, based on United States Census figures, it was necessary to visualize the country as a "nation of small towns" to which the country newspaper catered.[18] The indiscriminate placement of boilerplate material throughout a newspaper "usually without a pre-reading by the editors," was his reasoning for reaching the conclusion that the Connecticut papers were not "effective socializing agencies."[19]

In his article about Willey's findings and similar studies conducted on weeklies, Tulane professor Jesse Frederick Steiner emphasized that even though a weekly's content might be largely filled with non-local boilerplate material, most residents of rural towns preferred to have a community newspaper of their own and would support it "in spite of the desire to also read the city daily when available."[20]

Boilerplate Beats Out Ready-Print as "Less Objectionable" Use of Syndicate Material

The number of ready-print pages in weeklies dropped by roughly 40 percent in the mid-1920s, based on information contained in a 1936 monograph authored by longtime W.N.U. syndicate writer Elmo Scott Watson. The monograph incorporated information he wrote for a 1923 W.N.U. promotional pamphlet in which he credited the ready-print industry with "the swift increase in the number of papers and in the phenomenal increase in newspaper circulation" for more than half a century.[21]

Many of the ready-print subscribers switched to boilerplate because it allowed a newspaper editor to order only the material he wanted and to reject any matter deemed unsuitable for his readers, according to newspaperman turned historian Milton M. Quaife in his 1922 article in *The National Printer Journalist* on the Kellogg newspaper syndicate. He wrote, "Ready-print worked a revolution in the rural press of America, the far reaching consequences of which defy measurement. Yet our formal histories of the press, while devoting ample space to such matters as the general idiosyncrasies of certain famous New York editors utterly ignore this development and one will search in vain for any mention of the name of the man whom above any other it is due: Ansel Nash Kellogg."[22]

In his 1927 article on the rural press, Tulane professor Jesse Frederick Steiner wrote that many editors viewed the use of boilerplate as "less objectionable" than ready-print.[23] However, he lamented that some editors were not conscientious in this task and wound up selecting a "jumble of extracts" interspersed throughout their pages. For example, page three of the May 25, 1922 edition of the *Ackley (IA) World Journal* included boilerplate articles on trappers finding gold in Canada, "sensation mongers" in France, a stream in Washington state described as a "freak of nature," and belief in charms. The page also included an exchange item on a lost love and a humorous brief from *The New York Tribune*. According to its masthead, the newspaper was the result of a consolidation between the *Ackley World* and the *Ackley Inter-County Journal*. The *Ackley World* was established in 1893, succeeding the *Ackley Enterprise*, established in 1867. The *Ackley Inter-County Journal* succeeded the *Ackley Tribune*, subsequently, the *Ackley Phonograph*. Ackley, in the north-central part of Iowa, served readers in Hardin and Franklin counties.[24]

Another example of a weekly newspaper article containing information that did not apply to the readers was the women's page of the *Big Piney (WY) Examiner* which included a fashion article on a furred velvet evening wrap with matching shoes and handbag; clothing accessories that were not likely to be worn by the typical Big Piney housewife.[25]

Steiner said that even more regrettable than the "hit-and-miss assemblage of material" was the tendency to use boilerplate to "disseminate thinly disguised propaganda of various political, economic, and other interests, dressed up in a style intended to appeal to farmers."[26] For example, page one of *The Soda Springs (ID) Chieftain*, which represented a consolidation of *The Soda Springs Chieftain* and *The Caribou County Recorder*, contained a headline that boasted "J.C. Penney Retains Status of Farmer." The article (no author identified) praised the efforts of company namesake J.C. Penney for his ownership of purebred Guernsey cattle and for being "a steady advocate of better sires in the breeding program of dairy farms." The article also stated, "In the present attitude of business toward the farmer, Mr. Penney's opinion is widely sought in matters pertaining to crop diversification, stock raising and distribution of farm products."²⁷ Thus, even though the use of boilerplate gave weekly editors complete control over what syndicate matter was selected for publication, some editors were either lackadaisical or naive in their selection of material that often had understated political or product publicity purposes.

Non-controversial editorials distributed by the W.N.U. syndicate in the early twenties caught the attention of national publications such as *The New Republic*. An article in its April 11, 1923 issue observed that country newspapers were "without purpose." Author Lynn Montross, in his criticism of ready-print and boilerplate, wrote, "The editorial page, once the battlefield of charging opinions, is now filled with cheerful, watery blurbs prepared for a hundred papers." Critical of the tone of writing in weeklies, he asserted that a "mock sophistication" was being created in these small communities, because country newspaper readers were being exposed to material intended for a more sophisticated, metropolitan audience. The article likened country newspapers to the appendix, "an organ without a purpose," and charged that their readers suffered "boilerplate appendicitis" that brought complications to the "afflicted community" because country newspapers "upheld mediocrity and standardization of thought and custom and served as a breeding ground for propaganda."²⁸

In addition to determining the news value of product publicity, professor Charles L. Allen wrote in his handbooks for country editors and journalism students that the country editor also had to deal with pressure from local publicity agents representing non-local companies to have their information placed as news stories. Despite the pressured sales pitches of publicity agents for copy placement, he suggested that whenever product publicity had local news value "enough to make it interesting and informative for country readers" it would be appropriate to run as a regular news story. Allen stressed that "free advertising" stories should be avoided. He described free-advertising stories as containing these attributes: repetition of a company name, frequent compliments, exaggerated statements, subtle references to the worth of a certain thing, statements that are so all-inclusive as to be ridiculous, and repetition of a certain fact or facts in connection with the subject of the news.²⁹

Outspoken and longtime country editor Charles M. Harger wrote a 1928 article in *The Outlook* magazine that defended the philosophy of rural newspapers to make friends instead of enemies and turn away from local news content that is "intensely personal and often as prejudiced as the editorials." He claimed that the local political editorial column was of little interest to most except those involved in the situation. "Recognition of that principle marked the passing of the political organ, and today, the country newspaper dabbles little in politics," he wrote. He noted that this transition turned the more successful weeklies into business enterprises that, contrary to charges of being subservient to the business office, instead offered an editorial voice that was "timely, sane and positive" from an editor who did not "go around with a chip on his shoulder seeking quarrels."[30]

The previous year, Tulane professor Jesse Frederick Steiner had also defended a business-minded approach by many editors of the 1920s that differed from their predecessors. He wrote in *The Outlook* magazine that many small-town editors turned away from the "militant nature" of caustic comments and fiery editorials and instead turned their publications into nonpartisan organs because they had "an eye on increased profits through gaining the good will of the people."[31]

An ongoing campaign in *The New Republic* denouncing the use of propaganda by rural newspapers took a different turn in a 1926 article, "The Small Town Press Sells Out." Author and weekly editor Carroll D. Clark acknowledged that the influence of rural newspapers was "potent and far-reaching" in shaping attitudes and opinion. To Clark, the influence of weeklies was troubling because of their increased advertising from large corporations, widespread use of "boilerplate" material, increased economic and political partisanship, and "swelling columns of thinly camouflaged propaganda supplied by various organized interests." The weekly editor, Clark emphasized, reviewed and selected for publication articles from the aforementioned news sources. He identified the national or "foreign" advertisements of monopoly corporations, such as the Standard Oil Company, the American Telegraph and Telephone Company, various railroads, electric power companies, and other public utilities, that appeared in weeklies. The purpose for the advertisements, according to the author, was to develop "goodwill" not only to the corporations but to the economic and political systems under which they operated.[32] For example, a two-column Standard Oil Company advertisement in a 1922 edition of the Ackley, Iowa, weekly addressed the issue of misinterpretation of the term "by-product." The advertisement copy, which appeared and read like news copy, ran under the headline, "Every Standard Oil Product a Primary Product."[33]

In his article, Clark admitted that much of the boilerplate material was "innocent, harmless and commonplace," such as bulletins of the U.S. Department of Agriculture, but argued that other material could have been viewed as "veiled propaganda." He referred to articles from the American

Bankers' Association's Public Education Commission that explained how bankers worked to promote agriculture improvements in their communities.[34] Other "veiled propaganda" sources that he identified were the American Legion, the U.S. Bureau of Education, the Agriculture Extension Department, International Harvest Company, and the Sears-Roebuck Agriculture Foundation. For example, news items from the American Legion dominated three of four available columns of copy on an inside page of a 1923 edition of *The Wakefield* (MI) *Advocate*. The articles concerned a Legion hospital, the Michigan tour of a Legion leader, the opening of a Legion orphans' home, and a fundraising effort by the Legion to place world war grave markers in France.[35] The author also referred to political propaganda and observed that, despite its extensive use, it was at least more obvious than the aforementioned "veiled propaganda" because it promoted partisan political issues or individual candidates. As an example, he pointed to state political machines purchasing vast amounts of newspaper space, which represented valuable advertising revenue for the weeklies.

Steiner made similar observations about the use of propaganda in his 1927 article on the rural press, but noted that metropolitan dailies were also victims of legislative, political, and industrial propaganda efforts. He observed that the rural press appeared to be more gullible to such orchestrated efforts to mold public opinion only because of its greater use of syndicate material. He stated, "If the facts were known, it is likely that the rural press is no more hampered in its editorial policy by advertising interests than are the large-city dailies."[36] For example, in their 1920s study of Muncie, Indiana, the Lynds found that the city's two dailies, morning and afternoon papers, more closely resembled a community weekly because of their heavy use of syndication material. In contrast, the city's only weekly, a four-page Democratic organ that carried no retail advertising, reflected the editor's personality through its strong editorial opinions.[37]

But whatever the content of the weekly, whether it was awash in syndicate material or chock-full of local opinion and news items, the rural press was recognized for its influential role because of the economic potential of its readers and the editorial guidance it provided to a large portion of the country's populace. Charles L. Allen wrote about the influential role of the country press, especially in terms of the economic potential of its readers, in his 1928 textbook on country journalism. He observed, "Farm families have great spending potential for items beyond that needed to raise crops. There are six and one-half million farm families that look to their local newspapers for news and editorial guidance."³⁸

The Country Editor as an Influence Peddler, Even President

But it was the weekly editor himself, even more than his newspaper, who influenced the community argued Harris and Hooke in their 1923 work on the community newspaper. They explained that the community newspaper expressed the editor's conception of life in general and the life of the town. "... those who habitually read it [community newspaper] cannot fail to feel and respond in some degree to the influence which the editor both consciously and unconsciously exerts."³⁹ An example of a weekly that was a printed representation of its editor's personality and political persuasion was North Carolina's *The Chapel Hill Weekly*, according to Steiner in his article on the rural press.⁴⁰ He noted that the Chapel Hill newspaper contained no boilerplate or other syndicated matter, such as serial stories or cartoons. He observed, "Every paragraph in the paper is written by the editor, who also solicits the advertising and runs a job printing business."⁴¹ The strong influence of the small-town newspaper editor was addressed by *American Magazine* editor Merle Crowell at a 1929 session of the Southwestern Journalism Congress at which he said of country newspapers, "Their editors think saner and hit much straighter than some of their city cousins." He did, however, deride the "ordained-by-God" attitude of some editors who, he claimed, tended to talk down to their publics.⁴² American Press Association President John H. Perry also recognized the growing perceived influence of the rural press, particularly its editors. He was quoted as follows in Allen's textbook on country journalism: "The force that controls this country of ours, in the long run, is the rural editor, in his capacity as spokesman for sixty million Americans who live and earn their living on the farms and in the villages and towns of 5,000 population or less...."

According to Charles L. Allen, a successful country editor needed to be friendly, even-tempered, neat in personal appearance, well-read, cooperative, tactful, courteous, fair, and tolerant. In addition, he wrote that the country editor should serve as a leader and community booster, engage in community enterprises, develop others' talents, run a financially successful operation, connect with a church, have command of the English language, cultivate originality and resourcefulness, and know how his subscribers make their living.⁴³ While Allen's list of recommended attributes and activities were perhaps more idealistic than realistic, it did serve as a guide for country editors who viewed their role as much more than that of simply overseeing a local business operation.

In fact, country editors enjoyed a public endorsement of their prominence when they gained access and influence in the White House after one of their own, Ohio newspaperman Warren G. Harding, was elected to the presidency in 1920. Dr. George Tryon Harding Sr. owned *The Caledonia* (OH) *Argus*, where his son, Warren, learned the journalism trade. Warren Harding continued his journalism training at Ohio Central College in Iberia, Ohio, and also worked at *The Union Register* in Mount Gilead, Ohio. After completing his college studies, the future president and two friends purchased *The Marion* (OH) *Daily Star*, where he served as editor until entering politics full time. President Harding's brief term came to an end when he died of apoplexy and Vice President Calvin Coolidge assumed the presidency in August of 1923. Coolidge was re-elected in 1924 but did not seek re-election four years later.

During his presidency, Harding maintained his membership in the National Press Club. A March 1922 article in *The Washington Post* mentioned the president's attendance at a concert to mark the installation of a radiotelephone receiving set in the rooms of the National Press Club. At the event, the president spoke of the power of the press in "moulding [sic] public opinion" and said that public opinion was a greater power than all laws.⁴⁴ Harding also spoke at the 1923 banquet of the American Society of Newspaper Editors at which he endorsed the organization's adoption of a written code of ethics. An article in *The Washington Post* pointed out that he spoke "as a newspaper man and not as President of the United States."⁴⁵ After his August 1923 death in California, members of the National Press Club adopted a resolution expressing its grief at the loss of a "fellow craftsman."⁴⁶ From the time of the arrival of Harding's body in the nation's capital, newspapermen served as honor escorts throughout all of the funeral functions of state, including the train ride to Marion, Ohio, and the burial service there.⁴⁷

In fact, the weekly editorship was a job to which many men aspired, according to noted novelist and successful advertising copywriter Sherwood Anderson. He moved from Chicago and purchased a farm in southwest Virginia to enjoy a leisurely lifestyle and live off of the earnings from his short stories and novels. He soon became restless, however, and purchased the two weeklies in Marion County, Virginia. One was a Democrat publication, and the other, a Republican organ. In an article in *The Outlook* magazine, he explained his entry into the weekly profession by pointing out, "I think almost every man in the country has the belief, buried away in him somewhere, that he would make a successful editor." Anderson left the political writing to the party leaders and focused instead on his observations of the "comings and goings" of the people in the community, and editing submitted copy by local columnists. The celebrated author-turned-editor was impressed by the quality of his local writers. He observed, "There may be an opportunity for as good writing in weekly newspapers of this kind as in the magazines or in books ... Some of the best writing we get nowadays is being done by the newspaper men."[48]

Educating Small-Town Editors: Formal vs. Informal, Pride in Provincialism

Formal education of editors, or the lack thereof, was a popular topic of debate in the weekly newspaper field. Some weekly editors believed that formal training was necessary to learn how to operate a newspaper business more efficiently and to write editorials based on fact rather than emotion. Other editors believed that college journalism training was not necessary and that the best education could be received through the traditional apprenticeship. But readers generally respected their editors, who guided local political actions through the newspaper editorial page, for either their formal education or professional experience, as long as they were considered well read.[49]

In his article on country newspapers, Charles Harger observed that thousands of college journalism graduates had moved into country newspaper offices. He wrote, "Ability to write clear English, to know news when he sees it, to touch the human-interest events of the community and transfer them pleasingly to the printed page is no mean art."[50] However, some country editors took pride in the fact that they were not college-educated "journalists." One such editor was Don C. Wright of *The Crane* (MO) *Chronicle*. He responded to a column by Elmo Scott Watson of *The Publishers' Auxiliary* in which Watson derided a locally written column by Wright that expressed a preference for mechanics-printers as small-town editors as opposed to trained journalists. The Missouri editor's response letter, published in *The Publishers' Auxiliary*, identified "journalists" as those who had recently graduated from journalism schools. He added, "I deny the fact that I am a journalist. However, I believe that I spend more time doing purely journalistic work on my newspaper than any other editor in my section. I am developing more columns of original matter than any of them, and yet, I do not aspire to the dignified, but unfitting, title of journalist."[51]

Lack of a formal education among weekly editors in the South was not so much a sensitive issue as were the accusations by their peers in other parts of the country that they were too provincial in their thinking, leading to a writing tone that was unsophisticated and narrow-minded. For example, in the fourth of a series of articles on American journalism in a 1926 edition of *The Outlook*, magazine author D.C. Seitz wrote that "it would be hard to prove that it [country newspaper] has progressed intellectually."[52] Articles in the national press pointed to the Southern press and its unwillingness to embrace 1928 presidential Democratic candidate Governor Alfred E. Smith of New York because of his Catholic faith and anti-Prohibition stand. A December 1926 editorial in *The New York Times* opined that some Southern newspapers were resentful of the attention given to the attitude of the South toward Smith's candidacy. Acknowledging that southern states had their fair share of "fanatical prohibitionists" and "religious bigots," the southern editors argued that such persons existed in other parts of the country as well. The editorial, quoting some southern newspapers on Smith's candidacy, observed, "Perhaps the small-town newspapers are more outspoken than those of the cities." *The New York Times* editorial reprinted an excerpt from an editorial in *The Cordele (GA) Dispatch* concerning Smith that stated, "Protestant America is a fine country because it believes in religious freedom, but free Americans should never fall under Catholic rule."[53] Other articles referred to southern resistance to unionized workers and the prospective International Paper & Power Company purchase of a number of southern newspapers to provide "built-in" customers for the Northeast company's newsprint. A May 1929 *New York Times* article reported that regional textile strikes and interest of the International Paper and Power Company in purchasing southern newspapers gave some southern editors "an opportunity to declaim against communism" and restore stinging editorial words such as "predatory" and "plutocracy."[54]

Noted author and journalist W.J. Cash observed that there were signs that progressive thinking was moving into some southern editorial offices. He offered two reasons why many smaller southern newspapers during this period were getting more progressive and intelligent editing. He pointed out that the economic depression halted the exodus to the North of talented young journalists and that the development of standardized daily journalism improved the overall quality of newspapers.[55]

But despite the influx of new thinking, University of Kentucky professor Thomas D. Clark emphasized that southern editors had to move slowly when they presented new ideas because of the traditional mindset of their readers. "The effect of this type of journalism is to be determined in terms of the slow and patient way in which society was brought to make changes of its own accord."[56] But there were some southern editors who defied the "slow-go" approach and instead openly fought traditional ways of thinking. For example, community involvement, such as joining the local Kiwanis Club, was expected of the small-town community editor. But Julian Hall, who became editor of Dothan, Alabama's, *The Eagle* after his father's death in 1924, had to ponder an invitation to join the local Ku Klux Klan chapter. Hall wrote anonymously in *The American Mercury* that one of the first things that happened after he became editor was to receive the Klan membership invitation. Such an invitation was not so unusual during the 1920s in the South when a resurgent number of Klan chapters waged strong anti-Jew, anti-Catholic, and anti-sin campaigns. In fact, his invitation came from the local superintendent of education, a prominent member of the locally thriving group. The new editor refused to join the group and spent the next several months lambasting the Klan, all the while "estranging friends and making enemies." He wrote, "The country editor can either assert himself and defy the moguls of his community, in which case his life is an open hell; or he can knuckle under, in which case it's a secret purgatory. Mine has been for the most part the open-hell variety."[57]

Economic Boom before the Bust

For some time many smaller newspaper operations feared that metropolitan newspapers would attract their readers and advertisers and eventually run them out of business. But despite having a reputation for being poor businessmen, weekly publishers on the whole made significant progress in achieving financial stability. Publishers who were unwilling or unable to modernize their business practices, however, were forced to go out of business or sell their operations to the highest bidders.

This general upswing in the economic status of small-town journalism was acknowledged in a 1927 article in *Editor & Publisher*. Len Fieghner—vice president of the National Association of State Press Field Managers—spoke at the association's 1927 annual meeting in Detroit and summed up concerns about big-city newspapers taking over readership from small-town newspapers. He observed that weeklies no longer faced the threat of extermination but had instead established themselves more firmly because of the specialized audience they served. "No matter what quantity of small town local news is covered in the pages of the nearest large daily, there are always the seemingly trifling news items of local interest, which mean so much to the small town residents and which can be found only in their local newspaper ...."[58]

Not only were improved business practices welcomed in the weekly field, but they were a necessity, according to textbook authors Emerson Harris and Elizabeth Hooke, because of the high cost of producing a newspaper. They asserted it was "imperative that every unit of expense count toward service and income."[59] Backing up their assertion was the testimony of a weekly publisher in Nebraska who wrote in *The Publishers' Auxiliary* of his inability to handle the mechanical duties of the print shop after being injured in a car accident. He reluctantly hired a printer but feared that all of his profits would be absorbed in the printer's salary. Since he was temporarily free from the print shop duties but confined to a wheelchair, a friend took him around town to visit with townspeople and businessmen to collect news stories and solicit advertisements. His efforts paid off in increased subscriptions and local advertising. He wrote, "There is a moral in that story for every man who is attempting to run a weekly newspaper by doing the mechanical work in the back shop. They will achieve greater success when they hire a printer and keep themselves out on the street."[60]

Some publishers discovered the financial benefits of combining their newspapers and printing services with other businesses or public service roles. For example, a stationery and book store worked well in combination with a print job, according to author Millard V. Atwood in his book on the country weekly, and enabled a publisher to have a better business location on a town's main street. He also noted that the insurance business was another popular sideline endeavor for newspaper editors, as were political appointee roles such as city clerk or postmaster.[61] Any potential conflicts of interest were seemingly not a concern for some weekly editors who felt it more important to keep their newspapers operating rather than to close down an important communication tool within their community, especially in a one-newspaper town.

A 1928 column in *The Saturday Evening Post* that identified its writer only as "One Of 'Em," responded to an earlier article from *The Saturday Evening Post* expressing surprise that country weeklies were succeeding financially. The author, a country editor, explained how it was possible to be both a weekly editor and a successful businessman. He described himself as owner and editor of the oldest weekly in a southwestern state and in a town with a population of 3,500. He reported having 2,000 subscribers at $1.50 per year, plus a gross monthly income of more than $1,000, which brought his annual income to more than $15,000.[62] He estimated that 90 percent of his income came from the immediate territory and that "foreign advertising" was placed by agencies for national advertisers on behalf of local merchants that sold their particular products. His advertising rates were 20 cents per column inch for local advertisers and 30 cents for foreign advertising. Reader advertisements, more commonly known as classified ads, were sold for 10 cents per line. He reported having made as much as 80 dollars for a single issue and observed that in a town where a $200-a-month income was regarded with respect, "I'm one of the big boys, if not the big boy."[63]

It was fortunate that small-town newspapers did not depend heavily on circulation revenues for their financial success. At the end of the decade the prevailing price of an annual weekly subscription was two dollars. An editorial in *The Publishers' Auxiliary* observed that some publications charged as much as three dollars while others were sold for less than $1.50 a year, especially in the South. The editorial urged country editors to charge at least two dollars and "devote a portion of the increased revenue to producing a better newspaper that will better represent the community, be more interesting to the subscribers and a better medium for the merchants."[64]

As Weak Weeklies Fail, Others Enjoy New-Found Prosperity

Weeklies that could not increase subscribers or subscription and advertising revenues simply had to close their doors or merge with another newspaper or publication group. Signs that weaker publications folded or were merged into successful printing operations were indicated in a decrease in the number of community newspapers from roughly 15,000 in 1915 to fewer than 12,000 in 1924.[65] In his 1926 study of the country press, Malcolm M. Willey observed that during that same nine-year period, the number of towns in which a weekly paper was published decreased by only 1,116. Also during that period, the number of county seats from which a weekly newspaper originated increased by 50. He pointed out that those in the newspaper business interpreted the figures as a sign of strength "through the cleaning out of the marginal properties, and a consolidation of the stronger."⁶⁶ Even by the late 1920s, the weekly continued to hold on in communities with a population of less than 5,000. The 1927 *N.W. Ayer & Son's American Newspaper Annual and Directory* listed roughly 9,000 weeklies published in towns under 5,000. Community weeklies were most numerous in the north-central states, with Illinois and Iowa each having more than 500 small-town community weeklies.

Willey conducted a similar study with University of Minnesota colleague William Weinfeld that was published in the mid-1930s and looked at trends in numbers and distribution of the country weekly from 1900 to 1930. They found that the total number of weeklies declined from 11,310 in 1900 to 9,522 in 1930, a decrease of 2,280 or 19.3 percent. The study reported that among the 22 states that had a smaller percentage of papers in 1930 than in 1900, only four of them were west of the Mississippi River. Of the 26 states that in 1930 had a larger percentage of papers than at the outset of the century, only eight were east of the Mississippi River. Based on the data, the authors concluded that older sections of the country that had previously experienced growth in weekly journalism, reached a point of maximum numbers and "in the face of economic and social adjustment declined or reached a state of stability in numbers of papers." The study also found that the number of Democratic newspapers declined from 3,119 to 2,114, a decrease of 1,005 or 32.2 percent, the number of Republican newspapers declined from 3,537 to 2,567, a decrease of 970 or 27.4 percent, and the number of straight independent newspapers increased from 2,263 to 3,268, an increase of 1,005, or 44.4 percent. The newspapers with independent leanings (Democratic, Republican and neutral) increased in the same period from 2,866 to 4,272, an increase of 1,406, or 49.1 percent.⁶⁷

In his 1926 article on country journalism and its financial success in *The Outlook* magazine, D.C. Seitz emphasized that despite a seeming dominance of metropolitan dailies and *The Saturday Evening Post*, most of the country's weeklies—and some 2,000 dailies that he claimed could be considered country publications—enjoyed a new-found prosperity. He wrote, "To a far greater extent than their city brethren they [country weeklies] have improved in appearance and increased in opulence. Many of them are veritable gold mines. A look at the income-tax payments made by some of their owners makes even a well-paid, city-hired man sit up and wonder if he had been truly wise in lighting out for the metropolis."⁶⁸

Beginning in the latter half of the 1920s, John H. Casey—a University of Oklahoma professor and specialist in country newspapers—helped to identify some of the more successful weekly operations. Each year he named the All-American Country Weekly Newspaper team, which listed the top 10 or so weeklies in the country based on editorial content and business acumen. In a 1929 article in *The Publishers' Auxiliary* he listed three "stellar" weeklies that he suggested should be studied by other publishers. They were the *Wayne* (NE) *Herald*, the *Freehold* (NJ) *Transcript*, and the *Millford* (DE) *Chronicle*.[69] Each of these publications, according to the professor, was highly profitable, but more importantly, they were influential and beneficial to their respective communities.

In relation to profitability, newspapers that originated from county seats were considered the most desirable because of their potential for obtaining local retail advertising and legal notices. In their book on the community weekly, Emerson Harris and Elizabeth Hooke noted that it was not uncommon for the asking price of a weekly deemed "profitable and substantial" to have been more than twice the value of the physical plant and net tangible assets when earning potential and "goodwill" of the business was taken into consideration.[70] For example, a listing in the May 1929 issue of *The Publishers' Auxiliary* identified two Texas weeklies for the asking price of $35,000.[71] One of the weeklies was located in a town of 15,000, and the other in a town of 2,500, just 20 miles away.[72] Included in the offer was the purchase of one plant for the two papers, a warehouse, an adjacent vacant lot, and a long list of equipment to support both newspaper and job-printing operations. The owner listed net profits from the two previous years in excess of $17,000.[73] An alternate offer was also listed to include stock options, provided that the buyer was willing to organize a company and pay $55,000 for the additional purchase of two smaller weeklies, printed at the same plant, and would agree to start a semi-weekly or daily and employ the current owner on the "same terms as other stockholders of equal capacity."[74]

Country editors could not have foreseen the economic turmoil that would face smaller publications as they entered the next decade, as evidenced in a 1928 University of Missouri survey. Journalism professor T.C. Morelock conducted the survey of country editors that revealed that the weekly was holding its own despite the inroads of metropolitan dailies, large mail-order printing houses, and other competitors. Although the number of weeklies decreased steadily throughout the decade, the papers that survived were generally more financially stable and better established in their communities. In the survey, the editors stated that opportunities for public service and financial reward were good and steadily improving.[75] James Clifford Safley's 1930 textbook on country journalism—written prior to the stock market crash—hailed the community weekly field as a profession that provided its publishers financial stability and personal satisfaction, "... and that is more than the average-salaried job on a city newspaper offers, with its speed, its high pressure, its grind, and its uncertainty." Ownership of a country newspaper was "the most nearly ideal" goal in journalism, according to the text. "The man who owns a successful country newspaper," it added, "indeed is well situated."[76] This book was designed as a guide for a course in country newspaper work in schools of journalism and as a handbook for editors and publishers of country newspapers. The first chapter describes the general aspects of country journalism. Other chapter topics include country correspondence, auxiliary press services, selection of a location, financing a newspaper, and commercial printing.

The October 29, 1929 stock market crash, also referred to as "Black Tuesday," was not immediately portrayed as a national economic disaster in many small-town newspapers, although some editors could foresee economic troubles ahead. In a November 1929 issue of the *Sheffield* (AL) *Standard*, the local editor wrote, "The aftermath of the stock market debacle is bringing a series of stories, telling about bank closings, suicides, fortunes wiped out, and other evidences that it rarely pays to try to make money too fast, especially when you are fooling with forces that you do not understand."[77]

Notes

1 Emerson P. Harris and Elizabeth H. Hooke, *The Community Newspaper* (New York: D. Appleton and Company, 1923), 1.
2 "Keep Going," *The Brookshire* (TX) *Times*, January 13, 1922, 1. Brookshire, in Waller County, Texas, had a population of 10,292 in 1920. *Fourteenth Census of the United States*, "Population," volume 1, section 4, 641, Table 53. http://newspaperarchive.com/, http://www.census.gov/.
3 James Playsted Wood, *The Story of Advertising* (Garden City, NY: Ronald Press, 1958), 388.
4 "Helps Sick Women," *The Rocky Mount* (NC) *Weekly News*, September 17, 1920. Rocky Mount, in Nash County, is located in the northeastern section of North Carolina. Rocky Mount had a population of 12,742 in 1920. *Fourteenth Census of the United States*, "Population," volume 1, section 3, 268, Table 51. http://newspaperarchive.com/, http://www.census.gov/.
5 Wood, *The Story of Advertising*, 391.
6 "February Furniture Sale Ends Saturday," *Highland Mills* (NY) *Star*, March 3, 1927, 10. Highland Mills and Middletown, in Orange County, New York, had a population of 18,420 in 1920. *Fourteenth Census of the United States*, "Population," volume 1, section 2, 261, Table 51. http://newspaperarchive.com/, http://www.gov/.

7 Jesse Frederick Steiner, "The Rural Press," *The American Journal of Sociology* 33:3 (November 1927): 420.
8 Charles L. Allen, *Country Journalism* (New York: Thomas Nelson and Sons, 1928), 214.
9 Gleason L. Archer, *Big Business and Radio* (New York: American Book-Stratford Press, 1939), 67.
10 "Radio Programs for Week-End," *Highland Mills* (NY) *Star*, March 3, 1927, 11. http://newspaperarchive.com/.
11 Ibid.
12 "Radio Needs Newspaper Ads to Get Commercial Program Across," *N.E.A. Bulletin* 8:88 (May 1927): 10.
13 L.L. Thurstone, "The Significance of Psychology for the Study of Government and Certain Specific Problems Involving Both Psychology and Politics: Round Table on Politics and Psychology, Reports of the Second National Conference on the Science of Politics Held at Chicago, Illinois, Sept. 8–12, 1924," *The American Political Science Review* 19:1 (February 1925): 120.
14 Robert S. Lynd and Helen M. Lynd, *Middletown: A Study in American Culture* (New York: Harcourt, Brace & Co., 1929), 475–476.
15 Carl C. Taylor, "The Country Newspapers as a Town-Country Agency" (paper presented at the Fourth National Country Life Conference, New Orleans, LA, 1921), 45.
16 Millard V. Atwood, *The Country Newspaper*, The National Social Science Series (Chicago: A.C. McClurg & Co., 1923), 53, 55.
17 Malcolm M. Willey, *The Country Newspaper* (Chapel Hill, NC: The University of North Carolina Press, 1926).
18 In 1920 there were 14,946 towns in the United States with a population less than 10,000. Cities with a population of 10,000–25,000 numbered 459, and the number of cities with a population exceeding 25,000 was 287. *Fourteenth Census*, "Population," vol. 1, Table 31, 50. http://www.census.gov/.
19 Willey, *The Country Newspaper*, 8, 61, 65.
20 Steiner, "The Rural Press," 414–415.
21 Elmo Scott Watson, *A History of Newspaper Syndicates, 1865–1935* (Chicago: The Publishers' Auxiliary, 1936), 83–84.
22 Milton M. Quaife, "How A.N. Kellogg Revolutionized America's Country Press," *The National Printer Journalist* (February 1922): 21.
23 Steiner, "The Rural Press," 419.
24 *Ackley* (IA) *World Journal*, May 25, 1922, 3. Ackley had a population of 1,529 in 1920. *Fourteenth Census of the United States*, "Population," volume 1, section 2,196, Table 51. http://newspaperarchive.com/, http://www.census.gov/.
25 "Furred Velvet Evening Wrap, Shoes and Handbags to Match," *Big Piney* (WY) *Examiner*, November 4, 1926, 4. Big Piney was a part of Lincoln County in 1920, which is located in the central-western part of Wyoming. The town later became a part of Sublette County. The town's population numbered only 173 in 1920. *Fourteenth Census of the United States*, "Population," volume 1, section 3, 319, Table 51. http://newspaperarchive.com/, http://www.census.gov/.
26 Steiner, "The Rural Press," 419.

27 "J.C. Penney Retains Status of Farmer," *The Soda Springs* (ID) *Chieftain*, August 8, 1929, 1. Soda Springs, the county seat in Caribou County, is located in the southeast corner of Idaho. The county had a population of 935 in 1920. *Fourteenth Census of the United States*, "Population," volume 1, section 2, 196, Table 51. http://newspaperarchive.com/, http://www.census.gov/.
28 Lynn Montross, "Boiler Plate Appendicitis," *The New Republic*, April 11, 1923, 189–190.
29 Allen, *Country Journalism*, 214.
30 Charles Harger, "Opulent Country Newspapers," *The Outlook* 148 (February 29, 1928): 339–340.
31 Steiner, "The Rural Press," 415.
32 Carroll D. Clark, "The Small Town Press Sells Out," *The New Republic* 45 (January 20, 1926): 237.
33 "Every Standard Oil Product a Primary Product," *Ackley* (IA) *World Journal*, May 25, 1922, 7. http://newspaperarchive.com/.
34 Clark, "The Small Town Press Sells Out," 238.
35 *The Wakefield* (MI) *Advocate*, April 21, 1923, 3. Wakefield, in Gogebic County, is located in the northern part of Michigan near Lake Superior. Wakefield had a population of 4,151 in 1920. *Fourteenth Census of the United States*, "Population," volume 1, section 2, 234, Table 51. http://newspaperarchive.com/, http://www.census.gov/.
36 Steiner, "The Rural Press," 420.
37 Lynd and Lynd, *Middletown: A Study in American Culture*, 475.
38 Allen, *Country Journalism*, 3–4.
39 Harris and Hooke, *The Community Newspaper*, 93.
40 Chapel Hill is located in North Carolina's Orange County. The town had a population of 5,317 in 1920. Wakefield had a population of 4,151 in 1920. *Fourteenth Census of the United States*, "Population," volume 1, section 2, 18, Table 2. http://newspaperarchive.com/, http://www.census.gov/.
41 Steiner, "The Rural Press," 418.
42 "Crowell Pays a High Tribute to Country Press," *The Publishers' Auxiliary*, April 20, 1929, 5. Merle Crowell spoke at the third annual session of the Southwestern Journalism Congress at the College of Industrial Arts in Denton, TX.
43 Allen, *Country Journalism*, 10–13.
44 "President Under Roof with Wilson," *The Washington Post*, March 5, 1922, 1.
45 "President Discusses 'Shop' with Editors," *The Washington Post*, April 29, 1923, 1.
46 "National Press Club Grieves for President," *The Washington Post*, August 9, 1923, 5.
47 "Newspaper Men Form Continuous, Reverent Escort," *The Washington Post*, August 9, 1923, 5.
48 Sherwood Anderson, "Nearer the Grass Roots," *The Outlook* 148:1 (January 4, 1928): 3, 27.
49 Thomas D. Clark, *The New Rural Press and the New South* (Baton Rouge, LA: Louisiana State University Press, 1948), 75.
50 Harger, "Opulent Country Newspapers," 340.
51 Don C. Wright, "Not a Journalist," *The Publishers' Auxiliary*, November 2, 1929, 4.
52 D.C. Seitz, "The Country Press," *The Outlook* 142 (January 27, 1926): 137.
53 "Smith and the South," *The New York Times*, December 10, 1926, E12.

54 Julian Harris, "South Sees Unions Gaining a Foothold," *The New York Times*, May 26, 1929, E1.
55 W.J. Cash, *The Mind of the South* (New York: Random House, 1941), 374.
56 Clark, *The New Rural Press and the New South*, 110.
57 Julian Hall, "A Small-Town Editor Squawks," *The American Mercury* 185 (May 1939): 71.
58 "Motor Delivery No Menace to Small Papers," *Editor & Publisher* 60:14 (August 27, 1927): 5.
59 Harris and Hooke, *The Community Newspaper*, 303.
60 "Hire a Printer and Be a Publisher," *The Publishers' Auxiliary*, December 7, 1929, 4.
61 Atwood, *The Country Newspaper*, 33–34.
62 In 2022, according to the latest government figures based on the Consumer Price Index, $3,000 from 1928 was worth $52,686 and $15,000 from 1928 was worth $255,950. http://www.measuringworth.com/.
63 "How Did the Country Editor Get that Way?" *The Saturday Evening Post* 201 (July 14, 1928): 137.
64 "It's Worth $2.00 … Ask It!" *The Publishers' Auxiliary*, May 4, 1929, 4. In 2022, according to the latest government figures based on the Consumer Price Index, $2 from 1929 was worth $35. http://www.measuringworth.com/.
65 *N.W. Ayer & Son's American Newspaper Annual and Directory* (Philadelphia: N.W. Ayer & Sons, 1924), 11.
66 Willey, *The Country Newspaper*, 6–7.
67 Malcolm M. Willey and William Weinfeld, "The Country Weekly: Trends in Numbers and Distribution, 1900–1930," *Social Forces* 13:1 (October 1934–May 1935, 1934): 51–56.
68 Seitz, "The Country Press," 136.
69 "Casey Selects All-American Weekly Eleven," *The Publishers' Auxiliary*, March 2, 1929, 6.
70 Harris and Hooke, *The Community Newspaper*, 324.
71 In 2022, according to the latest government figures based on the Consumer Price Index, $35,000 from 1929 was worth $597,218. http://www.measuringworth.com/.
72 "Newspapers for Sale," *The Publishers' Auxiliary*, May 25, 1929, 5.
73 In 2022, according to the latest government figures based on the Consumer Price Index, $17,000 from 1929 was worth $290,077. http://www.measuringworth.com/.
74 "Newspapers for Sale," 5. In 2022, according to the latest government figures based on the Consumer Price Index, $55,000 from 1929 was worth $938,486. http://www.measuringworth.com/.
75 "Survey Reveals Country Paper Holding Its Own," *The Publishers' Auxiliary*, March 9, 1929, 1.
76 James Clifford Safley, *The Country Newspaper and Its Operation* (New York: D. Appleton and Company, 1930), 383.
77 "Aftermath of Stock Market Debacle," *The Sheffield* (AL) *Standard*, November 22, 1929, 4.

References

"Aftermath of Stock Market Debacle." *The Sheffield* (AL) *Standard*, November 22, 1929, 4.

Allen, Charles L. *Country Journalism*. New York: Thomas Nelson and Sons, 1928.
Anderson, Sherwood. "Nearer the Grass Roots." *The Outlook* 148:1 (January 4, 1928): 3–4, 27.
Archer, Gleason L. *Big Business and Radio*. New York: American Book-Stratford Press, 1939.
Atwood, Millard V. *The Country Newspaper*, The National Social Science Series. Chicago: A.C. McClurg & Co., 1923.
"Casey Selects All-American Weekly Eleven." *The Publishers' Auxiliary*, March 2, 1929, 6.
Cash, W.J. *The Mind of the South*. New York: Random House, 1941.
Clark, Carroll D. "The Small Town Press Sells Out." *The New Republic* 45 (January 20, 1926): 236–239.
Clark, Thomas D. *The New Rural Press and the New South*. Baton Rouge, La.: Louisiana State University Press, 1948.
"Crowell Pays a High Tribute to Country Press." *The Publishers' Auxiliary*, April 20, 1929, 5.
"Every Standard Oil Product a Primary Product." *Ackley* (IA) *World Journal*, May 25, 1922, 7.
"February Furniture Sale Ends Saturday." *Highland Mills* (NY) *Star*, March 3, 1927, 10.
Fourteenth Census of the United States. Population. 1920. edited by United States Bureau of the Census: Washington, DC: Government Printing Office, 1921.
"Furred Velvet Evening Wrap, Shoes and Handbags to Match." *Big Piney* (WY) *Examiner*, November 4, 1926, 4.
Hall, Julian. "A Small-Town Editor Squawks." *The American Mercury*, no. 185 (May 1939): 69–74.
Harger, Charles. "Opulent Country Newspapers." *The Outlook* 148 (February 29, 1928): 339–341, 355.
Harris, Emerson P., and Elizabeth H. Hooke. *The Community Newspaper*. New York: D. Appleton and Company, 1923.
Harris, Julian. "South Sees Unions Gaining a Foothold." *The New York Times*, May 26, 1929, E1.
"Helps Sick Women." *The Rocky Mount* (NC) *Weekly News*, September 17, 1920, 5.
"Hire a Printer and Be a Publisher." *The Publishers' Auxiliary*, December 7, 1929, 4.
"How Did the Country Editor Get that Way?" *The Saturday Evening Post* 201 (July 14, 1928): 137–138, 143.
"It's Worth $2.00... Ask It!" *The Publishers' Auxiliary*, May 4, 1929, 4.
"J.C. Penney Retains Status of Farmer." *The Soda Springs* (ID) *Chieftain*, August 8, 1929, 1.
"Keep Going." *The Brookshire* (TX) *Times*, January 13, 1922, 1.
Lynd, Robert S., and Helen M. Lynd. *Middletown: A Study in American Culture*. New York: Harcourt, Brace & Co., 1929.
Montross, Lynn. "Boiler Plate Appendicitis." *The New Republic*, April 11, 1923, 189–190.
"Motor Delivery No Menace to Small Papers." *Editor & Publisher* 60:14 (Aug. 27, 1927): 5.
"National Press Club Grieves for President." *The Washington Post*, August 9, 1923, 5.
"Newspaper Men Form Continuous, Reverent Escort." *The Washington Post*, August 9, 1923, 5.
"Newspapers for Sale." *The Publishers' Auxiliary*, May 25, 1929, 5.
N.W. Ayer & Son's American Newspaper Annual and Directory. Philadelphia: N.W. Ayer & Sons, 1924.
"President Discusses 'Shop' with Editors." *The Washington Post*, April 29, 1923, 1.
"President Under Roof with Wilson." *The Washington Post*, March 5, 1922, 1.

Quaife, Milton M. "How A.N. Kellogg Revolutionized America's Country Press." *The National Printer Journalist* (February 1922): 21.

"Radio Needs Newspaper Ads to Get Commercial Program Across." *N.E.A. Bulletin* 8:88 (May 1927): 10.

"Radio Programs for Week-End." *Highland Mills* (NY) *Star*, March 3, 1927, 11.

Safley, James Clifford. *The Country Newspaper and Its Operation*. New York: D. Appleton and Company, 1930.

Seitz, D.C. "The Country Press." *The Outlook* 142 (January 27, 1926): 136–138.

"Smith and the South." *The New York Times* December 10, 1926, E12.

Steiner, Jesse Frederick. "The Rural Press." *The American Journal of Sociology* 33:3 (November 1927): 412–423.

"Survey Reveals Country Paper Holding Its Own." *The Publishers' Auxiliary*, March 9, 1929, 1.

Taylor, Carl C. "The Country Newspapers as a Town-Country Agency." Paper presented at the Fourth National Country Life Conference, New Orleans, LA, 1921.

Thurstone, L.L. "The Significance of Psychology for the Study of Government and Certain Specific Problems Involving Both Psychology and Politics: Round Table on Politics and Psychology, Reports of the Second National Conference on the Science of Politics Held at Chicago, Illinois, Sept. 8–12, 1924." *The American Political Science Review* 19:1 (February 1925): 110–122.

The Wakefield (MI) *Advocate*, April 21, 1923, 3.

Watson, Elmo Scott. *A History of Newspaper Syndicates in the United States, 1865–1935*. Chicago: *The Publishers' Auxiliary*, 1936.

Willey, Malcolm M. *The Country Newspaper*. Chapel Hill, NC: The University of North Carolina Press, 1926.

Willey, Malcolm M., and William Weinfeld. "The Country Weekly: Trends in Numbers and Distribution, 1900–1930." *Social Forces* 13:1 (October 1934–May 1935): 51–56.

Wood, James Playsted. *The Story of Advertising*. Garden City, NY: Ronald Press, 1958.

Wright, Don C. "Not a Journalist." *The Publishers' Auxiliary*, November 2, 1929, 4.

www.measuringworth.com.

· 4 ·

THE 1930S: BOOSTERISM AND BUSINESS SURVIVAL

During the Great Depression of the 1930s, personal incomes, tax revenues, profits, and prices dropped, as did the demeanor of many Americans who fell into a personal depression after seeing their life savings drastically dwindle or become depleted. Although most community newspapers also experienced a downfall in profits, they also realized the importance of their business survival in relation to boosterism. Weeklies recognized their need to serve as confidence builders for the local business community as well as individual citizens who were also struggling to maintain a revenue source and keep bill collectors at bay. The weekly became a "must read" in terms of learning about the latest federal government jobs and relief programs. But it also served as a comforting reminder to its readers that life went on as usual—babies were born, brides were wed, and loved ones were buried. But weeklies had to be ever mindful of their balance sheet to keep their operations afloat. As a result, some weeklies quickly recognized the need to barter in terms of collecting subscription and advertising fees and paying bills, which kept their printing presses operating during challenging economic times.

A newspaper is a business; and by the 1930s, the majority of weekly publishers became increasingly professional. Unlike their predecessors who undersold their printed products or were negligent in collecting advertising and subscription fees, the community weekly publisher of the 1930s understood the importance of balancing his books to keep the presses rolling. But the Depression necessitated a willingness to bend some book-balancing rules, and bartering proved to be beneficial for the publisher, his newspaper readers, and business clients in order to maintain advertisers and subscribers.

As weeklies dealt internally with business viability concerns, they outwardly took on stronger roles as boosters for their communities, both in terms of supporting local merchants and boosting the morale of area residents with words of encouragement, advice on frugality, rural community updates, and actions of public service. Weeklies were the important link that kept communities together. The effects of the Depression were too easily recognizable in these small rural towns and villages; so, the weeklies and small-town dailies focused on positive news as a means of boosting morale. They took on community leadership roles and sponsored various community service projects and relief efforts. In fact, many publishers took on enlarged roles as community leaders because their business peers suffered economic and emotional losses.

Golden Rule Approach to Business: Coming to the Aid of Communities in Trying Times

Throughout the economically depressed 1930s, weeklies and small-town dailies maintained their operations with a "golden rule" approach to business. Printing words of encouragement and advice on frugality, participating in public service, and printing names of area residents in community columns to give readers a feeling of importance were just some of the ways the country editor maintained an optimistic tone in trying to boost the morale of area residents during difficult financial times. Textbook author James Safley wrote that the country newspaper was expected to serve as a leader in its community, to "be a guiding star in time of trouble, a counselor and a friend." By doing so, he asserted, the editor derived "a great measure of satisfaction in the knowledge that he has been of genuine service to the public."[1]

Although weekly newspapers traditionally declared their community service role across their nameplates, these "mottos" seemed to take on special significance during troubled times. For example, *The Richwood* (OH) *Gazette* staked its claim as "A Real Home Paper, Devoted to the Best Interests of the Community in Which It Is Published."[2] *The Cambridge City* (IN) *Tribune* professed on its nameplate to be "More Than a Newspaper—A

Community Institution."³ *The Deming* (NM) *Headlight* printed the following just below its name: "Deming—Always Deming."⁴

Weekly newspapers were certainly concerned about staying in business during hard economic times, but they were equally concerned about the well-being of their readers and community members. The financial well-being of community members had a direct impact on the newspaper's advertising and subscription revenues. A "distressed" community was less likely to provide willing advertisers and paying subscribers, but it also offered opportunities for community support and outreach—opportunities brought to the public's attention through the weekly newspaper. In February 1930, *The Sheffield* (AL) *Standard* published an editorial asking readers to look around them and see the ravages of an economic upheaval. It called on citizens to help those less fortunate. The editorial stated, "Colbert County may not be as prosperous as we might wish, but there is no famine, no pestilence, no dire danger. However, there are families in our community, hit by the hard hand of circumstance, unable to make satisfactory adjustment in life." The editorial added that many would deny such a state existed. But it provided examples of hardships endured by local citizens and ended with, "Isn't it about time for us to think along this line, not that there is any quick formula towards relieving distress, but rather that we may be more willing to assist established agencies?"⁵ *The Tuscumbia* (AL) *Times* addressed unemployed workers in a July 1930 editorial by stating, "There is no situation more discouraging to a man or a woman than to be dependent upon work for livlihood [sic] and yet be without a chance to sell their labor because of adverse economic conditions."⁶

In contrast to the "boosterism" role taken on by weeklies, many of the larger metropolitan dailies were accused of downplaying the severity of the Depression for the purposes of propping up local businesses to keep advertising linage up. For example, in their mid-1930s follow-up study of Muncie, Indiana, sociologists Robert and Helen Lynd found that the public's confident optimism did not begin to erode until late April 1930, when the city's evening paper began publishing articles about a local "bad slump" and the past hard winter for workers.⁷ Among metropolitan daily critics was a journalism education leader who accused the large-city newspaper owners of being more concerned about their stockholders and advertisers than the welfare of readers. Kenneth Olson, president of the American Association of Teachers of Journalism, delivered a speech at the association's 1935 annual gathering at which he criticized owners for not using their profits to help the poor and champion causes to improve their status in life.[8]

Taking on Community Leadership Roles

The Depression not only called upon weekly editors to become morale leaders through their writings, but also to take the helm of community booster organizations in voluntary and elective positions that were previously held by successful local merchants. Country editor C.M. Meredith Jr. observed in his 1937 textbook on country journalism, "A compilation of the names of the leading men and women in the community is not now complete without the inclusion of the editor." Chapter eight included an analysis of eight eastern Pennsylvania country newspapers that showed the relationship between the amount of business in each of the newspaper's towns, the number and amount of personal items and news stories, and the amount of advertising. Also analyzed was the amount of plate matter published, the amount of news published, and the amount of advertising and subscriptions. The number of commuters was also considered as bearing on the success of each newspaper, as were wages earned in the community and the amount of money spent in advertising. The presence or the absence of editorials, the number of news features, and the number of correspondents were analyzed to indicate each newspaper's general financial condition and standing in the community.[9]

University of Minnesota journalism professor Thomas Barnhart reinforced Meredith's observation in a study on editorial writing in weekly and small daily newspapers from 1930 through 1932. Writing about his findings in *Journalism Quarterly*, Barnhart emphasized that because of frequent bankruptcies and changes in business, many of the traditional community leaders, such as bank presidents and major store owners, were no longer in positions to take on leadership roles. Consequently, the newspaper editor often felt obliged to take on a leadership role to encourage the community to "carry on" during the trying times of the 1930s.

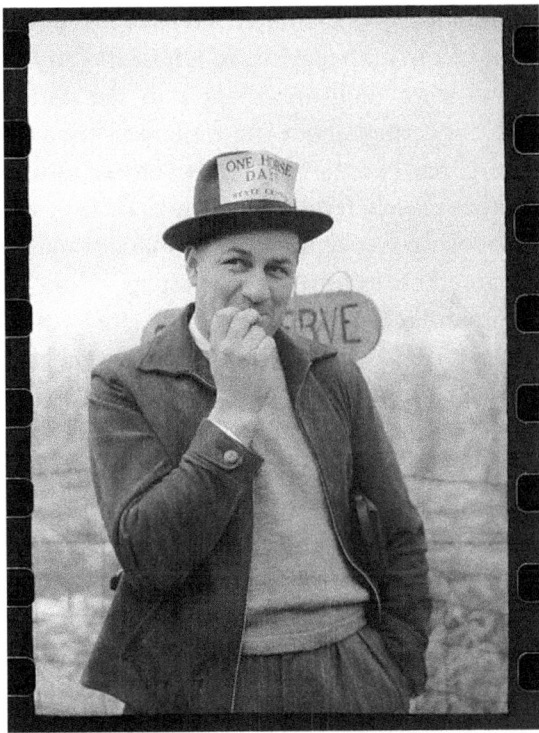

Figure 4.1 During hard economic times, weekly editors were expected to take the helm of community booster organizations in voluntary and elective positions that were previously held by successful local merchants. Local newspaper editor, cornhusking contest, Marshall County, Iowa. 1939. Contributor Arthur Rothstein. Retrieved from the Library of Congress. http://hdl.loc.gov/loc.pnp/fsa.8a12776.

In addition, Barnhart's study revealed that many citizens who were previously involved in service clubs dropped out to focus on their own financial problems, so many community newspaper editors volunteered to head up charitable drives and conduct campaigns for relief funds.[10] In his review of 486 newspapers in 43 states, Barnhart found that 470 papers provided aid to community welfare organizations, 430 aided in relief to the needy and unemployed, and 408 cooperated in miscellaneous relief projects, such as projects to provide psychological outlets for the unemployed. The study also revealed that of the weeklies studied, 361 cooperated with merchants to stimulate trade, 353 worked to bring relief to farms, 342 sought to reduce taxes, 207 gave aid to banks, 187 fought to oust corrupt and ineffective officials, 72 sought county and township government reorganizations, 70 urged consolidating rural schools, 54 contributed aid to continue schools, 40 sought lower utility rates, and 17 led movements to adjust the city's indebtedness.[11]

Weekly and small-town daily newspapers in the early 1930s not only appeared to be more concerned about the welfare of their readers than their metropolitan counterparts, but they were also better mirrors of the public. The content of weeklies closely represented the daily lives of their readers. In fact, Barnhart's textbook on weekly newspaper management emphasized how important it was for an editor to turn out a newspaper that "mirrored the lives of small-town and rural folk."[12]

Because of its close tie to the community, the weekly served as a valuable research source, according to some sociologists. A sociology professor at New Jersey College for Women, Rutgers University, described the content of the average weekly as being "consistent and repetitive in nature" and primarily concerned with local affairs. He acknowledged that while some weeklies reported inconsistently, varied their editorial policies, or were careless or negligent about omissions, average community newspapers were considered accurate and thus could be considered as reliable a source as public records that were "often badly kept." He observed, "The person who does not know America's small-town papers does not know rural America."[13]

Back-to-the-Country Movement Focuses on Food, Farming, Fellowship, and Fraud

The concept of country journalism being better connected to its readers and more concerned about their well-being was embraced as part of a "back-to-the-country movement." Proponents of the small-town press acknowledged that weeklies still contained a fair amount of syndicate material, but they argued that the community weekly had closer ties to small communities than regional dailies and were thus more concerned about reporting on local matters.

By the mid-1930s, it was estimated that the Western Newspaper Union syndicate supplied features to 9 of every 10 U.S. weekly newspapers. Local editors had the choice of hundreds of features including cooking, fashion, business, sports, religion, travel, celebrity news, comic strips, gossip columns, literary series, and photographic layouts. The Chicago-based W.N.U. sold 400 types of features to 10,732 daily and weekly newspapers. The company operated 34 U.S. plants. In addition to supplying syndicate material, the company produced a weekly trade paper, operated a magazine printing business, and sold printing machinery and wholesale paper. Described as the world's largest publishing syndicate, W.N.U. was valued by its owners at $8,500,000. In a 1936 *Time* magazine article, W.N.U. Editor-in-Chief Wright A. Patterson estimated that nearly 11,000 small-town and metropolitan editors used W.N.U. material on a regular basis. The syndicate also provided editorial commentary, including a regular column on the New Deal, a series of U.S. government relief programs, projects, reforms, and regulations enacted in 1933. Editors could choose from three categories of New Deal editorials: pro, con, and middle-of-the-road.[14]

A 1933 column in *The Nation* magazine, signed by the pseudonym "The Drifter," referred to a back-to-the-country movement that ensured better support for the small-town press as metropolitan dailies became more national in character and circulation. The columnist wrote, "Many of our metropolitan newspapers already are so general as to leave a field in their own area for regional journalism." The column bemoaned the death of a Georgia printer-editor who died after running a weekly for more than 40 years. The columnist observed, "The printer-editor is a disappearing type, but the personal journalism which he exemplified and the country newspaper where he flourished are on the upgrade." The article mentioned the death of William Benjamin Franklin Townsend, printer-editor of *The Dahlonega* (GA) *Nugget* who single-handedly put out the weekly on a hand press for more than 40 years. According to the author, the last words the editor wrote were "The editor is sick" at the end of a column on local news. Then the editor sat down to rest and died, at age 78.[15]

Metropolitan journalist Jay House, a former weekly newspaperman, also alluded to a back-to-the-country movement and growing influence of the weekly in a 1934 article in *The Saturday Evening Post*. He asserted that the weekly was more capably edited than in previous decades and had a "better grasp of its function as a local newspaper."[16]

But critics of the small-town press contended that printing mostly positive news or biased coverage in favor of a community's power elite while ignoring or downplaying negative issues involving its privileged and powerful hurt readers rather than helped them. As an example, the author of a 1935 magazine article in *The Nation* referred to local newspaper coverage of the press guild fight at the *Lorain* (OH) *Journal*. The article described how management-labor conflicts were usually covered in small-town newspapers. The author asserted that fair reporting on management-labor issues could be expected from wire reporters. But he said that fair coverage could not be expected from a small-town newspaper reporter because of the reporter's strong allegiance to his boss, who was often the owner of his town's only paper as well as a heavy shareholder in the local plant where labor conflicts might occur. The author argued that by serving as "organs of special and local pleading for privileged interests" the small-town press purposely ignored news that could potentially harm local businesses and business leaders.[17]

Another important element of the weekly's morale-boosting role during the Depression was to provide helpful advice on how to stretch a family's food supply and living expenses. For example, farmers could read regularly published agricultural columns provided to the weekly press via state and federal agricultural programs on such matters as types of crops to grow, and how to diversify and rotate them. Often these articles were backed by local editorial comment. A March 1931 editorial in *The Tuscumbia* (AL) *Times* discussed a newspaper investigator who visited farm families in the country's drought areas and found evidence of suffering and lack of material comforts. But, according to the editorial, the investigator also found comfortable families practicing what was termed "safe farming." The editorial concluded, "If more farmers would grow all the necessities possible and then devote time and labor to the money crops—drouths [sic]—low prices and other disasters wouldn't entail such material suffering." Throughout the Depression, the U.S. Department of Agriculture Office of Information provided educational materials for the press to disseminate to the general public for the purpose of improving farming practices and food supplies.[18]

A 1934 issue of *The Richwood* (OH) *Gazette* contained a news article on the growing trend of "part-time" farmers across the country—defined as industrial workers who were trying to grow a portion of their food, including keeping a flock of chickens or a sow on their property. According to the article, a survey of more than 200 "part-time" farm families in the vicinity of Columbus, Ohio, found that industrial workers were more successful in their farming efforts if they had some previous farming experience, as opposed to city workers who lacked farming know-how. The Rural Economics Department of the Ohio Experiment Station conducted the survey.[19]

Another helpful hint for those seeking out alternative food sources came in the 1936 edition of *The Pointer* in Riverdale, Illinois, that included a brief notice about the publishing of a 68-page leaflet describing and illustrating the most common species of mushrooms. According to the article, the leaflet was designed "to assist those interested in collecting mushrooms for food and to help them avoid the poisonous varieties." *The Pointer* served readers in Riverdale, Dolton, South Holland, and Lansing, communities outside of Chicago in Cook County, Illinois.[20]

Public service was another important task for the weekly editor as officers of local charitable and service organizations often asked the editor to lead or support community service programs and events. To promote community camaraderie, *The Journal-Advance and Benton County Gazette* in Gentry, Arkansas, advertised a 1933 community sale where items such as oil stoves, corn, hay, soybeans, cattle, and farm implements were sold. The promotion stated that ladies from the local Methodist church would serve lunch and community members were encouraged to "Enjoy lunch and a friendly visit with neighbors."[21]

Weeklies also inundated readers with real-life morality lessons by publishing articles about fraudulent business practices and unethical financial schemes. For example, an April 1930 issue of *The Sheffield* (AL) *Standard* contained the newspaper's first banner headline, "Hackworth, Ex-Banker, Given 15 Years."[22] The article told of a former vice president of the Tennessee Valley Bank who was found guilty of embezzlement and sentenced to 15 years in prison. Other editors found themselves warning readers about such illicit business practices as chain letters—a popular "get-rich-quick" scheme during the Depression that often targeted rural residents. These chain-letter campaigns—with names such as "Prosperity Club" or "Send-a-Dime"—contained messages that attempted to convince the recipients to make a certain number of copies and send them to a specified number of recipients. A single issue of the *Ada* (OK) *Weekly News* contained several cautionary tales about the buildup and the downfall of a local chain-letter system that lasted only one week.[23] One of the articles referred to chain-letter mania that had swept the town and noted that stenographers and notary publics were kept busy taking transfers in accordance with the rules of the game. An editorial in the same issue warned residents of the dangers of the risky financial game and compared it to going into battle. "Every man," the editorial stated, "knows somebody is going to be killed but thinks it is the other fellow who will be hit and that he himself will come through safely."[24] Two pages later, an article described the collapse of the Ada chain-letter business, with a sub-headline that read, "Exchanges for Five-Dollar Systems Move Out; All Is Quiet and Normal on Main Street as Once Enthusiastic Fans Return Attention to Business."[25] Ironically, the same issue also contained an article about the arrests of five chain-letter promoters from Oklahoma City on felony charges of drawing a lottery for operating two separate chain letters in Shawnee, Oklahoma.[26] Another article in the same issue reported on a civil suit for $35,840 in damages against seven purveyors of chain letters as "chainomania" reached its peak and disappointed investors sought to "get even with somebody." The *Ada Weekly News* served as a good example of the consolidation of weekly newspapers that took place in the early twentieth century. The weekly was established in 1901 and consolidated with the *Ada Weekly Democrat* in 1910, the *Pontotoc County Enterprise* in 1912, and the *Ada Star-Democrat* in 1919, becoming the *Ada Evening News* and *Ada Weekly News* by the 1920s.[27]

Taking a local leadership role during the severe economic downturn of the 1930s, weeklies often joined in efforts with other local merchants to encourage shopping at independent hometown merchants as opposed to national chain stores. For example, a headline in an April 11, 1930 edition of *The Sheffield* (AL) *Standard* proclaimed, "FACTS you should consider about the home-owned, home-controlled independent business men of Tuscumbia-Sheffield." The full-page message asked readers to ignore the claims of chain stores and mail-order houses that they sold goods and services for less. The message emphasized that a local merchant who sold the same goods for the same price also provided credit and delivery service and "carries you when you are short of money." The plea asked readers to trade with home businesses and keep profits at home."[28] A similar full-page message appeared in a March 1930 issue of *The Cambridge City* (IN) *Tribune* under the headline, "A Chain Is as Strong as its Weakest Link; a City Is as Weak as Its Strongest Chain." The message, sponsored by the city's independent hometown merchants, stated that chain stores took money out of the community and "neither directly nor indirectly will it [money] ever find its way back into circulation here."[29] In a July 1930 editorial, *The Tuscumbia* (AL) *Times* encouraged readers to buy from local independent merchants not only because they were local, but because the quality of their goods and services had risen to a competitive level with national chain stores. The editorial noted that merchants 20 years earlier did not understand that buy-it-at-home campaigns were permanently successful not because the businesses were locally operated, but because they remained competitive in goods and services. It said of the local merchants, "They sell goods now, instead of merely keeping them."[30]

Country Correspondents: Apostles of the Country Editor

Country correspondents, mostly farm wives who wrote about their communities and recorded everyday happenings, played an important role in boosting the morale of readers and the bottom line of weekly publishers. Correspondents wrote columns under the heading of a community's name that contained news about its residents, usually related to births, marriages and deaths, social events such as bridal showers and church receptions, out-of-town visitors, and travel. Correspondent reports from rural communities showed that, despite tough economic times, people still enjoyed their lives, attended church, visited friends and relatives, hosted social events, got married, and had babies—most of whom the newspapers described as "beautiful."

According to a country journalism textbook, country correspondents were "apostles of the country editor" because they sold the newspaper to hundreds that were "too far distant for him [editor] to reach directly."[31] Publishers recognized that correspondents maintained subscriptions because of their columns' popularity. In fact, the author of a textbook on weekly newspapers estimated that editors devoted more space to country correspondence than to any other single category because roughly half of the average weekly's circulation went to readers on rural routes and in small communities. State press associations and the National Editorial Association—also recognizing the importance of correspondents—joined forces in 1937 to publish a monthly informal, instructive magazine named *Folks*, which was described as "the Helpmate of the Newspaper Correspondent."[32]

An appreciation for these country scribes was voiced in a *Time* magazine article that profiled the 1935 winner of "The Best Country Newspaper Correspondent in the U.S." contest, sponsored by the Crowell Publishing Company's *Country Home* magazine. The contest winner was 58-year-old Mary Elizabeth Mahnkey of Oasis, Missouri, who had been a correspondent for 44 years for *The Taney County Republican* in Forsyth, Missouri. She had also contributed poetry, letters, and farm gossip to *Country Home* magazine over the years. Her community was like that of many country correspondents in that its population numbered less than 100. In fact, at the time the article was published, Oasis had only 21 residents while the town of Forsyth, from which the weekly—with a circulation of 871—was published, had a population of 281. As winner of the nationwide competition, she received 50 dollars, a "fine silver meat platter with a vegetable dish to match," a free trip to Manhattan, and the title of the best country correspondent.[33]

Thus, the country's view of rural journalism, as displayed among the pages of nationally syndicated magazines and newspapers, was both complimentary and critical. Critics of country journalism continued to raise questions of fairness and favoritism while supporters of the back-to-the-country-movement applauded the rural press for its microscopic examination of the intimate details of small-town life.

Business Survival: Budgeting, Bartering and Battling for Advertising Revenues

The Great Depression left many businesses struggling for survival, and weeklies were certainly not immune to the economic hardships that caused many businesses to close their doors or consolidate with financially stronger operations. Although there remained a strong demand for weeklies, readers simply could no longer afford to pay for subscriptions. Compounding the problem was the loss of advertising revenue from local businesses that either shut down or discontinued advertising, and from national advertisers that restricted their advertising budgets to metropolitan dailies and national magazines.

With the previous decade marked by the consolidations and closings of the country's weakest weeklies, it would have appeared that the remaining 9,522 weeklies in towns with a population of less than 15,000 were financially sound and ripe for expansion.[34] University of Minnesota professor Bruce McCoy conducted a 1929 study—prior to the October 1929 stock market crash—on competition and consolidation in the weekly newspaper field. He estimated that weeklies served 53 percent of the country's population. He predicted that the tendency toward consolidation of two or more newspapers published in the same city or town would lead to a new era of prosperity and service for the country press.[35] But many of the surviving publications did not become thriving business operations due to an unforeseen economic depression that changed the financial outlook for many small-town newspaper publishers. The economic downturn accelerated the number of weekly mergers and suspensions, and many journalists left small-town journalism altogether.

Personnel Budgeting: Job Demands Outweigh Job Openings

The loss of job opportunities at weeklies was especially frustrating for the growing number of college-educated reporters and editors who viewed the weekly newspaper field as the easiest way to enter into their chosen profession. But despite the fact that journalism education was well established by this time, there remained many editors and publishers who trained as apprentices and never received formal journalism training. In fact, University of Wisconsin journalism professor Grant Hyde asserted that some journalists were "quite unfitted" for the profession. He observed in a 1931 article on the state of journalism that, "Perhaps this dark year of depression may precede the dawn of a better day for journalism teaching."[36]

As part of the effort to graduate more students fit for journalism, the American Association of Schools and Departments of Journalism appointed a special committee in 1938 to review curriculum requirements. The committee recommended that students take specific courses in business and advertising in response to an increased demand among weekly and small daily papers for employees trained in these areas.[37] But despite these efforts, a 1939–1940 National Council of Professional Education for Journalism study found that there were more institutions providing professional education for journalism than placement opportunities warranted. For example, in 1939 the 32 schools of journalism in the United States had an enrollment of 6,295 students (undergraduate and graduate) and 216 institutions providing some journalism training had class enrollments of more than 13,000. But only 1,385 graduates were hired in the journalism field that year. The study also revealed that during the previous five years roughly 16 percent of journalism graduates took jobs in the weekly field, while 31 percent were hired at daily newspapers.[38]

Despite the fact that the Depression tightened the personnel budgets of many weekly and small-town newspapers and thus could be seen as a means to "weed out" poor-quality journalists, there remained a large contingent of experienced, better-trained reporters and editors who found themselves out of work. However, many of them eventually found jobs with the federal government after the Franklin D. Roosevelt administration established a number of federal agencies as part of an overall economic recovery effort known as the New Deal, which included the Works Progress (later renamed Projects) Administration employing roughly 8.5 million in this work-relief program. President Roosevelt's 1933 National Industrial Recovery Act allowed businesses to fix prices and create production quotas. It also established fair-practice codes that guaranteed improved working conditions and the right of collective bargaining for labor. Small newspapers were placed under the jurisdiction of the Graphic Arts Industries Code—which was adopted in 1934 and was established to set minimum wages for newspaper employees in cities of varying sizes. The National Editorial Association served as a national code authority to ensure newspaper compliance to the N.R.A. codes. The recovery act was later ruled unconstitutional by the U.S. Supreme Court. Writing for federal agencies such as the National Recovery Administration and the Agricultural Adjustment Administration, former newspaper editors and reporters often found their work turning up in the pages of their previous employers—small-town dailies and weeklies throughout the country. It was estimated that 6,600 individuals were hired as writers, editors, historians, researchers, and art critics for the Federal Writers' Project.[39]

For some weekly publishers who lacked funding to pay even a single reporter, the only newsgathering help came from local correspondents. Sometimes a correspondent's only pay was a free subscription to the newspaper, according to Charles Wilson, who wrote about weeklies in a 1934 article, "The Country Press Reawakens." Regarding country correspondents, he observed, "Few of them sign their work. Yet they write on, through flood and famine, drought and pestilence—miniature historians who expect neither money nor fame."[40] But while some correspondents received no cash compensation, C.F.R. Smith, editor of the country correspondents' magazine, *Folks*, conducted a survey covering a large sampling of rural weeklies in Minnesota that showed that 87.5 percent of rural correspondents received cash payment for their work. The survey revealed that column-inch rates paid to correspondents varied from two to five cents, while payment per column ranged from 25 cents to one dollar. The study also reported that monthly rates ranged from one to two dollars.[41]

To Barter or Not to Barter

Most weekly publishers had to consider a number of tough business-related strategies in order to remain in operation throughout the decade. One concern was whether or not to barter with subscribers. Thus, many small-town editors found themselves trading newspaper subscriptions or printed copies of previous issues that were lying around the newspaper office for coal, plumbing, medical services, and farm produce. For example, J. Milam, editor of *The Informer* in Jasper, Arkansas, was a one-man shop who kept his readers informed through trade outs of squirrel meat and bushels of squash for subscriptions. So despite the fact that subscription revenues might have been down, this did not necessarily mean that newspapers had fewer readers. Readers simply found more creative ways to "pay" for their subscriptions.[42]

Because newspapers contained valuable information such as where to get a job, where to find a hot meal or temporary shelter, and where to shop for the lowest prices on everyday necessities, newspapers themselves became necessities for local residents. Therefore those who could not afford to pay cash for a subscription found other means to "pay" for a copy because they were too proud to ask for free copies, according to weekly editor Bruce Crawford of Norton, Virginia, who wrote about his country journalism career in a 1933 issue of *The New Republic*.[43]

Weekly editors were encouraged by their professional peers to take pride in their businesses and not to openly complain about their financial struggles. In fact, a 1928 column in *The Publishers' Auxiliary* chastised editors who published the "poverty joke" because it appeared as if they were whining about unpaid subscriptions. The joke referred to a preacher who asked all in his congregation to stand if they were paying their debts. Only one man remained seated. He then stood, looking "careworn and hungry, wearing last-summer's suit" and explained that he could not pay his debt because "all of those who were paying their other debts were his subscribers." The unsigned column pointed out that by printing the joke, editors belittled their profession and perpetuated the obsolete idea that operating a weekly was a thankless and poor-paying job. The joke also sent the message, according to the columnist, that an editor was "a spineless man whose weakness everyone imposes [on] because he meekly accepts whatever his subscribers choose to give."[44]

Some country editors, though, were seemingly not as generous in offering free subscriptions for trade outs on handiwork or vegetables. *The Tuscumbia (AL) Times* listed its subscription rates on page four of each issue, along with the directive, "Cash in Advance."[45] *The Richwood (OH) Gazette* listed circulation rates with the disclaimer, "These rates are given only to cash in advance customers."[46] However, a published policy did not necessarily mean there was no opportunity for informal agreement and/or bartering.

Battling Radio and Dailies for Dwindling Advertising Dollars

A second key strategy for business survival in weekly publishing involved determining tactics that should be used to battle radio for dwindling advertising revenues. Potential weekly advertisers reduced their budgets and often considered an "either/or" advertising strategy as opposed to reducing advertising costs in various media outlets. Many merchants were drawn to the program sponsorship opportunities available in radio and turned their backs on advertising in the community weekly. Thus, weekly publishers began to recognize radio as the new advertising threat, and it became a theme for discussion in many meetings of national and state press associations in the early 1930s.[47] National Editorial Association Executive Secretary H.C. Hotaling voiced his concern about radio competition in his annual report to the association's 1931 convention in Atlanta. "There are country weeklies in America today," he stated, "... that are fighting for existence because of unrestricted radio competition."[48] In radio, the advertiser selected and often concocted the editorial background for his advertising through program sponsorship. Throughout the 1930s, big-name radio personalities became associated with advertised products such as coffee, gasoline, and tobacco products. In fact, by the end of the 1920s, radio advertisers had spent roughly $40 million for broadcast time alone.[49]

While weekly publishers early on determined the advertising threat of radio, they were not as quick to recognize the new medium as a serious news competitor. In fact, weekly editors initially welcomed the use of radio as a news source—by the late 1920s, radio was being utilized for news bulletins, such as ballgame scores or horse race results—because they viewed the radio news bulletins as a means of getting people interested enough to subsequently buy a newspaper "to get more details."[50] But they abruptly adopted tactics to lessen the advertising competition of radio. One such tactic included editing out the names of radio advertisers when publishing radio schedules. Most early radio programs—whether drama, music, entertainment, or news—had one advertising sponsor with the name of the sponsor included in the program's title. Weeklies also persuaded broadcasters to purchase advertising space in the newspapers to promote their programs.[51]

The loss of national advertising revenue was also a major concern for small-town publishers as the competition from dailies became more acute during the Great Depression. Edgartown, Massachusetts editor-publisher

Henry Beetle Hough observed that the increased advertising competition from daily newspapers resulted in the curious anomaly of his newspaper, *The Vineyard Gazette*, becoming too costly a medium for the nation's largest and wealthiest corporations. However, he said, his newspaper was a practical and economical advertising venue for the small grocer with a limited advertising budget. As a result, his newspaper employed economizing measures and sought multiple small advertising accounts instead of depending on a few large national advertisers.[52]

In their pursuit of national advertising agencies, weekly publishers argued that even though many of their subscribers also subscribed to a daily newspaper from a nearby community, the hometown newspaper was the best medium for advertising. Weekly publishers often referred to a 1930 study on the newspaper reading habits of rural and farm families that found a 61 percent preference for viewing advertisements in their home paper as opposed to the nearby metropolitan daily. The survey revealed that 100 families subscribed to 260 newspapers, the majority having subscribed to both a weekly and a daily newspaper from a larger nearby community.[53]

Merchant Partnerships, Job-Printing Services

Despite concerted efforts to attract national advertising, the weekly publisher was forever aware that the greatest potential for advertising revenue was located just outside his front doors, on Main Street. The importance of local merchants advertising in their home newspaper was affirmed in a University of Wisconsin Department of Agricultural Journalism 1935 study that found that local display, classified, and legal advertising accounted for more than 75 percent of total advertising revenue in 100 weeklies throughout the United States and Canada. In fact, survey respondents even offered advice on how weeklies could attract more local advertising—by eliminating the use of unpaid propaganda, or free publicity, from government agencies and businesses. Of the 100 weekly newspapers in the U.S. and Canada represented in this survey, 60 were from Wisconsin.[54] With the exception of entire ready-print pages, free publicity was utilized on a need-to-fill basis—meaning the articles were placed in spaces that were not sold for advertising. Also, local merchants sometimes purchased advertising in their community weekly because of the tie-ins provided in publicity articles to certain products or services that could be found at local businesses.

In a 1934 *Editor & Publisher* article, country editor Paul Bittinger offered advice to weekly editors on how to increase advertising linage. He proposed that weeklies use more aggressive business methods such as hiring an advertising solicitor to prepare attractive, timely, and seasonal advertising layouts in advance to potential advertising customers. He also recommended the use of syndicated advertising services to provide updated artwork. Another suggestion was that editors use promotional themes—such as back-to-school specials—and customer discount coupons so that advertisers would receive better returns on their advertising dollar. For example, he said that his newspaper promoted weekly grocery specials for smaller independent grocers and, later, larger chain grocery markets. In doing so, he built up his newspaper's food advertisement linage. He also encouraged the use of national theme weeks—such as Cotton Week, Insurance Week, etc.—for thematic advertising promotions and special sections.[55]

Some weeklies openly chastised local merchants for failing to advertise in their publications. A 1937 front-page personal column written by *The Alton* (IA) *Democrat* publisher George E. Bowers referred to a Kansas weekly that contained a dozen blank spaces, each surrounded by a rule or border to represent non-advertising merchants and a dying town. Bowers then suggested that every business in his town should be represented in each issue of the newspaper. He reminded local merchants that 10,000 northwest Iowans read *The Alton* (IA) *Democrat* on a regular basis. He wrote, "It's up to the business men to tell what they are doing. If they don't, the town's reputation as a business center is blasted."[56] *The Sheffield* (AL) *Standard* suggested that more local businesses advertise to encourage sales during an economic depression. One of the newspaper's editorials stated, "This year advertising is more needed, not because people have less money to spend, but they hesitate to spend it. It is far more logical to advertise when sales are hard than when they are easy."[57] Other newspapers also appealed for more local advertising, but their approach was less direct. *The Hopewell* (NJ) *Herald* reminded readers each week that their paper "Gets into the Home, Where Circulation Counts" in a proclamation printed above its nameplate. The advertising rates, listed on page four, were as follows: Cent-a-word Column, no less than 25 cents; Regarding Notices, 15 cents per line on first page; Cards of Thanks, $1.00; Resolutions of respect, condolences, etc., $2.00. The paper was listed as a foreign advertising representative for The American Press Association.[58]

And finally, one key strategy that kept many weeklies in operation during the decade was to expand their job-printing services to increase revenues that were not directly tied to their newspapers. Taking such action redefined the publisher's role from editor-publisher to printer-publisher, a common role among the country's earliest newspapermen. Especially in smaller towns with declining trade centers, publishers replaced lost advertising revenue with specialized printing and engraving jobs. Even though an emphasis on job-printing operations made a publisher more a merchant and less an editor, it did extend the life of weaker newspapers, observed the author of an article on competition and consolidation in the weekly newspaper field.[59]

One country editor who wrote about the merchant-versus-editor relationship asserted that it was difficult for the editor to demand economizing of town officials while at the same time seeking their business through legal notices and printing jobs. He stated, "In a depression more than at any other time, citizens clamor collectively for public service and economy, but howl individually for special favors. The small-town editor-publisher, if he must scrouge [sic] to survive, is no exception to the general run of pigs at the public teat."[60]

Ultimately, only the strongest weeklies survived to the end of the decade. For some, survivability required consolidation with weaker newspapers or a revision in style, staffing, design, and content of their publications to appeal to new readers and advertisers. As a result of newspaper consolidations, there was a decrease in advertising competition because nearby newspapers folded. Also, physical plants improved, and some weeklies even began using the latest technology—an offset press. Offset printing is a process by which an image is transferred by ink from a paper or metal plate onto a smooth rubber cylinder that then transfers the image to paper. The process was developed in the early 1900s. The equipment required for offset was less expensive than letterpress equipment required to produce the same size newspaper.

Although offset presses were somewhat experimental at the end of the decade, early proponents asserted that offset would ultimately be more cost-effective because it was cheaper to produce more photographs per newspaper issue. Offset would thus enable editors to respond to readers' demands for more photographs and illustrations. The weeklies that thrived during the decade began taking on some of the characteristics of the metropolitan dailies such as specialized staff reporters, separate editorial and business departments, and magazine-style design features that appealed to more readers and advertisers. For example, by the mid-1930s two Pennsylvania weeklies changed their formats, which were viewed at the time as innovations in the rural weekly field. The *Mount Pleasant* (PA) *Journal* added a 16-page tabloid magazine section, and *The Selinsgrove* (PA) *Times* discarded the traditional page-one design and replaced it with a magazine design style. The Selinsgrove newspaper also focused on developing local news that was not included in the area's daily, and added a carrier boy delivery system.[61]

Surviving and Thriving

During the 1930s, weeklies served as a morale booster by encouraging local citizens to keep the faith and keep their money in the banks—but they also kept other businesses alive through advertising trade outs, promotional campaigns, and reinforcement of positive economic news. In many cases, they finished the decade in better economic shape than they entered it. A 1938 *Time* article observed that of the country's 11,852 rural papers, nearly half of them were more than 50 years old, and 151 were more than 100 years old. Since the early 1930s, only 126 weeklies folded or were merged with other small-town papers. The average circulation of a weekly was 2,000. The article said of weeklies, "While their columns now include many of the features found in dailies, and streamlined autos have joined the pills among the ads, they remain the most authentic expressions of U.S. rural life." The article featured John Holliday Perry, described as "No. 1 in the rural press." In addition to having bought enough voting trust certificates and common stock shares the previous month to give him controlling interest of the Western Newspaper Union, he was elected its president—succeeding Herbert Henry Fish who served in that capacity for 20 years. Perry was also president of the American Press Association—which was a national advertising representative for 5,000 country newspapers. In 1938, A.P.A. placed $2.5 million of $7 million of its national advertising in country weeklies. Perry also owned *The American Press*—a trade paper for weeklies—and Publishers' Autocaster Service—which sold casting boxes for making plates to country publishers. Perry was an attorney for the James G. Scripps papers in the Northwest and national counsel for the United Press Association, the Scripps Newspapers, and the Newspaper Enterprise Association. He also owned four dailies in Florida and the *Reading* (PA) *Times*.[62]

The following year, *Time* magazine published an article that reported evidence of continued growth, financial success, and influence in the weekly field. The article was based on the findings of its survey of 100 typical weeklies and bi-weeklies throughout the country—estimated to have an audience of 17 million readers. The article noted that despite the decade's turbulent economic depression, weeklies had actually gained in numbers, circulation, and advertising lineage while dailies suffered declining numbers in those categories. The survey's general findings were that most had good business in 1938 and early 1939; boilerplate ads were disappearing; news was ably written but editorials were either purely boosterish, overly timid, or entirely lacking; and a wealth of local columns kept the print lively and entertaining.[63]

Newspaper chains became an important factor to the financial success formula of newspapers in the 1920s and 1930s. Among the largest were the Scripps-Howard, Hearst, and Gannett newspaper chains, known for their acquisition of dailies throughout the country. But they also began acquiring weeklies, many for the purpose of consolidation with other small-town publications. However, the most influential national chain of weeklies began at the weekly level. A testament to the findings of the *Time* survey was demonstrated in the success of a West Virginia newspaper family. In 1934, the three Woodyard brothers (Ted, Bill, and Henry Chapman) of West Virginia acquired control of eight weeklies on Long Island, New York's North Shore. Together with their 15 county-seat West Virginia weeklies, the Woodyards became owners of the largest weekly newspaper chain in the country. The second largest weekly chain was the 17-paper Procter group in Ohio, assembled by the late Colonel William Cooper Procter (Ivory Soap) and Charles Bond (Two-Pants Suits).[64]

Ted Woodyard bought out his brothers' interests in the group and extended the chain to 29 newspapers and two job-printing plants at the end of the 1930s. He also owned Woodyard Associates, Inc.—a New York-based cooperative of 2,113 small-town weeklies that was formed in 1938 to secure national advertising, buy paper and supplies, and set up a systematized accounting method. A 1939 profile in *The Saturday Evening Post* noted that his journalism career began in 1920 when his father, a United States congressman, purchased the weekly *Spencer* (WV) *Times-Record* for the three Woodyard sons to run. Their operating philosophy was to print as much local news as possible and eliminate most boilerplate copy.

As recalled in the article, the Woodyard operating philosophy was demonstrated firsthand when the publishing magnate returned for a visit to Spencer and greeted "Aunt Sarah"—a local woman everyone referred to using the familial title. The elderly woman explained to Ted Woodyard that she was walking with a cane because she had stubbed her toe. He proceeded to the newspaper office and told the editor to explain to readers that Aunt Sarah was forced to use a cane not because of old age, but because of an accident.

He instructed the editor, "Tell them that Aunt Sarah might break all 10 of her toes, but that the weight of 75 years can't break her indomitable spirit."[65] Thus, thanks to the careful editing of a wise publisher, Aunt Sarah became much more than a strong woman who refused to let a stubbed toe keep her down; she also became a symbol of determination and an example of strength for others in the community to rally around and imitate.

Notes

1. James Clifford Safley, *The Country Newspaper and Its Operation* (New York: D. Appleton and Company, 1930), 4, 383.
2. *The Richwood* (OH) *Gazette*, June 14, 1934, 1. Richwood, in Union County, is located in the northern-central part of Ohio. The newspaper, established in 1872, was circulated in Union, Delaware, and Marion counties. Richwood, in Claiborne Township, had a population of 1,573 in 1930. *Fifteenth Census of the United States*, "Population," volume 1, section 8, 869, Table 5. http://newspaperarchive.com/, http://www.census.gov/.
3. *The Cambridge City* (IN) *Tribune*, March 27, 1930, 1. The *Tribune* was established in 1868. Cambridge City, in Jackson Township of Wayne County, is located along Indiana's eastern-central border. Cambridge City had a population of 2,113 in 1930. *Fifteenth Census of the United States*, "Population," volume 1, section 4, 350, Table 5. http://newspaperarchive.com/, http://www.census.gov/.
4. *The Deming* (NM) *Headlight*, January 16, 1931, 1. The *Headlight* was identified as a member of the National Editorial Association. The *Headlight* was established in 1882. Deming, in Luna County, is situated on New Mexico's eastern-southern border. Deming had a population of 3,377 in 1930. *Fifteenth Census of the United States*, "Population," volume 1, section 7, 739, Table 5. http://newspaperarchive.com/, http://www.census.gov/.
5. "Who Suffers in Colbert," *The Sheffield* (AL) *Standard*, February 28, 1930, 4. Sheffield, in Colbert County, is located in the northwestern corner of Alabama. Sheffield had a population of 6,221 in 1930. *Fifteenth Census of the United States*, "Population," volume 1, section 2, 85, Table 5. http://www.census.gov/.
6. *The Tuscumbia Times*, July 1, 1930, 4. The *Times* was identified as a member of the Alabama Press Association. Tuscumbia, in Colbert County, is located in the northwestern corner of Alabama. Tuscumbia had a population of 4,533 in 1930. *Fifteenth Census of the United States*, "Population," volume 1, section 2, 86, Table 5. http://www.census.gov/.
7. Robert S. Lynd and Helen M. Lynd, *Middletown in Transition* (New York: Harcourt, Brace and Company, 1937), 17.
8. Kenneth E. Olson, "The Newspaper in Times of Social Changes," *Journalism Quarterly* 12:1 (March 1935): 9.
9. C.M. Meredith, Jr., *The Country Weekly* (Boston: Bruce Humphries, 1937), 11, 163–173.
10. Thomas F. Barnhart, "Newspaper Leadership in Times of Depression," *Journalism Quarterly* 10:1 (March 1933): 3.

11 Thomas F. Barnhart, *Weekly Newspaper Management* (New York: D. Appleton-Century, 1936): 5.
12 Ibid.
13 John Winchell Riley, Jr., "The Country Weekly as a Sociological Source," *American Sociological Review* 3:1 (February 1938): 41, 43.
14 "The Press: Big Boiler-Plate," *Time*, April 27, 1936, 32. In 2022, according to the latest government figures based on the Consumer Price Index, $8.5 million from 1936 was worth $179.25 million. http://www.measuringworth.com/.
15 "In the Driftway," *The Nation*, July 5, 1933, 17.
16 Jay E. House, "The Old Country Weekly," *The Saturday Evening Post*, May 12, 1934, 25.
17 Haywood Broun, "Lessons from Lorain," *The Nation*, July 31, 1935, 132.
18 "The Same Old Story," *The Tuscumbia* (AL) *Times*, March 3, 1931, 4.
19 "Farm Experience Asset to 'Part Time' Farmers," *The Richwood* (OH) *Gazette*, June 14, 1934, 6. http://newspaperarchive.com/.
20 "Leaflet Is Aid to Mushroom Pickers," *The Pointer*, July 31, 1936, 2. Riverdale, Illinois, in Thornton Township, had a population of 2,504 in 1930. *Fifteenth Census of the United States*, "Population," volume 1, section 4, 320, Table 5. http://newspaperarchive.com/, http://www.census.gov/.
21 "Community Sale," *The Journal-Advance and Benton County* (AR) *Gazette*, April 6, 1933, 2. Gentry, in Benton County, is located in the northwestern corner of Arkansas. Gentry had a population of 779 in 1930. *Fifteenth Census of the United States*, "Population," volume 1, section 3, 121, Table 5. http://newspaperarchive.com/, http://www.census.gov/.
22 "Hackworth, Ex-Banker, Given 15 Years," *The Sheffield* (AL) *Standard*, April 4, 1930, 1.
23 Ada, in Pontotoc County, is located in the southern-central part of Oklahoma. Ada had a population of 11,261 in 1930. *Fifteenth Census of the United States*, "Population," volume 1, section 8, 895, Table 5. http://newspaperarchive.com/, http://www.census.gov/.
24 "Ada Chain Letter Fans Panicky in Attempt to Keep $5 Systems Moving," *The Ada* (OK) *Weekly News*, May 16, 1935, 3–4. http://newspaperarchive.com/.
25 "Chain Letter Business Collapses Here as Late Investors Fail to 'Cash In,'" *The Ada* (OK) *Weekly News*, May 16, 1935, 6. http://newspaperarchive.com/.
26 "Chain Letters Bring Arrests," *The Ada* (OK) *Weekly News*, May 16, 1935, 7. http://newspaperarchive.com/.
27 "Disappointed Investors Sue Chain Promoters," *The Ada* (OK) *Weekly News*, May 16, 1935, 2. http://newspaperarchive.com/. In 2022, according to the latest government figures based on the Consumer Price Index, $8.5 million from 1935 was worth $762,992. http://www.measuringworth.com/.
28 "FACTS You Should Consider About the Home-Owned, Home Controlled Independent Business Men of Tuscumbia-Sheffield," *The Sheffield* (AL) *Standard*, April 11, 1930, 6.
29 "A Chain Is as Strong as Its Weakest Link; A City Is as Weak as Its Strongest Chain," *The Cambridge City* (IN) *Tribune*, March 27, 1930, 2. http://newspaperarchive.com/.
30 "Real Merchants Here," *The Tuscumbia* (AL) *Times*, July 8, 1930, 4.
31 Meredith, *The Country Weekly*, 63.
32 Thomas F. Barnhart, *Weekly Newspaper Writing and Editing* (New York: The Dryden Press, 1949), 191, 197.

33 "Crossroads Correspondent," *Time*, July 29, 1935, 40. In 2022, according to the latest government figures based on the Consumer Price Index, $50 from 1935 was worth $1,064. http://www.measuringworth.com/.
34 *N.W. Ayer & Son's Directory of Newspapers and Periodicals* (Philadelphia: N.W. Ayer & Sons, 1930).
35 Bruce McCoy, "Competition and Consolidation in the Community Weekly Field," *Journalism Quarterly* 7:1 (December 1930): 23.
36 Grant M. Hyde, "United States Journalism in 1931," *Journalism Quarterly* 8:4 (December 1931): 419–428.
37 "Journalism Schools to Improve Training of Students for Weekly and Small Daily Field," *The Publishers' Auxiliary*, January 8, 1938, 5.
38 "Only Half of Journalism Grads Hired by Papers," *The American Press* 59:7 (May 1941): 12.
39 William E. Berchtold, "Press Agents of the New Deal," *The Outlook* 164 (July 26, 1934): 25.
40 Charles M. Wilson, "The Country Press Reawakens," *The North American Review* 238 (September 1934): 262.
41 Barnhart, *Weekly Newspaper Writing and Editing*, 198.
42 Wilson, "The Country Press Reawakens," 263. Jasper, in Newton County, Arkansas, had a population of 385 in 1930. *Fifteenth Census of the United States*, "Population," volume 1, section 2, 114, Table 4. http://www.census.gov/.
43 Bruce Crawford, "A Country Editor," *The New Republic*, September 27, 1933, 180. Norton, an independent city in southwestern Virginia, had a population of 3,077 in 1930. *Fifteenth Census of the United States*, "Population," volume 1, section 2, 1,131, Table 4. http://www.census.gov/.
44 "Why Reprint the Poverty Joke?" *The Publishers' Auxiliary*, February 12, 1938, 4.
45 *The Tuscumbia* (AL) *Times*, July 1, 1930, 4.
46 *The Richmond* (OH) *Gazette*, June 14, 1934, 2.
47 James Playsted Wood, *The Story of Advertising* (Garden City, NY: Ronald Press, 1958), 417. Total advertising revenue dropped almost a billion dollars from a peak of $3.42 billion in 1929 to $2.60 billion in 1930. In 2022, according to the latest government figures based on the Consumer Price Index, $3.42 billion from 1929 was worth $58.36 billion and $2.60 billion from 1930 was worth $45.5 billion. http://www.measuringworth.com/.
48 H.C. Hotaling, "Executive Secretary's Annual Address" (paper presented at the 46th Annual Convention of the National Editorial Association, Atlanta, GA, 1931), 29.
49 Wood, *The Story of Advertising*, 413–415. In 2022, according to the latest government figures based on the Consumer Price Index, $40 million from 1929 was worth $682.5 million. http://www.measuringworth.com/.
50 F. Parker Stockbridge, "Radio vs. the Press," *Outlook and Independent* 156:18 (December 31, 1930): 692.
51 Hyde, "United States Journalism in 1931," 423.
52 Henry Beetle Hough, *Country Editor* (New York: Doubleday, Doran & Company, 1940), 264–265, 256–257.
53 W.A. Sumner, "Reading Interests and Buying Habits of the Rural and Village Subscribers of a Daily Newspaper," *Journalism Quarterly* 9:2 (June 1932): 185.

54 William K. Howison and W.A. Sumner, "Revenue Sources of Country Weekly Newspapers," *Bulletin, Department of Agricultural Journalism, College of Agriculture, University of Wisconsin*: 10 (1938): 5, 31.
55 Paul W. Bittinger, "Says Weeklies Must Try New Methods," *Editor & Publisher* 67:25 (November 3, 1934): 9.
56 G.E. Bowers, "It Seems to Us," *Alton* (IA) *Democrat*, August 6, 1937, 1. Alton, a part of Nassau Township in Sioux County, is located in the northwestern part of Iowa. It had a population of 10,000 in 1930. *Fifteenth Census of the United States*, "Population," volume 1, section 5, 388, Table 5. http://newspaperarchive.com/, http://www.census.gov/.
57 "The Way to Whip It," *The Sheffield* (AL) *Standard*, April 4, 1930, 2.
58 *The Hopewell* (NJ) *Herald*, February 17, 1932, 1. Hopewell, in Mercer County, is located along New Jersey's central-eastern border. Hopewell had a population of 1,467 in 1930. *Fifteenth Census of the United States*, "Population," volume 1, section 7, 720, Table 5. http://newspaperarchive.com/, http://www.census.gov/. In 2022, according to the latest government figures based on the Consumer Price Index, 25 cents from 1932 was worth $5.51, 15 cents was worth $3.30, $1 was worth $22, and $2 was worth $44. http://www.measuringworth.com/.
59 McCoy, "Competition and Consolidation," 28–29.
60 Crawford, "A Country Editor," 180.
61 "New Editorial Technique Seen as Need of Weekly Newspapers," *Editor & Publisher* 65:41 (February 23, 1935): 30. Mount Pleasant, in Pennsylvania's Westmoreland County, had a population of 10,918 in 1930. *Fifteenth Census of the United States*, "Population," volume 1, section 7, 957, Table 4. Selinsgrove, in Pennsylvania's Snyder County, had a population of 2,797 in 1930. *Fifteenth Census of the United States*, "Population," volume 1, section 7, 954, Table 4. http://newspaperarchive.com/, http://www.census.gov/.
62 "Rural Titan," *Time*, July 18, 1938, 36. In 2022, according to the latest government figures based on the Consumer Price Index, $2.5 million from 1938 was worth $5 million and $7 million was worth $149 million. http://www.measuringworth.com/.
63 "The Grass Roots Press," *Time*, February 20, 1939, 48.
64 "The Press: Woodyard Weeklies," *Time*, July 9, 1934, 52.
65 Thomas Gerber and Hal L. Curtis, "Home-Town Paper," *The Saturday Evening Post*, May 20, 1939, 14, 39, 42.

References

"Ada Chain Letter Fans Panicky in Attempt to Keep $5 Systems Moving." *The Ada* (OK) *Weekly News*, May 16, 1935, 3–4.
Barnhart, Thomas F. "Newspaper Leadership in Times of Depression." *Journalism Quarterly* 10:1 (March 1933): 1–13.
Barnhart, Thomas F. *Weekly Newspaper Management*. New York: D. Appleton-Century, 1936.
Berchtold, William E. "Press Agents of the New Deal." *The Outlook* 164 (July 26, 1934): 25–27.

Bittinger, Paul W. "Says Weeklies Must Try New Methods." *Editor & Publisher* 67:25 (November 3, 1934): 9, 37.
Bowers, G.E. "It Seems to Us." *The Alton* (IA) *Democrat*, August 6, 1937, 1–2.
Broun, Haywood. "Lessons from Lorain." *The Nation*, July 31, 1935, 132–133.
The Cambridge City (IN) *Tribune*, March 27, 1930, 1.
"A Chain Is as Strong as Its Weakest Link; A City Is as Weak as its Strongest Chain." *The Cambridge City* (IN) *Tribune*, March 27, 1930, 2.
"Chain Letter Business Collapses Here as Late Investors Fail to 'Cash In.'" *The Ada* (OK) *Weekly News*, May 16, 1935, 6.
"Chain Letters Bring Arrests." *The Ada* (OK) *Weekly News*, May 16, 1935, 7.
"Community Sale." *The Journal-Advance and Benton County* (AR) *Gazette*, April 6, 1933, 2.
Crawford, Bruce. "A Country Editor." *The New Republic*, September 27, 1933, 179–181.
"Crossroads Correspondent." *Time*, July 29, 1935, 40–41.
The Deming (NM) *Headlight*, January 16, 1931, 1.
"Disappointed Investors Sue Chain Promoters." *The Ada* (OK) *Weekly News*, May 16, 1935, 2.
"FACTS You Should Consider About the Home-Owned, Home-Controlled Independent Business Men of Tuscumbia-Sheffield." *The Sheffield* (AL) *Standard*, April 11, 1930, 6.
"Farm Experience Asset to 'Part Time' Farmers." *The Richwood* (OH) *Gazette*, June 14, 1934, 6.
Fifteenth Census of the United States. Population. 1930. Edited by United States Bureau of the Census. Washington, DC: Government Printing Office, 1931–1933.
Gerber, Thomas, and Hal L. Curtis. "Home-Town Paper." *The Saturday Evening Post*, May 20, 1939, 14, 39–40, 42.
"The Grass Roots Press." *Time*, February 20, 1939, 48–51.
"Hackworth, Ex-Banker, Given 15 Years." *The Sheffield* (AL) *Standard*, April 4, 1930, 1.
The Hopewell (NJ) *Herald*, February 17, 1932, 1.
Hotaling, H.C. "Executive Secretary's Annual Address." Speech presented at the 46th Annual Convention of the National Editorial Association, Atlanta, GA. 1931.
Hough, Henry Beetle. *Country Editor*. New York: Doubleday, Doran & Company, 1940.
House, Jay E. "The Old Country Weekly." *The Saturday Evening Post*, May 12, 1934, 25, 52, 55–56.
Howison, William K., and W.A. Sumner. "Revenue Sources of Country Weekly Newspapers." *Bulletin, Department of Agricultural Journalism, College of Agriculture, University of Wisconsin*, no. 10 (1938).
Hyde, Grant M. "United States Journalism in 1931." *Journalism Quarterly* 8:4 (December 1931): 419–428.
"In the Driftway." *The Nation*, July 5, 1933, 17.
"Journalism Schools to Improve Training of Students for Weekly and Small Daily Field." *The Publishers' Auxiliary*, January 8, 1938, 5.
"Leaflet Is Aid to Mushroom Pickers." *The Pointer*, Riverdale, IL, July 31, 1936, 2.
Lynd, Robert S., and Helen M. Lynd. *Middletown in Transition*. New York: Harcourt, Brace and Company, 1937.

McCoy, Bruce. "Competition and Consolidation in the Community Weekly Field." *Journalism Quarterly* 7:1 (December 1930): 23–30.

Meredith, C.M., Jr. *The Country Weekly*. Boston: Bruce Humphries, 1937.

"New Editorial Technique Seen as Need of Weekly Newspapers." *Editor & Publisher* 65:41 (February 23, 1935): 30.

N.W. Ayer & Son's Directory of Newspapers and Periodicals. Philadelphia: N.W. Ayer & Sons, 1930.

Olson, Kenneth E. "The Newspaper in Times of Social Changes." *Journalism Quarterly* 12:1 (March 1935): 9–19.

"Only Half of Journalism Grads Hired by Papers." *The American Press* 59:7 (May 1941): 12.

"The Press: Big Boiler-Plate." *Time*, April 27, 1936, 32.

"The Press: Woodyard Weeklies." *Time*, July 9, 1934, 52.

"Real Merchants Here." *The Tuscumbia* (AL) *Times*, July 8, 1930, 4.

The Richwood (OH) *Gazette*, June 14, 1934, 1.

Riley, John Winchell, Jr. "The Country Weekly as a Sociological Source." *American Sociological Review* 3:1 (February 1938): 39–46.

"Rural Titan." *Time*, July 18, 1938, 36.

Safley, James Clifford. *The Country Newspaper and Its Operation*. New York: D. Appleton and Company, 1930.

"The Same Old Story." *The Tuscumbia* (AL) *Times*, March 3, 1931, 4.

Stockbridge, F. Parker. "Radio vs. the Press." *Outlook and Independent* 156 (December 31, 1930): 692–694.

Sumner, W.A. "Reading Interests and Buying Habits of the Rural and Village Subscribers of a Daily Newspaper." *Journalism Quarterly* 9:2 (June 1932): 182–189.

The Tuscumbia Times, July 1, 1930, 4.

"The Way to Whip It." *The Sheffield* (AL) *Standard*, April 4, 1930, 2.

"Who Suffers in Colbert?" *The Sheffield* (AL) *Standard*, February 28, 1930, 4.

"Why Reprint the Poverty Joke?" *The Publishers' Auxiliary*, February 12, 1938, 4.

Wilson, Charles M. "The Country Press Reawakens." *The North American Review* 238 (September 1934): 260–267.

Wood, James Playsted. *The Story of Advertising*. Garden City, NY: Ronald Press, 1958.

www.measuringworth.com.

· 5 ·

THE 1940S: PATRIOTISM, PRODUCTION, PROFESSIONALISM, AND THE POSTWAR PERIOD

After spending the previous decade boosting the morale of their citizens and the retail offerings of local merchants during a lengthy economic depression, community weekly newspapers in the 1940s returned to the task of promoting patriotism when faced with a second world war and the wartime challenges of skilled worker shortages and difficulty in replacing or repairing worn equipment. Postwar challenges included increased production and personnel costs, pushing for recognition as a profession rather than as a trade, and responding to societal shifts in relation to population patterns and worldviews.

The role of a patriot press was not new to community newspapers, many of which had been established for the purpose of promoting or supporting a war effort. Fewer than 30 years prior, weeklies had proven to be valuable propaganda partners of the U.S. government during The Great War—later renamed World War I. Thus, it was not surprising when the federal government called upon them in late 1941 to serve as a propaganda partner after the United States declared war on Japan following the bombing of a U.S. military base in Pearl Harbor, Hawaii.

Another major challenge for weekly publishers in the 1940s was confronting production problems in relation to wartime and the postwar years. As was the case for many manufacturing industries during the war, preferences in terms of supplying raw materials and workers (often female) were given to the production of war-related products, such as weaponry and military supplies. During the war, newspaper operations had to deal with the loss of skilled pressmen, equipment failures, and difficulty in finding replacement parts. After the war, the returning soldiers who were small-town editors and publishers were confronted with equipment in need of repair, higher costs for new equipment and supplies, and prospective employees in search of higher paying union wages.

Weekly publishers yearned for the respect of their metropolitan daily peers and leaders in the political and business communities, specifically as a means to attract national advertising accounts. They engaged in concerted efforts to improve their printed product, to unite politically and advocate certain issues, and to market their product as a valued business partner. They were thus able to enhance their publication's status as a mass medium outlet for national advertisers. As a result, government and corporate publicity seekers, political operatives, and a growing number of national advertisers viewed the weekly newspaper business as a valuable delivery system for their publicity, promotions, and propaganda.

In addition to helping the U.S. government in the international war effort during the 1940s, weeklies also waged a battle on the home front to respond to the changing news interests of readers. The postwar period brought new challenges to the weekly as soldiers who returned home had a wider worldview and an interest in matters beyond their hometown's borders. Thus, editors had to carefully consider the balance between local and non-local news. But while there was an interest in news from afar, the more pressing issues at home included jobs, schools, public health concerns, racism, and housing for returning soldiers and their growing families.

War Propaganda: The Weapon of Printers' Ink

Weeklies of the 1940s reflected their predecessors of the 1910s in that they were heavily utilized by the federal government as a propaganda tool to promote patriotism in all areas of everyday life, from the products that citizens consumed or rationed, to the jobs they held or left behind to go to war. During World War I, weeklies became a vital partner with the federal government in publishing all manner of war-support information supplied through the government-sanctioned Committee on Public Information, better known as the Creel Committee. However, despite the fact that weeklies had a tradition of cooperating with the federal government to promote an international war effort, the preceding decade of difficult economic times turned the perspective of many weeklies inward. They had a stronger focus on local news and political issues and on community boosterism.

As a result, many weeklies during the 1930s decreased their subscriptions to nationally syndicated ready-print and boilerplate material companies and increased their use of government propaganda. By the late 1940s, there were an estimated 250 newspaper syndicates that produced 2,000 non-local features such as columns, editorial cartoons, and comic strips. Most of the country's estimated 10,000 weeklies purchased at least one non-local feature. The main syndicate source for weeklies was the Western Newspaper Union, which served an estimated three of every five of the country's non-dailies. By this time, W.N.U. was based in New York, with 35 branches throughout the country. According to country journalism textbook author Thomas Barnhart, the W.N.U.'s service to small-town newspapers was so complete that the company was referred to as "the Sears and Roebuck of the weekly newspaper field" in recognition of the popular national retailer and catalog-order business. Other syndicates that served weeklies were the National Weekly Newspaper Service, which was owned and managed by W.N.U., the Newspaper Enterprise Association of Cleveland, and King Features Syndicate of New York, the largest producer of syndicate material. Also, some state press associations sent out weekly news releases to members at little or no cost.[1]

A growing number of government agencies provided informational columns and articles on such pocketbook issues as family finance, consumer spending habits, and business and farming practices. So, even though there was an increased amount of government publicity in their publications, weekly editors continued to place a strong emphasis on local matters, as evidenced in the heavy use of community correspondent and locally written columns. Much of the local content concerned the impact of war on the community. Correspondents submitted community reports that told of American Red Cross projects. Soldiers stationed overseas sent columns home with their first-person accounts of battlefronts and foreign travels. Thus, when Japan's 1941 bombing of Pearl Harbor brought forth a declaration of war, weekly publishers had to decide how to balance local news with news from the war front, especially considering that syndicated news wire services made war news in the 1940s more affordable and accessible than during previous international conflicts.

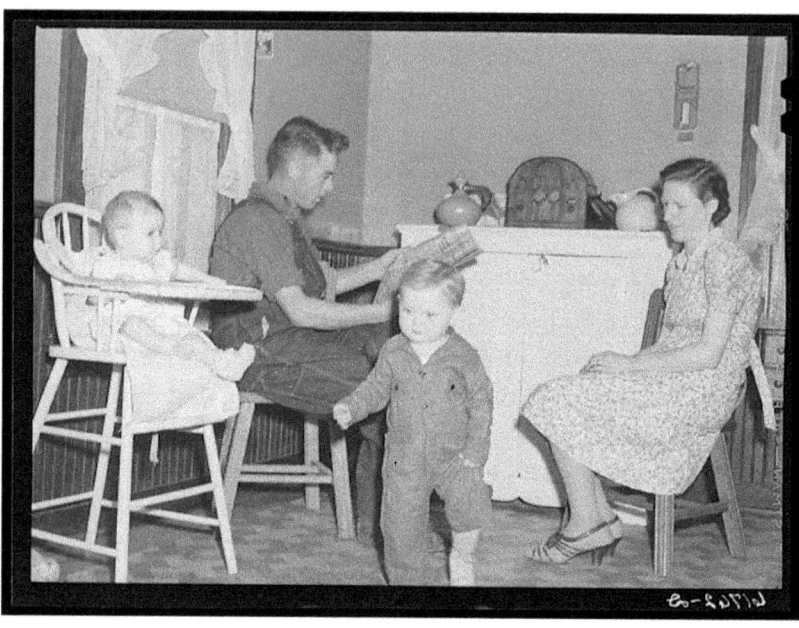

Figure 5.1 Printing words of encouragement and advice on frugality were just some of the ways the country editor tried to boost the morale of area residents during difficult financial times. Owner of 120-acre farm with family. Meeker County, Minnesota. 1940. Contributor John Vachon. Retrieved from the Library of Congress. http://hdl.loc.gov/loc.pnp/fsa.8c18248.

Henry Beetle Hough, editor of *The Vineyard* (MA) *Gazette*, in Edgartown, described the editorial battle of local news versus international news when he recalled hearing a radio report about Germany's 1939 bombing of Warsaw and invasion of Poland as he and his wife were riding in their car. The couple had just completed that week's edition of the paper, but his wife asked him whether or not they should return to the office and incorporate news of the Warsaw bombings in the newspaper. He wrote, "ordinarily the *Gazette* had no concern with outside news," but that given the seriousness of the situation, he decided to return to the office and re-make the front page to include the European war update.[2]

By the 1940s, radio was considered a legitimate alternative news source to newspapers, particularly for national and international news. But weekly publishers continued to print syndicate and wire stories of important national and international events. They did so because community newspaper readers tended to retain their back issues for at least a week's time and could refer to the articles for details and in-depth coverage.

It is no wonder that the government called on weeklies to help the war effort, especially in recruiting, given the military's own data that showed the rural male to be the ideal fighting soldier. Lt. North Callahan—who worked in the Recruiting Publicity Bureau at Governors' Island, New York—described the "Ideal Composite Recruit" in a 1940 article in *The Publishers' Auxiliary*. The description included physical traits such as age, height, weight, and waist measurements. It also included societal traits such as being a native-born citizen from a rural community and a high school attendee with some mechanical, clerical, or occupational training. According to Callahan, an analysis of recruiting methods revealed that advertisements in small-town and rural newspapers were the most productive for enlistment purposes. He encouraged weekly editors to incorporate human interest stories in their recruiting articles, such as the enlistment of twins or five sons from the same family. He concluded, "It is suggested that all editors and reporters keep in closer touch with recruiting officials and thereby serve the double purpose of obtaining good stories for their papers and doing a worthy, public-spirited service for their country."[3]

War Brings Staffing Shortages, Shutdowns or Suspensions, and a Few Startups

As in World War I, many printers, editors, reporters, and publishers of small-town newspapers joined the military during World War II, which led to understaffed publications. In many cases, federal government propagandists served as an "auxiliary staff" for these publications, providing columns and articles from various bureaucratic agencies. Some publishers who joined the military ranks relied on their wives and daughters to keep their newspapers operating. In fact, by 1941 more than 700 women served as editor-publishers of weeklies.[4]

The war also changed the gender makeup of college journalism programs and overall enrollment figures. An editorial in *The New York Times* observed that war had turned the nation's schools and departments of journalism "over to the women for the duration," adding, "Men are as rare today in journalism classrooms as women once were in the city rooms of newspapers." College journalism enrollment decreased 57 percent from 1939—the last year before the war began to affect enrollment—to 1943, according to the American Association of Teachers of Journalism. A.A.T.J. president Douglass W. Miller stressed that finding jobs for its graduates was one of the big problems faced by the average school of journalism before the war. Since the war, however, he said jobs were more plentiful than persons to fill them.[5]

Smaller newspapers, especially those struggling financially, permanently closed their doors after their publishers joined the armed forces, while other newspapers suspended operations and were revived after the war. A January 1942 issue of *The New York Times* ran an Associated Press article about a small-town Massachusetts weekly editor who suspended his paper's publication after signing up to serve in the armed forces. Twenty-seven-year-old Joseph S. Cotton of *The Turners Falls* (MA) *Herald* announced the suspension with the statement: "When you gotta go, you gotta go." He also wrote in his final article, "Opinion of the passing of *The Herald* is divided into two schools of thought—those who are sorry to see it go and those who are glad. The former includes persons about whom praise-worthy articles were written; the latter, persons who didn't like what the newspaper said about them."[6]

But even as the overall number of weekly newspapers decreased during the 1940s, from a high of 10,860 in 1940[7] to a low of 9,672 in 1945,[8] there were the occasional startups that owed much of their success to serving as an important home link for soldiers assigned overseas. Such was the case of *The Rowley* (MA) *News*—established in 1944 by 17-year-old Donald Kent. According to the young publisher, part of his newspaper's early success was that it came out during wartime. Under the tutelage of a neighbor who was a veteran newspaperman, Kent set the newspaper by hand and printed it on a foot-power press donated by his mentor. As success mounted, the operation was able to graduate to a larger press and typesetting machine the following year. Despite being a small publication, Kent said, "It [the newspaper] made a hit with the boys overseas to whom it was sent in an envelope with other mail from home."[9]

Also among the community newspapers that were established during World War II were the internment camp newspapers based in the 10 relocation camps located in the western half of the country that became home to more than 100,000 Japanese-Americans during the war. The camps—established in an effort to curb potential Japanese espionage—were located in Arizona, Arkansas, California, Colorado, Idaho, Utah, and Wyoming. The camp newspapers were established to disseminate government information and were under the direction of the War Relocation Authority.[10]

Hometown Bonds with Soldiers, Selling War Bonds

In keeping with their role as a morale-boosting link between soldiers and their loved ones back home, many weeklies featured news updates on local residents who served in the military and columns written by local soldiers or their family members.[11] The *Dispatch Democrat* in Ukiah, California, placed its standing column, "News of the Service Folks," on the front page.[12] The *McKean County Democrat* in Smethport, Pennsylvania, ran a regular column, "Bugle Calls," that featured letters sent home from service members stationed overseas.[13]

As they had during World War I, weeklies maintained a proud partnership with the U.S. government during World War II in campaigns to: promote war bond sales; collect rubber, scrap metal, cooking fats, and other waste products; encourage rationing and maintenance of equipment and supplies; donate blood; sew garments for soldiers and civilians; grow vegetables; and volunteer for civilian defense programs. Many weeklies printed two-word reminders to "Buy Bonds" that were often positioned just to the right and left of the newspapers' nameplates, the large-print name of a newspaper that usually appears at the top of the front page.

The war bonds campaigns were successful due in large part to the partnership of weeklies with the federal government to promote patriotism through bond purchases. A June 14, 1945 edition of Pennsylvania's *McKean County Democrat* included a front-page article that reported the number of bonds issued in the county for the Seventh War Loan Drive and attributed the drive's success to the appearance of a United States Army exhibit and show.[14] An expression of thanks for the key role that newspapers, particularly small-town newspapers, played in supporting the war effort came in the form of telegraphed messages from President Franklin Roosevelt and British Prime Minister Winston Churchill that were sent to members of the National Editorial Association gathered for the group's annual convention in Quebec in June 1942.[15]

Noted small-town publisher William A. White of the *Emporia* (KS) *Gazette* also praised the role of the press during the war, but from a different perspective. In an August 1942 article in *The Atlantic Monthly*—a condensed version appeared in *The Washington Post*—he observed that "all over the country newspapers, large and small, from the country weekly to the metropolitan daily, are discussing world politics with an intelligence that could not have been imagined 25 years ago when we entered the first World War." T.H. Thomas, a military historian who served on the general headquarters staff in World War I, asserted, however, that the credibility of war news and interpretation suffered from an overly optimistic slant.[16]

Advertisers also joined in the war bonds campaigns, making use of the opportunity to promote patriotism as well as their particular services or products. The same June 14 issue of the *McKean County Democrat* included a nearly full-page advertisement that implored local residents to "Buy Bigger Bonds in the Mighty Seventh [War Loan]." The advertisement listed 20 local business sponsors along with the declaration that "This advertisement is a contribution to America's all-out war effort."[17] A May 27, 1943 edition of the *Kerrville* (TX) *Mountain Sun* featured an advertisement from the local Charles Schreiner Bank that pleaded with patrons, "Don't Just Buy War Bonds ... Keep Them!" Essentially the advertising message explained that cashing in a war bond for much-needed cash was the equivalent of "giving aid to the enemy" and that patrons should instead seek out loans.[18]

Helpful Tips from the O.W.I. and Focusing on Women's Wartime Roles

The Office of War Information served as a type of federal clearinghouse that provided regular columns to weeklies on a wide range of topics, including rationing and conservation. For example, one single column from June 1945 referred to the sale of surplus trucks in farm areas and called for homeowners to buy coal in the summer months. The same column also announced the cancellation of state and regional fairs by the Office of Defense Transportation to reduce inter-city transportation, but noted that local and county fairs were allowed to continue.[19]

But just as the government war propaganda discouraged citizens from doing certain things—such as driving their automobiles—it also encouraged them to follow particular practices or engage in specific activities. For example, a March 6, 1942 article in the *Casa Grande* (AZ) *Dispatch* encouraged citizens to plant a vegetable garden—commonly called a victory garden—reminding them of the importance of good health and eating vegetables. It urged small-town and rural citizens to have a home garden rather than to rely on canned vegetables due to: a strained transportation delivery system; a greater demand for vegetables in army camps, factories, and cities; and reduced tin supplies and commercial canning facilities, many of which were converted to war-supply factories.[20]

Helpful tips for the homemaker on cost and supply savings during wartime were scattered throughout the women's pages of weeklies. The women's page of the *Dispatch Democrat* in Ukiah, California, published a "Ration Calendar" as well as a regular column titled "Mrs. America And The War," both supplied by the O.W.I. The column featured updates on ration books and news from the War Production Board on products that were available or prices that were altered. The April 7, 1944 column announced that a ban on metal scales to weigh babies was lifted so that metal scales could be used for the first time since April 1943. Other announcements included the availability of more leather at shoe repair shops, as ordered by the War Production Board, and reduced prices on lamps and lampshades due to new maximum prices that were set at the wholesale level by the Office of Price Administration. Column readers were also reminded of community pricing on 700 foods and other items. The column referred to the requirement that retailers were to post the community ceiling price on an item against the actual selling price. It was recommended that violations of ceiling prices first be addressed with the local retailer before being reported to the nearest Office of Price Administration bureau.[21]

In addition to a focus on women's wartime homemaking roles, there were also news articles and advertisements that reflected the growing role women had in the active military. The Women's Army Corps was organized in 1943. Other military branches soon followed with similar groups. A local Coca-Cola bottling company in Kerrville, Texas, utilized a quarter-page advertisement in the local weekly to salute women who had joined pre-graduation programs at universities that qualified them for auxiliary services of the armed forces. The May 27, 1943 advertisement pictured a young, athletic-looking woman walking briskly, with accompanying copy that began, "Girls are in training, too ..." A second photograph showed three young women in athletic attire enjoying a "refreshing," "ice-cold" Coca-Cola after exercising.[22] There were also reports about women joining the workforce to replace soldiers at war. A March 6, 1942 front-page article in the *Casa Grande* (AZ) *Dispatch* reported that a naval shipyard in Vallejo, California, would administer examinations in California, Nevada, and Arizona for potential female workers at the large military facility.[23]

Weeklies served as a community bulletin board to report on opportunities for wartime volunteer services. For example, a March 6, 1942 article in the *Casa Grande* (AZ) *Dispatch* referred to the start of "National Sew and Save Week," which was part of an ongoing campaign in which women were asked to make a million home-sewn garments to distribute to "suffering civilians and returning soldiers."[24] The women's page in the May 27, 1943 edition of the *Kerrville* (TX) *Mountain Sun* contained a headline without an accompanying article that stated simply, "Miss Raphel Announces Arrival of Army Yarn for Red Cross Knitting."[25]

War-Support Campaigns Reap Public Relations Benefits

War-support campaigns also gave local businesses a public relations opportunity to applaud the efforts of local volunteers while invoking goodwill among potential customers and clients. For example, the Arizona Edison Company ran a four-column, three-inch advertisement in the March 6, 1942 edition of the *Casa Grande* (AZ) *Dispatch* thanking local women for donating their time and talent to American Red Cross and United States Defense Council "war work—such as sewing and knitting and for attending classes in first aid, home nursing, and canteen work."[26] In that same issue, a Casa Grande, Arizona, Chevrolet car dealership gave a nod to conservation efforts, by encouraging residents to conserve their automobile tires. The advertisement listed 10 ways to conserve tires based on the "Chevrolet Car Conservation Plan."[27]

In addition to reaping public relations benefits from placing war-related messages of support in their local newspapers, businesses could also assist the country in its industrial recovery efforts through advertising, according to a U.S. Office of Censorship official. In a letter to the Association of National Advertisers, John H. Sorrells—assistant director of the Office of Censorship—reminded businesses of the importance of advertising to aid the country's war effort. The letter, issued in March 1942, stated in part, "Advertising, properly conceived, can help speed the industrial effort, as it has in the past been a tremendous factor in promoting the American system of mass production."[28]

As the war was drawing down, the National Editorial Association took steps to ensure its continued governmental support as postwar recovery efforts began. In January 1944, N.E.A. President Albert Hardy announced the association's formulation of a Community Development Committee. The committee was to serve as a clearinghouse through which all publishers could exchange ideas on community expansion, postwar rehabilitation, and employment opportunities.[29]

Although the war ended in September 1945 after President Harry Truman ordered that atomic bombs be dropped on Hiroshima and Nagasaki, Japan, weeklies continued to respond to reader fascination about the military and development of the atom bomb. An August 8, 1946 issue of the *Bedford* (PA) *Gazette* contained a 10-photograph spread titled, "Pictures Show Highlights of Atomic Year One."[30] Weeklies and local business sponsors also continued to promote military enlistment as patriotism was at a high level following the war's end. The *Bedford* (PA) *Gazette* included an August 8, 1946 article that announced higher monthly base and retirement salaries among various Army rankings.[31]

War Years Lead to Increased Use of Press Wire, Photographs

Weeklies remained much the same throughout the 1940s in terms of appearance and production quality due to an inability to employ enough skilled printers to maintain equipment during the war years. The "typical country weekly" of the early 1940s contained eight pages, with seven columns per page.[32] Not much had changed by the end of the decade, when most weeklies maintained a seven- or eight-column format with one-column stacked headlines and occasional illegible copy that resulted from the use of antiquated equipment and typefaces. In fact, a weekly editor advised his peers that it was more important to emphasize legibility and attractiveness in their publications than to be concerned with "aping the big-city daily style, with screaming streamers ...."[33]

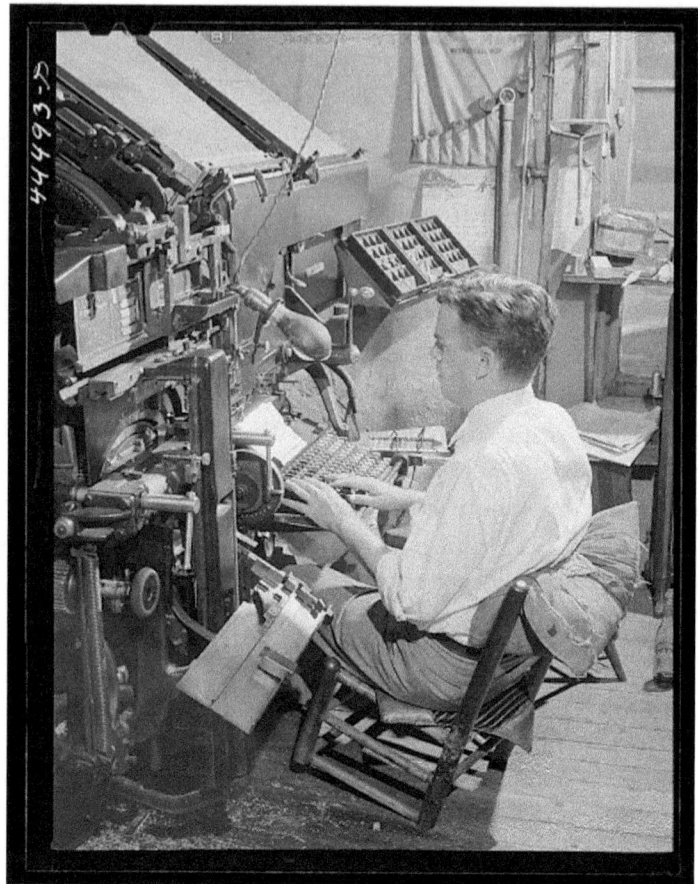

Figure 5.2 Cary Williams, editor of the *Greensboro* (GA) *Herald Journal*. 1941. Contributor Jack Delano. Retrieved from the Library of Congress. http://hdl.loc.gov/loc.pnp/fsa.8c05858.

Aside from antiquated equipment, weeklies also faced a shortage of skilled pressmen available to handle press equipment failures. To compound the problem, replacement parts for printing presses were hard to obtain because facilities that manufactured press parts were converted to produce war-related materials. An article in the August 6, 1949 issue of *The Publishers' Auxiliary* described the situation as "acute and alarming in some areas." The article estimated a loss of 10,000 printers annually due to death, retirement, and change of vocation. New recruits from printing schools and apprenticeships were not sufficient to meet employment demands. Printing schools provided the better preparation for qualified workers rather than individual apprenticeships, according to the article, which referred to the success of G.I. in-service training as an example. The G.I. Bill was officially titled the Servicemen's Readjustment Act of 1944. It provided college or vocational education to returning War World II veterans, commonly known as G.I.s.

To assure the quality of printing schools, the article recommended that instructors return to the print shop at "frequent intervals" in order to acquire experience with new tools, machines, operations, processes and ideas. It was also suggested that the classrooms be equipped with modern machinery.[34] A Veterans' Administration report issued in 1949 showed that 24,072 veterans studied printing and related subjects in shops and schools under the G.I. Bill. The report also revealed that on-the-job trainees outnumbered those enrolled in trade vocational schools by seven to one.[35]

During this decade, a number of large weekly newspapers (usually 16 or more pages) began subscribing to a syndicated wire news service, such as the Associated Press or the United Press, to provide content in place of hiring more reporters. In his 1949 textbook on weekly newspaper writing and editing, University of Minnesota journalism professor and former weekly publisher Thomas Barnhart outlined the specifics of becoming a wire press member. To become an A.P. member, he wrote, the weekly publisher had to negotiate with the nearest bureau manager or A.P. field representative. The publisher and A.P. representative had to agree on a membership fee, a contract indicating type of service, assessments for unusual services, and transmission charges. Barnhart explained that most weekly publishers signed up for a "pony" service, which consisted of a portion of the full service such as telephone reports of 5, 10, or 15 minutes. A pony service provided 500, 1,000, or 1,500 words daily and included the right to clip A.P. dispatches from incoming daily newspapers. Also included were E.O.S. (Extraordinary Service) calls or filings, which were described as fast-breaking A.P. stories to daily newspapers. In addition, as an A.P. member, weeklies were entitled to purchase A.P.-syndicated features. The cost for a typical pony service was $5 a week, plus toll charges, which ranged from $10 to $15 a month. The United Press served weeklies in cities where it did not serve a daily newspaper. The U.P. service consisted of a toll-collect telephone or telegraph file that contained 100 to 200 words in abbreviated form. U.P. costs ranged from $2.50 to $10 a week in addition to telegraphic tolls for unexpected news of importance. U.P. also mailed advance releases of news and features, referred to as "United Press Red Letter" material.[36]

Although photographs were used sparingly in many weeklies because of high costs and production delays, the use of photographs rose sharply among the few weeklies that converted to offset presses. A 1941 article in *The*

American Press about a survey of 16 weeklies that used offset printing—also referred to as lithography—found widespread use of local pictorial news coverage and that an average of 24 percent of the editorial space had been given over to photographs. One publisher surveyed for the study referred to the use of the offset press as a "revolution in printing" in the weekly newspaper business. He observed that through lithography it was possible "to inject life into a traditionally monotonous, almost dead in appearance publication—the small-town community newspaper." The article described offset printing as being in the experimental stage but noted that it was gathering momentum as more printers discovered the advantages of lithography.[37]

Finding qualified press workers also became a financial concern for small-town newspapers as many pressmen joined unions and began demanding the same union wages received by their peers at the metropolitan dailies. In his column "Experience Talks" in a January 8, 1945 issue of *The Publishers' Auxiliary*, Wright A. Patterson reported that some weeklies had to shut their doors because of increasing wage scales. He said the union workers had no choice but to stand by the wage demands dictated by their union, or else they would have lost their union membership. He advised newspaper workers to weigh the benefits of a job in their hometowns as opposed to a few extra dollars in their pockets, noting, "A depression may hit newspapers, and newspaper payrolls, just as it may hit all other lines of industry." He added, "Those papers that have been forced out of existence will not provide jobs at any wage scale."[38]

The high costs of starting a newspaper and the frustrations of working with antiquated, worn-out equipment might have discouraged some returning soldiers from publishing a weekly newspaper, but others overcame the difficult odds and enjoyed long, lucrative careers. Among them was William "Bill" Stewart of *The Monroe Journal* in Monroeville, Alabama. Described by peers as a shrewd businessman and a keen editor, Stewart bought *The Monroe Journal* in 1947 and several other Alabama weeklies during the next few years. It had not been too many years earlier (late 1930s and early 1940s) when he was a journalism student at the University of Alabama. In recognition of his long and respected career in Alabama weekly journalism, Stewart was inducted posthumously into the Alabama Press Association's Newspaper Hall of Honor in 2000. Auburn University journalism professor Ed Williams wrote a nominating letter on behalf of Stewart in which he recalled a conversation he had with Stewart about getting into the weekly newspaper field. As a college journalism student, Stewart took a class taught by the A.P.A.'s first field manager, Doyle Buckles. Stewart told his colleague that Buckles convinced him and many other classmates to enter the weekly newspaper field, adding, "He (Buckles) made it [weekly newspapering] sound so interesting. He persuaded us that the weekly field offered fully as many opportunities for service and livelihood as did the larger daily newspapers."[39]

A Push for Professionalism and Validation

A growing number of weekly publishers promoted formal journalism education and the use of textbooks about the weekly field as a means to promote professionalism. A leader in this push was noted University of Minnesota journalism professor and former weekly editor Thomas F. Barnhart, who, by 1949, had published a trilogy of books on weekly newspapering. His first book, *Weekly Newspaper Management*, was published in 1939, followed in 1949 by *Weekly Newspaper Writing and Editing* and *Weekly Newspaper Makeup and Topography*. In *Weekly Newspaper Writing and Editing*, Barnhart explained that the small-town newspaper provided its community with "a localized expression of our country's purpose." He wrote that the weekly served as its community's spokesman, "the voice of its spirit, ideals, activities, and achievements." Barnhart began his journalism career in 1920 at the *Snohomish* (WA) *County Tribune* and then served as an assistant to the Washington Press Association field manager while a journalism student at the University of Washington, where he edited the student newspaper. He accepted a faculty position at the University of Minnesota in 1931.[40]

A main reason for writing his series of textbooks, according to Barnhart, was that journalism students who entered the weekly field were perplexed by what defined news at a weekly newspaper, "as compared to what they've learned in a reporting textbook." He said most of the textbooks were framed in terms of writing news for metropolitan dailies. For example, he said that a typical journalism textbook defined news as a fact or idea that would interest a large number of readers. His definition was "anything timely that is selected by the news staff because it is of interest and significance to their readers or because it can be made so."[41] Editions of *The Publishers' Auxiliary* also helped students to understand small-town journalism. Robert L. Warren, of *The Wayne* (MI) *Dispatch*, wrote to *The Publishers' Auxiliary* and recalled that during his undergraduate days the "Ox," as it was affectionately known by the students, served as a supplementary text in his community newspaper class.[42]

To improve their business practices, many weekly publishers sought out textbooks and guides, but others also wanted to learn how to better understand and serve their audiences, so they called upon academics to conduct various studies, such as readership satisfaction surveys. The Rutgers University Department of Journalism conducted a 1940 readership survey for the *Hunterdon County Democrat* in Flemington, New Jersey. After examining a 16-page issue of the newspaper, 100 readers from Flemington and outlying areas marked the articles and advertisements they had read and then responded to questions about their reading selections. The survey found that among advertisements, illustrated motion picture announcements had the highest readership rating at 80 percent. The survey also revealed that two of the most popular features were obituaries and wedding notices. Some of the editorials were read by 95 percent of the male reviewers and 85 percent of the female reviewers. Classified advertisements were more popular with male readers, with 85 percent having read that section as compared to 70 percent among females. Most importantly, the survey found that 80 percent of the participants said that their local newspaper helped them to become informed about prices and values and where to purchase needed merchandise.[43]

Social and political scientists in the 1940s explored the importance of the community newspaper as a social instrument, advancing the 1920s work of sociologist Malcolm Willey. Iowa State College journalism professor Charles E. Rogers—who started in journalism at a rural newspaper—asserted that one of the most important roles of the weekly was serving as a socializing agent because it went about its business "unsensationally, narrating the story of town and trade area with the minimum of irritation to its readers." The weekly newspaper held special significance, he explained, "because the editor himself gets credit or blame for every expression, every shading of emphasis, and every omission." In other words, he observed, news had the same force as comment.[44]

In terms of earning professional respect, weekly publishers began to recognize the importance of joining various organizations as a sign of accountability both for potential advertisers and readers. At the start of the decade, weekly publishers were advised that their newspapers would attract more national advertisers if they complied with requirements to join the Audit Bureau of Circulations. For years, national advertisers had accused weekly publishers of fraudulently boosting their circulation numbers because they refused to adhere to the generally respected circulation reporting requirements of the Bureau, to which most daily newspapers subscribed. D. Howard Moreau—publisher of the *Hunterdon County* (NJ) *Democrat*—spoke at the Bureau's 1940 annual convention and emphasized that when competition threatened to cut advertising accounts for his weekly newspaper, he was well armed to meet the threat. As a Bureau member, he claimed, national advertisers were more prone to do business with his newspaper and other circulation-certified publications. He encouraged national advertisers to do business with Bureau-member weeklies, stating, "National advertisers can well afford to encourage weekly newspapers to join A.B.C. by favoring those that are pioneering in A.B.C. membership ... The small-town newspaper that is progressive enough to comply with A.B.C. requirements will be just as quick to render service to a national advertiser and its agency."[45]

Seeking More National Advertising, Stronger Editorializing, and Power Positioning

Weekly publishers were also advised to join forces through their national professional associations to attract more national advertising. At the start of the decade, two organizations handled advertising for hometown weeklies—the American Press Association and Western Newspaper Union. In 1943, the National Editorial Association launched the Newspaper Advertising Service, Inc., which similarly offered a unified sales and service program to national advertisers and advertising agencies. The N.A.S. eventually split from the N.E.A. and became the Weekly Newspaper Representatives.

Writing in *The American Press* in 1940, *The Stafford* (CT) *Press* publisher Robert Warner stressed that individual efforts to reach out to national advertising managers, agency space buyers, and agency account executives were usually ineffective. He also discouraged state press associations from contracting with a salesperson to represent their member newspapers in soliciting national advertising. "The only chance of national volume in the weekly field," he concluded, "is patient waiting for a change in the national advertising mind, plus patient plugging by our accredited representative, The American Press Association."[46] An experimental readership analysis of the April 11, 1946 issue of the *Hancock County Journal* in Carthage, Illinois—which was selected as a representative weekly paper—indicated that more people read weeklies than was generally assumed by newspaper advertising representatives. A.W. Lehman—managing director of the Advertising Research Foundation—told attendees at the 1946 annual convention of the Weekly Newspaper Bureau of the National Editorial Association in Estes Park, Colorado, that readers of weeklies read more pages of individual issues than previously thought. For example, the average readership per page was 89 percent for men and 93 percent for women. In addition, Lehman noted that the study was able to accurately determine the cost per reader for advertisements in a weekly newspaper.[47]

Many leaders in the weekly profession believed that some of their peers were too accommodating of publicity seekers who sought free publicity as opposed to paying for advertising space. Retiring National Editorial Association President Ray Brown spoke to members gathered at the association's 1941 convention during which he described the mass of free publicity sent to newspapers as "sabotage of news columns." He said that "this vicious circle will continue until some constructive method is arrived at whereby enormous funds that are now going into publicity can be diverted into the place they belong—advertising columns." He outlined the N.E.A. public relations program to promote the value of hometown advertising to national manufacturers and to persuade advertising agencies that hometown newspapers offered an equal economic value with metropolitan papers.[48]

There was much frustration on the part of weekly professional organizations in their attempts to "educate" weekly editors on the importance of not running publicity items due to laziness (not taking the initiative to gather more local news) or tightfistedness (refusing to hire additional staff to gather and write local news). Among the weekly organizations and publications that joined the fight against free publicity was *The American Press* magazine—which estimated that weeklies "gave away" $250,000 a week, or $13 million a year, in free publicity.[49] Its finding was based on an analysis of free publicity "of a national nature" that ran during one week in several hundred weekly newspapers nationwide. The advertising cost equivalency was figured at 32 cents an inch.[50]

Despite the negative connotation generally given to free publicity, weekly publishers were mostly critical of publicity seekers for commercial interests since their publications were much more welcoming of so-called propaganda pieces from various federal government agencies. A 1947 article in *The Public Opinion Quarterly* reported that 2,500 press releases were issued in an average year and that no newspaperman could possibly be a specialist so as "to interpret intelligently the work of specific scientists or administrators." The article's author surmised, therefore, that government information workers were valuable "time-savers" for scientists, administrators, and journalists.[51] A chapter on publicity in Thomas Barnhart's 1949 textbook on weekly newspaper writing and editing also emphasized the importance of government information workers. He referred to several federal departments, such as treasury, justice, interior, agriculture, commerce, and labor, which provided a steady flow of news and information to weeklies. Also helpful to small-town newspapers, according to the author, were the federal departments that dealt with federal loans, securities, public works, communications, labor relations, tax appeals, and employee compensation.[52] While public utilities were often viewed as potential advertisers, most weekly editors considered themselves to be providing a public service in the printing of free publicity from government agencies.

With their attention to preserving and gaining advertising accounts, weekly editors were harshly criticized, particularly by their metropolitan daily counterparts, for appearing to abandon strong editorial comment in order to avoid local controversy that could lead to loss of advertising revenue. A chapter on editorial writing in Barnhart's 1949 textbook acknowledged that a growing trend was that of replacing the editorial with a personal column.[53] However, Charles T. Duncan, an associate professor of journalism at the University of Minnesota, surveyed Minnesota's community newspapers and found that more than 77 percent of them regularly ran conventional-type editorials, editorial columns, or both. He pointed out that he conducted the survey in response to a widespread belief that editorials in the weekly press were "on the way out." He admitted that while there was greater reader interest in personal columns than in the standard editorial, the study found that if Minnesota weeklies could be regarded as being indicative of a general trend, then "the editorial function still flourishes" in community weeklies.[54]

The Publishers' Auxiliary conducted a 1949 survey of members of the 81st Congress that emphasized the potential influential power weekly newspaper editorials had among the country's leaders. The survey revealed that 276 legislators resided in 269 small towns of which 129 had dailies and/or weeklies and 110 had weeklies only. Writing on the congressional membership survey, Edward Farrell observed, "Inspection of this analysis shows the great potential influence of the non-metropolitan newspaper in national affairs. Newspapers speaking on behalf of their readers through editorial columns can carry extremely effective messages to congressmen—right from the home."[55]

In January 1949, *The Publishers' Auxiliary*, or "The Aux" as it was commonly referred to, moved its editorial, classified advertising, and printing facilities from Chicago to Frankfort, Kentucky. In an announcement about the move, it was stated, "We are much closer to the type of community to which we all are dedicated. In other words, perhaps we are trading something of an ivory tower in the city to a working re-acquaintance with the grassroots. We think that is proper." Wright A. Patterson and Elmo Scott Watson were listed as contributing editors, and George H. Bechtel was listed as editor.[56]

In an effort to promote the political voice of community weeklies, the University of Missouri began publishing the *Grass Roots Digest* in 1949—which was described as the "official publication of The Grass Roots Editors of America." The monthly digest contained a review of editorials from non-metropolitan newspapers across the country and was established "to recognize good editorial writing on timely subjects, to supply newspapers with good reprint editorials, and to furnish editors material that would help them write their own editorials."[57]

In an effort to seek the respect of politicians, peers at metropolitan dailies, and pundits—who had too quickly dismissed the weekly field as unsophisticated, unprofessional, and unimportant—community publishers referred to a 1940 national survey of weeklies conducted by Malcolm Forbes of the famous publishing family. The survey found weeklies to be the prime printed medium for more than half of the nation's population. The survey also indicated that a reported total circulation of 21 million among weeklies did not reflect their full readership. Among other survey findings was that the rural counties that the weeklies served controlled the nation's political majorities and contained 48 percent of all retail stores—with sales that totaled $14 billion, or 31 percent of the national total.

Malcolm Forbes, son of publisher B.C. Forbes, conducted the survey for a senior thesis project at Princeton University. He interviewed 75 weekly newspaper editors in 20 states and also interviewed 250 residents of Englewood, N.J., a suburb of New York City, concerning the *Englewood Press*. Of the 250 Englewood residents interviewed, 200 were subscribers to the *Englewood Press*. He also interviewed 50 Englewood merchants, heads of schools of journalism, and press association officers. After graduation from Princeton, he bought a leading Ohio weekly, *The Fairfield Times* of Lancaster, with a circulation of 6,500.[58]

In similar findings to the Forbes study, the Department of Commerce's Office of Small Business examined weeklies and found them to be in a stronger position than ever before through a "survival of the fittest" factor. The commerce department study, published in 1949, found that even though the number of weeklies had steadily decreased, overall circulation had increased to 165,000 from the two previous years. The study also stressed that the weekly field would continue to face increasing production costs and rising capital requirements. To assist prospective publishers, the Office of Small Business prepared a booklet, "Establishing and Operating a Weekly Newspaper," that was available for purchase (for 15 cents) through the superintendent of documents.[59]

Readers of Weeklies: Postwar Changes in News Preferences

The postwar period brought new challenges to the weekly, as it had to serve a changing reading audience of more women who worked outside of the home or became more concerned about non-local affairs, and soldiers who returned home after journeying far from the family farm or family-owned business. Even readers of weeklies who were not deployed developed a keen interest in news from beyond their town and surrounding communities. For example, as "war brides" began to populate many smaller towns, weeklies began to feature more news from their native countries.[60] Although many women who were employed during the war returned to full-time domesticity after their soldier husbands came home, others continued to work, often because their husbands entered college on the G.I. Bill. While female weekly newspaper readers retained a high level of interest in softer news, such as society columns and personal items, they were more likely than men to read the front page as well as the entire publication. In fact, the authors of a weekly newspaper readership survey asserted that the content of the weekly was designed to appeal to women because of their higher readership levels—particularly in the categories of local news and display advertising.[61] A 1948 feature on the modern farm wife in the *New York Times Sunday Magazine* observed that while "politicking" was still considered a novelty among farm women, for an increasing number it [politics] no longer stopped at the county line. "The war dead are coming home now—reminders of a disaster which mothers and wives, above all, hope can be averted again," it stated. "The war has made their world larger for having made their families smaller."[62]

In addition to a transition away from traditional gender roles, other domestic topics of importance included demands for improved education and health care—with particular attention paid to polio outbreaks. Challenges of surviving a postwar economic recession also became the topic of headlines.

In addition, weekly editors recognized the importance of addressing larger cultural issues, such as racism, and the growing international conflict that became known as the Cold War. So, just as domestic and international concerns changed in society, so did the news preferences of readers of weeklies. Thus, despite a long-held allegiance to local and "pocketbook" issues, weeklies began to include more news about cultural shifts and international relations.

More Leisure Time: TV Joins Print and Radio to Promote Time-Saving Products and Services

By the end of the decade, new products and technologies that had been placed on hold during the war were introduced to the average consumer who wanted to furnish a new home with an eye on convenience and more family and leisure time. In fact, at the end of the 1940s, farming families began to refer to "five o'clock" farming—meaning that with the exception of planting and harvesting seasons, farmers worked seven-hour days, leaving evening hours open for church and social gatherings, television viewing, or outdoor hobbies.[63]

Thus, "modern-day" conveniences such as washers and dryers allowed families to enjoy more leisure time, including watching television with its commercials for time-saving products. Referring to the country's obsession with convenience appliances, a syndicated columnist wrote in a September 29, 1949 edition of the Placerville, California, *Mountain-Democrat* about going into a department store where he saw one of the female workers coming up the stairs with a bundle of clean wash. He asked her if the owner was taking in laundry. She responded that the owner had put in a new automatic washing machine and was allowing store employees to do their laundry during their lunch break so they would have more time to relax at night and on weekends. The syndicated column, "From Where I Sit," written by Joe Marsh, was distributed by the United States Brewers Foundation.[64]

Although many were pleased with having television as a new entertainment option, some disliked the fact that the advertising industry had seemingly taken over television programming as a means to promote a wide range of new convenience and leisure-time products and services. A syndicated column, "The Once Over" by H.I. Phillips, commented on the difference in radio and television advertising and observed that it was easier to tune out one's ears than one's eyes. The July 1948 column quoted reader Elmer Twitchell, who remarked, "I object to my home being made a showroom for the assorted products of American industry. Why should my den be converted into a commercial exposition hall and my parlor made a sales manager's delight?" By the end of 1948 there were four television networks—NBC, ABC, CBS, and Dumont Television. The number of television sets in U.S. homes increased from 9,000 to 125,000.[65]

To promote new time-saving products and services, national advertisers and utility companies partnered with local businesses that sold their wares and services, and provided weeklies a steady stream of advertising revenue for a growing consumer-oriented society. For example, a June 14, 1945 advertisement in the *McKean County* (PA) *Democrat* from Bell Telephone Company of Pennsylvania asked potential customers, "Is a Telephone in your Post-War Plans?" The advertisement pointed out that, after the war, materials and manpower could again be used for civilian needs—such as the expansion of rural and city phone service. The advertisement concluded, "Until final Victory, expansion must wait, of course."[66] The Standard Oil Company of California ran a September 29, 1949 advertisement in the Placerville *Mountain-Democrat* that boasted about its company-developed "soapless" soaps, or detergents. The advertisement claimed that the detergents made water "wetter" to "attract dirt and grease like a magnet," resulting in dishes that sparkled when cleaned.[67] That same issue contained an advertisement for the Hotpoint brand automatic/electric dishwasher. The dishwasher advertisement featured illustrations of one woman toiling at a kitchen sink washing dishes, while another woman, dressed in a fashionable swimsuit, waited on her daughter to place the last dish in the dishwasher before they headed to a swimming pool. The headline read, "Decide Now ... Sink or Swim?"[68] The Pennsylvania Electric Company endorsed electric ranges in an August 8, 1946 *Bedford* (PA) *Gazette* advertisement that referred to the appliance as "the pride and joy of a housewife."[69]

What impact did implied pressures of domesticity through advertising messages and women's pages articles have on the typical female reader of weekly newspapers? A 1948 *New York Times Sunday Magazine* feature on farm wives by David Dempsey observed that farm women found themselves spending more time away from cooking and housekeeping chores and instead, spending money to replace coal stoves, outdoor plumbing, and hand pumps. They also developed a sense of fashion and spent time and money in nearby cities purchasing stylish clothing for "hat and glove" affairs—sometimes for a fashion consultant fee of $10. The Department of Agriculture reported that the average farm family income tripled in 1947 from the time of the Pearl

Harbor attack. One husband from Pekin, Illinois, stated in *The New York Times* article that "since the end of the war, my wife has bought everything the women in town brag about, including an expensive operation."[70]

Newspaper, Printing House, and Library

Along with better-equipped homes, there was a push for better-equipped schools and libraries, as many returning soldiers joined their children to become full-time students. In addition to writing editorials that endorsed the construction and support of public schools and libraries, some weekly editors went a step further—sponsoring book drives or even allowing their businesses to take on the multiple role of newspaper, printing house, and library. In 1946, when *The Wheaton* (MN) *Gazette* editor William B. Sweetland moved to Wheaton, he discovered that the town's only library existed at the local school. The school library's reading material was geared exclusively to young people. So, Sweetland started a library at the newspaper office with a $25 investment, and a few feet of wall space.[71] *The Wheaton Gazette* staff operated the library and wrote updates on new library books and reviews of "must reads" that appeared in regular columns in the newspaper's women's pages.[72]

Time-saving appliances gave rural women more time for leisure reading. In his 1948 profile on farm wives, author David Dempsey interviewed Mrs. Victor Schwarzentraub (no first name given) who lived on a 280-acre farm near Washington, Illinois. She admitted that she "gads about" more than she used to, attending meetings of the Women's Club, the American Legion Auxiliary, a church "Good Neighbor" society, a women's fraternal order, and the county Home Bureau. In addition to sewing her own dress for her son's wedding, she tended a large garden that produced 200 quarts of canned and frozen food. She and her husband subscribed to 10 magazines—half of which were farm journals and the rest were of general interest—including *The Readers' Digest, Life,* and *The Saturday Evening Post.* During the previous year, she completed two Home Bureau reading courses of nine books each. She observed that in the past, women read on the sly because "a woman wasn't supposed to have time to read and keep her house clean."[73]

Fighting Polio, Racism, Communism, and a Recession

In addition to quality education, good health care was an important quality-of-life issue to the growing number of young families with preschool and school-age children. However, quality of life became a more serious concern when several large epidemics of poliomyelitis occurred in the United States immediately following the war's end.[74] A November 1948 article in *The Washington Post* reported that the number of infantile paralysis cases was expected to exceed 27,000 that year, just shy of the 26,000 cases reported in 1946. The article also reported that the record year for polio in the United States was 1916, with 30,000 cases reported.[75]

So, after fighting a second world war abroad, Americans found themselves fighting a battle against infantile paralysis on their home shores.

In the mid-1940s, newspaper reports on polio cases started appearing with more frequency and increased to multiple articles within single weekly editions in the latter part of the decade. For example, a June 14, 1945 issue of the *McKean County Democrat* in Smethport, Pennsylvania, contained a brief article about a third case of infantile paralysis having been reported that year in Buffalo, New York.[76] However, a single page of a July 15, 1948 edition of *The Mexia* (TX) *Weekly Herald* contained an advertisement for a family polio insurance policy as well as three United Press wire stories about polio outbreaks, and another article about a statewide campaign to fight polio.[77] One of the articles referred to an increase in reported polio cases in North Carolina.[78] The second article focused on a study presented to the First International Poliomyelitis Conference in New York that revealed an increase in polio among teenagers and young adults.[79] The third article reported on the number of polio cases reported for the week (89) and year to date (736) in the state of Texas.[80] A fourth polio-related article on the same page reported on the Texas governor's announcement of a statewide "Clean-up and Fight Polio Week."[81] The following page contained a United Press article that addressed concerns about polio being linked to the use of public swimming pools.[82] In Placerville, California, a band concert to aid a local Emergency Polio Fund was mentioned in a page-one article of a September 29, 1949 issue of the *Mountain-Democrat*.[83]

Weekly newspaper coverage during the postwar period also began to turn an eye to domestic concerns related to racism, particularly in the South. Hodding Carter—editor of the weekly *Delta Democrat-Times* in Greenville,

Mississippi—brought much attention to the issue when he received a Pulitzer Prize in 1946 for his work against racism.[84] Some weekly editors in other parts of the country acknowledged that racism was not unique to the South and joined in the fight as well. For example, an August 8, 1946 editorial in the *Bedford* (PA) *Gazette* applauded members of the First Methodist Church of Monroe, Georgia, for adopting a resolution that condemned the lynching of two local black couples. The editorial referred to the sensitivity of Southerners that too much finger-pointing was turned their way and emphasized that racial violence occurred in the North as well. The editorial stated, "They [southerners] will not be helped by silence. ... They need assurance that they do not work alone or unnoticed...."[85] Despite an occasional reference to racial strife in the South, most general-news community weeklies throughout the country represented the majority white population. News from the black community was occasionally referenced with the word "Negro" appearing in the headline or standing headline. For example, the July 15, 1948 issue of *The Mexia* (TX) *Weekly Herald* contained a two-paragraph article at the bottom of the front page announcing "Negro Methodists Hold District Meet in Mexia July 12–16."[86] As Charles Rogers observed in a 1942 article on the American country weekly, "Its society column almost never shows favoritism on class and racial lines, except of course toward the 'blacks' and 'browns' and the people born on the wrong side of the track, though they do have their birth and death notices announced."[87]

While there was fear of change and misunderstanding among races within the country, there was also a growing fear and resentment of communists. In fact, the fear and resentment of communists grew to the point that the United States became engaged in what was popularly referred to as the Cold War against an expanding Soviet Union and other communist countries. Weekly editors—generally perceived as more patriotic and conservative than most journalists—took it upon themselves to educate their readers about the ills of communism. For example, a July 15, 1948 editorial in *The Mexia* (TX) *Weekly Herald* referred to a religious society communism experiment in Amana, Iowa, beginning in the late 1850s. The experiment failed—according to the editorial writer—because individuals rebelled against sharing equally with those who did not contribute as much to the general welfare of the society. The editorialist quoted a younger member of the Amana Society who said, "What Communists never seem to realize is that man isn't a bee."[88]

By the end of the decade there were signs that the economy was slowing down, so a July 1949 editorial in *The Publishers' Auxiliary* encouraged weekly publishers to join another fight—to "mount a defense against the up-swing [sic] of recession psychology." The editorial warned, "The greatest danger in this perfectly normal trend is that the people will develop a depression psychology." Editors and reporters were reminded of their role to objectively present both gains and losses in business. The editorial continued, "It will be remembered that the people make prosperity—and they make depressions. They do both with the editor's help."[89]

The 1940s ended as they had begun, with an economic recession. However, the later recession was not as severe as the earlier one that required a world war to bring the country out of the depths of a depression. But as the weeklies published familiar stories of how to spend wisely and support local businesses, they also focused on new concerns from home and abroad that threatened their readers' lives and security. The 1948 profile of 1940s Midwest farm wives recounted Mrs. Victor Schwarzentraub's story of attending the 1948 Illinois meeting of the Home Bureau at which there was talk about the Marshall Plan—also known as the European Recovery Program—which was a United States plan to rebuild Western Europe after World War II. Weeklies responded to growing readers' interests as headlines about domestic wars on polio and racism and a Cold War on communist nations were regularly interspersed among articles about a Kiwanis Club pancake supper, the travel itinerary of a local couple, and the results of the pickle-eating contest at the county fair. But because of rural and small-town residents' increased sophistication and concern about issues beyond their county's borders, it was not uncommon to find the topic of discussion at a Kiwanis picnic, a Women's Club meeting, or a church supper, to be the growing communist threat, hunger in Europe, or the pros and cons of the Marshall Plan.[90]

Notes

1 Thomas Barnhart, *Weekly Newspaper Writing and Editing* (New York: The Dryden Press, 1949), 202–206.
2 Henry Beetle Hough, *Country Editor* (New York: Doubleday, Doran & Company, 1940), 1–2. Edgartown is in Dukes County in Massachusetts, which had a population of 1,370 in 1940. *Sixteenth Census of the United States*, "Population," volume 1, section 5, 481, Table 4. http://newspaperarchive.com/, http://www.gov/.
3 Lt. North Callahan, "Army Seeks Help of Editors in Rural Recruiting Work," *The American Press* 59:2 (December 1940): 6.
4 "Women Publish 704 Weekly Newspapers in the United States," *The National Publisher* (July 1941): 10.

5 "War Changes Schools of Journalism," *The New York Times*, December 19, 1943, E9.
6 "Publisher Stops Paper to Join Armed Forces," *The New York Times*, January 17, 1942, 12. Turner Falls, was an unincorporated village in Montague in Franklin County, Massachusetts. Montague had a population of 7,582 in 1940. *Sixteenth Census of the United States*, "Population," volume 1, section 5, 481, Table 4. http://newspaperarchive.com/, http://www.gov/.
7 *N.W. Ayer & Son's Directory of Newspapers and Periodicals* (Philadelphia: N.W. Ayer & Sons, 1940).
8 *N.W. Ayer & Son's Directory of Newspapers and Periodicals* (Philadelphia: N.W. Ayer & Sons, 1945).
9 "Kent, at 17, Is a Veteran," *The Publishers' Auxiliary*, July 30, 1949, 4. Rowley, in Essex County, Massachusetts, had a population of 1,533 in 1940. *Sixteenth Census of the United States*, "Population," volume 1, section 5, 481, Table 4. http://newspaperarchive.com/, http://www.gov/.
10 Merriman Smith, "Roosevelt Sets up Works Corps for Aliens from Coast Areas," *The Washington Post*, March 22, 1942, B6. Rennie Taylor, "Resettlement of Japanese Involves Unusual Problems," *The Washington Post*, May 4, 1942, 11. Catherine A. Luther, "Reflections of Cultural Identities in Conflict: Japanese American Internment Camp Newspapers during World War II," *Journalism History* 29:2 (Summer 2003): 70, 73.
11 Sgt. Robert L. Spencer, "Sgt. Robert L. Spencer Writes of Experiences with Overseas Army," *Kerrville* (TX) *Mountain Sun*, May 27, 1943, 9. Kerrville, in Kerr County, is located north of San Antonio in southeast Texas. Kerrville had a population of 5,572 in 1940. *Sixteenth Census of the United States*, "Population," volume 1, section 9, 1,058, Table 5. http://newspaperarchive.com/, http://www.gov/.
12 "News of the Service Folks," *Dispatch Democrat*, April 7, 1944, 1. Ukiah, in Mendocino County, is located in the northwestern part of California. Ukiah had a population of 3,731 in 1940. *Sixteenth Census of the United States*, "Population," volume 1, section 3, 128, Table 5. http://newspaperarchive.com/, http://www.census.gov/.
13 "Bugle Calls," *McKean County* (PA) *Democrat*, June 14, 1945, 3. Smethport, in McKean County, is located in the northwestern part of Pennsylvania near the New York state line. Smethport had a population of 1,840 in 1940. *Sixteenth Census of the United States*, "Population," volume 1, section 8, 927, Table 5. http://newspaperarchive.com/, http://www.census.gov/.
14 "County 'E' Bond Sales Reach $649,000; 43 Percent of McKean's Quota Is Sold," *McKean County* (PA) *Democrat*, June 14, 1945, 1. http://newspaperarchive.com/. In 2022, according to the latest government figures based on the Consumer Price Index, $649,000 from 1945 was worth $10.5 million. http://www.measuringworth.com/.
15 "Roosevelt and Churchill Praise Editors," *The Washington Post*, June 24, 1942, 19.
16 William A. White, "Editor Praises Press Coverage of War: But Noted Military Expert Thinks News Slant of American Papers Is 'Too Rosy,'" *The Washington Post*, July 26, 1942, SP8.
17 "He Can't Ask You Now!" *McKean County* (PA) *Democrat*, June 14, 1945, 6. http://newspaperarchive.com/.

18 "Don't Just Buy War Bonds... Keep Them!" *Kerrville* (TX) *Mountain Sun*, May 27, 1943, 10. http://newspaperarchive.com/.
19 Office of War Information, "Town and Farm in Wartime," *McKean County* (PA) *Democrat*, June 14, 1945, 6. http://newspaperarchive.com/.
20 "Home Garden Vital due to Lack of Tin," *Casa Grande* (AZ) *Dispatch*, March 6, 1942, 2. Casa Grande, in Pinal County, is located in the southern-central part of Arizona. Casa Grande had a population of 1,545 in 1940. Sixteenth Census of the United States, "Population," volume 1, section 3, 91, Table 5. http://newspaperarchive.com/, http://www.census.gov/.
21 "Mrs. America and the War," *Dispatch Democrat*, Ukiah, CA, April 7, 1944, 4. http://newspaperarchive.com/.
22 "That Extra Something!... You Can Spot It Every Time," *Kerrville* (TX) *Mountain Sun*, May 27, 1943, 7. http://newspaperarchive.com/.
23 "Arizona Women Will Be Given Chance to Work in Shipyards," *Casa Grande* (AZ) *Dispatch*, March 6, 1942, 3. http://newspaperarchive.com/.
24 "Million Garments for War Sufferers Goal Set in U.S.," *Casa Grande* (AZ) *Dispatch*, March 6, 1942, 2. http://newspaperarchive.com/.
25 "Miss Raphel Announces Arrival of Army Yarn for Red Cross Knitting," *Kerrville* (TX) *Mountain Sun*, May 27, 1943, 10. http://newspaperarchive.com/.
26 "The Army of Patriotic Women," *Casa Grande* (AZ) *Dispatch*, March 6, 1942, 3. http://newspaperarchive.com/.
27 "Goff Lists 10 Ways to Conserve Tires During War Period," *Casa Grande* (AZ) *Dispatch*, March 6, 1942, 2. http://newspaperarchive.com/.
28 "Advertising Is Aid to War Effort, OC Director Declares," *Casa Grande* (AZ) *Dispatch*, March 6, 1942, 7. http://newspaperarchive.com/.
29 "Publishers to Aid in Community Work," *Christian Science Monitor*, January 7, 1944, 12.
30 "Pictures Show Highlights of Atomic Year One," *Bedford* (PA) *Gazette*, August 8, 1946, sec. 2, 4. Bedford, in Bedford County, is located in the southwestern part of Pennsylvania. Bedford had a population of 3,268 in 1940. Sixteenth Census of the United States, "Population," volume 1, section 8, 923, Table 5. http://newspaperarchive.com/, http://www.census.gov/.
31 "New Higher Pay for the Army!" *Bedford* (PA) *Gazette*, August 8, 1946, sec. 2, 4. http://newspaperarchive.com/.
32 Malcolm Forbes, "Is Your Newspaper a 'Typical Country Weekly'?" *The American Press* 59:12 (October 1941): 8.
33 Raymond Wild, "Urges Modernization of Out-Dated Weeklies," *The American Press* 59:1 (November 1940): 17.
34 Leroy Brewington, "Shortage of Skilled Printers Requires Plans for Training," *The Publishers' Auxiliary*, August 6, 1949, 8.
35 "More Colleges Call on Active Journalists as Teachers; 24,072 Students Taking On-the-Job Printing Training," *The Publishers' Auxiliary*, September 24, 1949, 8.
36 Barnhart, *Weekly Newspaper Writing and Editing*, 206. In 2022, according to the latest government figures based on the Consumer Price Index, $2.50, $5, $10 and $15 from 1949 was worth, $15 was worth $31, $63, $126, and $189. http://measuringworth.com/.

37 William B. Marsh, "Survey Shows Most 'Offset' Newspapers Are Making Progress," *The American Press* 59:5 (March 1941): 4.
38 Wright A. Patterson, "Papers Declining as Costs Increase," *The Publishers' Auxiliary*, January 8, 1949, 4.
39 Ed Williams, nominating letter for Bill Stewart to be inducted into Newspaper Hall of Honor, March 13, 2000.
40 William T. Koester, "Barnhart Rates as 'Editors' Man of the Week' for Educational Devotion to Weekly Newsmen," *The Publishers' Auxiliary*, December 10, 1949, 4.
41 Barnhart, *Weekly Newspaper Writing and Editing*, 35, 57–58.
42 Robert L. Warren, "The Open Forum-Faithful 'Ox' Reader," *The Publishers' Auxiliary*, January 22, 1949, 4.
43 Frank B. Hutchinson, "Weekly Newspaper Readership Studied," *The American Press* 59:7 (May 1941): 8.
44 Charles E. Rogers, "The Role of the Weekly Newspaper," *Annals of the American Academy of Political and Social Science* 219 (January 1942): 151.
45 "Weeklies Will Join A.B.C. if It Means More Ads, Moreau Explains," *The American Press* 59:1 (November 1940): 9.
46 Robert Warner, "United Effort Only Way to Get More Ads, Says Warner," *The American Press* 59:2 (December 1940): 4.
47 "Advertising News," The *York Times*, June 15, 1946, 30.
48 "N.E.A. President Attacks Publicity as 'Sabotage,'" *The American Press* 59:7 (May 1941): 3.
49 In 2022, according to the latest government figures based on the Consumer Price Index, $250,000 from 1941 was worth $5.029 million and $13 million from 1941 was worth $261.5 million. http://measuringworth.com/.
50 "Free Space in Weeklies Worth $13,000,000 a Year," *The American Press* 59:8 (June 1941): 2.
51 T. Swann Harding, "Genesis of One 'Government' Propaganda Mill," *The Public Opinion Quarterly* 11:2 (Summer 1947): 233–234.
52 Barnhart, *Weekly Newspaper Writing and Editing*, 62.
53 Ibid., 272.
54 Charles T. Duncan, "Editorials Not 'On Way Out' Among Minnesota Weeklies," *Journalism Quarterly* 26 (March 1949): 57.
55 Edward J. Farrell, "Survey Reveals Political Power of 'Grassroots,'" *The Publishers' Auxiliary*, March 12, 1949, 1.
56 "Movement of Aux Creates Confusion; It Also Opens Way to Bright Future," *The Publishers' Auxiliary*, January 29, 1949, 2.
57 "Missouri Paper Digests Opinion of Grassroots," *The Publishers' Auxiliary*, July 16, 1949, 1.
58 "Future of Weekly Newspapers Promising, Evaluation Shows," *The American Press* 59:10 (August 1941): 4. In 2022, according to the latest government figures based on the Consumer Price Index, $13 billion from 1940 was worth $278.7 billion. http://measuringworth.com/.
59 Walter A. Snead, "Department of Commerce Examines Weeklies, Finds Their Position 'Stronger Than Ever,'" *The Publishers' Auxiliary*, August 27, 1949, 4.

60 "War Brides Arrive in U.S. from Britain," *McKean County* (PA) *Democrat*, June 14, 1945, 1.
61 Wilbur Schramm and Merritt Ludwig, "The Weekly Newspaper and Its Readers," *Journalism Quarterly* 28 (Summer 1951): 306, 310, 312.
62 David Dempsey, "That Midwest Power—The Farmer's Wife," *The New York Times*, October 3, 1948, SM46.
63 Ibid.
64 Joe Marsh, "From Where I Sit," *The Mountain-Democrat*, September 29, 1949, 3. Placerville, in El Dorado County, is located northeast of Sacramento, California. According to its nameplate, the newspaper was established in 1852 and was a member of the Audit Bureau of Circulations and the California Press Association. Placerville had a population of 3,064 in 1940. *Sixteenth Census of the United States*, "Population," volume 1, section 3, 127, Table 5. http://newspaperarchive.com/, http://www.census.gov/.
65 H.I. Phillips, "The Once Over," *The Mexia* (TX) *Weekly Herald*, July 15, 1948, 4. http://newspaperarchive.com/.
66 "Is a Telephone in Your Post-War Plans?" *McKean County* (PA) *Democrat*, June 14, 1945, 5. http://newspaperarchive.com/.
67 "Easier Dish Washing... You'll Find the Secret in Petroleum," *The Mountain-Democrat*, September 29, 1949, 10. http://newspaperarchive.com/.
68 "Decide Now... Sink or Swim?" *The Mountain-Democrat*, September 29, 1949, 8. http://newspaperarchive.com/.
69 "The Pride and Joy of a Housewife—The New Electric Range," *Bedford* (PA) *Gazette*, August 8, 1946, sec. 2, 3. http://newspaperarchive.com/.
70 Dempsey, "That Midwest Power—The Farmer's Wife," SM12. In 2022, according to the latest government figures based on the Consumer Price Index, $10 from 1948 was worth $123. http://measuringworth.com/.
71 In 2022, according to the latest government figures based on the Consumer Price Index, $25 from 1946 was worth $379. http://measuringworth.com/.
72 Charles T. Duncan, "Sweetland Wouldn't Wait for Public Library, He Founded One—In His Newspaper's Office," *The Publishers' Auxiliary*, March 12, 1949, 1.
73 Dempsey, "That Midwest Power—The Farmer's Wife," SM12, SM46.
74 Alton L. Blakeslee, "Medical Detectives Hunt Polio 'Trigger' in Epidemic Localities," *The Washington Post*, September 7, 1947, B2.
75 "Polio Heading for Its Second Worst Year," *The Washington Post*, November 26, 1948, 18.
76 "Polio in Buffalo," *McKean County* (PA) *Democrat*, June 14, 1945, 4. http://newspaperarchive.com/.
77 "Polio Policy," *The Mexia* (TX) *Weekly Herald*, July 15, 1948, 3. http://newspaperarchive.com/.
78 "North Carolina Battles Against Polio Outbreak," *The Mexia* (TX) *Weekly Herald*, July 15, 1948, 3. http://newspaperarchive.com/.
79 "Report Shows Polio Is Attacking More Teen Agers, Adults," *The Mexia* (TX) *Weekly Herald*, July 15, 1948, 3. http://newspaperarchive.com/.
80 "89 Polio Cases This Week," *The Mexia* (TX) *Weekly Herald*, July 15, 1948, 3. http://newspaperarchive.com/.

81 "Jester Proclaims Statewide 'Clean-up, Fight Polio Week,'" *The Mexia* (TX) *Weekly Herald*, July 15, 1948, 3. http://newspaperarchive.com/.
82 "Health Departments Agree Swimming Pool Polio Not Connected," *The Mexia* (TX) *Weekly Herald*, July 15, 1948, 4. http://newspaperarchive.com/.
83 "Band Concerts Aid Polio Fund," *The Mountain-Democrat*, September 29, 1949, 1. http://newspaperarchive.com/.
84 Greenville, in Washington County, part of the Mississippi Delta Region, had a population of 20,892 in 1940. *Sixteenth Census of the United States*, "Population," volume 1, section 6, 568, Table 2. http://newspaperarchive.com/, http://www.census.gov/.
85 "The South Can Stop It," Bedford (PA) *Gazette*, August 8, 1946, sec. 2, 2. http://newspaperarchive.com/.
86 "Negro Methodists Hold District Meet in Mexia July 12–16," *The Mexia* (TX) *Weekly Herald*, July 15, 1948, 1.
87 Rogers, "The Role of the Weekly Newspaper," 151.
88 George Peck, "Man Is Not a Bee," *The Mexia* (TX) *Weekly Herald*, July 15, 1948, 4. http://newspaperarchive.com/.
89 "Newspapers Play Vital Role in Fight Against Recession," *The Publishers' Auxiliary*, July 16, 1949, 4.
90 Dempsey, "That Midwest Power—The Farmer's Wife," SM12.

References

"89 Polio Cases This Week." *The Mexia* (TX) *Weekly Herald*, July 15, 1948, 3.
"Advertising Is Aid to War Effort, OC Director Declares." Casa Grande (AZ) *Dispatch*, March 6, 1942, 7.
"Advertising News." *The New York Times*, June 15, 1946, 30.
"Arizona Women Will Be Given Chance to Work in Shipyards." Casa Grande (AZ) *Dispatch*, March 6, 1942, 3.
"The Army of Patriotic Women." Casa Grande (AZ) *Dispatch*, March 6, 1942, 3.
"Band Concerts Aid Polio Fund." *Mountain-Democrat*, Placerville, CA, September 29, 1949, 1.
Barnhart, Thomas F. *Weekly Newspaper Writing and Editing*. New York: The Dryden Press, 1949.
Blakeslee, Alton L. "Medical Detectives Hunt Polio 'Trigger' in Epidemic Localities." *The Washington Post*, September 7, 1947, B2.
Brewington, Leroy. "Shortage of Skilled Printers Requires Plans for Training." *The Publishers' Auxiliary*, August 6, 1949, 8.
"Bugle Calls." McKean County (PA) *Democrat*, June 14, 1945, 3.
Callahan, Lt. North. "Army Seeks Help of Editors in Rural Recruiting Work." *The American Press* 59:2 (December 1940): 6.
"County 'E' Bond Sales Reach $649,000; 43 Percent of McKean's Quota Is Sold." McKean County (PA) *Democrat*, June 14, 1945, 1.
"Decide Now… Sink or Swim?" *Mountain-Democrat*, Placerville, CA, September 29, 1949, 8.

Dempsey, David. "That Midwest Power—The Farmer's Wife." *The New York Times*, October 3, 1948, SM12, SM13, SM46–SM47.

"Don't Just Buy War Bonds… Keep Them!" *Kerrville* (TX) *Mountain Sun*, May 27, 1943, 10.

Duncan, Charles T. "Editorials Not 'On Way Out' Among Minnesota Weeklies." *Journalism Quarterly* 26 (March 1949): 57–60.

Duncan, Charles T. "Sweetland Wouldn't Wait for Public Library, He Founded One–In His Newspaper's Office." *The Publishers' Auxiliary*, March 12, 1949, 1.

"Easier Dish Washing… You'll Find the Secret in Petroleum." *Mountain-Democrat*, Placerville, CA, September 29, 1949, 10.

Farrell, Edward J. "Survey Reveals Political Power of 'Grassroots.'" *The Publishers' Auxiliary*, March 12, 1949, 1.

Forbes, Malcolm. "Is Your Newspaper a 'Typical Country Weekly'?" *The American Press* 59:12 (October 1941): 8.

"Free Space in Weeklies Worth $13,000,000 a Year." *The American Press* 59:8 (June 1941): 2–3.

"Future of Weekly Newspapers Promising, Evaluation Shows." *The American Press* 59:10 (August 1941): 4.

"Goff Lists 10 Ways to Conserve Tires During War Period." *Casa Grande* (AZ) *Dispatch*, March 6, 1942, 2.

Harding, T. Swann. "Genesis of One 'Government' Propaganda Mill." *The Public Opinion Quarterly* 11, no. 2 (1947): 227–235.

"Health Departments Agree Swimming Pool Polio Not Connected." *The Mexia* (TX) *Weekly Herald*, July 15, 1948, 4.

"He Can't Ask You Now!" *McKean County* (PA) *Democrat*, June 14, 1945, 6.

"Home Garden Vital Due to Lack of Tin." *Casa Grande* (AZ) *Dispatch*, March 6, 1942, 2.

Hough, Henry Beetle. *Country Editor*. New York: Doubleday, Doran & Company, 1940.

Hutchinson, Frank B. "Weekly Newspaper Readership Studied." *The American Press* 59: 7 (May 1941): 8.

"Is a Telephone in your Post-War Plans?" *McKean County* (PA) *Democrat*, June 14, 1945, 5.

"Jester Proclaims Statewide 'Clean-up, Fight Polio Week.'" *The Mexia* (TX) *Weekly Herald*, July 15, 1948, 3.

"Kent, at 17, Is a Veteran." *The Publishers' Auxiliary*, July 30, 1949, 4.

Koester, William T. "Barnhart Rates as 'Editors' Man of the Week' for Educational Devotion to Weekly Newsmen." *The Publishers' Auxiliary*, December 10, 1949, 4.

Luther, Catherine A. "Reflections of Cultural Identities in Conflict: Japanese American Internment Camp Newspapers during World War II." *Journalism History* 29, no. 2 (2003): 69–81.

Marsh, Joe. "From Where I Sit." *Mountain-Democrat*, Placerville, CA, September 29, 1949, 3.

Marsh, William B. "Survey Shows Most 'Offset' Newspapers Are Making Progress." *The American Press* 59:5 (March 1941): 4.

"Million Garments for War Sufferers Goal Set in U.S." *Casa Grande* (AZ) *Dispatch*, March 6, 1942, 2.

"Missouri Paper Digests Opinion of Grassroots." *The Publishers' Auxiliary*, July 16, 1949, 1.

"Miss Raphel Announces Arrival of Army Yarn for Red Cross Knitting." *Kerrville* (TX) *Mountain Sun*, May 27, 1943, 10.

"More Colleges Call on Active Journalists as Teachers; 24,072 Students Taking On-the-Job Printing Training." *The Publishers' Auxiliary*, September 24, 1949, 8.

"Movement of Aux Creates Confusion; It Also Opens Way to Bright Future." *The Publishers' Auxiliary*, January 29, 1949, 2.

"Mrs. America and the War." *Dispatch Democrat*, Ukiah, CA, April 7, 1944, 4.

"N.E.A. President Attacks Publicity as 'Sabotage.'" *The American Press* 59:7 (May 1941): 3.

"Negro Methodists Hold District Meet in Mexia July 12–16." *The Mexia* (TX) *Weekly Herald*, July 15, 1948, 1.

"New Higher Pay for the Army!" *Bedford* (PA) *Gazette*, August 8, 1946, 4.

"News of the Service Folks." *Dispatch Democrat*, Ukiah, CA, April 7, 1944, 1.

"Newspapers Play Vital Role in Fight Against Recession." *The Publishers' Auxiliary*, July 16, 1949, 4.

"North Carolina Battles Against Polio Outbreak." *The Mexia* (TX) *Weekly Herald*, July 15, 1948, 3.

N.W. Ayer & Son's Directory of Newspapers and Periodicals. Philadelphia: N.W. Ayer & Sons, 1940.

N.W. Ayer & Son's Directory of Newspapers and Periodicals. Philadelphia: N.W. Ayer & Sons, 1945.

Office of War Information, "Town and Farm in Wartime," *McKean County* (PA) *Democrat*, June 14, 1945, 6. http://newspaperarchive.com/.

Patterson, Wright A. "Papers Declining as Costs Increase." *The Publishers' Auxiliary*, January 8, 1949, 4.

Peck, George. "Man Is Not a Bee." *The Mexia* (TX) *Weekly Herald*, July 15, 1948, 4.

Phillips, H.I. "The Once Over." *The Mexia* (TX) *Weekly Herald*, July 15, 1948, 4.

"Pictures Show Highlights of Atomic Year One." *Bedford* (PA) *Gazette*, August 8, 1946, 4.

"Polio Heading for Its Second Worst Year." *The Washington Post*, November 26, 1948, 18.

"Polio in Buffalo." *McKean County* (PA) *Democrat*, June 14, 1945, 4.

"Polio Policy." *The Mexia* (TX) *Weekly Herald*, July 15, 1948, 3.

"The Pride and Joy of a Housewife—The New Electric Range." *Bedford* (PA) *Gazette*, August 8, 1946, 3.

"Publisher Stops Paper to Join Armed Forces." *The New York Times*, January 17, 1942, 12.

"Publishers to Aid in Community Work." *Christian Science Monitor*, January 7, 1944, 12.

"Report Shows Polio Is Attacking More Teen Agers, Adults." *The Mexia* (TX) *Weekly Herald*, July 15, 1948, 3.

Rogers, Charles E. "The Role of the Weekly Newspaper." *Annals of the American Academy of Political and Social Science* 219 (January 1942): 151–157.

"Roosevelt and Churchill Praise Editors." *The Washington Post*, June 24, 1942, 19.

Schramm, Wilbur, and Merritt Ludwig. "The Weekly Newspaper and Its Readers." *Journalism Quarterly* 28 (Summer 1951): 301–314.

Sixteenth Census of the United States: 1940: Population. Edited by United States Bureau of the Census. Washington, DC: Government Printing Office, 1942–1943.

Smith, Merriman. "Roosevelt Sets up Works Corps for Aliens from Coast Areas." *The Washington Post*, March 22, 1942, B6.

Snead, Walter A. "Department of Commerce Examines Weeklies, Finds Their Position 'Stronger Than Ever'" *The Publishers' Auxiliary*, August 27, 1949, 4.

"The South Can Stop It." *Bedford* (PA) *Gazette*, August 8, 1946, 2.

Spencer, Sgt. Robert L. "Sgt. Robert L. Spencer Writes of Experiences with Overseas Army." *Kerrville* (TX) *Mountain Sun*, May 27, 1943, 9.

Taylor, Rennie. "Resettlement of Japanese Involves Unusual Problems." *The Washington Post*, May 4, 1942, 11.

"That Extra Something!... You Can Spot It Every Time." *Kerrville* (TX) *Mountain Sun*, May 27, 1943, 7.

"War Brides Arrive in U.S. from Britain." *McKean County* (PA) *Democrat*, June 14, 1945, 1.

"War Changes Schools of Journalism." *The New York Times*, December 19, 1943, E9.

Warner, Robert. "United Effort Only Way to Get More Ads, Says Warner." *The American Press* 59:2 (December 1940): 4.

Warren, Robert L. "The Open Forum-Faithful 'Ox' Reader." *The Publishers' Auxiliary*, January 22, 1949, 4.

"Weeklies Will Join ABC if It Means More Ads, Moreau Explains." *The American Press* 59:1 (November 1940): 9.

White, William A. "Editor Praises Press Coverage of War: But Noted Military Expert Thinks News Slant of American Papers Is 'Too Rosy.'" *The Washington Post*, July 26, 1942, SP8.

Wild, Raymond. "Urges Modernization of Out-Dated Weeklies." *The American Press* 59:1 (November 1940): 17.

Williams, Ed. nominating letter for Bill Stewart to be inducted into Newspaper Hall of Honor, March 13, 2000.

"Women Publish 704 Weekly Newspapers in the United States." *The National Publisher* (July 1941): 10.

www.measuringworth.com.

· 6 ·

THE 1950S: BECOMING LOCALIZED IN NEWS, CENTRALIZED IN OPERATIONS

Community journalism experienced a resurgence in the 1950s due to several key factors. Urban sprawl moved more citizens into once-rural communities. Advanced technologies enabled small printing operations to discard ready-print pages and produce a financially feasible professional product. Chain ownership and central printing operations introduced a new business model for weeklies to remain competitive. And finally, weeklies concentrated more on local news.

A surging housing market that began in the late 1940s continued into the new decade. Veterans of World War II and the Korean War were the main contributors to the surge. They returned to the workforce and sought more affordable housing outside of the country's large metropolitan centers. The result was the settlement of areas that became known as suburbs. An interstate construction program that President Dwight Eisenhower promoted made the suburbs more accessible. Just as pioneer settlements had become important links along the rail lines a century before, the interstate highway system transformed agriculturally based communities into important links on new roadways in the 1950s.

New residents of the suburbs and rural communities expected a town newspaper that focused on their interests and activities. Along with their journalistic expectations, they brought disposable incomes to support Main Street merchants who trumpeted their products and services in the pages of the community weekly. In response to a postwar emphasis on consumption, weeklies competed head-on with "shoppers" or printed their own—which featured a heavy concentration of display and classified advertising and brief community-calendar listings and/or articles.

Technology developments in the 1950s revolutionized the printing industry as a whole—allowing for reduced overhead and operations costs that proved especially beneficial to small-town newspapers. Teletypesetters produced punch tape that activated a typesetting machine, eliminating the costly and time-consuming hand-set type. Offset printing—which expanded in the 1940s—became more prevalent among weekly press operations. Offset shops were less expensive to operate and turned out high-quality products in relation to type readability and illustration reproduction.

A new business model was introduced during the decade when a number of weekly publishers in the 1950s purchased competing weeklies and consolidated their staffs and printing operations to cut production costs and reach an expanded geographic base. Weekly chains, central printing presses, and advertising collectives—designed specifically to serve weekly newspaper groups—sprang up during the decade. Chain ownership allowed weekly publishers to boast of larger circulations that attracted merchants because the businesses could place their advertisements in multiple publications. The larger circulations and multiple publications also proved to be a draw for national advertisers.

Weeklies, for the most part, became even more distinctively community oriented in the 1950s. Weekly publishers realized that the major advantage weeklies had over their media competitors was the ability to intimately cover local issues because of close personal and business ties to the community. In addition to the traditional country correspondents who wrote columns from surrounding rural communities, weeklies began adding reporters to their staffs. Reporters provided in-depth coverage on local issues since weeklies could not compete with the time-sensitive, news-announcement format of dailies, and radio and television stations.

New Pioneer Printers: Weeklies Follow Population Movement

Just as their predecessors had a century before, small-town editors in the 1950s found it necessary to follow shifting populations. They established publishing roots in newly formed suburban communities or newly discovered rural crossroads as a means of survival. A 1959 analysis by *The American Press*, based on the *N.W. Ayer Directory of Newspapers and Periodicals*, determined there were 434 weekly newspapers in the United States that were 100 years or older. New York state had the most papers, with 73 having passed the century mark. Pennsylvania and Illinois were tied for second with 38 each. Among the oldest weeklies was *The Virginia Gazette*, established in 1736 in Williamsburg.[1]

Both World War II and the Korean War brought a large drop in the number of weeklies, many in small, rural communities. In fact, since World War II there had been a steady decrease in weeklies, dropping to 8,892 in 1952—with a total circulation of 17.2 million, according to the first *Directory of Country and Suburban Home Town Newspapers*. This particular directory—published by the Weekly Newspaper Representatives, Inc.—was a combination of the directories formerly published by the American Press Association and the Newspaper Advertising Service. A.P.A. had published its own directory every year for the previous 32 years. The largest number of newspapers was in the state of Illinois with 622, followed by Texas with 557, and New York with 484. The directory showed there were roughly 75.1 million people living on farms or in towns of under 10,000 population.[2] At the end of the decade, the number of weeklies totaled about 9,000—with a record 22.8 million in paid circulation in 1959—representing an increase of slightly more than 100,000 copies per issue from the previous year. Of these newspapers listed in the "weekly" category, 8,990 came out once a week.[3]

University of Iowa professor Wilbur Peterson looked at a decrease in the number of weeklies in the United States from 1950 to 1959. He found that suspensions of weeklies occurred in 488 towns with a population of 1,000 or less—which left those communities without local papers. The total of all weeklies (in 48 states) dropped 788—with 703 of the decreases in small towns. Only 5 percent of country weekly towns retained competitive newspapers by the end of the decade. Peterson also reported that in the cities where a daily was published, 173 weeklies died. Of the 173 papers that failed, some of them were owned by a daily newspaper and were established for no other reason than to discourage a competitive weekly from entering the market. In addition, the study—which used figures from the 1950 and 1959 issues of the *N.W. Ayer & Sons Directory of Newspapers and Periodicals*—found a trend to one-newspaper places continuing. Only a few communities remained in the weekly field with multiple newspaper ownerships.[4]

For example, University of Minnesota journalism professor John Cameron Sim found that 58 weeklies had shut down in Minnesota since 1942. Of the 58 weeklies, 20 suspended operations during the Korean War, but 36 were revived by 1954. Of these 36 papers, only eight were in towns with a population of less than 500. Newspapers in towns of less than 500 people were in jeopardy of shutting down. Residents of these smallest communities often moved to larger towns and metropolitan suburbs. Also, the smaller towns had fewer retail outlets, which meant the loss of potential advertising revenue. Thus, Sim asserted that weekly publishers would have to emulate the pioneer printer and move to new or growing rural communities that needed newspapers.[5]

Sim and others in the weekly field believed that metropolitan dailies would not be able to cover the need for local news in the new suburban communities. He wrote, "The opportunities for community newspapers are not being sharply diminished by this shift of population; they are merely altered. Better a transplanted paper than a dead one."[6]

Several articles published in the mid-to-late 1950s provided examples of the explosive growth of a suburban weekly press. A June 22, 1959 *Newsweek* article, "Making Publishing Hay in the Suburbs," explained how small-town newspapers were building circulation and profits on local news.[7] A 1960 *Editor & Publisher* article highlighted the expansion of the Moreau Publications plant in Orange, New Jersey. The company purchased adjacent property, built a new plant wing, and installed additional machinery and equipment. By the end of the decade the plant turned out 11 newspapers and produced 46 "shoppers" that averaged 20 tabloid pages in size.[8] Shoppers were newspapers mailed free of charge to homeowners that provided large coverage areas for advertisers—something small-town newspapers could not do. The content was usually confined to advertisements, and perhaps a few community items or community-calendar listings.

The prize-winning Cleveland area weeklies, *Sun-Press* and *Sun-Messenger*, also expanded into the suburban market, serving 19 eastern Cleveland suburbs with a population of 225,000. Publisher Harry Volk reported a combined "saturation" circulation of 62,000. The *Sun-Press* was founded in 1946 by Volk and Milton Friedlander to serve an area Volk described as a "neglected news field." Volk recalled, "We were certain that if we could produce a weekly that was professionally written and edited and keyed to the suburbs, the advertising would follow." The papers specialized in "work-up" or in-depth reporting stories to attract readers. Several stories that drew attention included a series on well-to-do women who shoplifted in the suburbs, a series on mental health, and stories on social drinking and alcoholism.[9]

Among the new "pioneer printers" who ventured into small towns previously without a newspaper was John Henry Cutler. The university professor and freelance writer had no previous newspaper experience when he founded the *Duxbury* (MA) *Clipper* in 1950 in a coastal resort town of less than 2,000. Cutler described himself as "the poor man's William Allen White." He wrote about his adventures of running a weekly, or "ragbag," which he learned was another term for a weekly. He started the *Clipper* with an outlay of $100 and turned down a $25,000 offer in 1959 to sell the paper.[10]

An April 1960 *Editor & Publisher* article told of Lake Grove, Oregon—located 10 miles southwest of Portland—which had no newspaper throughout the 1950s. In the spring of 1960 the town's 4,000 residents suddenly had two weeklies both named the *Lake Grove News*. According to the article, two weekly publishers in nearby towns had the same idea at the same time and chose the same name for their publications. However, one of the papers was renamed the *Lake Grove Press* after its second week of operation.[11]

But there were some metropolitan dailies fighting back against Sim's challenge that they would not be able to respond to the need for local news in the new suburban communities. A May 1960 *Editor & Publisher* article featured Baltimore's *The Evening Sun's* answer to the problem of readers and advertisers spreading to the suburbs. The daily began publishing its own weekly inside the daily. *The Evening Sun* weekly included typical features of the small-town press. According to the article, small retailers liked the fact that their advertisements—which previously seemed lost among the big displays in the daily publication—received more prominent placement in the weekly edition. An added bonus was that they were able to use newspaper techniques such as pictures and maps that were not readily available at the average country newspaper.[12]

In a negative nod to rural weeklies, whose practices they deemed more provincial and less sophisticated in tone, some larger metropolitan chains preferred to use suburban newspapers as a training ground for their newspaper management personnel. The metropolitan chains made a distinction between rural and suburban weeklies, and chose only the weekly suburban field as a training ground because its reader level of sophistication, retail options, and local concerns were similar to that of the metropolitan daily reader. For example, Knight Newspapers (Detroit, Akron, Charlotte, and Miami) bought two weeklies in Florida. The company moved younger men from their dailies into Florida suburban weeklies for grassroots training. "Employees who come from a weekly operation," said James L. Knight, the *Miami Herald's* general manager, "tended to place proper values on selling, production, and editorial matters."[13]

Signs of urban sprawl were evident in articles and advertisements scattered throughout the pages of weeklies. For example, in response to the quick spread of suburb and tract housing, a January 19, 1950 issue of *The Bessemer* (MI) *Herald* featured a three-column architectural drawing and blueprint of a new home model. The Claridge—as the model was called—featured an "attached garage under the same roof to give a larger appearance, two-bedroom, living room, kitchen-dinette." Interested buyers were encouraged to contact the Small House Planning Bureau in St. Cloud, Minnesota.[14] The same issue advertised kitchen cabinet installation from a local wood products company under the enticing headline, "How to Get Your Dream Kitchen—and SAVE."[15]

Ready-Print Out, Offset In

A single headline in the March 1952 edition of *The American Press* summed up a major shift in the production of weeklies: "Ready-Print Pages No Longer Available." The only remaining ready-print service in the country—Western Newspaper Union—discontinued its ready-print service that dated back to the Civil War. For decades, ready-print contributed the preprinted "insides" of thousands of weekly newspapers. W.N.U. President Farwell Perry cited rising costs of newsprint, production, and distribution as reasons for eliminating the service. Also, there was less of a need for ready-print as more weeklies tied their success to an emphasis on local news, according to the article. During its peak, more than 7,000 newspapers used the W.N.U. ready-print service. By 1952 that number had dwindled to 1,412, accounting for only 5 percent of W.N.U.'s total business.[16]

At the same time that the national syndicate announced the discontinuation of its ready-print service, W.N.U. stated that it would increase the number of features available in mat and plate form. These services were already provided by a number of private and public concerns to assist newspapers with "filler" material.[17] Corporations, businesses, trade associations, non-profit agencies, and governmental departments provided a wealth of boilerplate material for weeklies. Boilerplate was provided either free of charge or for purchase, usually on a contractual basis.

Alexander Brook recalled the boilerplate material contained in his first issue as publisher of the Kennebunk (ME) *Star* in 1958. The issue included two mats from the Dodge (automobile) safety consultant, three free "Did You Know?" mats, and "a variety of others inviting people to buy savings bonds, support the Heart Fund, and join the female branch of the Marine Corps." At the time of Brook's purchase of the paper in 1958 for $30,000, it contained a four-page broadsheet—meaning one folded sheet. Brook's first issue had 51 inches of legal advertising, 17 classifieds and 190 column inches of display advertising at 40 cents per column inch—for advertising revenue totaling $109. Subscriptions were $2 a year, or 5 cents off the rack. The paper had a circulation of 1,254, but, Brook wrote, "350 were mailed free to former publishers' friends, advertisers, potential advertisers, or people who had died." The total newspaper income amounted to about $8,000 a year.[18]

Clippings from other newspapers also remained a popular option for "filler" material. Some weeklies purchased pre-set columns from another newspaper, usually a nearby daily, published at the same central printing press. Former weekly newspaper employee and author Charles Harter recalled that in the mid-1950s, the *Garrett* (IN) *Clipper* purchased (at 5 cents an inch) pre-set county news left over from the press run of the nearby county seat daily paper in Auburn. He worked 14 years in small-town journalism in Ohio, Indiana, Illinois, and Kentucky, beginning in 1951.[19]

As weeklies moved away from ready-print and its supply of low- or no-cost printing paper and pre-sold national advertisements, their job-printing services offered an important income stream to help finance their newspaper publishing operations. In fact, some weeklies had to disband their newspaper operations and remain solely in the job-printing service. An anonymous Midwest weekly publisher wrote about his two-year, financially losing venture from 1956 to 1958. He stated that he endured 88-hour work weeks, an $80 weekly return on his $20,000 investment, an average $10,000 yearly profit, and limited family time. After shutting down the paper, he became owner of a job-printing plant and freelance photojournalist. He wrote, "I published a small weekly for more than two years while I watched a life-long dream turn into a frightening nightmare."[20]

The American Press printing trade journal conducted a 1952 survey of weeklies that revealed that 54 percent of press-operating time was devoted to job printing. The survey concerned the press-operating times and types of equipment of the average weekly newspaper publishing plant. More than 600 weeklies responded to the survey, representing a 7 percent cross-section of the country's estimated 8,500 weekly newspaper plants.[21]

It was not unusual to find countless promotional advertisements among the pages of weeklies touting the quality of printed products from their press plants. For example, a one-third-page advertisement in a November 12, 1959 edition of *The Wright County* (IA) *Monitor* promoted the newspaper's job-printing business as "Wright County's Most Complete Office Supply Store." The advertisement listed office supplies, printing specials, and new merchandise—such as wedding announcements, business or professional cards, and daily calendars.[22]

A 1952 survey report in *The American Press* also found that only one in eight—or more than 1,000 weeklies—operated offset presses. Offset lithography—better known as photo-offset—made plates from photographs of pasted-up material for reproduction. The photograph of pasted-up material was known as a "master copy." The reproduction quality for photographs was much better than letterpress and the equipment could be purchased for a 10th the cost of a letterpress plant to produce the same size newspaper.[23] The survey even revealed that a majority of weeklies still used hand-set presses.[24] One such weekly was the *Garrett Clipper* in DeKalb County, Indiana. Publisher, professor, and author Eugene Harter recalled his apprentice days there from 1953 to 1956. He wrote that the "Country Campbell press dominated the room, resting on a rough tobacco- and ink-stained pine floor. Equipment was arranged as it would have been in the late 1900s." He observed that the Campbell press occasionally "threw inked sheets of paper all about, especially during winter days when static electricity hung in the air" and that the printers responded by pouring buckets of water over the floor to moisten the air.[25]

Despite the small percentage of weeklies using offset—also referred to as "cold type"—a growing number of production managers preferred offset and declared it the method of the future. One such manager was B.G. Burke—production manager at *The San Diego Union* and San Diego's *Evening Tribune*—who recounted his company's transition to offset in 1956 in an article in *The Publishers' Auxiliary*. He described how the company acquired two Intertype Fotosetters and auxiliary equipment and set up a separate cold-type department. He explained that hot-type machine operators received additional pay to train in the cold-type process. The transition was a gradual process, according to Burke, but the result was a more professional looking product that could be turned around in the same amount of time.²⁶

Victor Leiker—publisher of *The Courier* in Middletown, New Jersey — suggested to attendees at the 1960 Mid-Atlantic Newspaper Mechanical Conference in Philadelphia that they incorporate his use of both offset and rotary printing as a possible solution to the rising costs of production. Leiker acknowledged that "better looking ads" could be produced using hot type so he advised publishers not to throw out their type-casting machines if they switched to offset. But he also pointed out that weeklies lost valuable national advertising because they continued to use the old hot-type method. He suggested that a group of independent weekly publishers establish a central offset plant to handle national advertising and other special printing projects. He concluded, "Offset is the nearest thing to solving the weekly problems today."²⁷

Walter Rae, author of *Editing Small Newspapers* (revised in 1952 from its 1943 edition), encouraged publishers to use "photo-offset," as he termed it, because it made excellent reproductions of illustrations. Also, the equipment could be purchased for a 10th of the cost of a letterpress plant. The only disadvantage to offset, according to Rae, was the lack of distinctive typefaces. However, he offered that the new eight-point I.B.M. Electric Typewriter with justified lines, using the typeface called "text type," closely resembled a letterpress product. Rae explained that offset newspapers were generally of a tabloid size because the offset presses—which printed 6,500 copies an hour—were not large enough to print a double-truck standard-size 8-column paper.²⁸

By the late 1950s and early 1960s, evidence of the growth of offset in the weekly newspaper industry could be seen in the number of articles and classified listings in trade publications. Articles and classifieds told about the switch to offset or advertised the sale and setup of offset presses. For example, one classified page in a 1960 edition of *The Publishers' Auxiliary* had several boxed advertisements with the following headlines, "Save $15,000 on one year old Vanguard Rotary offset press," "Complete offset set up," and "Going offset February 1st."²⁹ An article in the same trade publication related the switch to offset at the *Sharon* (PA) *Herald* as described by the newspaper's production manager, Robert C. Schemback. He addressed the topic at the 1960 Mid-Atlantic Newspaper Mechanical Conference. Schemback stated that the failure of newspapers in the past 20 years was often related to the lack of modernization in equipment and that offset allowed an advertising sales department to offer more options to potential customers such as halftones, line cuts, and better layout design choices.[30]

Just as offset presses were scarce, photo-engraving equipment was found only sparingly in weekly production facilities in the 1950s. Only 763 plants responded to a 1952 equipment survey conducted by *The American Press* stating they used photo-engraving equipment. The most popular brand was called a Scan-A-Graver—which was an electronic engraving machine that made halftones by boring holes into plastic sheets.[31] In his article on trends in the weekly newspaper field, University of Minnesota journalism professor Thomas F. Barnhart observed that the plants that used photo-engraving equipment were part of a movement in technological advancement that "ushered in a new era for the weekly as well as the small daily press."[32] The Scan-A-Graver—a product of Fairchild Graphic Equipment, a division of Fairchild Camera and Instrument Corporation—was promoted as a precision electronic engraving machine that could provide the highest quality reproduction. In addition to the Scan-A-Graver, the Fairchild Company also sold Scan-A-Plate—engraving material that could be easily cut for mortises, silhouettes, and other effects.[33] Thus, the Scan-A-Graver—which allowed the addition of high-quality photographs—not only gave weeklies a more professional appearance but also added a new element of localism to stories: names AND faces.

Group Ownership: Risky Initially, Often Paid Off

Weekly publishers had an obvious reason to pursue group ownership, centralized printing, and advertising collectives—their profits were sagging due to increased costs for shop wages, newsprint, and job shop paper and supplies. The Pennsylvania Newspaper Publishers Association conducted a study of 40 weeklies in Pennsylvania, New York, New Jersey, and Ohio. The study revealed that gross income for weekly newspapers increased roughly 15.7 percent in 1951 over 1950, but profits continued to show a decrease. The Weekly Newspaper Bureau of the National Editorial Association conducted a similar study using the reports of 153 papers in 33 states. It found that net income before income taxes for 1951 was 11.2 percent, compared with 13.2 percent for 1950.[34]

Thomas F. Barnhart—often referred to as "Mr. Weekly Newspaper" because of his extensive research and writing on that subject—revised his

Weekly Newspaper Management textbook in 1952 (introduced in the 1930s) to address the changing business model of weeklies. His research for the updated textbook—which also served as a valuable resource guide for weekly publishers and editors—was based on personal visits to 232 small-town newspapers during the summer of 1952.[35] Barnhart found that newspaper buyers continued to show an interest in acquiring medium and large weekly papers that earned an adequate profit. But buyers were only slightly interested in papers located in communities with a population of less than 1,000—unless they were proven retail centers. As a consultant, Barnhart participated in the redesign of more than 50 weekly and daily newspapers.[36]

In response to the struggles that publishers had in deriving profits from single newspaper ownership, a number of weekly publishers looked to group ownership for financial stability. Group ownership proved to be risky initially—especially for family-owned operations because of the heavy financial borrowing often required to purchase another newspaper. But it often paid off in increased subscribers and local and national advertising accounts. In fact, a number of business concerns with no background in community journalism also viewed weekly newspaper group ownership as a profit-making venture and hired trained journalists to run their news operations.

Group ownership came in several forms—a conglomerate of weeklies or dailies, a combination of weeklies and dailies, and a combination of newspapers (weeklies and/or dailies), and/or radio, and/or television. In 1952, Review Publishers, Inc. purchased the weekly *The Freeport* (TX) *Facts*. The company also purchased *The Angleton* (TX) *Times* and ran *The Daily Facts-Review* in Brazosport, Texas. C.P. Kendall, Jr.—whose father bought the paper in 1914 when it merged with the Kendall-family-owned *Valasco* (TX) *World*—edited *The Freeport Facts* for more than 20 years. He assured *The Freeport Facts* readers that the weekly would continue to be published every Thursday, but he also encouraged them to subscribe to the *The Daily Facts-Review*.[37]

A concern among small-town newspaper readers was that the combination or consolidation of their hometown newspaper into a group or chain would mean the loss of a newspaper that focused on their particular community issues. But weekly publisher Alexander Brook responded to reader concerns about the loss of a hometown paper when he purchased and later combined two small Maine weeklies. Although there was a single edition for both communities, the front page was changed to reflect the news from that particular community. The nameplate was changed to match the front-page community of interest. Also a few minor changes were made to inside stories. Advertising and copy of general interest appeared in both editions. The newspaper mailing was separated so that residents received their community's name emblazoned on the front page. Brook observed that although the copy and layout changes meant more work for the staff, the effort quelled complaints about the two towns not having a paper of their own.[38]

A similar effort gave residents in the Pennsylvania towns of New Oxford and East Berlin a sense that they still had their own community newspaper after the papers of the towns combined to form the *New Oxford Item-East Berlin News-Comet*. A four-column nameplate for *East Berlin News-Comet* appeared on page 5, along with a heading for "E.B. Classified." News and classified listings on that particular page related specifically to East Berlin and its surrounding villages.[39] The villages were close enough geographically that event and classified listings would have been of interest to readers residing in the general vicinity. Two East Berlin newspapers, the *East Berlin News* and *East Berlin Comet*, had consolidated prior to joining with the New Oxford Item. In the masthead on page 4, it was noted that the *New Oxford Item* was established in 1871 and the East Berlin *News-Comet* in 1880.

Profitability Plans Include Central Plants and Advertising Cooperatives

A major benefit of group ownership was the ability to consolidate printing operations into one central plant. Many single-paper owners reached agreements to pool resources with other newspapers and jointly own a printing plant. Other publishers simply made arrangements with commercial printers to print their newspapers. Although publishers of small newspapers might have disliked the loss of control in having their newspapers printed at another location, they reasoned that this was the only way to stay in the news business. Publisher J.W. Rockefeller, Jr. wrote in a 1958 *Modern Lithography* article that an investment of a few thousand dollars and the use of a central [printing] plant enabled someone to enter the newspaper business. He added, "Here indeed lies hope for a reversal in the decreasing trend in dailies and weeklies."[40]

The profitability plan of group ownership assumed that advertising revenue would increase because advertisements could appear in all of the publications, thus serving larger audiences and geographical areas. But in some cases, although a group's geographic range was expanded, population totals remained too low for paid-circulation publications to compete with the free-circulation shoppers. Alexander Brook explained that as he added new communities and newspaper editions to his southern Maine weekly newspaper group, it was, initially, not feasible to charge higher advertising rates. Despite an expansion of his group's coverage area, he explained, overall circulation was not high enough to warrant increased advertising rates. In his words, advertising revenues were greatest if newspapers operated in "condensed, isolated, competition-free, high-income areas."[41]

Just as weekly publishers found it financially beneficial to cooperate with other weeklies in a central printing operation, they also realized the benefits of advertising cooperatives. The elimination of the Western Newspaper Union ready-print service in 1952 also meant the loss of an advertising cooperative for the weekly publisher. Although the majority of advertising revenue went to the syndicate, the subscribing publisher did reap some benefits for any local advertising sold on the ready-print pages. Around the same time, other advertising cooperatives were making changes as the American Press Association and the Newspaper Advertising Service merged and the Greater Weeklies Associates reorganized to 100 percent publisher ownership.[42] In Deep River, Connecticut, *The New Era* publisher Curtiss S. Johnson—a former advertising agency executive—encouraged other weekly publishers to hire a national advertising representative rather than worry about soliciting national advertisements. He explained in a February 1952 article in *The American Press*, "An [advertising] agency likes to place its business through a representative just like a publisher likes to put his copy through a machine rather than set the type by hand."[43]

Another means to fill the advertising hole left by ready-print national advertisers came from syndicate services and non-profit concerns that were established to offer weeklies "themed" messages—to which local businesses could attach their names in the form of an endorsement. For example, 30 local businesses in Clarion, Iowa, sponsored a weekly church message in the local newspaper with a sponsor line that read, "in the interest of Stronger Churches and a Better Community by the following business and professional men of Clarion." A syndicate service in Strasbourg, Virginia, provided the sponsored message.[44] A non-profit concern—Better Schools, of New York City—joined with the Public Service Advertising Council to solicit local business sponsors for a community message encouraging attendance at school board meetings. Seven local businesses—including grocers, the local electric cooperative, an insurance agent, a materials company, and a motor company—sponsored a message that appeared in an August 1, 1957 edition of *The Sikeston* (MO) *Herald*. It stated, "Remember, Better Schools come from the personal interest of people like you!"[45]

Localness: Community Bulletin Board Journalism

Weekly publishers who wanted to stay competitive with daily newspapers, radio newscasts, and the emerging television news industry, realized they should concentrate on doing what community weeklies could do best—provide in-depth coverage on local issues. These points were credited to Florida Governor Leroy Collins addressing the fall meeting of the New England Weekly Press Association—held in Crawford Notch, New Hampshire—in an October 1959 article in *The American Press*. The governor's main message was that weekly newspapers—rather than fading into obscurity—were becoming increasingly important. The sub-headline of the article read: "Bigness of dailies re-opens field for coverage of activities of individuals by small town and neighborhood newspapers."[46]

No longer could weeklies rely on ready-print and boilerplate material to fill news holes within their pages. A 1951 review of 30 surveys and studies of weekly newspaper reading conducted during the previous 12 years affirmed the unique role that weeklies had in connecting residents to their community. University of Illinois journalism professor Wilbur Schramm and research assistant Merritt Ludwig found that "localness" and especially the publishing of local names made for high readership in weekly newspapers. Despite the fact that nearly all weekly newspaper readers surveyed relied on radio for current news—and roughly half also subscribed to a daily or Sunday newspaper—Schramm and Ludwig found that the weekly did a better job of "knitting together its readers with the little understandings which are the essence both of communication and community." They asserted that the daily served more as a bulletin board of the latest political, economic, and commercial news, while the weekly served as a "great wide window through which readers look out into their community and into the lives of their friends and acquaintances." As an example of the strong community of interest developed by a weekly, the researchers found that it was difficult to find readers who were away from their communities for more than a few weeks without having their hometown newspaper mailed to them to addresses in all parts of the world.[47]

So instead of serving as a bulletin board of news briefs from near and far, like the dailies, the weekly practiced "community bulletin board" journalism. For example, a June 16, 1955 edition of the *National Road Traveler* of Cambridge City, Indiana, included a two-columned box that ran down the entire length of a page and featured a list of piano students of Mrs. Hoyt Vanderbeek and the program of pieces they were to perform at their upcoming recital. The *National Road Traveler* proclaimed to be the largest weekly in the state, offering a "complete weekly review of eastern Indiana."[48] In an August 1, 1957 edition of *The Sikeston* (MO) *Herald*, the police chief provided helpful hints on ways to avoid home break-ins as part of the city's declared "Burglary Prevention Week." The burglary prevention article appeared beside other front-page stories related to: injuries and a death from local car accidents; Jaycees and Lions club announcements; five obituaries; a school-opening schedule; an upcoming election for community committee members; and the appointment of a person to oversee free food distribution.[49] A September 12, 1958 edition of *The Weimar* (TX) *Mercury* featured a front-page article on prices for various types of meat and eggs. After a slight space between lines, a new paragraph noted that "Mr. and Mrs. C.F. Havar of El Campo were Weimar visitors Wednesday." Other front-page items included a leading story on arrests that solved 30 local burglaries, and four obituaries.[50] A November 12, 1959 front-page article in *The Wright County Monitor* of Clarion, Iowa, also listed upcoming musical performances by local students that were to be held in celebration of American Education Week. The two-column article listed pieces to be performed by the Clarion High School band, string quartet, mixed chorus, and drama troupe. Other front-page articles included: accident reports; agriculture news for dairy farmers and corn growers; church and civic club announcements; student awards; and an obituary.[51] A February 8, 1951 edition of *The Boyden* (IA) *Reporter* contained these front-page standing headlines: Sick and Injured; Resolutions of Condolence; Card of Thanks; Celebrate Birthdays; Men in Service; School News; Many Move in Past Week; Club Meetings; Legion Auxiliary Meets; and Sioux County Court News.[52]

Some academics and journalism association leaders speculated that weeklies would die out if they failed to do an adequate job of covering local news. James Ford—dean of the school of journalism at Montana State University—said in a 1952 speech before a meeting of the North Dakota State Press Association, "In the little time that your reader has to sit down in the evening it is generally a question of whether he will read your paper or be snared away by the beautiful four-color picture of the charming, ravishing blonde illustrating a story in *The Saturday Evening Post*." Most newspapers made it a real chore for the reader to get the news, let alone in readable form, but, he added, "You don't have to work very hard to listen or look at it in pictures, by comparison!" He suggested that weeklies not rely so heavily on syndicate and press service material and focus instead on covering local issues.[53]

So, how did weekly editors, reporters, and correspondents stay in touch with their communities? Mabel Temby—editor of the *Kewaunee* (WI) *Enterprise*—wrote in a May 1959 article in *National Publisher* that she worked 70 to 80 hours a week and that her phone rang constantly. "The farmers get up at five o'clock," she said, "and before they go out into the fields, they call to tell me about the hay they have for sale, or the cow they want to buy." She even received calls in the middle of the night, recalling, "The taverns close at one, and they sleep mornings, so when my phone rings at 1:30 I know before I pick up the receiver that it will be one of them."[54]

Newspaperman and *Boilerplating America* author Eugene Harter seemed to imply that some weekly reporters became too closely involved in their readers' personal affairs, blurring the line between news and gossip, when he recalled working with a society editor who penciled in wedding dates and another date nine months later. She'd then check the "Blessed Events" column, according to Harter, and match it to her chart. "Some weeks she would rush to the phone," he wrote, "and amid much tittering, reveal the results of her biological research to her friends."[55]

There was no blurring of the lines between news and gossip in "The Spillway," a popularly read gossip column that ran for more than 40 years in *The Florence* (AL) *Herald*. The column, named for the spillway of Wilson Dam on the nearby Tennessee River, was written by several anonymous authors throughout the years. "Nobody knew who wrote it except me and dad," recalled John D. "Jack" Martin in a 2009 interview. He said that most of the authors were women but "a couple of men did it at times," adding, "It was a well-guarded secret." To avoid being discovered, Martin said it was often under the cover of night that he went to the author's home to collect that week's column. An emphasis on gossip made the column "wildly popular" throughout the years, according to Martin. Following is a typical "Spillway" item: "A little bird has whispered to us that Louise Jones' visit in North Wilkesboro, North Carolina, which delayed her arrival here and shortened her vacation with us by several days, was a significant one. We don't know a thing but how we are a-guessin'."[56] "The Spillway" not only focused on who's who, but who's with whom, according to Martin. "If you were with your boyfriend instead of your husband, everyone knew about it," he added with a chuckle.⁵⁷

Marcy B. Darnall, John D. Martin's grandfather, bought *The Florence (AL) Herald* in 1921. He had been editor of the *Key West (FL) Citizen*. His son, Marcy B. Darnall, Jr., and daughter, Louise Darnall Martin, inherited the paper from their father. Marcy Jr. ran the paper. His sister lived in Atlanta with her husband, Albert L. Martin. Marcy Jr. served in World War II as a Navy pilot. Before going to war, he asked his sister to take over the paper if he died while serving his country. After receiving his discharge papers in 1945, Marcy Jr. was tragically killed in a plane accident on his return to the States. So his brother-in-law, Albert L. Martin—who had never worked in the newspaper business—came from Atlanta with his wife, Louise, to northwest Alabama to run the paper. Their son, Jack, worked in various positions, mostly in the print shop, from the 1950s until the paper was sold in the mid-1970s. *The Florence Herald*—a member of the Alabama Newspaper Advertising Service, Alabama Press Association, and National Editorial Association—was established in 1884. The banner claimed that the paper served "agriculture, commerce, industry, and education in the Muscle Shoals District."⁵⁸

Commenting on the importance of covering a wide span of local issues, including social and gossip columns, Alexander Brook—publisher of the *Kennebunk (ME) Star*, which later combined with several area weeklies to become the *York County Star*—wrote in his book on small-town journalism that to be the community weekly of record meant it was important to report on what appealed "to the thoughtless as well as the thoughtful of all ages."⁵⁹ But, based on the local political climate and media competition, weekly newspaper local coverage was not always as detailed as it could be. In the early 1950s, University of Oregon journalism professor Charles T. Duncan surveyed more than 300 weeklies throughout the United States and found that city council meetings ranked much higher in news value than did school board or county board meetings. He also found that competition was a significant factor in determining a newspaper's diligence in reporting the news of local government. For example, he said that there was less contention between the press and local government in communities served by a monopoly newspaper than in those where there were competing newspapers. The survey also revealed that relations between the weekly press and local government news sources were more on the harmonious side. Also, he found that lack of time and shortage of staff were the most frequently mentioned reasons for failure to provide readers with regular, direct reporting of public affairs. Duncan was critical of weeklies that were more thorough in covering local government offices and departments but ignored the regular meetings of various governing bodies. "If fewer than half of the weekly newspapers give on-the-spot coverage to the public sessions of three key units of local government," he wrote, "then the community press is not doing its job [or] living up to the obligations of its self-assumed and widely proclaimed 'grass roots' role."[60]

Page 1 of the April 6, 1954 issue of *The Landmark* in Statesville, North Carolina, provided a good example of the importance of local news in a small-town weekly in relation to national or international affairs. Juxtaposed against stories about the resignation of the N.A.T.O. commander of Central Europe, and Congress tackling President Dwight D. Eisenhower's budget, was an article about a barn, some hay, a cow, and several chickens being destroyed in a fire, and another concerning the city's decision to hire a dog catcher and purchase a truck.[61]

Rapid Turnover in Reporter Staffs, Search for Alternate Newsgatherers

In attempting to offer more in-depth reporting on local issues, editors found it necessary to hire staff reporters. But this sometimes became a human resources nightmare because the weeklies had to find the money to pay the additional staff members. Then, they often ended up losing the newly trained employees to larger newspapers in better-paying markets. *The American Press* featured a *Nieman Reports* analysis of weeklies that served as a training school for reporters who sought jobs at metropolitan dailies. In his analysis, Charles T. Duncan found that pay scales for reporters on small newspapers had gone up sharply in recent years and that beginner salaries were often equal to or higher than at city dailies. Yet, he observed, gas stations in Eugene, Oregon, offered nearly as much for beginner attendants (college education not required) as most of the state university's journalism graduates received as starting salaries. Aside from low salaries, he also raised the question of what could be done about making the small town more than a way station for young persons of talent and ambition. "To provide more lifetime careers," he observed, "in both the editorial and business phases, careers short of ownership itself, to open a third road between the one leading to the publisher's desk and the one leading yonder and away—that is certainly one of the great challenges confronting the community newspaper today."[62] However, publisher Alexander Brook discovered that reporters were more likely to stay if a sense of community was developed among reporters and they were offered incentives to stay once they acquired a strong community tie. He observed that the best young reporters would accept modest salaries "if the newspaper is vital and their coworkers compatible."[63]

In an effort to increase staff but not the amount paid out in salaries, many weeklies relied on local "experts" or high school journalism students to contribute regular columns or sections. A popular contributor in rural newspapers was the county agricultural or home economics agent. For example, *The Wright County* (IA) *Monitor* featured a November 12, 1959 column titled "Get Acquainted with Squash Clan," written by home economist Geraldine Steele. She encouraged housewives to explore some new dishes to put on their fall table. The article described the four main types of squash and how to select them for purchase.[64] County agent Doyle Moore ran a regular column, "County Agent's Notebook," in *The Weimar* (TX) *Mercury*. His September 12, 1958 column referred to extension, research, and commercial chemical company representatives participating in the county's annual Brush Evaluation Tour. The same column also listed October 20 as the stalk destruction deadline for Colorado County cotton growers.[65] Other examples of non-paid staff were the high school journalism students who wrote articles for the one- or two-page sections in a weekly issue devoted solely to local school news. The journalism department of Texas A & M College found in 1952 that 89 representative Texas weekly newspapers devoted 11.3 percent of their news space to school news.[66]

A Need for Informed and Independent Editorial Comment

A strong emphasis on local issues sometimes went beyond reporting to advocating a particular action or way of thinking in an editorial, usually written by the editor. In fact, weekly editors who promoted a strong editorial voice joined forces in 1954 to establish the International Society of Weekly Newspaper Editors. The organization's purpose was to encourage and promote informed and independent editorial comment in weekly newspapers. Their actions followed a meeting two years earlier of the Freedom of Information Committee of Sigma Delta Chi—the oldest organization representing journalists in the United States and renamed the Society of Professional Journalists in 1960—at which it was reported that the tendencies of public officials and public agencies to withhold information were due "in part at least, to a decline in vigilance, in enterprise, and in aggressiveness on the part of local newspapers." A freedom of information panel held at Sigma Delta Chi's 1952 convention in Denver addressed the need for greater vigilance and enterprise on the part of newspapers. Gene Cervi, publisher of the weekly *Rocky Mountain Journal* in Denver, served on the panel.67

On the advocacy side, *The Bessemer* (MI) *Herald* was a strong proponent in 1950 for the construction of a youth recreation center and ran a January 19, 1950 advocacy headline over its nameplate stating, "We Need Recreational Facilities for Bessemer." A front-page, two-column article described a well-attended community meeting to discuss the building of a youth recreation center. In fact, all of the front-page articles pertained to local issues—obituary notices, club meetings and social gatherings, city government, and local postal and air service issues.68

However, some editors made it a policy never to indulge in local politics through their writings, especially if it meant offending a potential advertiser or subscriber. For example, when hired for his first newspaper position in 1951 at a small weekly in Ohio, newspaperman-author Eugene Harter recalled that the publisher advised him to avoid "rambling editorial wind" and warned, "We don't look fer trouble, no writin' of opinions—not like the ol' days."69

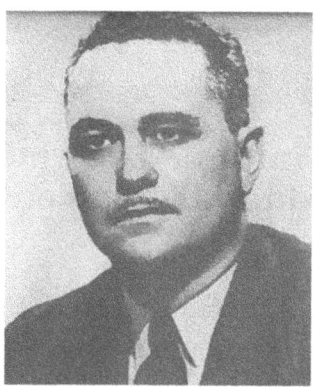

Figure 6.1 William Hodding Carter II, Pulitzer-Prize winning editorialist, editor of the *Delta Democrat-Times* in Greenville, Mississippi and prolific author of works including *Southern Legacy, The Winds of Fear, Flood Crest, Where Main Street Meets the River, First Personal Rural* and *Their Words Were Bullets.* 1956. Retrieved from the Library of Congress. http://hdl.loc.gov/loc.pnp/cph.3c28422.

Pulitzer Prize-winning weekly editor Hodding Carter of the *Delta Democrat-Times* in Greenville, Mississippi was among the editors who vehemently disagreed with their weekly counterparts that newspapers were better served by remaining detached from their communities—"encouraging the good and denouncing the bad, but not taking personal part in the good or the bad of civic life." In his book about his career in small-town journalism, Carter—who won the Pulitzer Prize for editorial writing in 1946—wrote, "I don't see how I can stand apart in Greenville, praising and deriding and warning, and expect to be taken as anything but a town scold." For years it was an accepted practice that country editors served as presidents or on the boards of local merchant clubs and charitable organizations. Some editors saw no conflict of interest as they ran the post office or ran for mayor or town council member. But Carter said an editor should not run for public office and that he, himself, probably should not have served on his town's school board. However, he considered it appropriate that he served on the library board. He concluded that a free press and individual freedoms would be endangered if he became "afraid to print every story that has meaning for my town or to comment upon the controversial happenings."[70]

Defending Unpopular Causes Riles Pressure Groups, Threatens Safety and Stability

Two southern weekly editors followed Carter's award-winning ways, earning the coveted Pulitzer Prize for campaigns against the Ku Klux Klan. The 1953 award went to North Carolina editors Willard Cole of the *Whiteville News-Reporter* and Horace Carter of the *Tabor City Tribune*.[71]

Delivering the third annual Joseph Pulitzer Memorial Lecture at the Columbia University graduate School of Journalism in 1958, Hodding Carter also warned that pressure groups in small communities threatened the independence and survival of small weekly newspapers. He said pressure groups attempted to destroy "weekly newspapers that defend unpopular causes and civil liberties." He observed, "The pressure groups frighten advertisers, and the papers come under the gun of the local merchants and local political bosses." He cited the case of Hazel Brannon Smith, editor of *The Lexington* (MS) *Advertiser* and *The Durant* (MS) *News*, who became the target of advertising boycotts and physical threats from white Citizens Council members and local officials after she accused them of discrimination and physical abuse of Negroes.⁷² In 1952, Park F. Stone, weekly editor of *The Maynard* (MA) *Enterprise*, was awakened twice in one night when a dozen shots were fired into his home. He speculated the attacks came because of his crusading editorials against liquor violators in Maynard and adjacent towns.⁷³ Horace V. Wells, Jr., editor of *The Clinton* (TN) *Courier-News*, received the 1957 Elijah P. Lovejoy Award for Courage in Journalism for his newspaper's stance during the community's contentious clash over school integration. As the award's recipient, Wells was cited for "his realistic devotion to the principles of law and order while subjected to the scorn and abuse of a large segment in his community." The award was presented by the International Conference of Weekly Newspaper Editors, an organization founded in 1955 at Southern Illinois University. The award is named for Elijah Parish Lovejoy, a crusading abolitionist editor murdered by a mob in Alton, Illinois, in 1837 for his antislavery editorials.⁷⁴ The home of *The Mount Dora* (FL) *Topic* editor Mabel Norris Reese was attacked twice with homemade bombs following her editorials that urged a calm approach to school integration and criticized local violent reactions to the 1954 U.S. Supreme Court decision to ban segregation in public schools.⁷⁵

During the 1950s, P.D. East was another Mississippi weekly editor who, like Hodding Carter, made a name for himself by writing fearlessly on local racial issues. However, unlike Carter, he averted from soft scolding and preferred instead to run lampooning advertisements and use sophisticated sarcasm that local readers often mistook for words of praise. For example, he printed an editorial in his paper on April 21, 1955 that compared Mississippi's progress to that of the crawfish. He wrote of the state symbol, the magnolia, that "once you have smelled a magnolia, you have smelled them all—every magnolia looks alike and smells alike." But concerning the crawfish he observed that although they came in numerous shapes, colors, and sizes "there is one thing common to them all, and that's the direction of movement." He suggested that the state legislature adopt the crawfish as the state symbol, replacing the magnolia. The crawfish represented the state's progress, according to East, which was "downhill, backward, toward the mud." He described the state's deliberations related to voting literacy tests, school segregation, and screening speakers before they were allowed to address public school and college students. He also listed the names of the state's "great leaders" and purposely lower-cased their names as a sign of disrespect. East described being surprised that he did not receive a phone call the day that the editorial appeared. He received two calls the next day. Both men, fooled into falling for East's sophisticated, sarcastic wordplay, became subscribers to his paper as a result of the editorial. One remarked to East, "P.D., that's telling them niggers where their place is, by God."[76]

East wrote that he did not intend to become a controversial newspaperman when he started *The Petal (MS) Paper* in 1953, but, rather, a financially successful one who abided by what he sarcastically termed the dictates of success in the weekly field—"loving mother and hating sin." All the news stories and photographs from this small community near Hattiesburg were local. But he soon drew the ire of local advertisers and subscribers when he ran a front-page feature on the anniversary of Abraham Lincoln's death, which he described as "unfortunate." East recalled that a couple of subscribers took issue with him, saying that the only thing unfortunate about Lincoln's death was that it did not come sooner. But East was most widely known for his lampooning advertisements aimed at Mississippi U.S. Senator James Eastland, the White Citizens Councils, and the Ku Klux Klan. The lampoons became widely distributed and resulted in out-of-state subscriptions to his paper outnumbering local circulation. East's most famous "fake ad" appeared on a full page in the March 15, 1956 edition of *The Petal (MS) Paper*. It invited subscribers to join "The Glorious Citizens Clan," with an accompanying illustration of a jackass and the proclamation that "You Too Can Be Superior."[77]

Publisher Bill Stewart of *The Monroe Journal* in Monroeville, Alabama, was not as sarcastic as East in his criticism of racism in his south Alabama community. On one occasion he was straight-forward in his scolding of local Ku Klux Klan members. A December 17, 1959 editorial, placed in a prominent position on page 1, began, "The race hate mongers are at it again. At a time when there should be peace and good will among all men, they have reared their mean, ugly heads and have decreed that a Negro high school band should not march in the Christmas parade that was to be held in Monroeville today." Although the band had marched in the parade during the previous eight years, school leaders declined that year's invitation in an effort to avoid violence. Stewart also complimented the schools' leaders on exercising "extremely sound and careful judgment in efforts to avert any crises which both white and colored alike might regret." The editorial concluded, "The fact that the Negro leaders pulled their band out of the parade is positive proof that they desire no violence."[78]

Syndicated Opinions, Local Editorials, Perceived Influential Power, and Profits

Unlike Carter, East, Stewart, and other weekly editors who preferred to comment editorially on local, national, and international issues of concern, most weeklies avoided editorials altogether. Instead, they offered syndicated opinion columns on such issues as the Korean War, the spread of communism, public school desegregation, and the space race against Russia. Opinion columns about newsmakers—such as presidents Harry Truman and Dwight D. Eisenhower, executed spies Julius and Ethel Rosenberg, anti-communist Senator Joseph McCarthy, and hip-swinging entertainer Elvis Presley—were also popular. A weekly Wisconsin editor took a personal interest in one Wisconsin U.S. senator's anti-communist fervor. Editor Leroy Gore of *The Sauk-Prairie Star* in Sauk City, Wisconsin, headed a petition drive in 1954 to force Senator Joseph McCarthy to stand for a recall election. After appearing on several New York radio and television shows, Gore received support and donations for his "Joe-Must-Go" club to print recall petitions and place them in Wisconsin's 350 small newspapers. Residents in Sauk City and nearby Prairie Du Sac (3,100 population of the two villages)—displeased with his petition efforts—waged their own campaign, "Door-for-Gore," to encourage the editor to leave town. In less than a month, the editor had obtained 200,000 petition signatures (400,000 were needed to force a recall election). Gore was unsuccessful in the recall effort and sold his paper in 1955, citing "post-recall repercussions" and the success of the anti-Gore club to drive "a tough wedge of personal hatred into the community." The Wisconsin Supreme Court in June 1955 reversed a circuit judge's ruling that found the "Joe-Must-Go" club guilty of organizing as a corporation and spending money for political causes in violation of the state law that prohibited such action by a corporation.[79]

However, because of a heavy reliance on syndicated opinions as opposed to local commentary, a controversy arose about the lack of editorial writing in weeklies and the perceived influential power of publishers. A survey among Ohio's weekly editors showed that those who did editorialize considered it vital to their newspaper. But, they added, the fear of losing advertisements was one reason for keeping out of local squabbles. Of the 151 newspapers inspected for the survey, 83 had no editorial page or local column of comment, while 68 contained columns or editorials. Some of the Ohio editors felt strongly about the use of local editorials and indicated so in their survey comments. Despite the fact that his weekly newspaper had to compete with four large weeklies, a daily published within 10 miles, and the metropolitan dailies of Akron and Cleveland, Lee Cavin, editor of *The Seville (OH) Chronicle*, asserted, "I believe editorials are the small weekly's only hope of individuality in a tight competitive field. We sell strong in the face of close superior competition." *The Seville Chronicle* had a circulation of 1,012 in a town of 963. It had a strict policy of no advertising on the editorial page. All the material on the editorial page was written by editor Lee Cavin and his wife, except a small syndicated cartoon. Another editor felt equally passionate about the importance of editorials, having stated in the survey, "An editor who doesn't use editorials should get the hell out of the business."[80]

The controversy surrounding the lack of locally written editorial opinion and assertions that editors held little political sway in their communities was sparked by the responses of country editors to 25 separate opinion polls conducted by *The American Press*. Results from the early-1950s polls indicated that the opinions among weekly editors were largely conservative and did not conform to the majority opinions of Americans. In one such poll in February 1952, *The American Press* queried 718 editors and found that only six out of 169 southern editors said President Harry Truman was their choice for the 1952 presidential election. Many said they would vote for a Republican rather than for Truman. It also found that the majority of country editors expected U.S. Senator Robert A. Taft of Ohio to win the Republican nomination but they did not think he had as much chance of winning a race against Truman as would General Dwight Eisenhower. President Truman later announced that he would not seek another term. Republican Gen. Dwight Eisenhower defeated Democrat U.S. Senator Adlai Stevenson in the 1952 general election.[81]

John C. Obert—a Nieman Fellow at Harvard University and editor of the *Alexandria (MN) Park Region Echo*—wrote about the conservatism of country editors and their lack of political influence in a July 1959 *Nieman Reports* article. He observed, "Far too many of the nation's 9,000 country editors share a grand illusion that they run the country."[82] Obert's article drew a variety of responses, most of them defensive, from country editors across the country. Dwight Payton—an editorial writer for *The Daily Oklahoman* in Oklahoma City and former editor and publisher of the *Overbrook (KS) Citizen*—wrote a response column in *The Daily Oklahoman* that was reprinted in *The American Press*. He was unapologetic for country editors' "old-fashioned philosophies" in support of the Ten Commandments, the teachings of Christ, and the U.S. Constitution. He observed that the country editor "believes in the dignity and glory of the individual and holds that the 'social group', which is the liberals' great love, is a soulless monstrosity typified by communists."[83] Other editors, such as Weimer Jones of the *Franklin* (NC) *Press*, offered a tempered response. As past president of the North Carolina Press Association, he accepted that "there's enough truth in what he [Obert] says to warrant some soul-searching." Jones acknowledged that some weekly editors were ill-informed and that others suffered from provincialism. However, when he considered whether or not the country press had lost its influence to run the country, he responded, "I don't think you can lose something you never had." But he noted that it was a time of opportunity for the country weekly because people had less confidence in the daily press and television and radio to cover local issues of importance. As a result, he observed, "the country press has become both a stabilizing influence and a dynamic, constructive force." The *Franklin* (NC) *Press* editor published a book in 1960, *My Affair with a Weekly*, featuring a compilation of his weekly column, "Strictly Personal." A former city newspaperman, he bought the *Franklin Press*, his hometown paper, in 1945, and his writings dealt with running a weekly and life among mountain people.[84]

The dynamic force of weekly journalism was on public display during the 1959 United States visit of Nikita Khrushchev when—at the request of *The American Press*—weekly editors from across the country delivered to the Soviet premier copies of their newspapers.[85] In soliciting editorials, newspaper copies, and letters explaining the free press to send to the Soviet leader, the trade magazine explained, "Mr. Khrushchev needs to be taught that the man who makes the decisions in our country is not the President but the voter on Main Street. He needs to learn that if he has anything to 'sell' us, he must sell the people."[86] According to the 92nd annual edition of the *N.W. Ayer & Son's Directory of Newspapers and Periodicals*, weekly newspapers climbed to a record 22.8 million (22,818,335) in paid circulation in 1959, an increase of slightly more than 100,000 copies per issue from the previous year. Of these newspapers listed in the "weekly" category, 8,990 came out once a week.[87]

A May 21, 1960 *Editor & Publisher* article titled, "The Weekly Editor: More Income," stated that there was an increase in total income for 1959 of 9.1 percent over 1958, as reported by the weekly newspapers participating in the 9th annual National Weekly Newspaper Cost Study. Expenses increased by 7.6 percent for the same period. The 1959 "composite" paper had a circulation of 3,952, 117 more than the previous year. The average newspaper income per subscriber was $30.88, up from $28.31 in 1958. The composite paper had 13.9 employees and a 1959 income of $8,757 per employee, and 284 subscribers for each employee. Advertising occupied 59 percent of the paper in 1959, compared with 54.6 percent in 1958. Local advertising was 78.5 percent, national was 9.5 percent, classified was 9 percent, and legal was 3.4 percent. The typical weekly paper published 1,101 pages in 1959, compared to 1,052 in 1958.[88] In addition, a five-year financial study of weeklies in the state of Washington found that newspapers grossed more money but kept less of it as net profit after bills were paid. The survey—sponsored by the University of Washington and the Washington Newspaper Publishers Association—looked at the financial report of 76 newspapers over five years, 1954–1958. The survey also found that 15 of those newspapers lost money after a decent salary for the publisher was deducted.[89]

So, despite criticism from their own ranks that they were too provincial and avoided controversy so as not to run off advertisers, small-town newspapers experienced resurgence during the decade. More citizens moved to the suburbs or once-rural areas and supported their new or renewed community newspaper, both in readership and advertising. As a result of the population shifts throughout the 1950s, weekly publishers happened upon a successful business model of consolidations and group ownership, centralized printing, advertising cooperatives, and localized news to sustain them into the next decade.

Notes

1 "434 Weekly Newspapers Are 100 Years Old, or Older," *The American Press* 77 (October 1959): 10.
2 "Total Circulation of Weeklies Now 17,269,183," *The American Press* 70 (July 1952): 1.
3 *N.W. Ayer & Son's Directory of Newspapers and Periodicals* (Philadelphia: N.W. Ayer & Sons, 1959).
4 Wilbur Peterson, "Loss in Country Weekly Newspapers Heavy in 1950s," *Journalism Quarterly* 38 (Winter 1961): 15, 20, 22.
5 John Cameron Sim, "Weekly Newspapers Again Facing Challenge to Move," *Journalism Quarterly* 35 (Spring 1958): 195–196.
6 Ibid., 197.
7 "Making Publishing Hay in the Suburbs," *Newsweek* 53:25 (June 22, 1959): 88.
8 "The Weekly Editor: Plant Expansion," *Editor & Publisher* 93 (September 10, 1960): 59.
9 Max Price, "The Weekly Editor," *Editor & Publisher* 93 (May 7, 1960): 32.
10 John Henry Cutler, *Put It on the Front Page, Please!* (New York: Ives Washburn, 1960). Duxbury, in Plymouth County, Massachusetts, had a population of 3,167 in 1950. *Seventeenth Census of the United States*, "Population," volume 1, section 7, 21–11, Table 6. In 2022, according to the latest government figures based on the Consumer Price Index,

$100 from 1950 was worth $1,230.53, and $25,000 from 1959 was worth $254,038. http://measuringworth.com/.

11 "The Weekly Editor: Thursdata, One for Each Hand," *Editor & Publisher* 93 (April 2, 1960): 34.
12 Bramwell Terrill, "Weekly-Inside-Daily Reaches to Suburbia," *Editor & Publisher* 93 (May 7, 1960): 14.
13 Kenneth R. Byerly, *Community Journalism* (New York: Chilton Company, 1961), 16.
14 "The Claridge-Small House Planning Bureau," *The Bessemer* (MI) *Herald*, January 19, 1950, 5. Bessemer, in Gogebic County, is located in the western upper peninsula of Michigan. Bessemer had a population of 3,509 in 1950. *Seventeenth Census of the United States*, "Population," volume 1, section 7, 22–22, Table 7. http://newspaperarchive.com/, http://www.census.gov/.
15 "How to Get Your Dream Kitchen—and SAVE," *The Bessemer* (MI) *Herald*, January 19, 1950, 7. http://newspaperarchive.com/.
16 "Ready-Print Pages No Longer Available," *The American Press* 70 (March 1952): 1, 26.
17 Ibid.
18 Alexander B. Brook, *The Hard Way: The Odyssey of a Weekly Newspaper Editor* (Bridgehampton, NY: Bridge Works Publishing Co., 1993), 20. Kennebunk, in York County, is located along the southern coastline of Maine. Kennebunk had a population of 2,576 in 1950. *Seventeenth Census of the United States*, "Population," volume 1, section 7, 19–13, Table 7. In 2022, according to the latest government figures based on the Consumer Price Index, $30,000 from 1958 was worth $307,376, 40 cents was worth $4.10, $109 was worth $1,116, $2 was worth $20, and 8,000 was worth $81,967. http://measuringworth.com/.
19 Eugene C. Harter, *Boilerplating America: The Hidden Newspaper* (Lanham, MD: University Press of America, 1991), 77. Garrett, in Indiana's DeKalb County had a population of 4,291 in 1950. *Seventeenth Census of the United States*, "Population," volume 1, section 7, 14–13, Table 6.
20 "The Weekly Editor," *Editor & Publisher* 93 (December 31, 1960): 30. In 2022, according to the latest government figures based on the Consumer Price Index, $80 from 1958 was worth $819.67, $20,000 was worth $204,917, and $10,000 was worth $102,458. http://measuringworth.com/.
21 "What Kinds of Equipment Are Being Used in the Country Newspaper Shops of America?" *The American Press* 70 (May 1952): 28, 34.
22 "Bargains Unlimited," *The Wright County* (IA) *Monitor*, November 12, 1959, 5. http://newspaperarchive.com/. Iowa's Wright County had a population of 19,652 in 1950. *Seventeenth Census of the United States*, "Population," volume 1, section 7, 15–21, Table 6.
23 Walter Rae, *Editing Small Newspapers*, 2nd ed. (New York: M.S. Mill Co. & William Morrow & Co., 1952), 189.
24 "What Kinds of Equipment Are Being Used in the Country Newspaper Shops of America?" 10–11.
25 Harter, *Boilerplating America*, 76.
26 "Says Cold Type Method of Future," *The Publishers' Auxiliary*, January 2, 1960, 2.
27 "The Weekly Editor: The Types to Wed," *Editor & Publisher* 93 (April 9, 1960): 32.

28 Rae, *Editing Small Newspapers*, 189, 190, 194.
29 "Big Opportunities," *The Publishers' Auxiliary*, January 16, 1960, 6.
30 "Paper's Switch to Cold-Type Told," *The Publishers' Auxiliary*, May 14, 1960, 2. Sharon, in Mercer County, Pennsylvania is located 75 miles northwest of Pittsburgh. Sharon had a population of 25,267 in 1960. *Eighteenth Census of the United States*, "Population," volume 1, part 2, section 40, 40–20, Table 5. http://www.census.gov/. In 2022, according to the latest government figures based on the Consumer Price Index, $15,000 from 1960 was worth $150,000. http://measuringworth.com/.
31 "What Kinds of Equipment Are Being Used in the Country Newspaper Shops of America?" 12.
32 Thomas F. Barnhart, "Recent Trends in the Weekly Newspaper Field," *Journalism Quarterly* 31 (Fall 1954): 462.
33 "Top-Quality Engravings in Your Newspaper," *The Publishers' Auxiliary*, April 9, 1960, 3.
34 "Gross Income of Weeklies Rose 15% in '51," *The American Press* 70 (July 1952): 14.
35 Don Robinson, "Barnhart Has Monopoly on Textbooks for Weekly Papers," *The American Press* 70 (October 1952): 14.
36 Barnhart, "Recent Trends in the Weekly Newspaper Field," 460–461.
37 "Weekly Publication of Facts Will Continue," *The Freeport* (TX) *Facts*, March 27, 1952, 1. Angleton, in Brazoria County, is located on the gulf coast of Texas, to the southwest of Galveston. Angleton had a population of 3,399 in 1950. *Seventeenth Census of the United States*, "Population," volume 1, section 10, 43–29, Table 7. Freeport, in Brazoria County, is located on the gulf coast of Texas, to the southwest of Galveston. Freeport had a population of 6,012 in 1950. *Seventeenth Census of the United States*, "Population," volume 1, section 10, 43–30, Table 7. http://newspaperarchive.com/, http://www.census.gov/.
38 Brook, *The Hard Way: The Odyssey of a Weekly Newspaper Editor*, 53.
39 *New Oxford* (PA) *Item-East Berlin News-Comet*, July 12, 1956, 4–5. New Oxford, in Adams County, is located in southeast Pennsylvania. New Oxford had a population of 1,366 in 1950. *Seventeenth Census of the United States*, "Population," volume 1, section 9, 38–30, Table 7. http://newspaperarchive.com/, http://www.census.gov/.
40 J.W. Rockefeller, Jr., "What's the Future of Offset for Newspapers?" *Modern Lithography* 26:5 (May 1958): 32–33, 127, 129, 131.
41 Brook, *The Hard Way: The Odyssey of a Weekly Newspaper Editor*, 120.
42 "Ready-Print Pages No Longer Available," 26.
43 Curtiss S. Johnson, "Weeklies Can't Afford to 'Go It Alone' on National Ads," *The American Press* 70 (February 1952): 16. Deep River was an unincorporated city in Connecticut's Middlesex County. Deep River had a population of 2,034 in 1950. *Seventeenth Census of the United States*, "Population," volume 1, section 10, 7–9, Table 7. http://www.census.gov/.
44 "One Great Certainty," *The Wright County* (IA) *Monitor*, November 12, 1959, 3. http://newspaperarchive.com/.
45 "These People Are Deciding Your Child's Future," *The Sikeston* (MO) *Herald*, August 1, 1957, sec. B, 6. http://newspaperarchive.com/.
46 "Weeklies Becoming Increasingly Important, Says Florida's Governor," *The American Press* 77 (October 1959): 18.

47 Wilbur Schramm and Merritt Ludwig, "The Weekly Newspaper and Its Readers." *Journalism Quarterly* 28 (Summer 1951): 301, 304, 314.
48 "Piano Recitals," *National Road Traveler*, June 16, 1955, 8. Cambridge City, in Wayne County, is located in the east-central part of Indiana. Cambridge City had a population of 2,559 in 1950. *Seventeenth Census of the United States*, "Population," volume 1, section 5, 14–19, Table 7. http://newspaperarchive.com/, http://www.census.gov/.
49 "Don't Hang Out an Invitation to Burglars to Call, Chief Bruce Warns People Going on Trips," *The Sikeston* (MO) *Herald*, August 1, 1957, 1. Sikeston, in New Madrid and Scott counties, is located in the southeastern part of Missouri. The newspaper was listed as a member of the National Editorial Association and the Missouri Press Association. Sikeston had a population of 11,640 in 1950. *Seventeenth Census of the United States*, "Population," volume 1, section 7, 25–25, Table 7. http://newspaperarchive.com/, http://www.census.gov/.
50 "Produce Prices," *The Weimar* (TX) *Mercury*, September 12, 1958, 1. Weimar, in Colorado County, is located in southeast Texas, west of Houston. Weimar had a population of 1,663 in 1950. *Seventeenth Census of the United States*, "Population," volume 1, section 10, 43–31, Table 7. http://newspaperarchive.com/, http://www.census.gov/.
51 "Climaxing American Education Week," *The Wright County* (IA) *Monitor*, November 12, 1959, 1. The *Monitor* was listed as a member of the National Editorial Association and the Iowa Press Association. Clarion, in Wright County, is located in north-central Iowa. Clarion had a population of 3,150 in 1950. *Seventeenth Census of the United States*, "Population," volume 1, section 6, 15–21, Table 7. http://newspaperarchive.com/, http://www.census.gov/.
52 *The Boyden* (IA) *Reporter*, February 8, 1951, 1. Boyden, in Sioux County, is located in northwest Iowa. Boyden had a population of 541 in 1950. *Seventeenth Census of the United States*, "Population," volume 1, section 6, 15–21, Table 7. http://newspaperarchive.com/, http://www.census.gov/.
53 "Country Papers Must Cover Local News to Survive," *The American Press* 70 (June 1952): 36.
54 Mabel Temby, "Hometown Editor Says Country Journalism Is for Me," *The National Publisher* (May 1959): 21. Kewaunee, in Kewaunee County in Wisconsin had a population of 2,583 in 1950. *Seventeenth Census of the United States*, "Population," volume 1, section 10, 49–20, Table 7. http://www.census.gov/.
55 Harter, *Boilerplating America*, 7.
56 "The Spillway," *The Florence* (AL) *Herald*, January 2, 1958, 4. Florence, in the northwest Alabama county of Lauderdale, had a population of 23,879 in 1950. *Seventeenth Census of the United States*, "Population," volume 1, section 10, 2–18, Table 7. http://www.census.gov/.
57 John D. Martin, "In-person Interview with Author" (June 23, 2009).
58 Ibid.
59 Brook, *The Hard Way: The Odyssey of a Weekly Newspaper Editor*, 141.
60 Charles T. Duncan, "How the Weekly Press Covers News of Local Government," *Journalism Quarterly* 29:2 (Summer 1952): 292–293.

61 "Barn, Cow, Hay Lost to Fire," *The Landmark*, April 6, 1954, 1. http://newspaperarchive.com/. Statesville, in Iredell County in North Carolina, had a population of 16,901 in 1950. *Seventeenth Census of the United States*, "Population," volume 1, section 10, 33–20, Table 7. http://www.census.gov/.
62 "Weeklies Too Often Viewed as Training School for City Jobs," *The American Press* 70 (January 1952): 29.
63 Brook, *The Hard Way: The Odyssey of a Weekly Newspaper Editor*, 141.
64 Geraldine Steele, "Get Acquainted with Squash Clan," *The Wright County* (IA) *Monitor*, November 12, 1959, 2. http://newspaperarchive.com/.
65 Doyle L. Moore, "County Agent's Notebook," *The Weimar* (TX) *Mercury*, September 12, 1958, 2. http://newspaperarchive.com/.
66 "11.3% of News in Weeklies is About Schools," *The American Press* 70 (January 1952): 12.
67 William M. Blair, "Greater Vigilance Urged for Press," *The New York Times*, November 22, 1952, 36.
68 "We Need Recreational Facilities for Bessemer," *The Bessemer* (MI) *Herald*, January 19, 1950, 1. http://newspaperarchive.com/.
69 Harter, *Boilerplating America*, 4.
70 Hodding Carter, *Where Main Street Meets the River* (New York: Rinehart & Company, 1953), 323, 336. Greenville, in Washington County in Mississippi, had a population of 29,936 in 1950. *Seventeenth Census of the United States*, "Population," volume 1, section 10, 24–13, Table 7. http://www.census.gov/.
71 Whiteville, in Columbus County in North Carolina, had a population of 4,238 in 1950. *Seventeenth Census of the United States*, "Population," volume 1, section 10, 33–21, Table 7. Tabor City, in Columbus County in North Carolina, had a population of 2,033 in 1950. *Seventeenth Census of the United States*, "Population," volume 1, section 10, 33–20, Table 7. http://www.census.gov/. http://www.census.gov/.
72 "Publisher Warns that Pressure Groups Threaten Survival of Small Weeklies," *The New York Times*, April 26, 1958, 40. Lexington, in Holmes County in Mississippi, had a population of 3,198 in 1950. *Seventeenth Census of the United States*, "Population," volume 1, section 10, 24–10, Table 6. Durant, in Holmes County in Mississippi, had a population of 2,311 in 1950. *Seventeenth Census of the United States*, "Population," volume 1, section 10, 24–10, Table 6. http://www.census.gov/.
73 "Shots Spatter Home of Crusading Editor," *The New York Times*, September 3, 1952, 12. Maynard, in Middlesex County in Massachusetts, had a population of 6,690 in 1950. *Seventeenth Census of the United States*, "Population," volume 1, section 10, 21–12, Table 7. http://www.census.gov/.
74 "Clinton Editor Is Cited," *The New York Times*, July 16, 1957, 18.
75 "Editor's Home Bombed," *The New York Times*, February 25, 1956, 22.
76 P.D. East, *The Magnolia Jungle: The Life, Times, and Education of a Southern Editor* (New York: Simon and Schuster, 1960), 139–143.
77 Ibid., 15, 121, 124, 128. Petal, in Forrest County in Mississippi, had a population of 2,148 in 1950. *Seventeenth Census of the United States*, "Population," volume 1, section 10, 24–9, Table 6. http://www.census.gov/.

78 "Peace, Good Will—Ku Klux Klan Version," *The Monroe Journal*, December 17, 1959, 1. Monroeville, in Monroe County, is located in the south-central part of Alabama. Monroeville had a population of 2,772 in 1950. *Seventeenth Census of the United States*, "Population," volume 1, section 4, 2–18, Table 7. http://www.census.gov/.

79 "Editor Pushes Drive to Recall McCarthy," *The New York Times*, March 20, 1954, 7; "McCarthy Critic Supported Here," *The New York Times*, April 10, 1954, 9; "McCarthy Attacker Attacked," *The New York Times*, April 16, 1954, 13; "Gore Sells Newspaper," *The New York Times*, February 25, 1955, 19; "'Joe Must Go Club' Wins," *The New York Times*, June 2, 1955, 33. Sauk City, in Sauk County in Wisconsin had a population of 1,755 in 1950. *Seventeenth Census of the United States*, "Population," volume 1, section 10, 49–21, Table 7. Prairie Du Sac, in Sauk County in Wisconsin had a population of 1,402 in 1950. *Seventeenth Census of the United States*, "Population," volume 1, section 10, 49–20, Table 7. http://www.census.gov/.http://www.census.gov/.

80 Ted Conover, "Only 42% of the Smaller Ohio Weeklies Publish Editorials," *The American Press* 77 (September 1959): 10.

81 "Less than 4% of Southern Papers for Truman; Taft, Eisenhower Run Neck and Neck as Favorites in Nation-Wide Poll of Country Editors," *The American Press* 70 (April 1952): 1.

82 John C. Obert, "Whatever Happened to the Country Press?" *Nieman Reports*, July 1959, 14.

83 "Says 'Nieman Fellow' Portrays Country Editors as 'Moss-Brains,'" *The American Press* 77 (September 1959): 18.

84 Weimer Jones, "Liberalism and the Country Press," *The Iowa Publisher* (November 1960): 4–5; Weimer Jones, *My Affair with a Weekly* (Winston-Salem, NC: J.F. Blair, 1960). Franklin, in Macon County in North Carolina, had a population of 1,975 in 1950. *Seventeenth Census of the United States*, "Population," volume 1, section 10, 33–19, Table 7. http://www.census.gov/.

85 "List 9,353 Weekly Papers with 22 Million Subscribers," *The Publishers' Auxiliary*, May 7, 1960, 1.

86 "Khrushchev Bombarded with Weekly Newspapers While Visiting in Washington," *The American Press* 77 (October 1959): 14.

87 *N.W. Ayer & Son's Directory of Newspapers and Periodicals* (Philadelphia: N.W. Ayer & Sons, 1959).

88 "The Weekly Editor: More Income," *Editor & Publisher* 93 (May 21, 1960): 34. In 2022, according to the latest government figures based on the Consumer Price Index, $30.88 from 1959 was worth $344.27, $28.31 from 1958 was worth $290, and $8,575 from 1959 was worth $87,135. http://measuringworth.com/.

89 Lee Irwin, "Weeklies' Profits Sink While Incomes Rise," *The Publishers' Auxiliary*, March 5, 1960, 6.

References

"11.3% of News in Weeklies Is About Schools." *The American Press* 70 (January 1952): 12.

"434 Weekly Newspapers Are 100 Years Old, or Older." *The American Press* 77 (October 1959): 10, 28, 30, 34.

"Bargains Unlimited." *The Wright County* (IA) *Monitor*, November 12, 1959, 5.
"Barn, Cow, Hay Lost to Fire." *The Landmark*, Statesville, NC, April 6, 1954, 1.
Barnhart, Thomas F. "Recent Trends in the Weekly Newspaper Field." *Journalism Quarterly* 31 (Fall 1954): 459–465.
"Big Opportunities." *The Publishers' Auxiliary*, January 16, 1960, 6.
Blair, William M. "Greater Vigilance Urged for Press." *The New York Times*, November 22, 1952, 36.
The Boyden (IA) *Reporter*, February 8, 1951, 1.
Brook, Alexander B. *The Hard Way: The Odyssey of a Weekly Newspaper Editor.*
Byerly, Kenneth R. *Community Journalism.* New York: Chilton Company, 1961.
Carter, Hodding. *Where Main Street Meets the River.* New York: Rinehart & Company, 1953.
"The Claridge-Small House Planning Bureau." *The Bessemer* (MI) *Herald*, January 19, 1950, 5.
"Climaxing American Education Week." *The Wright County* (IA) *Monitor*, November 12, 1959, 1.
"Clinton Editor Is Cited." *The New York Times*, July 16, 1957, 18.
Conover, Ted. "Only 42% of the Smaller Ohio Weeklies Publish Editorials." *The American Press* 77 (September 1959): 10.
"Country Papers Must Cover Local News to Survive." *The American Press* 70 (June 1952): 36.
Cutler, John Henry. *Put It On The Front Page, Please!* New York: Ives Washburn, 1960.
"Don't Hang Out an Invitation to Burglars to Call, Chief Bruce Warns People Going on Trips." *The Sikeston* (MO) *Herald*, August 1, 1957, 1.
Duncan, Charles T. "How the Weekly Press Covers News of Local Government." *Journalism Quarterly* 29:2 (Summer 1952): 283–293.
East, P.D. *The Magnolia Jungle: The Life, Times, and Education of a Southern Editor.* New York: Simon and Schuster, 1960.
"Editor Pushes Drive to Recall McCarthy." *The New York Times*, March 20, 1954, 7.
"Editor's Home Bombed." *The New York Times*, February 25, 1956, 22.
"Gore Sells Newspaper." *The New York Times*, February 25, 1955, 19.
"Gross Income Of Weeklies Rose 15% In '51." *The American Press* 70 (July 1952): 14.
Harter, Eugene C. *Boilerplating America: The Hidden Newspaper.* Lanham, MD: University Press of America, 1991.
"How To Get Your Dream Kitchen—and SAVE." *The Bessemer* (MI) *Herald*, January 19, 1950, 7.
Irwin, Lee. "Weeklies' Profits Sink While Incomes Rise." *The Publishers' Auxiliary*, March 5, 1960, 6.
"'Joe Must Go Club' Wins." *The New York Times*, June 2, 1955, 33.
Johnson, Curtiss S. "Weeklies Can't Afford to 'Go It Alone' on National Ads." *The American Press* 70 (February 1952): 16.
Jones, Weimer. "Liberalism and the Country Press." *The Iowa Publisher* (November 1960): 4–5.
Jones, Weimer. *My Affair with a Weekly.* Winston-Salem, NC: J.F. Blair, 1960.
"Khrushchev Bombarded with Weekly Newspapers While Visiting in Washington." *The American Press* 77 (October 1959): 14.

"Less than 4% of Southern Papers for Truman; Taft, Eisenhower Run Neck and Neck as Favorites in Nation-Wide Poll of Country Editors." *The American Press* 70 (April 1952), 1.

"List 9,353 Weekly Papers with 22 Million Subscribers." *The Publishers' Auxiliary*, May 7, 1960, 1.

"Making Publishing Hay in the Suburbs." *Newsweek* 53:25 (June 22, 1959): 88–89.

Martin, John D. "In-Person Interview with Author." June 23, 2009.

"McCarthy Attacker Attacked." *The New York Times*, April 16, 1954, 13.

"McCarthy Critic Supported Here." *The New York Times*, April 10, 1954, 9.

Moore, Doyle L. "County Agent's Notebook." *The Weimar* (TX) *Mercury*, September 12, 1958, 2.

New Oxford (PA) *Item-East Berlin News-Comet*, July 12, 1956, 4–5.

N.W. Ayer & Son's Directory of Newspapers and Periodicals. Philadelphia: N.W. Ayer & Sons, 1959.

Obert, John C. "Whatever Happened to the Country Press?" *Neiman Reports*, July 1959, 14–17.

"One Great Certainty." *The Wright County* (IA) *Monitor*, November 12, 1959, 3.

"Paper's Switch to Cold-Type Told." *The Publishers' Auxiliary*, May 14, 1960, 2.

"Peace, Good Will—Ku Klux Klan Version." *The Monroe Journal*, Monroeville, AL, December 17, 1959, 1.

Peterson, Wilbur. "Loss in Country Weekly Newspapers Heavy in 1950s." *Journalism Quarterly* 38 (Winter 1961): 15–24.

"Piano Recitals." *National Road Traveler*, Cambridge City, IN, June 16, 1955, 8.

Price, Max. "The Weekly Editor." *Editor & Publisher* 93:19 (May 7, 1960): 32, 34.

"Produce Prices." *The Weimar* (TX) *Mercury*, September 12, 1958, 1.

"Publisher Warns that Pressure Groups Threaten Survival of Small Weeklies." *The New York Times*, April 26, 1958, 40.

Rae, Walter. *Editing Small Newspapers*. 2nd ed. New York: M.S. Mill Co. & William Morrow & Co., 1952.

"Ready-Print Pages No Longer Available." *The American Press* 70 (March 1952): 1, 26.

A Report of the Seventeenth Dicennial Census of the United States, Census of Population: 1950. edited by United States Bureau of the Census: Washington, D.C.; Government Printing Office, 1952.

Robinson, Don. "Barnhart Has Monopoly on Textbooks for Weekly Papers." *The American Press* 70 (October 1952): 14.

Rockefeller, J.W., Jr. "What's the Future of Offset for Newspapers?" *Modern Lithography* 26:5 (May 1958): 32–33, 127, 129, 131.

"Says Cold Type Method of Future." *The Publishers' Auxiliary*, January 2, 1960, 2.

"Says 'Nieman Fellow' Portrays Country Editors As 'Moss-Brains.'" *The American Press* 77 (September 1959): 18.

Schramm, Wilbur, and Merritt Ludwig. "The Weekly Newspaper and Its Readers." *Journalism Quarterly* 28 (Summer 1951): 301–314.

Seventeenth Census of the United States: 1950: Population. Edited by United States Bureau of the Census. Washington, DC: Government Printing Office, 1953.

"Shots Spatter Home of Crusading Editor." *The New York Times*, September 3, 1952, 12.

Sim, John Cameron. "Weekly Newspapers Again Facing Challenge to Move." *Journalism Quarterly* 35 (Spring 1958): 195–198.

"The Spillway." *The Florence* (AL) *Herald*, January 2, 1958, 4.

Steele, Geraldine. "Get Acquainted with Squash Clan." *The Wright County* (IA) *Monitor*, November 12, 1959, 2.

Temby, Mabel. "Hometown Editor Says Country Journalism Is for Me." *The National Publisher* (May 1959): 21.

Terrill, Bramwell. "Weekly-Inside-Daily Reaches to Suburbia." *Editor & Publisher* 93:19 (May 7, 1960): 14.

"These People Are Deciding Your Child's Future." *The Sikeston* (MO) *Herald*, August 1, 1957, 6.

"Top-Quality Engravings in Your Newspaper." *The Publishers' Auxiliary*, April 9, 1960, 3.

"Total Circulation of Weeklies Now 17,269,183." *The American Press* 70 (July 1952): 1.

"Weeklies Becoming Increasingly Important, Says Florida's Governor." *The American Press* 77 (October 1959): 18.

"Weeklies Too Often Viewed as Training School for City Jobs." *The American Press* 70 (January 1952): 29.

"The Weekly Editor." *Editor & Publisher* 93:53 (December 31,1960): 30.

"The Weekly Editor: More Income." *Editor & Publisher* 93:21 (May 21, 1960): 34.

"The Weekly Editor: Plant Expansion." *Editor & Publisher* 93:37 (September 10, 1960): 59.

"The Weekly Editor: Thursdata, One For Each Hand." *Editor & Publisher* 93:14 (April 2, 1960): 34.

"The Weekly Editor: The Types to Wed." *Editor & Publisher* 93:15 (April 9, 1960): 32.

"Weekly Publication of Facts Will Continue." *The Freeport* (TX) *Facts*, March 27, 1952, 1.

"We Need Recreational Facilities for Bessemer." *The Bessemer* (MI) *Herald*, January 19, 1950, 1.

"What Kinds of Equipment Are Being Used in the Country Newspaper Shops of America?" *The American Press* 70 (May 1952): 10–13, 34–35.

www.measuringworth.com.

· 7 ·

THE 1960S: A TIME TO RETHINK, REDEFINE, RECRUIT, AND REGIONALIZE

The 1960s brought rethinking, redefining, recruiting, and the regional concept to the community weekly newspaper field. First, a newly defined approach to journalism, referred to as "community journalism," became popular as journalists took on a more activist role in shaping the news. Second, there was a concerted effort on the part of many weekly journalists to remove the term "country" or "rural" and any stereotypes related to those terms from the weekly newspaper field. Third, aggressive recruitment tactics were undertaken in the areas of staffing, circulation, advertising, and professional associations to hold back growing competition from encroaching dailies, suburban weeklies, and free-circulation shoppers. Fourth, a regional concept enabled weeklies to expand their circulation base and production capabilities to reduce operating costs and increase their attractiveness to national advertisers.

Several important books and articles published in the 1960s related to the community leadership role of the small-town newspaper and its influence on community decision-making. The role of the editorial, opinion column and personal column was explored, as was the impact of the community newspaper in creating news as opposed to reporting it. However, this so-called new approach of "community journalism" merely acknowledged something that weeklies had been doing all along.

For decades the stand-alone community weekly was most often referred to as a "rural" or "country" newspaper. The majority of weeklies did operate from small towns that were miles away from metropolitan areas during the first half of the twentieth century. However, that changed during the 1950s when once-rural communities grew and suburbs sprang up around metropolitan areas. Thus, the weeklies that served the newly established and growing communities expanded their coverage from mostly agriculture issues. Weekly journalists believed that the "rural" and "country" labels were too confining for their profession and should be eliminated.

Weeklies throughout the 1960s aggressively sought highly skilled production staffs to handle modern printing equipment. Only a handful of hand-set type shops remained that required only family members plus a few vagabond printers to produce a newspaper. The period experienced a shortage of skilled labor; so, the centralized printing plant became a workable option for newspaper groups to staff the advanced technological operations.

Recruiting more subscribers also became a concern for weeklies as free-circulation newspapers and shoppers threatened their financial livelihood. Weeklies also had to compete with metropolitan dailies that—in their attempt to fight for suburban readers—began to insert "weeklies" within their papers to cater to nearby neighborhood communities.

Recruiting for advertisers continued as weeklies explored ways to offer incentive packages and appeal to the ever-expanding suburban shopping centers that were closing down many family-owned stores in the small-town business districts. Weeklies also devised attention-getting stunts and promotions to bring attention to their advertisers.

Professional organizations specifically geared to weeklies aggressively recruited members and focused attention on certain areas of interest or business models, such as editorial writing or the growing suburban weekly field.

And finally, the regional concept changed the business landscape of the weekly newspaper industry to the point that it became the survival model for most weeklies. The regional concept included such practices as group ownership, joint operating arrangements, and centralized printing to manage personnel and costs.

Community Journalism: New Term, Old Practice

In 1961, Kenneth R. Byerly published *Community Journalism*—which had the distinction of defining in its title the type of journalism practiced in community weeklies. Previous texts on the small-town press referred to "country journalism" and "rural editors"—which seemed to describe more the geography of the subject matter than the nature of the news. An exception was the 1923 book, *The Community Newspaper*, co-authored by Emerson P. Harris and Florence Harris Hooke.[1] In Byerly's 1961 work, the University of North Carolina journalism professor explored the type of journalism practiced at weeklies that distinguished them from their metropolitan daily counterparts. He had personal knowledge of the subject, having served as the owner of a semi-weekly in Virginia and as the owner and publisher of weekly and daily newspapers in Wyoming and Montana.

Certainly a distinguishing characteristic among many weeklies was that they reported news from areas that no other print media outlets covered, or that were only minimally mentioned in regional dailies. *The Titonka Topic* in Titonka, Iowa—a member of the Iowa Press Association and the National Editorial Association—made the claim above its front-page banner that it "[t]horoughly covers a territory that is reached by no other paper."[2] *The Seguin* (TX) *Gazette* promised its readers in the paper's policy statement, "To publish the news as it happens, pointing out its significance to Guadalupe County ...."[3] So, not only did the *The Seguin Gazette* cover the area's news—which might be included in a regional daily—but it also explained the significance of events to its readers. For example, in reporting on the upcoming publication of the city's directory, *The Seguin Gazette* emphasized the importance of the directory as a resource for community residents. "Everyone gets his name in print without dying, marrying, running for office (and being elected or defeated), having an accident, being arrested, being quoted as to his opinion on some public question, or winning a sweepstakes jackpot," the article observed.[4] *The Seguin Gazette* was a member of the Texas Press Association, South Texas Press Association, National Editorial Association, Advertising Checking Bureau, Weekly Major Markets, and other booster organizations. The paper promoted itself as being Texas' First Triple Service Award Winner for community service in 1958–1962, agriculture in 1959, and industry in 1960. The paper was established in 1846 as the *Seguin Mercury*, later incorporating the *Western Texian*, *The Journal*, *The Seguin Times*, *The Seguin Record*,

The Seguin Anchor, The Guadalupe Gazette, The Seguin Zeitung, The Seguin Bulletin, The Guadalupe Gazette-Bulletin, and finally, *The Seguin Gazette.*

So, while national leaders wrestled with larger issues—communism, a space race with the Soviets, the threat of nuclear war and the Cuban missile crisis, assassinations of political leaders, civil rights protests, a black power movement, a burgeoning psychedelic drug culture, peaceful and violent anti-Vietnam War demonstrations, race riots, and a growing feminist movement—community weekly publishers and editors attempted to help their readers make sense of it all. Efforts to localize larger issues and explain their significance to local residents were the challenge of small-town newspapers engaged in community journalism.

Studies Explore Weeklies' Role in Leadership, Decision-making

Several academic studies in the 1960s explored the concept of community journalism as it related to community leadership and decision-making. Among them were: Alex S. Edelstein and Otto N. Larsen, "The Weekly Press' Contribution to a Sense of Urban Community," *Journalism Quarterly* 37 (Autumn 1960); William V. D'Antonio et al., "Institutional and Occupational Representatives in Eleven Community Influence Systems," *American Sociological Review* 26:3 (June 1961); Alex S. Edelstein and J. Blaine Schultz, "The Weekly Newspaper's Leadership Role as Seen by Community Leaders," *Journalism Quarterly* 40 (Autumn 1963); Alex S. Edelstein and Joseph J. Contris, "The Public View of the Weekly Newspaper's Leadership Role," *Journalism Quarterly* 43 (Spring 1966); Phillip J. Tichenor, Clarice N. Olien, and George Donohue, "Predicting a Source's Success in Placing News in the Media," (*Journalism Quarterly* 44:1, 1967); and Clarice N. Olien, George A. Donohue, and Phillip J. Tichenor, "The Community Editor's Power and the Reporting of Conflict," *Journalism Quarterly* 45 (Summer 1968).

A 1961 sociological study summarized the findings of 11 case studies pertaining to community power and concluded that—contrary to the tendency for editors and their newspapers to be ignored in these studies—"understanding the local decision-making process may not be possible without giving adequate attention to the strategy position of the newspaper editor." Authors of the study noted that "major issues have been successfully resolved or blocked by the position taken by the newspaper editor."[5]

There were numerous efforts within the weekly field to engage in community journalism. For example, editors of the *Burlington* (WI) *Standard Press* hosted a panel discussion with 10 leading citizens and their wives to establish a newspaper code of ethics. The panel was held following the publication of a story concerning a sex scandal that involved a Burlington alderman. The community reaction against the story was strong although the meeting participants agreed that a double standard on whether or not to print a story should not exist, regardless of the individual involved. The panel decided that people who committed sex offenses were mentally ill and their offenses should not be reported because it would embarrass family and friends, and children could be corrupted by reading sexually offensive stories. Editor William E. Branned said that the community members gave the impression that newspapers should protect the offender rather than the offended. He said that reporting unfavorable news was not an enjoyable task, but a serious one, and that, "a moral obligation can never be modified."[6]

It is not surprising that the Burlington panel participants had such strong opinions about their newspapers' ethics because active citizens were more likely to read the local newspaper, according to author Robert Dahl. In his 1961 work, *Who Governs?*, he pointed out that if politicians were convinced that the newspaper influenced public opinion, a publisher had some control over the choices politicians were likely to make. However, a politician skeptical of a publisher's influence on the attitudes of voters—or confident of his own capacity to offset editorial criticism—was more likely to chance a fight with the newspaper.[7]

Alex Edelstein and J. Blaine Schulz also explored community leaders' perceptions of the weekly editor's leadership role. Writing about their findings in a 1963 issue of *Journalism Quarterly*, they reported on a panel discussion among 46 community leaders, of which only one believed that it was the newspaper's role to initiate community projects. The majority of panelists said newspapers should work jointly with community leaders to initiate projects. Nearly 40 percent, however, said the newspaper's role was merely to provide publicity on community projects. As in the Burlington panel discussion, these 46 community leaders were also questioned about controversial content in the local newspaper. Two-thirds of the leaders said the newspaper should publish controversy only when it could not avoid doing so. Only one-third said that newspapers should take the initiative to bring controversies to the public's attention. Edelstein and Schulz then asked the same questions about newspaper leadership roles to a group of weekly editors gathered for an annual meeting of the Washington Newspaper Publishers' Association. In addition to a survey, the authors conducted personal interviews with 117 weekly newspaper publishers in the state. They found that the editors who had the clearest perception of the power structure tended to work with community leaders before "initiating" any community project. Working jointly with community leaders appeared to be typical for "community editors" as opposed to "journalist-editors" who had a much stronger identification with the traditional watchdog role of the press.[8]

After community and newspaper leaders were surveyed for their views on the weekly newspaper's leadership role, Alex Edelstein and Joseph J. Contris conducted a similar study to examine the views of the general public on the subject. Reporting on the study in a 1966 issue of *Journalism Quarterly*, it was revealed that 20 percent of persons surveyed approved of "action" or "avoidance" behavior, while 75 percent asked that the newspaper "print both sides." This was interpreted to mean that the public did not want the newspaper to polarize community attitudes on highly controversial issues—a value shared with community leaders, or "elites." In addition, the study revealed that the public expected the newspaper to monitor tax spending, to discover and expose political corruption, and to report crime incidents. However, the public preferred a limited editorial role in publicizing and criticizing actions of government officials.[9]

To Uphold or Scold: A Can-Do or Can't-Do Approach to Advocacy

In its role as a community advocate, it was not uncommon for a weekly to become a rallying force in times of hardship rather than simply a reporter of doom and gloom. For example, publisher Charles Deal of the *Keynoter* in the Florida Keys placed a new slogan across the masthead of his weekly following the heavy destruction of the central Florida Keys in 1960 from Hurricane Donna. The slogan bragged, "A Freebootin' Newspaper What Covers What's Left!" Even though the area was heavily damaged—including a portion of the *Keynoter* plant—the paper became a rallying force for the community. Deal observed, "If we've kept up spirits and nudged people into action, then we've done what any good newspaper of any size would want to do."[10] In Telluride, Colorado, some might say that a community newspaper saved the town from extinction in the early 1960s. John and Bettye McPhee started *The Telluride*

Times in 1963, some 50 years after the town's coal mining industry shut down and started a steady decline of industry and inhabitants. The newspaper initiated a "Clean-up, Paint-Up" campaign and was a motivating force to improve roadways to attract more tourists to the area.[11]

The close relationship between a community and its weekly was not only expressed in a "can do" attitude, but also included a scolding on occasion. For example, the *Kennebunk* (ME) *Star* publisher printed his feelings about some of his readers above the front-page banner. After a rough day with difficult subscribers who canceled their subscriptions, publisher Alexander Brook picked out the initials of what he'd been muttering—T.H.W.T.B.—and printed it in small type over the paper's price amount. A few observant readers asked Brook what the letters stood for, as did a *Time* magazine reporter who did a story on bragging mastheads. The September 29, 1961 *Time* article reported that when asked about the mysterious initials, Brook "halfheartedly explained that they stood for THE HARD WAY'S THE BEST. In fact, they represented the classic cry of exasperated newsmen everywhere: To Hell with the Bastards!" Brook kept the initials on the nameplate until he sold the paper—renamed the *York County Star*—in 1977.[12]

Debate continued throughout the decade on whether a weekly had to maintain a strong editorial voice to be considered a community leader. There remained a group of weekly editors who were too timid to criticize town officials or merchants for fear of boycotts or lost advertising revenue. But a stronger voice seemed to be emerging in favor of editorial leadership. In response to the push for more local editorial writing, a new quarterly magazine for the weekly newspaper field began publishing in 1960. The magazine, *Grassroots Editor*, was the official organ of the International Conference of Weekly Newspaper Editors—headquartered at Southern Illinois University. The goal of the magazine and the organization was to enhance the editorial effectiveness of the small community newspaper. A similarly titled publication, the *Grass Roots Digest*, had been established in 1949 on the campus of the University of Missouri. The International Conference of Weekly Newspaper Editors also annually presented its Elijah P. Lovejoy awards—named for the martyred abolitionist printer—which were given to weekly and small daily editors for courageous performance in the face of economic, political, or social pressures against them and their publications.[13] After reading a number of I.C.W.N.E. conference reviews written by weekly editors in their local columns, *Editor & Publisher* columnist Rick Friedman observed that instead of the usual "shop talk" that prevailed at most newspaper professional meetings,

I.C.W.N.E. conference participants were able to focus on independent editorial comment and leadership in weekly newspapers.[14]

The importance of a strong editorial role among weeklies was further explored in 1967 when Trinity University journalism professor Paul R. Busch surveyed 30 award-winning weeklies across the country. The newspapers were from 30 states representing all regions of "the lower 48" and Alaska and Hawaii. They were selected for the study based on the number of national and state general excellence awards each had received from professional newspaper associations. He found that the editors of these papers supported strong editorial pages. Of the papers, 27 had an editorial page, and eight used their own editorial cartoonist. He also found, however, that many of them included editorial page columns from their congressmen.[15]

Among weeklies with a strong local editorial voice was *The Florence (AL) Herald*. A 1963 column in *The Florence Herald* on the topic of editorials observed, "The editorial you read from time to time may not present the side you like or the side you are familiar with but they [editorials] reflect thought and their importance in stimulating interest for issues that concern the average citizen cannot be taken lightly." It added that, fortunately, "most of those who follow the newspaper calling know their responsibility and follow it well."[16]

Some weekly editors gained notoriety for not mincing words, while others took a more diplomatic approach to defend their stance or explain why certain issues were not addressed. "I write it like I see it, and I talk like I feel," stated longtime *New Richmond* (WI) *News* editor-publisher John Van Meter. A November 1964 *Editor & Publisher* article described him as "one of the last of the breed of gadfly weekly journalists, a man alternately hated, feared, applauded, loved and always regarded with awe in his own home town." Also serving as his town's mayor, he wrote a column that carried the motto, "Don't undertake vast projects with half-vast ideas." The title of his editorial column was "IMPORTANT-if true." The *New Richmond News* was founded by Van Meter's grandfather, Abe Van Meter, in 1869. Of its 2,800 circulation, about 800 papers were sold on the newsstands to people who claimed they would not subscribe just on general principles.[17]

The Guthrian in Guthrie Center, Iowa, used a November 26, 1963 editorial as a means to explain to its readers how some items were included in the newspaper and others not. The editorial stated that shortage of space was the most common reason for excluding material. It further explained that most newspapers used what it termed "time filler" for unanticipated open spaces. The editorial concluded, "Some filler is good, and some is just junk." The newspaper's nameplate featured a hawk eye illustration with two banners below—to the left, "agriculture and livestock" and to the right, "in Iowa where the tall corn grows." It was noted that *The Guthrian* was the county's official newspaper.[18]

But despite strong advocacy by *The Grassroots Editor* and individual editors to have a strong editorial voice, the overall record among weeklies was spotty. For example, a study of 215 non-daily Iowa newspapers (published during November 1960) found only 41 percent with editorial pages, compared to 63 percent in a similar 1930 study. More specifically, the study, reported in a 1962 *Journalism Quarterly* issue, found that only 27 percent of Iowa weeklies with a circulation of less than 2,500 had editorial pages.[19] In fact, the editor of Michigan's largest and most successful weekly challenged what he described as the "so-called" political power of the country's "rural newspapers" because so few of them ran editorials. In a 1962 interview with *Time* magazine, Robert Myers, publisher of the 13,000-circulation *Lapeer County Press* outside of Detroit, observed that more than half of the country's weeklies did not print editorials. Thus, he asserted that America's rural newspapers were "valueless, lily-livered and moribund" and run by "printers" who stuffed their pages with syndicated "hayseed" features.[20]

Stronger words concerning the lack or misuse of editorials in weeklies came from media critic Ben H. Bagdikian in a 1964 *Harper's Magazine* article. He criticized the weekly press for not writing local editorials and for diluting or misusing syndicate editorials in which the true source was concealed or minimized. He explained that the syndicates provided editorial services free of charge to weeklies and made their money by charging an association or a company a fee to place its point of view or a hidden commercial pitch within the editorial copy. As a result, Bagdikian asserted that "almost any private citizen or special group can buy his way into the editorial columns of smaller papers with relative ease and low cost."[21]

Editorial complaints similar to those Bagdikian leveled against the weeklies were echoed in the criticisms of John C. Obert, editor of the *Park Region (MN) Echo*, in the April 1964 issue of *Quill* magazine. He claimed that weekly editors shied away from controversy in editorials because they were concerned about not upsetting local businessmen. A June 1964 editorial in *The American Press* agreed with Obert's assertion that newspapers should incorporate editorials. However, it observed that running a controversial editorial each week could be "laying it on a little heavy, both for the community and the busy editor." It added that the solution was not "rippin' 'em up" once a week but rather "an editorial menu of fresh thinking" based on whether it was possible to accomplish an editorial's aim.[22]

Progressive, Provincial, or Politically Conservative

In his book on community journalism, Kenneth R. Byerly asserted that the term "country weekly" was misleading because it gave the tonal impression that country weeklies "have the rustic quaintness so often depicted by fiction and scenario writers." Byerly's work looked at the leadership role of small-town newspapers as opposed to homespun tales of trivia in the aforementioned fiction and non-fiction works. He quoted well-known retail magnate John Wanamaker as saying, "Give me a strong newspaper, and I'll show you a thriving town. Show me a weak newspaper, and I'll show you a town that's going backward. A progressive town means a progressive newspaper. No community is any stronger than its own newspaper. It's the life blood of every community."[23]

However, publishing at least one newspaper in every county was no longer a certainty because of a changing business climate. In fact, by 1960 there were only two weeklies (28 in 1910) in Missouri that were published in towns of 200 or less and only 105 weeklies (345 in 1910) in towns of less than 1,000.[24] John W. Hughes, secretary and business manager of weeklies in and around Calhoun, Georgia, noted that emigration from some rural areas meant that a newspaper exclusively "for that particular political subdivision [county] cannot be justified economically." He said that a central, jointly owned printing plant was the only means possible to reduce capital investments to a level that would allow newspapers to continue operating in low-population areas. A central printing plant was especially beneficial to weekly publishers, who were "by talent and inclination editors rather than businessmen or production specialists," added Hughes.[25]

"Country" editors had to fight accusations of being provincial and more politically conservative than the general population. Mississippi editor and author Hodding Carter criticized rural journalism critics and their use of the word "provincialism" as applied to behavior and folkways associated with the "American hinterlands." In his 1963 book, *First Person Rural*, he observed that "you can find hicks in New York City" and "world citizens in Lawrence, or Emporia, or Greenville." While he acknowledged that small newspapers had only limited political influence, he stressed that "their local news columns give a sense of individual existence and individual worth to millions of Americans."[26] A September 19, 1963 editorial in *The Florence* (AL) *Herald* stated that the editor of a small-town weekly was in a unique position because he knew all members of his community and they knew how to reach him at all times. It further observed that the editor had the "heavy responsibility" of recording not only local news, but state, national, and international news as well. It concluded, "Local editors and school teachers are largely responsible for the thinking that will protect America from forces, both within and without, that would destroy the freedom we enjoy."[27]

But some weekly editors were just as likely as daily newspapermen to criticize their peers for being too provincial. Outspoken critic Robert Myers, of the *Lapeer County* (MI) *Press*, claimed that part of his success in publishing the country's largest weekly was to get rid of some "sacred cows" in rural journalism. For example, he refused to participate in community drives or censor unfavorable coverage for a large advertiser. Also, he printed drunk-driving charges, regardless of the offender.[28] He did, however, retain one characteristic of country weeklies, the personal column, and incorporated it multiple times to the extent that his newspaper ran 16 columns each week. Of these, 10 columns were written by non-staffers—but all of the columnists were local residents. In addition, 16 correspondents contributed regularly to the publication. Column features included "Farm Program News," "The Green Thumb," "Rural Route One," and "Got a Problem?" Publisher Robert Myers wrote two regular columns, one on farming, and "Owner's Report," on the newspaper. Editor Jim Fitzgerald also contributed two columns, "Side Roads," containing local comments, and "If it Fitz," a wide-ranging commentary with a humorous twist.[29]

The assertion of weekly editors being more politically conservative than the general population was often supported in presidential polls that found them supporting the conservative candidate in larger percentages. This factor was affirmed in a 1960 presidential poll by *The Publishers' Auxiliary* that predicted Vice President Richard M. Nixon would defeat Massachusetts U.S. Senator John F. Kennedy "if the newspaper executives accurately reflect their community's feelings." Roughly 62 percent of weekly editors and publishers said their communities would support Nixon, while their personal preference for Nixon was upped to 65 percent. Nearly 4,000 surveys were returned from daily and weekly editors, although the exact number of weekly editor responses was not indicated. Senator John F. Kennedy later won the race by a narrow margin.[30] A similar result was found four years later when *The American Press* conducted a pre-election poll in September 1964 on the Lyndon Johnson-Barry Goldwater race. The poll asked daily and weekly publishers in the under-50,000 circulation category which candidate their readers would support. The results found that of the 500 publishers from 46 states who responded to the poll, U.S. Arizona Senator Barry Goldwater won the straw poll, 60.6 percent to 39.4 percent for President Lyndon Johnson, who was returned to office in a landslide vote.[31]

But, despite criticisms of being politically conservative and "soft" in news coverage, weekly editors asserted that their writers and editors practiced journalism just as vigorously and professionally as their daily counterparts. Letters sent to a September 17, 1960 issue of *Editor & Publisher's* "The Weekly Editor" column strongly decried an earlier column by a New York weekly associate editor who labeled country weeklies as provincial. One letter writer noted that more weeklies were being established or taken over by former daily newspapermen—many of them journalism school graduates with "a real nose for news and understanding of and practice in good typography and makeup." The letter speculated that daily journalists took satisfaction in "looking down their collective noses" at the weekly press only because they were disconcerted that weeklies were more widely read and enjoyed an editorial influence and community prestige beyond most dailies, and that weeklies filled a need and fulfilled a responsibility "which no other publication of any kind achieves."[32]

Sociologists Point to "Self-congratulatory" Reporting in Weeklies

Arthur J. Vidich and Joseph Bensman were not so concerned that weeklies were "rustic" or "quaint" in their coverage, but that they provided an unrealistic reflection of their communities. Vidich and Bensman explored the foundations of social life of a small northeastern town in their 1968 work—*Small Town in Mass Society*—and pointed out that "the belief in the superiority of local ways of living actually conditions the way of life." Their premise was based on the observation that the weekly emphasized the positive side of life, such as—job promotions, school achievements, local boy makes good in big city, man opens own business, contest winners, and athletic high scorers. The authors described such news items as "self-congratulatory newspaper articles."

According to the authors, a constant newspaper focus on warm and human qualities in all public situations resulted in the public character of the community taking on those qualities—a tone that was distinctly different from city life.[33]

A 1965 study of Minnesota weeklies had similar findings. Sociologists Clarice Olien, George Donohue, and Phillip Tichenor hypothesized that the location of the editor or publisher in the community power structure had some bearing on conflict reporting. They studied four issues each from the month of February 1965 of 88 Minnesota weeklies. They found that half of the newspapers reported no controversy and thus determined that whether a paper reported conflict was associated with how power was divided within a community. For example, in larger, more pluralistic communities where power was divided among more groups and individuals, there tended to be more reporting of community conflict in the local newspaper than in smaller communities where the power structure was more centralized and controlling of the local press. The study also added insight into the relationship of the editor to the community power and leadership structure.[34]

Certainly, as was the tradition of small-town journalism, there were numerous examples of "self-congratulatory" types of reporting in community newspapers during the time of the Vidich and Bensman study. A large, front-page photo in the March 8, 1962 issue of *The Desert Sentinel*—a Desert Hot Springs, California, weekly—showed a local high school student in front of his award-winning display at the 21st Westinghouse Science Talent Search in Washington, D.C.[35] An editorial viewpoint column in the January 29, 1964 issue of *The Seguin* (TX) *Gazette* titled "The Unsung Builders" promoted the area's advertising merchants, who were described as "intelligent and brave enough to invest in the community." The editorial encouraged readers to "support them because they're supporting you."[36] *The Titonka* (IA) *Topic* carried a weekly report, "The Bowler's Corner," in the upper left corner of its front-page featuring scores from local bowling league teams.[37] *The Rock Valley* (IA) *Bee*—proclaiming itself as serving Iowa's newest city—contained a June 9, 1966 front-page photo and article about a local businessman as part of an ongoing series, "Businessman of the Week."[38] *The Hubbard* (OH) *News and Reporter* posted a page-one photo and article on November 6, 1968 that extended happy birthday greetings to a local set of triplets. The paper's nameplate identified *The Hubbard News and Reporter* as the home newspaper of the Hubbard, Brookfield, and Vienna, Ohio, communities and boasted of it being "Ohio's Prize-Winning Weekly Newspaper." The paper earned awards in the

1968 Ohio Newspaper Contest for news coverage, advertising, sports news, and layout design. *The Hubbard News and Reporter* was published by Niles Suburban Newspaper, Inc., and was a member of the National Newspaper Association (formerly National Editorial Association).[39]

"Unpleasant Happenings" Headlines and Courage in Coverage

However, Vidich's and Bensman's claim that the community weekly did not report on local arrests, shotgun weddings, mortgage foreclosures, lawsuits, bitter exchanges in public meetings, suicide, "or any other unpleasant happening" was misleading. There were plenty of examples of "unpleasant happenings" scattered among the so-called "self-congratulatory" news. For example, the front page of the July 11, 1963 edition of *The Florence* (AL) *Herald* reported on a city commission meeting where a group of Negro ministers sought the establishment of a biracial committee to avert strife in reaction to desegregation. The article also referred to a request from the local president of the International Brotherhood of Electrical Workers for the commission to adopt an ordinance that would prohibit the licensing and sale of goods made in communist-controlled countries.[40] Interspersed among Christmas greetings and photos of busy postal workers processing greeting cards and holiday gifts was a December 20, 1967 page-one story in *The Upland* (CA) *News* about narcotics possession leading to the expulsion of two local students. Other articles in the same issue reported on a hit-and-run accident that killed a local youth, a forklift accident that killed an Upland man, and the arrests of four juveniles who fired shots during an after-party fracas. *The Upland News*—established in 1894—included *The Cucamonga Times* (published each Wednesday) and combined classifieds serving the *News-Tribune-Times* California towns of Upland, Montclair, Alta Loma, Cucamonga, Etiwanda, and Mt. Baldy.[41]

Not all weeklies ignored or attempted to diminish local corruption or the racial strife of the decade, as critics of the "country" press accused them of doing. Many editors endured advertising boycotts, threatening phone calls, gunshots, and fires as they refused to back down from bullying law enforcement tactics or threats to stop promoting the equal rights of Negroes. In 1964, Hazel Brannon Smith, editor and publisher of *The Lexington* (MS) *Advertiser* (and three other weeklies near Lexington), won the Pulitzer Prize, the Elijah P. Lovejoy Courage in Journalism Award—which she had previously won in

1960—and the Women of Conscience Award from the National Council of Women of the United States, for journalistic courage. The then-28-year newspaper veteran fought for equitable law enforcement and took on slot machine operators, liquor law violators, gamblers, and corrupt local politicians in her editorials. She contended, however, that from the time she bought her first newspaper in 1936 to the bombing of the fourth weekly in her group on August 27, 1964, she was not a crusader but "only an editor printing what she believed to be the truth." The same year she won the Pulitzer, she also faced an ongoing (since 1954) advertising boycott from the White Citizens Council initiated against "Hazel, the Nigger Lover," a $10,000 libel suit, and the loss of her husband's job as a hospital administrator, because of her editorials. She earned the Council's moniker after reporting on a 1954 shooting of a 27-year-old black man by a county sheriff and editorially deplored the shooting as unwarranted. In a two-part October (24 and 31) 1964 *Editor & Publisher* profile, she defended her condemnation of the shooting, adding, "But I had gone against the prevailing code. Suddenly they were calling me 'Nigger Lover.'"[42] Also, her rivals started a newspaper to try to put her out of business, though they were unsuccessful.[43]

Gene Wirges—editor of the 3,000-circulation *The Morrillton (AR) Democrat*—received the Elijah P. Lovejoy Courage in Journalism Award in 1962 for fighting the city and county political machine. As recalled in a September 22, 1961 *Time* article, a local resident told Wirges not long after he bought the paper in 1957 that local politicians were not "elected," but rather, "selected." While bringing to light corrupt practices of local politicians, the editor's home was stoned and he was shot at, beaten, and threatened in person and over the phone. At one point he sent his wife and children to Little Rock, out of concern for their safety, and neighbors felt compelled to stand guard at his home. Wirges discovered that Conway County's longtime sheriff—who was a personal friend of Arkansas Governor Orval Faubus—ran the local political machine.[44]

Another 1960s Elijah P. Lovejoy Courage in Journalism Award winner was J.R. Freeman—editor and publisher of the less-than-1,000-circulation *Frederick (CO) Farmer and Miner*. A July 1, 1967 *Editor & Publisher* feature recounted how he bravely executed a one-man mission to inform the country about a scandal surrounding shale oil deposits. Following an 18-month investigation, he reported on an alleged federal giveaway of millions of acres of shale oil deposits in Colorado, Utah, and Wyoming. He received numerous threatening phone calls and letters, and three shots were fired into his car while he was on his way to meet two investigation sources. In addition to the Lovejoy award, Freeman also received the National Newspaper Association's Herrick Editorial Award for service in the national interest. A fellow weekly publisher in Long Island, New York, wrote an editorial on Freeman's behalf, calling for the establishment of a fund to help Freeman and other newsmen who put their lives and businesses on the line for the sake of press freedom. The editorial was picked up by the International Conference of Weekly Newspaper Editors—of which Freeman was a member—and was reprinted for a mass mailing to weekly editors throughout the country. Editors were encouraged to subscribe to the *Frederick Farmer and Miner* to support Freeman's efforts and run the series in their own newspapers.[45]

Speaking at Sigma Delta Chi's 1967 annual subscription dinner in St. Charles, Missouri, Freeman told of an 80-year-old man who hobbled into his office and said he wanted to subscribe to the newspaper. The man pulled out five $20 bills and said he wanted to give that amount for a $3.50 subscription. Freeman said he refused the overpayment, but the old man explained that he wanted to help Freeman continue his reporting and "give the readers at least a $100 more worth of the story." After Freeman refused the cash a second time, the man said, "What are you trying to do? Break an old man's heart?"[46]

Free Publicity Denounced and "Personals" Defended

Another stereotype of "country journalism" was that weeklies, unlike their metropolitan counterparts, willingly rolled out the welcome mat to any and all free publicity. That simply was not the case. A campaign began several decades prior to discourage weeklies from "giving away" valuable space that could be sold as advertising. An example of the success of the anti-publicity campaign came in a 1960 report of a major trucking association. The association surveyed 133 Florida editors and publishers and decided to drop weeklies from its news release mailing list because of a poor response to those willing to trade editorial space for ads.[47] Also, a 1960 editorial in *The Publishers' Auxiliary* referred to a Missouri Press Association publicity control committee study of Missouri weekly newspapers. The study found that the newspapers received 50 to 100 pieces of free publicity releases weekly. Half of the newspapers did not print any of it, and the other half said they used a story or releases occasionally. Also, 50 percent thought the publicity material had some value,

25 percent said it was worthless, and the remainder said they would rather not receive the material.⁴⁸

There were a number of weekly editors like William "Bill" Stewart—longtime publisher of *The Monroe Journal* in Monroeville, Alabama—who, according to his son Steve Stewart, reluctantly ran "free press releases" only when there was not enough local copy to fill the paper. The younger Stewart worked for his father in different capacities, from cleanup boy and inserter in the late 1950s to publisher in the mid-1990s. He added, "We almost never bought outside materials. Our goal was to fill the paper with local copy." Newsmen throughout the state mimicked the elder Stewart's emphasis on local news. Their admiration for Bill Stewart was demonstrated in 1959 when they elected him as president of the Alabama Press Association. In 2000, Alabama journalists honored his outstanding journalism career when he was inducted posthumously into the Alabama Press Association Newspaper Hall of Honor.⁴⁹

Critics of country journalism were especially harsh when it came to discussing the "personals" that reported on the social gatherings and comings and goings of area residents. A personal is a short news item of local interest that features names. But proponents of community journalism argued that the personals helped the community stay connected. The society columns of dailies usually mentioned only the financially well-connected, but the personals included folks from varied income classes—although Negroes were routinely excluded from the general-circulation publications. An example of how closely readers perused the personals was relayed in a March 5, 1960 *Editor & Publisher* news brief. It noted that the *Walton* (NY) *Reporter* published an apology to two of its readers after the weekly reported that a couple was leaving for New York on a Thursday. The report implied that the couple would spend the entire weekend there. They returned Saturday, and the wife—a church organist and choir director—went to church for a choir rehearsal, but no one else was there. The janitor told her they thought she would be out of town, as stated in the paper; so the rehearsal was canceled. That evening, the couple surprised other invited guests at a dinner party, because the paper indicated they would be out of town.⁵⁰

Rural journalism's traditions and a "personalized" style of writing were defended by the city editor of Portland's *The Oregon Daily Journal* who was a former weekly editor-publisher. Responding to a September 24, 1960 *Editor & Publisher* column arguing that suburban weekly newspapers were better than country weeklies, William J. Cary, Jr. said the assertion of the suburban weekly's superiority was based on the "false premise that anything bigger is automatically better." Cary's October 22, 1960 *Editor & Publisher* column also addressed criticism about the quaint wording of personals. "The fact that Mrs. Jones served a delicious dinner, as did Mrs. Smith and Mrs. Brown, probably will continue to appear in the news columns of the country weekly for a long time," he wrote. "Few of suburbia's editors have had to explain to an irate Mrs. Jones why, after 30 years, her dinner for the quilting club suddenly is no longer delicious."[51]

In the same October 22, 1960 *Editor & Publisher* issue, Annabel Atterbury—editor of the *Hustiford* (WI) *News and Rural Route Flyer*—submitted a letter to the editor addressing the supposed superiority of suburban newspapers. She wrote there were many high-quality weeklies in the country and listed several as recommended reading for the author who derided country weeklies. "In Montclair and Wellesley the residents don't have time for cows and corn." But, she added. "In the corn and dairy country, the readers have little time for drama and music except as it comes over radio and TV. Who's the snob?"[52]

Recruiting Workers, Advertisers, Subscribers, and Organization Members

By the 1960s, it had become more difficult for the traditional family-owned weekly to retain qualified, trained reporters and print laborers as family-owned businesses dwindled and fewer publishers could count on succeeding generations to stay in the newspaper business. Marking his 10th anniversary in the weekly publishing field, John C. Bond of Rockland, Massachusetts, stated in a September 12, 1964 *Editor & Publisher* article that he owed his early success "to a wife who knew bookkeeping, a son who turned out to be a good newspaperman, and an excellent general manager who answered his classified ad in *Editor & Publisher*."[53]

At an Arizona weekly, the publisher's family members realized in a tragic way the difficulties of staffing a small newspaper when *Tombstone* (AZ) *Epitaph* publisher Layton Smith was killed in a 1964 plane crash. According to a February 22, 1964 *Editor & Publisher* article, Illinois weekly publisher G.C. Terry and his wife were staying at a Tucson motel when they heard about the crash. They drove to Tombstone to assist the *Tombstone Epitaph* staff in putting out that week's edition under "very trying circumstances."[54]

So, with an increasing loss of the family-owned newspaper tradition, more and more weeklies had to recruit employees from journalism and trade schools. But recruiting staff was not an easy task for weeklies even though college journalism enrollment was up. Communication students favored dailies over weeklies as well as the higher salaries of advertising and public relations. For example, a 1960 survey of University of Oklahoma journalism seniors found that the students viewed newspaper reporting and radio broadcasting jobs as the lowest paying in the field of journalism.[55]

In 1960, Northern Illinois University established a department to increase cooperation among community newspapers and college journalism programs in response to the growing problem of attracting college graduates. Department Chairman Dr. Donald Grubb explained in a July 23, 1960 article in *The Publishers' Auxiliary* that the program would help alleviate the shortage of "grassroots" journalists through several initiatives. The initiatives included enhancing recruiting efforts at the high school level, offering more scholarships in community and rural newspapering, re-examining salary scales and benefits, and working with the industry to recruit professionals.[56] In another recruiting effort, the *Elgin (IL) Courier-News* ran a series of articles on journalism schools in the Midwest to encourage high school students to pursue a journalism degree. Fred Whiting—assistant dean of the Medill School of Journalism at Northwestern—applauded the *Elgin Courier-News* article series. In an April 9, 1960 article in *Editor & Publisher*, he praised publisher C. Raymond Long for being willing to tackle the number one problem of journalism, "the failure of most media to sell themselves to young people who might be interested in entering our field."[57]

There were, however, some encouraging signs that aggressive staff recruiting could make a difference. The School of Journalism at the University of Nebraska reported that in 1958 and 1959, 10–20 percent of graduates sought a career in the weekly field. In fact, the report—mentioned in a January 2, 1960 article in *The Publishers' Auxiliary*—revealed that more students went into the weekly field in 1958 than into any other single medium—including dailies and public relations. The university attributed the results to a three-pronged approach by the Nebraska Press Association, the journalism school, and the Nebraska High School Press Association, to improve their recruiting programs.[58]

By the end of the decade, hirings and salaries reached levels more attractive to college graduates and highly skilled labor as evidenced in the 19th annual cost study of the Newspaper Association Managers and the National

Newspaper Association. The 1969 study found that the average weekly newspaper employed 9.2 persons and had an average of 379 subscribers per employee.[59] In 1967, weekly employees working full-time received an average salary of $12,524.[60]

Employment practices changed in the weekly field with the advent of centralized printing operations. Recruiting highly skilled labor became important because of heavy press demands and equipment maintenance. John Cameron Sim—in his book on the grassroots press—observed that a central plant was in a better position to train apprentices, to offer better fringe and retirement benefits and working conditions, and to control work hours more effectively.[61] Because of available equipment and skilled labor employed at centralized plants, it was easier for weeklies to publish extras. An extra was an additional issue that came out between regularly scheduled publishing dates. The most common reason for publishing an extra was if a big story broke between publishing dates, usually from Thursday through Monday. For example, a large number of weeklies published an extra following President John F. Kennedy's 1963 assassination, which occurred on a Friday.[62]

Women—especially homemakers—found growing employment opportunities in freelance writing, advertising sales, and production. A September 1964 article in *The American Press* discussed the cost benefits of converting from letterpress to offset printing. In the article, Ohio weekly publisher Bill Mussey said that women made excellent compositors and that "one housewife can replace one printer, too."[63] A number of "housewife columnists" expanded their traditional correspondent roles to commenting on their daily lives and families in a more sophisticated and often, humorous manner. Housewives also found employment opportunities in classified and display advertising sales.[64]

Recruiting top salesmen and changing publishing tactics to draw more advertisers also became a major concern as the competition for advertising dollars grew fiercer in the 1960s. Weeklies not only had to go up against dailies, outdoor advertising, radio, and television, but also a growing number of shoppers, suburban weeklies, free-circulation weeklies, and weeklies within dailies. A New Jersey publisher was one of many weekly publishers who found that the best solution to fend off the advertising competition of an area shopper was to establish one of his own. Michael J. Torpey, general manager of the 7,000-circulation *Freehold* (NJ) *Transcript*, told attendees at the 1960 Mid-Atlantic Newspaper Mechanical Conference that with $15 worth of equipment (two blades and a set-screw) he converted one of his presses to put out an eight-page tabloid on Mondays—in addition to his regular standard-size

Thursday edition. Torpey boasted in a May 14, 1960 *Editor & Publisher* article that within four months he drove the competition away by offering a combination rate for the area merchants in both the shopper tab and the regular weekly.[65]

Despite the threat of suburban weeklies to take away advertisers, some weeklies benefited as they were pushed to bi-weekly and tri-weekly publication schedules in order to have enough space to accommodate a growing demand for advertising—largely from car dealers, realty brokers, and suburban supermarkets. The March 26, 1960 issue of *Editor & Publisher* gave the example of the *Buena Park News-West Orange County* (CA) *Progress* that became a semi-weekly in need of a bigger building and new equipment to accommodate multiple weekly issues and more advertisers.[66]

Another factor in attracting new advertisers to weeklies was the rapid growth of offset printing—which provided a more professional-looking advertisement, and illustration and photo options. While only 27 percent of the 327 weeklies (averaging 12 pages or more) that responded to a 1964 trade survey used offset, another 13 percent planned to convert to offset within two years.[67] By 1969, the 19th annual cost study of the Newspaper Association Managers and the National Newspaper Association found that two-thirds of weeklies were printed on offset presses, as compared to one-third in 1965. Of the 111 offset papers that participated in the 1969 study, 68 shared presses in central printing plants.[68]

Editors were quick to embrace offset because the process was based on photography and did not involve processes that required the use of union labor workers at larger printing presses. Since weeklies were not tied to labor contracts they could make the progression to offset more quickly than dailies.

Offset changed the appearance of many small-town newspapers—which attracted advertisers because of increased uses of illustrations, borders, screens, and color. For example, photographers were hired not only to take news photos, but advertisement photos as well. Also, the offset press brought about a more uniform tabloid page size of 17 inches in length and 11 inches in width. Most weeklies were printed on broadsheets—referred to as broadsides—meaning a page of 22 inches in length and 17 inches in width. The switch to tabloid pages for weeklies made it easier for advertisers to place the same advertisement in multiple publications without having to make changes.

Weeklies were quick to promote their visual enhancements and increased production capabilities to attract advertisers and readers. The *Emmetsburg* (IA) *Democrat* boasted about its use of photographs. Under the nameplate it stated,

"Get the Whole Story—ILLUSTRATED—in the Reporter and Democrat." A November 9, 1961 issue included 17 news photos (12 head shots) and five advertising photos. The newspaper was designated the official city and county paper and was listed as a member of the Iowa Press Association, National Editorial Association, Weekly Newspaper Bureau, and National Advertising Representatives, Inc.[69]

Although *The Desert Sentinel* in Desert Hot Springs, California, stated that it did not have darkroom facilities for processing pictures, readers were invited to submit pictures and feature articles for publication. The photos were then taken to a centralized plant for offset production. The March 8, 1962 issue of *The Desert Sentinel* included six community news photos and three advertising photos.[70] Editor Harvey Smalley, Jr.—of the *Perham* (MN) *Enterprise-Bulletin*—sent a special run of his paper around the state that featured a red flag on the front page. The back page was a full-page grocery ad in two colors. A paper company paid for the promotional. A write-up about the promotional in an October 15, 1960 *Editor & Publisher* issue stated that Smalley considered the added cost of color a minor consideration if the results were increased national advertising. Smalley pointed out that a major drawback to national accounts for weeklies was the poor quality of reproduction, failure to follow printing instructions, and lack of merchandising services.[71]

One Texas weekly was apparently very successful in attracting local and national advertising through its extensive use of photos and illustrations. About 70 percent of the contents of the December 15, 1960 edition of *The Commerce* (TX) *Journal* were local and national advertising—including four full pages (of a 14-page edition) for Piggly Wiggly and A&P grocery advertisements. There were also local advertisements sponsored by department stores, appliance stores, pharmacies, insurance agents, carpet and tile stores, a movie theatre featuring an Elvis Presley film, auto supply stores, a Chevrolet dealer, furniture stores, a Coca-Cola bottling company, optometrists, hardware stores, banks, the gas company, the power and light company, a barbershop, the telephone company, and a group-sponsored, full-page message urging Commerce residents to "attend the church of your choice Sunday."[72]

Albion (NY) *Advertiser* publisher Peter Dragon used typefaces and trust to draw advertisers and maintain a financially successful weekly. His "Dragon System" offered Albion businessmen exclusive one-year use of a certain typeface for their advertisements. His advertisers even trusted him to determine the appropriate size of an advertisement. For example, a shoe repair store that planned to run a full-page advertisement tried to cancel at the last minute. But at Dragon's urging, the advertiser agreed to run an advertisement—although reduced in size and cost. Dragon convinced the shop owner that a smaller advertisement would be just as effective. So, despite losing some advertising revenue, he retained a satisfied customer.[73]

Clean typography was also a hallmark of *The Florence* (AL) *Herald*. Longtime print shop manager John D. "Jack" Martin observed that his family-owned newspaper was not successful at drawing many national advertisers but that it did attract a high percentage of local advertisers because of its readability and layout design. "Our paper was very easy to read," he recalled.[74]

An unprecedented example of the growing appeal of weeklies among national advertisers came with a $500,000 Camel cigarette campaign in 1960.[75] A 500-line advertisement was placed in every general-circulation weekly throughout the country to promote the cigarette brand manufactured by the R.J. Reynolds Tobacco Company. *Jackson* (GA) *Herald* editor N.S. Hayden noted in a published letter in the December 17, 1960 edition of *Editor & Publisher* that his paper gave the advertisement prime position "as requested" in the campaign he termed "a major breakthrough" for weekly advertising. Hayden wrote that he was stopped by several readers who remarked that the Camel advertisement added "prestige" to "their little hometown weekly."[76]

The printing of supplements—which are magazine-type "themed" inserts that sought paid sponsors—became more common in weeklies in the 1960s. The supplements were usually slick, full-color tabloids of varying length that required little staff effort—containing a few brief local features, but mostly photographs—and acquired special advertising revenue beyond contracted accounts. Supplement themes were often tied to local businesses and industries. For example, the *Dearborn* (MI) *Press* promoted local tourist sites—such as the Ford Motor Company's Rouge Plant and the Henry Ford Museum—in its annual Vacation-Fun-in-Dearborn supplement. The auto industry and Dearborn Chamber of Commerce provided advertising support for the supplement. Dearborn-area tourist centers and motels received extra copies of the tourism-themed supplement. During a Wayne State University Press Club panel discussion on problems associated with publishing supplements, Kenneth Weaver of the *Birmingham* (MI) *Eccentric* reported that his paper published seven supplements a year. They varied in topics such as spring and fall fashion, gardening, new automobiles, and Christmas gifts. He agreed with other panelists that it was appropriate to include features about an advertiser's history or product, but that an advertiser's request for an "editorial puff" should be refused.[77]

Photographs, illustrations, and improved printing quality were not the only attractors that brought more advertising to weeklies. Business-boosting stunts and sponsored special events also became popular. One publisher purchased some hens and a few guineas. Then, he asked local merchants to each donate a prize—such as a pocket knife or a shirt—for which they received an advertisement in his paper. The day of the stunt, a tag bearing the name of a merchant and its prize was attached to the leg of each hen and guinea. The publicity said the chickens would "fly from the top of the tallest (two stories) building" and that whoever caught a chicken or guinea would win a prize. According to a March 12, 1960 write-up in *Editor & Publisher*, the stunt drew a large crowd from miles around and was declared a success by the publisher.[78]

The end result of increased national advertising and sponsored supplements was that weeklies were less tied to their job shops. In fact, some independent weeklies were able to relinquish outside printing jobs altogether—while chain and group newspapers found it profitable to continue to print other newspapers and specialty print jobs at the centralized plants.

Subscription-Enticing Contests/Prizes and Professional Association Benefits

Some weeklies found that sponsorship of special events paid off not only in advertising, but also in circulation. For example, the four-paper Walnut Creek Sun Group in California sponsored political candidate nights, travel and basketball nights, rifle safety programs, swim meets, and journalism clinics. It sponsored a workshop showing how to prevent shoplifting and published carpool lists during bus strikes. The company also offered free want ads each spring to job-seeking teens.[79]

Weeklies had to battle free-circulation publications to maintain their paid subscribers despite their best efforts at promotions and community service. However, the classification of weeklies into "paid" and "free" did not necessarily mean that all circulation was paid at "paid" weeklies or free at "free" weeklies. Some issues were given away at paid weeklies, and some free copies were paid for—particularly if mailed out of town. Weekly paid circulation had continuously grown since the mid-1950s and set a record-breaking high of $24,399,490 in 1962.[80]

The incentives for a weekly to become a paid-circulation publication were to gain legal status as a newspaper, to win less costly second-class postal privileges, and to become a vehicle for public notice advertising. But new postal regulations made it tougher for newspapers to get second-class mail privileges. The regulation required that a publication with a second-class permit have at least a 65 percent paid circulation. During this time, the U.S. Postal Manual, Section 132.225 read:

> List of Subscribers. Publications must have a legitimate list of persons who have subscribed by paying or promising to pay for copies to be received during a stated time." Section 132.227 read: "Free Circulation Publications. Publications designed primarily for free circulation may not qualify for second-class privileges. Publications are designed primarily for free circulation when the total number of copies furnished during any 12-month period to legitimate paid subscribers (see 132.225) and to the purchasers of single copies constitutes less than 65 percent of the total number of copies distributed by mail at the second-class pound rates or the transient rate, by the publishers' carriers, and by other means for any purpose. See 132.31a. NOTE: The 65 per centum paid circulation standard established by this paragraph is effective upon publication. Publications which do not meet this standard but which now have second-class permits must maintain at least 55 per centum paid circulation until December 31, 1961, after which date the 65 per centum standard must be complied with.

Papers belonging to the Audit Bureau of Circulations had no problem with the ruling because a 75 percent paid circulation was a requirement for A.B.C. membership.[81]

As their competition for subscriptions increased, weeklies became more aggressive in their tactics to maintain and attract new readers—such as sponsoring contests and offering prizes. A University of Washington Weekly Newspaper survey revealed that the average subscription rates in 1960 were $3.38 for the more prosperous weeklies and $3.21 for the less prosperous.[82] For example, a December 20, 1967 edition of *The Upland* (CA) *News* used a full page to promote the "Greater Upland Stores ... Gift-O-Rama." The grand prize was a $539 color television set. The promotional included a coupon for the grand-prize drawing along with instructions to fill out the coupon and return it to one of the 14 participating merchants. The sponsoring merchants also included in-store coupons or small advertisements on the promotional page.[83] *The Hubbard* (OH) *News and Reporter* sponsored a 1968 bingo contest that had five business sponsors and ran for more than two months. A headline in the November 6, 1968 edition—"We Goofed!"—explained that the bingo number for the previous week's issue was accidentally omitted. The *Hubbard News and Reporter* issued an apology along with the aforementioned bingo number, printed on a cartoon drawing of a bug labeled, "Bingo Bug No. 64." As a result of the omission, contestants were given an extended deadline to turn in a winning card. The same *Hubbard News and Reporter* edition included a two-thirds page promotional headlined, "Enjoy a Fabulous Football Holiday in Sunny Miami." The newspaper group that owned the *Hubbard News and Reporter* sponsored a Super Bowl weekend tour for a special reduced-price group rate.[84]

The Super Bowl trip represented the kind of "trade out" advertising often practiced in the travel industry. Publishers received discounts and giveaways as incentives for subscribers in exchange for "free" advertising space. For example, a Chicago-based travel agency advertisement in the December 17, 1960 issue of *Editor & Publisher* encouraged publishers to trade out advertising space for travel accommodations that would be "ideal for prizes, contests, awards, or your family vacation." The advertisement listed various trade-out options—such as Caribbean cruises and resort accommodations along the Gulf and East coasts.[85]

An Arizona publisher opted for the personal touch instead of promotions as a means to attract subscribers. W.H. Shurtleff III, of the *Marana (AZ) Times*, spent one afternoon a week visiting homes in outlying rural communities. He wrote up the folksy news and sent marked copies to the families he visited who were not subscribers. He also encouraged local merchants to tell him who frequented their stores so that he could make a mention of local shoppers in the newspaper.[86]

However, a March 5, 1960 *Editor & Publisher* article questioned whether a weekly could have too many subscribers. Billy Smith argued that properly guided circulation was as important to the small weekly as it was to the large daily. As an example, he referred to a North Carolina weekly that, on press day, needed three persons working steadily for two hours to handle single-wrap subscriptions—many going out of state.[87] But publisher Henry Beetle Hough of *The Vineyard Gazette* in Edgartown, Massachusetts, took issue with that observation, responding in a letter in the April 16, 1960 *Editor & Publisher* issue that, "The only limit to the circulation a weekly should have is the circulation it can get, no matter where."[88]

In fact, by the end of the decade, circulation among weeklies totaled more than 3.3 million. Audit Bureau of Circulation weekly newspaper members reported total circulations during 1969 of 3,303,942—the highest U.S. total since 1965. Average circulation of A.B.C. weeklies increased to 8,341 during 1969—as compared to 8,019 the previous year. Increases in total weekly circulation were reported in 24 of the 42 states with A.B.C. weekly newspapers. The 396 weeklies included in the study showed a net increase of 16,274. The largest circulation increases were reported in California, Ohio, and Pennsylvania. All figures for the report were taken from publisher's statements for the period ending September 30, 1969.[89]

Recruitment also became an important issue for professional associations that catered to the weekly newspaper field because of an increased focus on member services—such as publications and advertising services, and political lobbying on behalf of the industry. In 1961, the Weekly Newspaper Representatives—serving as a national advertising service for weeklies—wanted to expand its business into the small-daily field and was renamed American Newspaper Representatives. A.N.R. bought Greater Weeklies in 1965—adding a professional listing service to its rate-setting, uniform billing program. In 1962, the National Editorial Association purchased *The Publishers' Auxiliary* trade newspaper from the F.W.P. (Farwell W. Perry) Corporation—which was a successor to the national newspaper syndicate Western Newspaper Union. The N.E.A.'s publication, *National Publisher*, was absorbed by *The Publishers' Auxiliary* in 1968. In 1964, the N.E.A. officially changed its name to the National Newspaper Association.

The rapid growth in suburban weeklies resulted in the 1960 formation of a group of eight Chicago publishers into the Suburban Press Foundation, which by 1967 had grown to 52 publishers who represented 200 weeklies in major metropolitan areas. At first, most of them also retained their membership in the larger National Editorial Association, but they soon felt the need for a professional association that addressed the specific needs of the suburban weekly industry. Some suburban weekly publishers speaking at a workshop of the 79th annual meeting of the N.E.A. in New York cited a sharp line of distinction between the suburban paper and the typical hometown weekly. They said N.E.A. was unable to serve their interests and pointed to Suburban Press Foundation as an organization that better addressed their problems of labor, competition, and distribution. The suburban press publishers asked N.E.A. to consider S.P.F. as a supplementary or subsidiary group, rather than as a replacement. They wanted to remain with N.E.A. because it was important in terms of staging conventions, providing a Washington voice and national advertising representation, and sponsoring travel study missions.[90] N.E.A. did not approve the request; so, the Suburban Newspapers of America—an offshoot of N.E.A.—was formed in 1964. Two years later the National Newspaper

Association (formerly N.E.A.) board approved a Suburban Newspaper Section with the N.N.A.

Other professional media groups also began to respect the business acumen and professional work of their peers in the non-daily newspaper field. For example, in 1960 the International Press Institute—with 1,300 members worldwide including 326 United States members—let down its barrier for membership to weekly, semi-weekly, and tri-weekly newspapers in the United States.[91]

The Regional Concept Introduces New Operating Agreements

Although gradually introduced in the previous decade, "regional concept" was the new label given to the varied operating agreements that developed among weeklies during the 1960s. According to *Editor & Publisher* writer Rick Friedman, in the June 20, 1964 issue, the term generally took two forms. One form was a group operation of separate editions offering combined advertising rates and local coverage to large chunks of population. The second form was a single, large, free-circulation newspaper, falling somewhere between the shopper's distribution patterns and the community weekly's feature approach.[92]

The regional concept was incorporated into eight Kentucky papers—with a combined circulation of 40,000—that joined together to form Greater Kentucky Publishing, Inc. As described in a February 25, 1967 issue of *Editor & Publisher*, a 4,000-square-foot printing plant was constructed near the town of Shelby, from capital raised through a Small Business Administration loan and equal stock purchases among the eight owners. Each paper prepared its own pages at their respective locations, while camera, plate-making, and presswork were conducted at the plant. A bonus for advertisers was that they received the 40,000-circulation audience without an extra charge. Also, a 12–16-page classified tabloid was inserted weekly, although sales, billing, and composition were handled separately by each paper.[93]

Another example of the regional concept was Hartley Newspapers of Columbus, Ohio—which was also featured in the *Editor & Publisher* article on the regional concept. The group operated seven weeklies and a metropolitan daily. Duplication of pages (including classifieds) in various editions saved time, personnel, and composing room costs, but each paper had a separate front page, sports page, society page, church page, and several inside pages.

The article pointed out that the operation drew large advertisers who would not have considered advertising in the smaller, individual papers.[94]

The regional concept included some quirky combinations as well. An August 29, 1964 *Editor & Publisher* article featured a husband-and-wife team in Minnesota that operated the *Trimont Progress* and the *Ceylon Herald* in which a double front page made the *Trimont Progress* two newspapers in one. *Trimont Progress* subscribers got their Trimont (population, 942) news on the first four pages of an eight-page paper, with Ceylon (population, 554) news on the back four pages. It was the reverse for *Ceylon Herald* subscribers, with Ceylon news featured on the first four pages. A fold in the middle of the paper made the switch in news sections possible. Gordon Spielman edited the *Trimont Progress*, and his wife, Phyllis Spielman, edited the *Ceylon Herald*.[95]

Another regional concept was the twin-weekly—a longtime operation model for Clarion County, Pennsylvania, publisher William C. Hearst. In a November 7, 1964 *Editor & Publisher* article, Hearst claimed to oversee Pennsylvania's first dual political operation. Active in Republican politics, he bought the *Clarion Republican* in 1941 and added the *Clarion Democrat* seven years later. Reasoning that the town should support two cooperating as well as two competitive newspapers, he changed the publishing schedule to Tuesday for the *Clarion Democrat* and left it at Thursday for the *Clarion Republican*. The partisan papers were still going strong in the 1960s, during which time the news editor, a Democrat, was responsible for editorials for that partisan publication. Hearst continued to write editorials for the *Clarion Republican*. The operation included merged advertising, bookkeeping, circulation, general-news departments, and production and printing facilities. Subscribers paid $5 a year for the two newspapers, although they were not required to accept both.[96]

A major advantage to operating by the regional concept was that it helped weeklies to bring down the cost-per-thousand in advertising. The higher cost of placing advertisements in smaller-circulation newspapers was going against the weekly in local and national advertising prospects, according to Al Stanford, publisher of *The Milford* (CT) *Citizen*. As he explained in a February 18, 1967 *Editor & Publisher* article, it cost the same to set a newspaper, whether 1,000 copies or 500,000. He said the weekly had to offer larger circulations or lower its composition cost dramatically to overcome the disadvantage of cost-per-thousand estimates. Compton was one of the three founding partners of the Compton Advertising Agency in New York before World War II. He later became the Bureau of Advertising's director and developed the slogan, "All Business is Local" for newspapers.[97]

Looking Ahead

Overall, weeklies were financially sound at the end of the 1960s. A 19th annual cost study by the Newspaper Association Managers and the National Newspaper Association found that the average weekly newspaper in 1969 earned a net income of 8.5 percent—almost equal to the profit in the previous year. The average income per subscriber for all newspapers participating in the study was $43.15—an increase of $7.95 per paper over the previous year.[98] The distribution of income per subscriber was $25.60 (advertising), $3.54 (circulation), $12.23 (printing), and $4.48 (miscellaneous). Income for the paper per employee was $15,238—a drop of $357 from the previous year. The study received 161 survey responses from publishers in 40 states. The net income was figured after deducting a uniform and modest salary for the publisher.[99]

But in considering the business outlook for weeklies in the coming decade, David Bowers wrote in the Spring 1969 issue of *Journalism Quarterly* that centralized printing was a key factor from which two conflicting trends were emerging. One was the growth of chain or group ownership—which would bring new newspapers and the revival of competition in one-newspaper communities. The other trend was the impact that centralized printing of weeklies could have in a mass society—especially at the grassroots level. The tremendous growth of centralized printing of weekly newspapers could be significant to communications at the grassroots level, he reasoned, because it permitted anyone with little capital to start a newspaper.[100]

The American Press's 1968 industry forecast survey among weekly, suburban, and daily newspaper publishers indicated that new computer technology with photocomposition was "fast becoming an accepted way of producing the words," and offset was "entrenched" as the printing process. The survey noted that these technological advances occurred during the 1960s, "a decade which saw the greatest advances in newspaper mechanical production since Gutenberg in the 15th century." And finally, survey participants observed that "progressive" newspapers would have to invest in large capital expenditures to purchase computerized equipment and offset presses, but that the new devices would enable them to cut production costs and produce a better product.[101]

Notes

1 Emerson P. Harris and Elizabeth H. Hooke, *The Community Newspaper* (New York: D. Appleton and Company, 1923), 245–246, 252.
2 *The Titonka* (IA) *Topic*, February 18, 1965, 1. Titonka, in Kossuth County, is located in north-central Iowa. Titonka had a population of 547 in 1960. *Eighteenth Census of the United States*, "Population," volume 1, part 17, section 2, 17–27, Table 8. http://newspaperarchive.com/, http://www.census.gov/.
3 *The Seguin* (TX) *Gazette*, January 29, 1964, 2. Seguin, in Guadalupe County, is located in south-central Texas, east of San Antonio. Seguin had a population of 14,299 in 1960. *Eighteenth Census of the United States*, "Population," volume 1, part 45, section 2, 45–40, Table 8. http://newspaperarchive.com/, http://www.census.gov/.
4 "New Directories Being Distributed," *The Seguin* (TX) *Gazette*, January 29, 1964, sec. 2, 2.
5 D'Antonio, et al, "Institutional and Occupational Representatives in Eleven Community Influence Systems," *American Sociological Review* 26:3 (June 1961), 445.
6 William E. Branned, "Community and Paper Meet, Decide Code of Ethics," *The Publishers' Auxiliary*, September 10, 1960, 2. Burlington, in Wisconsin's Racine County, had a population of 5,856 in 1960. *Eighteenth Census of the United States*, "Population," volume 1, part 51, section 2, 51–18, Table 7. http://www.census.gov/.
7 Robert A. Dahl, *Who Governs?: Democracy and Power in an American City* (New Haven: Yale University Press, 1961), 258–259.
8 Alex S. Edelstein and J. Blaine Schultz, "The Weekly Newspaper's Leadership Role as Seen by Community Leaders," *Journalism Quarterly* 40 (1963), 567, 571–573.
9 Alex S. Edelstein and Joseph J. Contris, "The Public View of the Weekly Newspaper's Leadership Role," *Journalism Quarterly* 43 (1966), 20, 24.
10 "The Weekly Editor: Freebooter," *Editor & Publisher* 93:41 (October 8, 1960): 68.
11 "The Weekly Editor: Killed Ghost Town," *Editor & Publisher* 97:33 (August 15, 1964): 10. Key West, in Florida's Monroe County, had a population of 33,956 in 1960. *Eighteenth Census of the United States*, "Population," volume 1, part 11, section 2, 11–10, Table 5. Telluride, in Colorado's San Miguel County, had a population of 677 in 1960. *Eighteenth Census of the United States*, "Population," volume 1, part 7, section 2, 7–12, Table 7. http://www.census.gov/.
12 "Maxims & Moonshine," *Time*, September 29, 1961, 58. Kennebunk, in Maine's York County, had a population of 4,551 in 1960. *Eighteenth Census of the United States*, "Population," volume 1, part 21, section 2, 21–13, Table 7. http://www.census.gov/.
13 "New Magazine for Weekly Editors," *The Publishers' Auxiliary*, January 16, 1960, 1.
14 Rick Friedman, "The Weekly Editor: Comments on a Conference," *Editor & Publisher* 100:34 (August 26, 1967): 30.
15 Paul R. Busch, "The Weekly Editor: Among the Best," *Editor & Publisher* 100:5 (February 4, 1967): 36–37.
16 "That Important Editorial," *The Florence* (AL) *Herald*, March 28, 1963, 2. Florence, in Lauderdale County, is located in northwestern Alabama. Florence had a population of 31,649 in 1960. *Eighteenth Census of the United States*, "Population," volume 1, part 2, section 2, 2–15, Table 8. http://www.census.gov/.

17 "The Weekly Editor: The Van Meter Reader," *Editor & Publisher* 97:47 (November 21, 1964): 40. New Richmond, in Wisconsin's St. Croix County, had a population of 3,316 in 1960. *Eighteenth Census of the United States*, "Population," volume 1, part 51, section 2, 51–19, Table 7. http://www.census.gov/.

18 "Here's Reason Why Items Do Not Always Get in Paper," *The Guthrian*, November 26, 1963, 2. Guthrie Center, in Guthrie County, is located in southwest Iowa, west of Des Moines. Guthrie Center had a population of 2,071 in 1960. *Eighteenth Census of the United States*, "Population," volume 1, part 17, section 2, 17–24, Table 8. http://newspaperarchive.com/, http://www.census.gov/.

19 Wilbur Peterson and Robert Thorp, "Weeklies' Editorial Effort Less than 30 Years Ago," *Journalism Quarterly* 39 (Winter 1962): 53–54.

20 "Success in the Sticks," *Time*, December 21, 1962, 42.

21 Ben H. Bagdikian, "Behold the Grass-Roots Press!" *Harper's Magazine* 229:1375 (December 1964): 102–105, 110.

22 "Charge: Irresponsible," *The American Press* 82:8 (June 1964): 4. Fergus Falls, in Minnesota's Otter Tail County, had a population of 13,733 in 1960. *Eighteenth Census of the United States*, "Population," volume 1, part 25, section 2, 25–22, Table 7. http://www.census.gov/.

23 Kenneth R. Byerly, *Community Journalism* (New York: Chilton Company, 1961), 5–6.

24 Ibid., 12.

25 "The Weekly Editor: News Brief," *Editor & Publisher* 93:48 (November 26, 1960): 38.

26 Hodding Carter, *First Person Rural* (Garden City, NY: Doubleday & Company, 1963), 246.

27 "The Editor's Job," *The Florence* (AL) *Herald*, September 19, 1963, 2.

28 "Success in the Sticks," 42.

29 "Local Columns Sell Subs for America's Largest Rural Weekly," *The American Press* 82:1 (November 1963): 18–19.

30 "Most Editors See Nixon Victory," *The Publishers' Auxiliary*, November 5, 1960, 1.

31 "Publishers Predict Goldwater Victory," *The American Press* 82:12 (October 1964): 14.

32 "The Weekly Editor: Mail Bagged," *Editor & Publisher* 93:38 (September 17, 1960): 34.

33 Arthur R. Vidich and Joseph Bensman, *Small Town in Mass Society* (Princeton, NJ: Princeton University Press, 1968), 31, 44–45.

34 Clarice N. Olien, George A. Donohue, and Phillip J. Tichenor, "The Community Editor's Power and the Reporting of Conflict," *Journalism Quarterly* 45:2 (June 1968), 245–246, 252.

35 "Young Desert Hot Springs Scientist," *The Desert Sentinel*, March 8, 1962, 1. *The Desert Sentinel*, founded in 1940, was listed as a member of the National Editorial Association. Desert Hot Springs, in Riverside County, is located in southern California, just north of Palm Springs. Desert Hot Springs had a population of 1,472 in 1960. *Eighteenth Census of the United States*, "Population," volume 1, part 6, section 2, 6–28, Table 8. http://newspaperarchive.com/, http://www.census.gov/.

36 "Editorial Viewpoint: The Unsung Builders," *The Seguin* (TX) *Gazette*, January 29, 1964, 2. http://newspaperarchive.com/.

37 "The Bowler's Corner," *The Titonka* (IA) *Topic*, February 18, 1965, 1. Titonka, in Iowa's Kossuth County had a population of 647 in 1960. *Eighteenth Census of the United States*,

"Population," volume 1, part 17, section 2, 17–14, Table 2. http://newspaperarchive.com/, http://www.census.gov/.

38 "Businessman of the Week," *The Rock Valley* (IA) *Bee*, June 9, 1966, 1. The *Bee* was a member of the Iowa Press Association and the National Editorial Association. Rock Valley, in Sioux County, is located in northwest Iowa. Rock Valley had a population of 1,693 in 1960. *Eighteenth Census of the United States*, "Population," volume 1, part 17, section 2, 17–27, Table 8. http://newspaperarchive.com/, http://www.census.gov/.

39 "Happy Birthday Palko Triplets!" *The Hubbard* (OH) *News and Reporter*, November 6, 1968, 1. Hubbard, in Trumbull County, is located in east-central Ohio, just north of Youngstown. Hubbard had a population of 7,137 in 1960. *Eighteenth Census of the United States*, "Population," volume 1, part 37, section 2, 37–28, Table 8. http://newspaperarchive.com/, http://www.census.gov/.

40 "Negro Ministers Seek Biracial Group; Communists Hit," *The Florence* (AL) *Herald*, July 11, 1963, 1.

41 *The Upland* (CA) *News*, December 20, 1967, 1, 4, 10. Upland, in San Bernardino County, is located in southern California, just east of Los Angeles. Upland had a population of 15,918 in 1960. *Eighteenth Census of the United States*, "Population," volume 1, part, 6, section 2, 6–30, Table 8. http://newspaperarchive.com/, http://www.census.gov/.

42 Rick Friedman, "The Weekly Editor: Women's Angle," *Editor & Publisher* 97:43 (October 24, 1964): 40, 42. Lexington, in Mississippi's Holmes County, had a population of 2,839 in 1960. *Eighteenth Census of the United States*, "Population," volume 1, part 26, section 2, 26–12, Table 7. http://www.census.gov/. In 2022, according to the latest government figures based on the Consumer Price Index, $10,000 from 1964 was worth $95,491. http://measuringworth.com/.

43 Rick Friedman, "The Weekly Editor: Women's Angle (part 2)," *Editor & Publisher* 97:44 (October 31, 1964): 27.

44 "Varieties of Violence," *Time*, September 22, 1961, 75. Morrillton, in Arkansas' Conway County, had a population of 5,997 in 1960. *Eighteenth Census of the United States*, "Population," volume 1, part 2, section 5, 5–12, Table 7. http://www.census.gov/.

45 Rick Friedman, "The Weekly Editor: Three Bullet Holes," *Editor & Publisher* 100:26 (July 1, 1967): 15. Frederick, in Colorado's Weld County, had a population of 595 in 1960. *Eighteenth Census of the United States*, "Population," volume 1, part 2, section 7, 7–12, Table 7. http://www.census.gov/.

46 Rick Friedman, "The Weekly Editor: A Call for Help," *Editor & Publisher* 100:32 (August 12, 1967): 40. In 2022, according to the latest government figures based on the Consumer Price Index, $100 from 1967 was worth $887.16, $20 was worth $177, and $3.50 was worth $31. http://measuringworth.com/.

47 "What to Do with Publicity Releases," *The Publishers' Auxiliary*, January 16, 1960, 4.

48 "PR Men Told: Include Local Angles," *The Publishers' Auxiliary*, April 2, 1960, 4.

49 Steve Stewart, "E-mail Interview with Author," (June 25, 2009). Monroeville, in Alabama's Monroe County, had a population of 3,632 in 1960. *Eighteenth Census of the United States*, "Population," volume 1, part 2, section 2, 2–16, Table 7. http://www.census.gov/.

50 "The Weekly Editor: Thursdata, Welcome Home?" *Editor & Publisher* 93:10 (March 5, 1960): 30. Walton, in New York's Delaware County, had a population of 5,753 in 1960. *Eighteenth Census of the United States*, "Population," volume 1, part 2, section 34, 34–15, Table 7. http://www.census.gov/.

51 William J. Cary, Jr., "The Weekly Editor: Rural Press Defended," *Editor & Publisher* 93:43 (October 22, 1960): 56.

52 "The Weekly Editor: Mail Bagged," *Editor & Publisher* 93:43 (October 22, 1960): 56. Hustiford, in Wisconsin's Dodge County, had a population of 708 in 1960. *Eighteenth Census of the United States*, "Population," volume 1, part 2, section 51, 51–15, Table 7. http://www.census.gov/.

53 "The Weekly Editor: Wife, Son & G.M.," *Editor & Publisher* 97:37 (September 12, 1964): 30. Rockland, in Massachusetts' Plymouth County, had a population of 13,119 in 1960. *Eighteenth Census of the United States*, "Population," volume 1, part 2, section 23, 23–12, Table 7. http://www.census.gov/.

54 "The Weekly Editor: Thursdata, Lends a Hand," *Editor & Publisher* 97:8 (February 22, 1964): 55. Tombstone, in Arizona's Cochise County, had a population of 1,283 in 1960. *Eighteenth Census of the United States*, "Population," volume 1, part 2, section 4, 4–8, Table 7. http://www.census.gov/.

55 "Students Rate Newspaper Jobs as Low Paying," *The Publishers' Auxiliary*, February 20, 1960, 1.

56 "Smaller Newspaper Employee Problem Studied at N.I.U.," *The Publishers' Auxiliary*, July 23, 1960, 3.

57 Robert U. Brown, "Shop Talk at Thirty: Journalism Recruiting," *Editor & Publisher* 93:15 (April 9, 1960): 76. Elgin, in Illinois' Kane County, had a population of 46,555 in 1960. *Eighteenth Census of the United States*, "Population," volume 1, part 2, section 15, 15–13, Table 2. http://www.census.gov/.

58 Jerry Petsche, "Publishers Seek Ways to Interest J-School Graduates," *The Publishers' Auxiliary*, January 2, 1960, 1.

59 "Net Income of Average Weekly Dips," *Editor & Publisher* 103:27 (July 4, 1970): 34.

60 "The Weekly Editor: Financial Report," *Editor & Publisher* 100:25 (June 24, 1967): 28. In 2022, according to the latest government figures based on the Consumer Price Index, $12,524 from 1967 was worth $111,107. http://measuringworth.com/.

61 John Cameron Sim, *The Grass Roots Press: America's Community Newspapers*, 1st ed. (Ames, Iowa: The Iowa State University Press, 1969, Reprint 1970), 152.

62 Rick Friedman, "The Weekly Editor: Extra!" *Editor & Publisher* 97:1 (January 4, 1964): 42.

63 "Here's One Way to Compare Offset vs. Letterpress Cost," *The American Press* 82:11 (September 1964): 18.

64 Rick Friedman, "The Weekly Editor: Housewife Columnists," *Editor & Publisher* 100:38 (September 23, 1967): 42.

65 "The Weekly Editor: $15 Conversion," *Editor & Publisher* 93:20 (May 14, 1960): 74. In 2022, according to the latest government figures based on the Consumer Price Index, $15 from 1960 was worth $150. http://measuringworth.com/. Freehold, in New Jersey's Monmouth County, had a population of 9,140 in 1960. *Eighteenth Census of the United States*, "Population," volume 1, part 2, section 32, 32–14, Table 7. http://www.census.gov/.

66 "The Weekly Editor: Unforeseen Demand," *Editor & Publisher* 93:13 (March 26, 1960): 127. Buena Park, in California's Orange County, had a population of 46,401 in 1960. *Eighteenth Census of the United States*, "Population," volume 1, part 2, section 6, 6–25, Table 7. http://www.census.gov/.

67 "1964 Newspaper Equipment Survey," *The American Press* 82:6 (April 1964): 14.

68 "Net Income of Average Weekly Dips," 34.

69 *The Emmetsburg* (IA) *Democrat*, November 9, 1961, 1. Emmetsburg, in Palo Alto County, is located in northwestern Iowa. Emmetsburg had a population of 3,887 in 1960. *Eighteenth Census of the United States*, "Population," volume 1, part 2, section 17, 17–24, Table 8. http://newspaperarchive.com/, http://www.census.gov/.

70 *The Desert Sentinel*, March 8, 1962, 2. http://newspaperarchive.com/.

71 "The Weekly Editor: News Brief," *Editor & Publisher* 93:42 (October 15, 1960): 58. Perham, in Minnesota's Otter Tail County, had a population of 2,019 in 1960. *Eighteenth Census of the United States*, "Population," volume 1, part 2, section 25, 25–22, Table 7. http://www.census.gov/.

72 *The Commerce* (TX) *Journal*, December 15, 1960. Commerce, in Hunt County, is located in northeast Texas, east of Dallas, and is the home of East Texas State College. Commerce had a population of 5,789 in 1960. *Eighteenth Census of the United States*, "Population," volume 1, part 2, section 45, 45–36, Table 8. http://newspaperarchive.com/, http://www.census.gov/.

73 "This Is the Story of a Dragon Named Peter… And What He Has Done to Make His Paper Profitable, Efficient and Award-Winning," *The American Press* 82:12 (October 1964): 28, 30. Albion, in New York's Orleans County, had a population of 6,416 in 1960. *Eighteenth Census of the United States*, "Population," volume 1, part 2, section 34, 34–18, Table 7. http://www.census.gov/.

74 John D. Martin, "In-Person Interview with Author," June 23, 2009.

75 In 2022, according to the latest government figures based on the Consumer Price Index, $500,000 from 1960 was worth $5 million. http://measuringworth.com/.

76 "The Weekly Editor: Mail Bagged," *Editor & Publisher* 93:51 (December 17, 1960): 30. Jackson, in Georgia's Butts County, had a population of 2,545 in 1960. *Eighteenth Census of the United States*, "Population," volume 1, part 2, section 6, 6–12, Table 2. http://www.census.gov/.

77 Rick Friedman, "The Weekly Editor: Supplements," *Editor & Publisher* 97:5 (February 1, 1964): 29. Dearborn, in Michigan's Wayne County, had a population of 112,007 in 1960. *Eighteenth Census of the United States*, "Population," volume 1, part 2, section 24, 24–21, Table 7. Birmingham, in Michigan's Oakland County, had a population of 25,525 in 1960. *Eighteenth Census of the United States*, "Population," volume 1, part 2, section 24, 24–20, Table 7. http://www.census.gov/.

78 Billy Smith, "The Weekly Editor: Prizes to the Swift," *Editor & Publisher* 93:11 (March 12, 1960): 57.

79 Rick Friedman, "The Weekly Editor: Promotion Pays Off," *Editor & Publisher* 97:24 (June 13, 1964): 40. Walnut Creek, in California's Contra Costa County, had a population of 9,903 in 1960. *Eighteenth Census of the United States*, "Population," volume 1, part 2, section 16, 16–24, Table 7. http://www.census.gov/.

80 Kenneth R. Byerly, "The Future of America's Weeklies," *The Grassroots Editor* 4:3 (July 1963): 3.
81 "Publishers Are Finding it Tougher to Get Second Class Entry," *The National Publisher* (April 1961): 15.
82 Billy Smith, "The Weekly Editor: Newspaper Survey," *Editor & Publisher* 93:17 (April 23, 1960): 148. In 2022, according to the latest government figures based on the Consumer Price Index, $3.38 from 1960 was worth $33.81 and $3.21 was worth $32.11.
83 "Greater Upland Stores… Gift-O-Rama," *The Upland* (CA) *News*, December 20, 1967, 11. In 2022, according to the latest government figures based on the Consumer Price Index, $539 from 1967 was worth $4,781.79. http://newspaperarchive.com/, http://measuringworth.com/. Upland, in California's San Bernardino County, had a population of 15,918 in 1960. *Eighteenth Census of the United States*, "Population," volume 1, part 2, section 6, 6–22, Table 5. http://www.census.gov/.
84 *The Hubbard* (OH) *News and Reporter*, November 6, 1968, 3, 16. http://newspaperarchive.com/.
85 "Reciprocal Trades," *Editor & Publisher* 93:51 (December 17, 1960): 30.
86 Billy Smith, "The Weekly Editor: More on Circulation," *Editor & Publisher* 93:16 (April 16, 1960): 30. Marana, in Arizona's Pima County, had a population of 4,805 in 1960. *Eighteenth Census of the United States*, "Population," volume 1, part 2, section 4, 4–8, Table 7. http://www.census.gov/.
87 Billy Smith, "The Weekly Editor: Too Much Circulation?" *Editor & Publisher* 93:10 (March 5, 1960): 30.
88 Smith, "The Weekly Editor: More on Circulation," 30. Edgartown, in Massachusetts' Dukes County, had a population of 1,474 in 1960. *Eighteenth Census of the United States*, "Population," volume 1, part 2, section 23, 23–11, Table 7. http://www.census.gov/.
89 "The Weekly Editor: Circulation Gain," *Editor & Publisher* 103:14 (April 4, 1970): 30.
90 "N.E.A.," *The American Press* 82:9 (July 1964): 16.
91 "Press Group Opens Doors to Weeklies," *The Publishers' Auxiliary*, August 13, 1960, 8.
92 Rick Friedman, "The Weekly Editor: Regional Concept," *Editor & Publisher* 97:25 (June 20, 1964): 42.
93 Rick Friedman, "The Weekly Editor: Kentucky Central Plant," *Editor & Publisher* 100:8 (February 25, 1967): 38.
94 Friedman, "The Weekly Editor: Regional Concept," 42.
95 Gene Malott, "The Weekly Editor: His and Hers," *Editor & Publisher* 97:35 (August 29, 1964): 30. Trimont, in Minnesota's Martin County, had a population of 942 in 1960. *Eighteenth Census of the United States*, "Population," volume 1, part 2, section 25, 25–21, Table 7. Ceylon, also in Minnesota's Martin County, had a population of 554 in 1960. *Eighteenth Census of the United States*, "Population," volume 1, part 2, section 25, 25–20, Table 7. http://www.census.gov/.
96 Rick Friedman, "The Weekly Editor: Twin Weekly's Politics," *Editor & Publisher* 97:45 (November 7, 1964): 49. Clarion, in Pennsylvania's Clarion County, had a population of 4,958 in 1960. *Eighteenth Census of the United States*, "Population," volume 1, part 2, section 40, 40–24, Table 7. In 2022, according to the latest government figures based on the Consumer Price Index, $5 from 1964 was worth $48.64. http://measuringworth.com/.

97 Rick Friedman, "The Weekly Editor: The Fourth Criterion," *Editor & Publisher* 100:7 (February 18, 1967): 49. Milford, in Connecticut's New Haven County, had a population of 41,662 in 1960. *Eighteenth Census of the United States*, "Population," volume 1, part 2, section 8, 8–4, Table 2.
98 In 2022, according to the latest government figures based on the Consumer Price Index, $43 from 1969 was worth $347.46 and $7.95 was worth $645.24. http://measuringworth.com/.
99 "Net Income of Average Weekly Dips," 34. In 2022, according to the latest government figures based on the Consumer Price Index, $25.60 from 1969 was worth $206.86, $3.54 from 1969 was worth $28.60, $12.23 from 1969 was worth $98.82, $4.48 from 1969 was worth $36.20, $15,238 was worth $123,130, and $357 from 1968 was worth $3,039. http://measuringworth.com/.
100 David R. Bowers, "The Impact of Centralized Printing on the Community Press," *Journalism Quarterly* 46 (Spring 1969): 43.
101 "The Year that Was… and the Years Ahead," *The American Press* 86:3 (January 1968): 27, 29.

References

"1964 Newspaper Equipment Survey." *The American Press* 82:6 (April 1964): 14–20.
Bagdikian, Ben H. "Behold the Grass-Roots Press!" *Harper's Magazine* 229:1375 (December 1964): 102–105, 110.
Bowers, David R. "The Impact of Centralized Printing on the Community Press." *Journalism Quarterly* 46 (Spring 1969): 43–46.
"The Bowler's Corner." *The Titonka* (IA) *Topic*, February 18, 1965, 1.
Branned, William E. "Community and Paper Meet, Decide Code of Ethics." *The Publishers' Auxiliary*, September 10, 1960, 2.
Brown, Robert U. "Shop Talk at Thirty: Journalism Recruiting." *Editor & Publisher* 93:15 (April 9, 1960): 76.
Busch, Paul R. "The Weekly Editor: Among the Best." *Editor & Publisher* 100:5 (February 4, 1967): 36.
"Businessman of the Week." *The Rock Valley* (IA) *Bee*, June 9, 1966, 1.
Byerly, Kenneth R. *Community Journalism*. New York: Chilton Company, 1961.
Byerly, Kenneth R. "The Future of America's Weeklies." *The Grassroots Editor* 4:3 (July 1963): 3–5, 64.
Carter, Hodding. *First Person Rural*. Garden City, NY: Doubleday & Company, 1963.
Cary, William J., Jr. "The Weekly Editor: Rural Press Defended." *Editor & Publisher* 93:43 (October 22, 1960): 56.
"Charge: Irresponsible." *The American Press* 82:8 (June 1964): 4.
The Commerce (TX) *Journal*, December 15, 1960.
Dahl, Robert A. *Who Governs?: Democracy and Power in an American City*. New Haven: Yale University Press, 1961.

D'Antonio, William V., et al. "Institutional and Occupational Representatives in Eleven Community Influence Systems." *American Sociological Review* 26:3 (June 1961): 440–446.

Edelstein, Alex S., and Joseph J. Contris. "The Public View of the Weekly Newspaper's Leadership Role." *Journalism Quarterly* 43 (1966): 17–24.

Edelstein, Alex S., and Otto N. Larsen. "The Weekly Press' Contribution to a Sense of Urban Community." *Journalism Quarterly* 37 (1960): 489–498.

Edelstein, Alex S., and J. Blaine Schultz. "The Weekly Newspaper's Leadership Role as Seen by Community Leaders." *Journalism Quarterly* 40 (1963): 565–574.

"Editorial Viewpoint: The Unsung Builders." *The Seguin* (TX) *Gazette*, January 29, 1964, sec. 2, 2.

"The Editor's Job." *The Florence* (AL) *Herald*, September 19, 1963, 2.

The Eighteenth Dicennial Census of the United States, Census of Population: 1960. Edited by United States Bureau of the Census. Washington, DC: Government Printing Office, 1961.

The Emmetsburg (IA) *Democrat*, November 9, 1961, 1.

Friedman, Rick. "The Weekly Editor: A Call for Help." *Editor & Publisher* 100:32 (August 12, 1967): 40.

Friedman, Rick. "The Weekly Editor: Comments on a Conference." *Editor & Publisher* 100:34 (August 26, 1967): 30, 32.

Friedman, Rick. "The Weekly Editor: Extra!" *Editor & Publisher* 97:1 (January 4, 1964): 42.

Friedman, Rick. "The Weekly Editor: The Fourth Criterion." *Editor & Publisher* 100:7 (February 18, 1967): 48–49.

Friedman, Rick. "The Weekly Editor: Housewife Columnists." *Editor & Publisher* 100:38 (September 23, 1967): 42, 44.

Friedman, Rick. "The Weekly Editor: Kentucky Central Plant." *Editor & Publisher* 100:8 (February 25, 1967): 38.

Friedman, Rick. "The Weekly Editor: Promotion Pays Off." *Editor & Publisher* 97:24 (June 13, 1964): 40.

Friedman, Rick. "The Weekly Editor: Regional Concept." *Editor & Publisher* 97:25 (June 20, 1964): 42.

Friedman, Rick. "The Weekly Editor: Supplements." *Editor & Publisher* 97:5 (February 1, 1964): 29.

Friedman, Rick. "The Weekly Editor: Three Bullet Holes." *Editor & Publisher* 100:26 (July 1, 1967): 15, 50–51.

Friedman, Rick. "The Weekly Editor: Twin Weekly's Politics." *Editor & Publisher* 97:45 (November 7, 1964): 49.

Friedman, Rick. "The Weekly Editor: Women's Angle." *Editor & Publisher* 97:43 (October 24, 1964): 40, 42.

Friedman, Rick. "The Weekly Editor: Women's Angle (part 2)." *Editor & Publisher* 9:44 (October 31, 1964): 27–28.

"Greater Upland Stores... Gift-O-Rama." *The Upland* (CA) *News*, December 20, 1967.

"Happy Birthday Palko Triplets!" *The Hubbard* (OH) *News and Reporter*, November 6, 1968, 1.

Harris, Emerson P., and Elizabeth H. Hooke. *The Community Newspaper*. New York: D. Appleton and Company, 1923.

"Here's One Way to Compare Offset vs. Letterpress Cost." *The American Press* 82:11 (September 1964): 18–20.

"Here's Reason Why Items Do Not Always Get In Paper." *The Guthrian*, Guthrie, IA, November 26, 1963, 2.

The Hubbard (OH) *News and Reporter*, November 6, 1968

"Local Columns Sell Subs for America's Largest Rural Weekly." *The American Press* 82:1 (November 1963): 17–20.

Malott, Gene. "The Weekly Editor: His and Hers." *Editor & Publisher* 97:35 (August 29, 1964): 30.

Martin, John D. "In-Person Interview with Author." June 23, 2009.

"Maxims & Moonshine." *Time*, September 29, 1961, 57–58.

"Most Editors See Nixon Victory." *The Publishers' Auxiliary*, November 5, 1960, 1.

"N.E.A." *The American Press* 82:9 (July 1964): 16–17.

"Negro Ministers Seek Biracial Group; Communists Hit." *The Florence* (AL) *Herald*, July 11, 1963, 1.

"Net Income of Average Weekly Dips." *Editor & Publisher* 103:27 (July 4, 1970): 34.

"New Directories Being Distributed." *The Seguin* (TX) *Gazette*, January 29, 1964, sec. 2, 2.

"New Magazine for Weekly Editors." *The Publishers' Auxiliary*, January 16, 1960, 1.

Olien, Clarice N., George A. Donohue, and Phillip J. Tichenor. "The Community Editor's Power and the Reporting of Conflict." *Journalism Quarterly* 45:2 (June 1968): 243–252.

Peterson, Wilbur and Robert Thorp. "Weeklies' Editorial Effort Less than 30 Years Ago." *Journalism Quarterly* 39 (Winter 1962): 53–56.

Petsche, Jerry. "Publishers Seek Ways to Interest J-School Graduates." *The Publishers' Auxiliary*, January 2, 1960, 1.

"PR Men Told: Include Local Angles." *The Publishers' Auxiliary*, April 2, 1960, 4.

"Press Group Opens Doors to Weeklies." *The Publishers' Auxiliary*, August 13, 1960, 8.

"Publishers Are Finding it Tougher to Get Second Class Entry." *The National Publisher* (April 1961): 15.

"Publishers Predict Goldwater Victory." *The American Press* 82:12 (October 1964): 14.

"Reciprocal Trades." *Editor & Publisher* 93:51 (December 17, 1960): 30.

The Seguin (TX) *Gazette*, January 29, 1964, 2.

Sim, John Cameron. *The Grass Roots Press: America's Community Newspapers*. 1st ed. Ames, IA: The Iowa State University Press, 1969. Reprint, 1970.

"Smaller Newspaper Employee Problem Studied at N.I.U." *The Publishers' Auxiliary*, July 23, 1960, 3.

Smith, Billy. "The Weekly Editor: More on Circulation." *Editor & Publisher* 93:16 (April 16, 1960): 30.

Smith, Billy. "The Weekly Editor: Newspaper Survey." *Editor & Publisher* 93:17 (April 23, 1960): 148.

Smith, Billy. "The Weekly Editor: Prizes to the Swift "*Editor & Publisher* 93:11 (March 12, 1960): 57.

Smith, Billy. "The Weekly Editor: Too Much Circulation?" *Editor & Publisher* 93:10 (March 5, 1960): 30.

Stewart, Steve. "E-mail Interview with Author." June 25, 2009.
"Students Rate Newspaper Jobs as Low Paying." *The Publishers' Auxiliary*, February 20, 1960, 1.
"Success in the Sticks." *Time*, December 21, 1962, 42.
"That Important Editorial." *The Florence* (AL) *Herald*, March 28, 1963, 2.
"This Is the Story of a Dragon Named Peter... And What He Has Done to Make His Paper Profitable, Efficient and Award-Winning." *The American Press* 82:12 (October 1964): 28, 30.
Tichenor, Phillip J., Clarice N. Olien, and George Donohue. "Predicting a Source's Success in Placing News in the Media." *Journalism Quarterly* 44:1 (March 1967).
The Titonka (IA) *Topic*, February 18, 1965, 1.
The Upland (CA) *News*, December 20, 1967.
"Varieties of Violence." *Time*, September 22, 1961, 75.
Vidich, Arthur J., and Joseph Bensman. *Small Town in Mass Society*. Princeton, NJ: Princeton University Press, 1968.
"The Weekly Editor. $15 Conversion." *Editor & Publisher* 93:20 (May 14, 1960): 74.
"The Weekly Editor: Circulation Gain." *Editor & Publisher* 103:14 (April 4, 1970): 30.
"The Weekly Editor: Financial Report." *Editor & Publisher* 100:25 (June 24, 1967): 28.
"The Weekly Editor: Freebooter." *Editor & Publisher* 93:41 (October 8, 1960): 68.
"The Weekly Editor: Killed Ghost Town." *Editor & Publisher* 97:33 (August 15, 1964): 42.
"The Weekly Editor: Mail Bagged." *Editor & Publisher* 93:38 (September 17, 1960): 34.
"The Weekly Editor: Mail Bagged." *Editor & Publisher* 93:43 (October 22, 1960): 56.
"The Weekly Editor: Mail Bagged." *Editor & Publisher* 93:51 (December 17, 1960): 30.
"The Weekly Editor: News Brief." *Editor & Publisher* 93:42 (October 15, 1960): 58.
"The Weekly Editor: News Brief." *Editor & Publisher* 93:48 (November 26, 1960): 38.
"The Weekly Editor: Thursdata, Lends a Hand." *Editor & Publisher* 97:8 (February 22, 1964): 55.
"The Weekly Editor: Thursdata, Welcome Home?" *Editor & Publisher* 93:10 (March 5, 1960): 30.
"The Weekly Editor: Unforeseen Demand." *Editor & Publisher* 93:13 (March 26, 1960): 127.
"The Weekly Editor: The Van Meter Reader." *Editor & Publisher* 97:47 (November 21, 1964): 40.
"The Weekly Editor: Wife, Son & G.M." *Editor & Publisher* 97:37 (September 12, 1964): 30.
"What to Do with Publicity Releases." *The Publishers' Auxiliary*, January 16, 1960, 4.
www.measuringworth.com.
"The Year That Was... and the Years Ahead." *The American Press*, 86:3 (January 1968): 27–29.
"Young Desert Hot Springs Scientist." *The Desert Sentinel*, Desert Hot Springs, CA, March 8, 1962, 1.

· 8 ·

THE 1970S: CAREERS, CONTENT, CONSUMERS, CONSOLIDATIONS, AND COMPUTERIZATION

In the 1970s, mass media academics and sociologists, journalism educators and students, and newspaper industry and association professionals closely examined or considered community weeklies in terms of career opportunities, content, consumers, consolidations, and computerization. A tight hiring market in journalism led a growing number of college graduates and unemployed metropolitan daily workers to seek a career in the weekly field. Just as more college graduates reached out to community newspapers, so did their professors who initiated more academic studies in the areas of weekly newspaper content and consumers. In addition, consolidations of business operations, production, facilities, and staffing became more aggressive in the 1970s, due in large part to rapidly advancing technology, particularly in computerized operations.

A record number of journalism graduates, technology that reduced staffing requirements, and an economic recession that reduced hiring, led to a critical mass in the newspaper job market during the 1970s. As a result, more college graduates turned to weekly newspapers for long-term career choices as opposed to a steppingstone on the way to a metropolitan daily. Even career daily journalists began to view the weekly as an opportunity rather than a temporary stay-over between daily newspaper positions. Journalism education and job preparation became a topic of discussion in the tight job market. Job satisfaction also came into the discussion as former daily journalists came to recognize the value of the multitasking skills required of a non-daily staff member.

The content of weeklies had long been the subject of criticism and ridicule among the metropolitan press and academic elites. But there was difficulty in conducting content analyses of weeklies because many small-town publications were not available in original, microfilm, or microfiche form—except in their local libraries. However, as weeklies became more accessible at metropolitan and university libraries, a growing number of academics conducted content analysis studies to accurately depict the types of information available in the weekly press. Likewise, more aggressive academic and industry studies looked at the societal aspects of the weekly newspaper consumer. Thus, the important questions of who read a weekly and what were they reading were answered more scientifically and less anecdotally. In addition, some weeklies faced the threat of invasive weekly zoned editions from metropolitan dailies that attempted to tap into "localism" and weeklies' advertising and readership markets.

Consolidations of weeklies into group and chain ownership and the resulting loss of independent family-owned newspapers became a major topic of discussion among newspaper businessmen and their professional associations. The consolidation concept of drawing strength in numbers also related to circulation as weekly owners debated the advantages and disadvantages of paid versus free circulation in terms of cost and competition.

Finally, computer technology changed every facet of operations, from newsgathering and writing, to production and distribution. Veteran personnel became perplexed as they had to abandon traditional practices and procedures to comply with new technology standards. It was a move some were not willing to take. Many veteran personnel opted for retirement—which created job openings for more newcomers to join the weekly employee ranks.

In Tight Economy, Weeklies Appeal More to Veteran Journalists and Recent Graduates

The perceived role that *The Washington Post* reporters Bob Woodward and Carl Bernstein had in bringing down the Richard Nixon presidency in the 1974 Watergate scandal was often linked to an explosion in college journalism enrollment in the mid- to late-1970s. But some academics argued that there were several other factors that drew students to the field even before Watergate. A January 1974 article in *Journalism Educator* revealed statistics from the country's 158 journalism schools and departments that reported more than 48,000 students in four-year and graduate college and university programs majored in journalism, which was a 15.9 percent increase from the previous year. This increase in journalism enrollment was compared to level or slight decreases in other academic disciplines (although not specified in the article). In 1970, the journalism enrollment increase was only 5.9 percent from the previous year, but then began rising steadily with increases of 10.8 percent in 1971 and 13.6 percent in 1972.[1] Despite the "obvious glamour of Watergate" and its "getting the credit, or blame, for creating a flood of academic journalism groupies," American University professor Robert Blanchard outlined several other reasons why journalism enrollment had increased to 55,000 in 1975, based on statistics from the Association for Journalism in Education. He said journalism enrollment increases were part of a national student rebellion against higher education—which began in the mid-1960s. And similar to business and law schools, journalism schools provided "preparation for careers with specific, applicable skills." He referred to a waning appreciation for a broad liberal arts education and observed that students found "particularly refreshing, journalism's traditional adversary relationship with government." Also, journalism schools addressed the emerging mass communication field of study, whereas other academic disciplines had not. And finally, Blanchard asserted that the skills, values, and applied knowledge taught in media studies could be used in a variety of fields upon graduation.[2]

A rapid enrollment growth in college journalism programs—coupled with an economic recession—resulted in a tight job market for the newspaper industry overall. Not only were graduates struggling to find positions, but also veteran reporters. Therefore, some college graduates and veteran reporters who previously would not have considered seeking a position at a non-daily publication, did so.

Responding to those who snubbed their noses at weekly newspaper work, Clemson, South Carolina, *Messenger* editor George Padgett was quoted in a June 9, 1973 *Editor & Publisher* article about misconceptions concerning the weekly field. He said that beliefs among some journalists that working on a weekly was "non-professional, non-challenging, and lacking in the excitement and glamour of a daily" were "pure bunk." He speculated that out-of-work newsmen who sought weekly jobs as "last resorts" would find that the weekly staffer worked long hours for what, admittedly, was low pay as compared to dailies. However, the weekly staffer enjoyed a "variety of experiences the likes of which the daily reporter may never have." Also, Padgett pointed out that weekly reporters had an opportunity to do more demanding in-depth coverage of events—such as informing readers what the passage of a sewer bond referendum would do to local taxes.[3]

In an effort to determine what weekly newspapers paid newsroom employees, Northeastern University and the New England Press Association sponsored a salary survey in 1974. It reviewed the salaries of reporters, reporters-photographers, editors, advertising salesmen, advertising managers, and general managers from 73 New England weeklies and small dailies (up to 25,000 circulation) in a six-state area. It found that reporters with up to five years' experience earned a median salary of $148.50 per week ($7,722 per year) while those with more experience received median salaries of $187.50 per week, or $9,750 per year.[4] An editor of a paper with more than five years' experience—who more than likely doubled as a reporter—earned a median salary of $200 per week ($10,400 per year). Assistant publishers or general managers were paid an average of $282.50 per week, or $14,690 yearly.[5] A 1975 National Newspaper Association study showed that weekly publishers—with a volume of $200,000 to $400,000—paid themselves on average $19,211. The study noted that since publishers reaped both salary and profits, the two figures should be considered together. For example, weekly publishers, on average, provided a net profit before income of $26,909, on an average gross income of $286,090.[6] In comparison, a college graduate starting at a daily in 1975 earned a median salary of $140 per week, or $7,280 annually.[7]

A 1976 survey by The Dow Jones Newspaper Fund showed that nearly seven of every 10 college graduates who majored in a news-editorial sequence found daily or weekly newspaper jobs. In 1958, editors of *The Wall Street Journal* established The Dow Jones Newspaper Fund to improve the quality of journalism education and the pool of applicants for jobs in the newspaper business. *The Publishers' Auxiliary* reported that only 3 percent of weeklies planned to reduce staff in 1975 while nearly one-fifth looked to hire college graduates. Among daily newspapers, 90 percent anticipated either staff reductions or no increases in staffing for 1975. The survey also revealed that weeklies found other newspapers to be their second-best source for recruiting newsroom employees—indicating an overall shift to more dependence on skilled personnel.[8] So, despite the fact that many college journalism graduates had ignored weeklies because of perceptions of less professionalism and lower salaries, more turned to small-town newspapers by the mid- to late-1970s because of better job opportunities.

Given job demand, how well were colleges and universities preparing students for the community newspaper field? Not very well, according to a 1978 Association of Education in Journalism and N.N.A. survey. Results showed that only five schools of journalism (of a possible 300) offered a sequence, option, or emphasis in community journalism, and 25 more colleges taught one or more courses in community journalism.[9] A few textbooks published in the 1970s were specific to community journalism work. They included Bruce M. Kennedy's *Community Journalism: A Way of Life*,[10] John McKinney's *How to Start Your Own Community Newspaper*,[11] and *How to Produce a Small Newspaper* by Edward Miller, Kathleen Cushman, and Larry Anderson.[12]

A 1976 debate took place about the practicality of a formal journalism education. Some small-town editors asserted in an April 1976 *Journalism Educator* article that college training focused too much on theory and not enough on the practical side of the profession. They complained that some journalism schools tended to point students to the big dailies and did not give students a proper background for the self-starting responsibilities demanded on a community newspaper. Most of the editors interviewed for the article agreed that more attention should be given to courses about the newspaper business. Ro [sic] Gardner—publisher of the *Lake Elsinore* (CA) *Valley Sun*—said, "The more students can learn about doing a little bit of everything—even if it be pricing job printing in a Franklin catalogue, the economics of country journalism, and practical plumbing—it will help on a small weekly."[13]

University of Missouri publications manager John Inglish and journalism professor David Martinson countered in an October 1976 *Journalism Educator* article that it was especially important for their students who took positions at small dailies and weeklies to be well versed in First Amendment rights and "the societal obligations of the press, particularly at the grassroots level." The authors observed that an enrollment explosion in journalism gave smaller newspapers an opportunity to hire outstanding journalism students "who before would not have considered anything but the prestigious metropolitan dailies."[14]

However, there were college journalism students like Ben Kocher who never viewed the weekly newspaper field as a second-best choice to working at a metropolitan daily. A January 17, 1970 *Editor & Publisher* feature on Kocher noted that at age 24, he formed a self-named company and purchased his hometown weekly—*The Millersburg* (PA) *Sentinel*. As the only member of his high school graduating class to return to Millersburg after attending college, Kocher said townspeople viewed his purchase of the paper "in terms of hope that the youth drain from the town could be reversed." The history and political science major joined *The Millersburg Sentinel* staff shortly before college graduation, advancing to associate editor before purchasing the paper.[15]

The debate on theoretical versus practical skills courses in journalism education continued as some critics described journalism graduates as "academic zombies." Others countered that theory courses comprised only 30–40 percent of the curriculum. To improve journalism education, some professionals suggested that more emphasis be placed on the student newspaper as a training ground and on master's degrees and professional internships.[16]

Practical journalism experience became the cornerstone of a University of Arizona community journalism project in 1975 when students began publishing the 59-year-old *Tombstone* (AZ) *Epitaph*. The weekly circulated 400 local copies and sent 4,100 copies by mail. It focused on historical articles and local news. But the publisher realized that out-of-town readers were not as interested in local news; so, he separated the newspaper into two publications. Publisher Harold O. Love—a Detroit lawyer—continued writing articles with a heavy emphasis on historical Tombstone and western lore for the *Tombstone Epitaph Journals*. The students took over publication of the *Tombstone Epitaph, Local Edition*, which focused on community news.[17]

Some professionals considering ways to improve journalism education also suggested that "mid-career" educational programs be made available to young journalists who were already working in the profession. In response to a call for educational opportunities for working journalists, the National Newspaper Association and the National Editorial Foundation established a program in 1976 to help working small-town journalists broaden their skills. The N.E.F. also sponsored the National Blue Ribbon Newspaper "accreditation" program and served as a support member of the American Council on Education in Journalism.[18]

Women Have Greater Management Opportunities at Weeklies

Aside from entry-level jobs, management opportunities for women were more readily available at weeklies than dailies—although men continued to hold a large majority of the better-paying positions. A 1977 Indiana University survey found that 18 percent of female weekly employees held management positions, as compared to only 2.4 percent at dailies. Management positions defined in the study were publisher, assistant publisher, editor, manager, director, and assistant editor, manager, or director. The survey was based on 182 weekly respondents from all geographical regions in the United States. The survey also found that men owned, entirely or in part, 72 percent of the 182 weeklies responding to the national survey. Females owned only 16 percent of the 182 papers, and 12 percent of the papers were jointly owned by male-female partnerships. In addition, 86 percent of female weekly employees made less than $15,000 as compared to 45 percent of men.[19] According to respondents, there were several key reasons that employment opportunities were better for women at weeklies than dailies. These included lower salaries, fewer male applicants, heavy employment turnover, less competition for positions, and more part-time jobs.[20]

The *Duncannon (PA) Record* and the *Perry County (PA) Times*—featured in an October 24, 1970 *Editor & Publisher* article—represented typical employment patterns among females in family-owned newspapers. Richard Swank—publisher and editor of both papers—had one daughter serve as an assistant editor and the other as a photographer. Both women were in their early 20s. Another female employee in her 20s—whom Swank described as a "gal-Friday"—was the backbone of the papers, according to the 53-year-old publisher. The *Duncannon Record*'s masthead promoted the publication as "An old newspaper with a young outlook."[21]

One female editor in the 1970s who did not rely on marital status or family connections to land her the title of editor-publisher started her own paper. In 1970, Hazel Hout McKinnon founded the *Northeast Arkansas Town Crier*—which served nine communities. The former school teacher began writing news on a typewriter and soliciting advertisements from a home office in Manila, Arkansas. The paper was printed at an offset plant 90 miles away. McKinnon also served as photographer and employed three part-time workers to help with production and distribution of the 12–20-page publication. She told *Editor & Publisher* in a July 21, 1973 feature, "We've got an Addressograph (mailing label) machine in the kitchen, makeup tables on the back porch, which also serves as the main office, and I work from an old-fashioned roll-top desk in the den." She said the *Northeast Arkansas Town Crier* concentrated on "chatty" news, which she distinguished from "country-type" news because it referred to local events and individual accomplishments as opposed to the comings and goings of residents.[22]

Other women were finding success on the business side of the weekly news operation. Employment surveys regularly found classified departments heavily staffed with women, largely due to part-time job opportunities. But Marianne O'Neil found success as manager of the classified advertising department that served Long Island, New York's, Community Newspaper Inc.—which included five weeklies. At the time of an October 17, 1970 *Editor & Publisher* feature article, O'Neil's strategies worked to boost the classified pages total to six per week, published in a section carried by all five papers. One strategy she proposed was to write down the phone numbers listed on the sides of commercial trucks and contact the owners to solicit advertising. Of her 11 full- and part-time staff members, the two male employees were designated to handle out-of-office, recruitment real-estate, and automotive advertisements.[23]

More Personal Journalism, More Personal Attacks

Did weeklies aspire to be simply smaller versions of metropolitan dailies, or did they view their community role differently, and thus purposely differ in content choices and performance expectations of their college-trained employees? This question was explored by California State University-Long Beach journalism professor Gerald C. Stone and student Janet Morrison. They considered whether small-circulation newspapers lacked standards or if they served different purposes than the metropolitan press. They reviewed various studies in the community newspaper field that seemed to show hometown newspapers met a different set of goals. They conducted a content analysis of community weeklies and small-circulation dailies to compare content. Content reviewed was wire news, local news, local society, local sports, paid features, public relations, editorials-columns, correspondent copy, obituaries, wire pictures, free pictures, miscellaneous, national ads, local ads, classified ads, legal ads, and political ads. The study found that weekly and daily newspapers tended to carry similar types of content. However, they found that circulation had a bearing on the proportions of various types of content. For example, their findings indicated that lower-circulation newspapers stressed grassroots copy and legal advertising, and contained more "soft" society news from correspondents' copy. Smaller papers also had a higher ratio of publicity material but contained fewer paid features, local pictures, and national advertising.[24] In another content study summarized in the Summer 1964 *Journalism Quarterly* issue, Bradley S. Greenberg's 1964 investigation of community newspapers concluded that the small-town newspaper served as a tool of unification in the community. In printing local news and pictures that the larger urban daily newspapers did not publish, the community press supplemented rather than substituted for the larger papers, Stanford University's Greenberg asserted.[25]

Content, political relationships, and finances were the dependent variables of a follow-up study in which California State University-Long Beach journalism professor Gerald C. Stone and student Patrick Mazza considered the impact of consensus theory on the community newspaper organization. The study considered the independent variables of length of time the publisher lived in a community, whether the publisher identified himself as a top community leader, and the size of the community. The authors observed that consensus between the publisher and the community power structure did not interfere "with the normal flow of news or editorial comment, at least not in the percentages of news or editorial matter carried." The publisher could not expect financial gain—advertising revenue, in particular—from close associations with members of the community power structure, according to the study. The authors thus concluded that motives for "boosterism" were either the publisher's own civic pride or "a desire by him to lessen potential strain between himself and his friends in the power structure."[26]

The new owners of the *Deer Park* (TX) *Progress* made a front-page promise to its readers on the type and tone of content they could expect in their hometown weekly. The January 1, 1970 open letter to the community stated that community news, church news, school news, official news of the city, and personal news of "everyone who lives in Deer Park" would be the "backbone" of the *Deer Park Progress*. It continued, "There is much to be done in the community as Deer Park continues its meteoric growth, and *The Progress* hopes to be in the middle of this effort to publicize what ought to be done, what is being done and, if necessary, what ought not be done."[27]

So, despite decades of avoiding "crusading" editorials in favor of placating the business community and local political power structure, more weekly editors in the 1970s deemed it important to use their perceived influence to advocate ideas and actions, and to scold local officials when necessary. However, reporting "what ought not be done" was more challenging—and, yes, even more threatening—to the weekly publisher than the daily publisher because of familiarity among small-town residents. Despite earlier studies that pointed to an inconsistent use of locally written editorials among weeklies, a 1979 survey of 359 non-daily editors revealed a perceived importance placed on editorials and editorial pages. An overwhelming majority of the editors indicated that editorials and editorial columns were an important segment of their newspapers that could be used to influence readers—particularly on local issues.[28]

Throughout the 1970s, there was no shortage of examples of crusading reporting among weeklies. For example, in January 1970 attackers tossed a fire bomb that destroyed the composing room of *The Monroe County Democrat* in Madisonville, Tennessee. The firebomb followed two shooting attempts, a beating, a robbery/ransom attempt, and other minor intimidations designed to convince editor Dan Hicks, Jr. to stop "telling it like it is"—which was in reference to his ongoing campaign against corrupt local officials. Despite the damage, there was only a one-day delay in getting that week's edition out. In 1969, Hicks had been awarded a Golden Quill Editorial Award and the Elijah P. Lovejoy Award for Courage in Journalism by the International Conference of Weekly Newspaper Editors for his ongoing fight against local corruption.[29]

Another east Tennessee paper, the *Newport Plain Talk* in Cocke County, faced new competition in 1970 when local officials invested in a weekly to try to run the *Newport Plain Talk* out of business. The Cocke County officials were unhappy the *Newport Plain Talk* reprinted an article from the *Knoxville (TN) News-Sentinel* that revealed alleged graft and corruption in the county. The *Newport Plain Talk* also ran a full-page account of an indictment against several local officials for civil rights violations. An overwhelming majority of the *Newport Plain Talk's* 7,000 subscribers—responding to a questionnaire—suggested that the paper should "keep on telling it like it is." The *Newport Plain Talk's* owner, John M. Jones, was also partial owner of the *Monroe County Democrat* that had come under attack in nearby Sweetwater for uncovering local corruption.[30]

A local political machine was also a threat to a southeast Georgia weekly published in the town of Ludowici. *Long County (GA) Press* editor William P. Durrence charged political machine officials with arson in a 1973 *Long County Press* fire. He also linked the machine to 10 other burnings in the previous four years and threats of arson to other Long County businesses—particularly *Long County Press* advertisers. The *Long County Press* was started in 1969 by 50 community residents who wanted a newspaper "just to print the truth." Durrence explained in a March 17, 1973 *Editor & Publisher* article that at the time of the paper's founding, Long County had a political machine that bought votes, used phony absentee ballots, and hand-picked juries and public servants. The 1973 arson incident followed local elections in which the anti-boss faction—supported by the Long County Press—elected three county commissioners (of five) and a new clerk.³¹

As publisher of the Marblehead (MA) Messenger, Bill Kirtz did not have to endure physical threats—only verbal charges of being a "troublemaker." Some residents of this upper-middle-class yachting village on the state's north shore did not approve of Kirtz's type of advocacy journalism. In a May 26, 1973 Editor & Publisher profile, he said some of the investigative reports created a stir among residents because the findings "didn't tell them what they wanted to hear." For example, Marblehead Messenger articles pointed to a community indifference to the problems in low- or middle-income housing, and allegations against a local yacht club for excluding Jews and Blacks from membership.³²

Supporters of community newspapers argued that because of close associations to their readers, community newspapers better understood the concerns and challenges of local residents than did nearby small dailies and large-circulation state and regional papers. Joseph Weston—editor of the Sharp Citizen in Cave City, Arkansas—asserted in a February 10, 1973 Editor & Publisher profile that because the metropolitan press could not reach out to regular people and interpret their problems, weeklies were being established at a rapid pace. The crusading editor founded his paper in 1972 and was an advocate of "personal journalism"—which included attacking politicians throughout the state. As a result, Weston regularly faced physical, economic, and legal threats.³³

Alexander Brook, publisher of the York County (ME) Star, was more cynical in his explanation of why dailies ignored controversy in the "outback." In fact, he leveled the same types of accusations against dailies that metropolitan reporters and editors charged against weeklies for decades: avoiding controversy in favor of commercialism. He asserted in his book, The Hard Way: The Odyssey of a Weekly Newspaper Editor, that the daily's only interest in rural areas was readership numbers for potential advertisers. As a result, he said, the dailies merely served as "scribes," recording events rather than reporting them. Dailies did not probe for "the story behind the story," he added, "because that can be dangerous—and why bother? It doesn't wage community service campaigns or investigate outback official shenanigans, because so what? It doesn't waste editorial breath on outback improvement, because who cares?"³⁴

But metropolitan dailies continued to fight back in their efforts to garner readers and advertisers from suburban weeklies. In 1975, The Washington Post began delivering zoned editions to the tri-state suburbs of Washington, D.C.,

Virginia, and Maryland. An August 1975 article in *The Publishers' Auxiliary* noted that several weekly zoned editions had appeared in markets across the country. The Suburban Newspapers of America organization knew of no situation where a metropolitan weekly zoned edition forced a suburban newspaper out of business, but the threat was real. *The Washington Post* reported that its first zoned editions generated 90,000 lines of advertising. Publishers of Sentinel Newspapers that circulated in Virginia and Maryland considered court challenges on charges of monopolistic practices by *The Washington Post*.[35] The following year, several weekly publishers in Cook County, Illinois, challenged *The Chicago Tribune's* Suburban Trib network—which published suburban zoned editions—for publishing legal notices. Illinois state law required that legal notices be published in a "newspaper circulated generally in the area." The plaintiff publishers contended that the Trib's zoned editions were printed in another county—and thus were first issued in a place other than Cook County.[36]

Weeklies also endured legal and business threats as a result of covering questionable practices at institutions and among the business community. For example, a September 29, 1973 *Editor & Publisher* article recounted the arrest of James Stewart—a 19-year-old reporter for the *Collegeville (PA) Independent*—for defiant trespass by the warden of the nearby Graterford Prison. Stewart—working for his family-owned paper—wrote about corruption, hushed-up escapes, and prisoner assaults. The *Collegeville Independent* published a nine-part series on the prison prior to Stewart's arrest. As a result of the series, the *Collegeville Independent* pushed for prison reform alleging that the prison offered no work or schooling programs.[37]

Editor-publisher Rupert Phillips of *The Mountain Home (AR) Baxter Bulletin* learned that the local Realtor board voted to withhold advertising because it disliked his paper's coverage of fires, accidents, floods, hospital conditions, and city council meetings and controversies. In 1973, visitor numbers were up at the resort community but real estate business was down. The Realtor board president complained about one article in *The Mountain Home Baxter Bulletin* on unusually high water in nearby lakes. He charged that the paper never pointed out "how it was going to make the fishing better." The Realtor board called off the advertising boycott after it began receiving national attention. *The Mountain Home Baxter Bulletin* was the largest weekly in Arkansas with a circulation of 11,500. The same year of the advertising boycott, the paper received the Arkansas Press Association sweepstakes award as the state's overall best weekly.[38]

Despite occasional boycotts, readers and merchants overall showed relative satisfaction with the content of their hometown weekly. For example, a 1970 University of Utah study found that 67 store managers in 12 Utah counties indicated they were satisfied with their hometown papers as an effective spokesman for the community in dealing with social, political, education, and economic problems.[39] A 1975 Syracuse University survey found that local content and features were the most popular items among newspaper readers and that newspapers were preferred five to one over television as a source of local news.[40]

A Priority in Personal Content over Product Promotion, Political Posturing

At the other end of the content spectrum from investigative reports and personal crusades was the community correspondent column. Correspondent columns rarely drew criticism unless a name was omitted or misspelled. Even into the so-called modern era of the 1970s, traditional correspondent columns persisted in weeklies throughout the country. *The Monroe Journal* in Monroeville, Alabama, ran columns from a dozen correspondents when Steve Stewart became the paper's editor in 1973.[41] A 1977 edition of the *Santa Rosa (NM) News* published columns from correspondents in the communities of La Loma, Newkirk, Cuervo, Dahlia, Dilia, Pasgura, Vaughn, Encino, Puerto de Luna, and Anton Chico.[42] News from the rural communities of Riverton, Watson, Locust Grove, and Farragut in Fremont County, Iowa, were regular features of *The Hamburg (IA) Reporter*.[43]

It was not uncommon to find some correspondents whose length of service equaled or nearly equaled that of the number of years their community received designated column space in a nearby weekly. Among the faithful correspondents was Bruna McGuire, who began writing for Ray County, Missouri, weeklies in the early 1900s. In 1970, she was still going strong at age 86, as was her column, "With Homefolks."[44] But one noticeable change in the columns by the 1970s was the correspondent byline. In previous decades, the common practice was to precede a married female columnist's name with the courtesy title of "Mrs." However, a 1979 issue of *The Democrat* in Emmetsburg, Iowa, identified female correspondents by first and last name only.[45]

Local content in small-town weeklies operated on the premise that "everyone knows everyone." Evidence of the small-town paper's tonal approach to news from a "we're all family" standpoint perhaps explained the photograph of six dateless but identified boys—lined up at their high school junior-senior prom. The caption under the photo in the April 27, 1972 issue of *The Hamburg* (IA) *Reporter*, read, "The proverbial stag line."[46] Also, it would have been difficult to find a metropolitan daily with a local restaurant promotional for "Rabbit Suppers Served This Friday Night," as was printed in a May 9, 1973 *Greene* (IA) *Recorder* advertisement for Sonny's Lounge in Greene, Iowa.[47]

Despite a push for personal journalism that included personal crusades and people-oriented features, weeklies were persistently labeled the conduit for free publicity. Whether for product promotion or political posturing, academics and media elites viewed weeklies as dumping grounds for publicity-type "news." But several content analyses showed that locally generated content—as opposed to syndicate or publicity "news" material—was at a higher percentage in weeklies than major and second-tier (smaller market) dailies.

A 1973 University of Wisconsin-Eau Claire study looked at the use of political publicity in one of the state's U.S. congressional districts during a non-election year. The sample included 50 weeklies in the Third Congressional District (including southwest and central-west Wisconsin counties) from a two-week period in October. The 32 press releases sent from the district's one congressman and two senators were compared to their placement success rate. Also observed were subject matter, placement, length, and copy editing of the releases. Of the 50 weeklies, 33 did not print any of the releases. Eight of the papers published 30 percent of the releases sent, and were thus deemed "easy marks" for free publicity. The study authors refuted generalized claims and criticisms of extensive use of publicity in the weekly press. They concluded that the politicians studied were "minimally successful" in placing their releases in weeklies, adding, "Editors are not so gullible and do not passively accept Capitol Hill press releases."[48]

A Summer 1976 issue of *Journalism Quarterly* highlighted a study that looked at the placement of news releases provided to Georgia weeklies from the University of Georgia Cooperative Extension Service. The extension service sent weekly packets to 168 weeklies with information about agriculture, home economics, and other related areas. The researchers reviewed a year's content of 14 weeklies and compared the placement of the materials to the total amount of information distributed. They found that the 14 papers used 15.7 percent of the available information. The heaviest use was material related to agricultural subjects—especially "how-to-do-it" stories.[49]

Some publishers fought back against the industrial icons that looked to weeklies for free space, while spending large advertising budgets on television and dailies. A December 15, 1973 *Editor & Publisher* article reprinted a cover letter sent to weekly publishers throughout the country from the R.J. Reynolds Industries Corporate Publications Manager. The letter accompanied a "news" service packet that contained articles to promote cigarette sales. *Editor & Publisher* also published a reply letter sent to Reynolds from David Kramer, president of the Illinois Press Association and publisher of six weeklies at Gibson City. Kramer's letter stated that for years he watched Reynolds pump huge amounts of advertising money into television, radio, magazines, billboards, and dailies—but not weeklies. He pointed out that the company would not get free space in the other media, but appeared to expect it from weeklies. He concluded, "You spent your money with the other media and we've made it okay without it. Now get them to run your 'news.'"[50]

In relation to overall content, one editor-publisher found he spent too little time concerned with the quality of his newspaper's content because so much of his time was required on layout and design. By the early 1970s, the *Brown County Democrat* in Nashville, Indiana—a 2,700-circulation weekly that averaged from 8 to 12 pages a week—moved to a modular, quasi-magazine-style makeup. The content was compartmentalized—using a lot of photographs and jumped stories. In fact, publisher Bruce Temple won several design awards for his efforts. He recalled to *Editor & Publisher* in a May 12, 1973 article, "I was brought up on metropolitan dailies where the emphasis was on helping the reader wade through scores and even hundreds of pages each day." Convinced that weekly community newspapers had a different mission, he redesigned the *Brown County Democrat* to have a nineteenth-century look, meaning one-column headlines and no photographs on the front page. One reader complained that he had to "read the whole paper" to find certain items, which was Temple's goal from the outset.[51]

Who Reads Weeklies and What Do They Read?

Several studies were conducted during the decade to determine who read weekly newspapers and their preferred news sources for various types of information. Many studies pointed to the fact that most readers of weeklies also subscribed to a nearby daily. In fact, longtime publisher Mel Ruder—of the

Hungry Horse News in Columbia Falls, Montana—recommended to his subscribers that they read a daily as well as a weekly. He even phoned in stories to the dailies—after his paper went to press.[52] But a 1977 Newspaper Readership Project survey revealed that only one in three daily newspaper readers also read a paid weekly. However, another third of the daily readers indicated that they regularly read a free weekly or shopper.[53]

A study of Pennsylvania weeklies offered a snapshot of readers who could be considered more community-minded because they submitted letters to the editor. Researchers Michael Singletary and Marianne Cowling reviewed the content of 25 non-daily newspapers in 22 Pennsylvania counties for a six-week period in the summer of 1977. They collected the names and addresses of writers of letters to the editor and sent them questionnaires. Of the 115 questionnaires sent out, 84 were returned. Among the responding letter writers, a third were under the age of 40, most held professional jobs, more than half attended college, and three-fourths were male. Nearly 40 percent of the letters related to community problems, while 30 percent concerned state, national, and local government or politics.[54]

An Autumn 1978 *Journalism Quarterly* article discussed a study by University of Minnesota journalism professors Clarice Olien, George Donohue, and Phillip Tichenor that looked at news source preferences among residents who resided in weekly newspaper communities in Minnesota. At the time of the study, Minnesota had 293 communities with populations of 10,000 or less. Of those, all but four had weekly or twice-weekly newspapers. They analyzed data from survey studies conducted in 19 communities since 1969. Survey respondents were adults who had been interviewed in their homes. They were asked to choose among television, radio, and newspapers as their preferred source of news in general (did not specify type of news: local; national; or international). The analysis showed that television was the preferred choice among communities in which the local newspaper was a weekly. They also found that while 90 percent of the weeklies' news space was devoted to local news—as compared to 40 percent in regional dailies—the bulk of news in smaller papers covered social events and athletics. Therefore, the weekly newspaper readers relied more on television and regional dailies to provide their public affairs news.[55]

A 1978 study of media use among rural Louisiana residents also found a heavy reliance on television for news about local government issues. University of Alaska professor George Winford analyzed survey data from 277 rural Louisiana households on media source preference (television, radio, weeklies, or dailies) in four categories. The categories were: local government; local community events; agriculture and homemaking news; and advertising information. He found that television was the preferred source for local government news (64 percent), while weeklies led as the preferred source for news about community events. Television and weeklies were nearly equal in importance for providing agriculture and homemaking news—74 and 72 percent respectively. Weeklies were the most relied on source for advertising information (80 percent).[56]

Editorial and news content of small-town papers often reflected the assumed political leanings of readers of weeklies. For example, *The Florence* (AL) *Herald* apparently believed strongly that its readers were stand-up, patriotic citizens as evidenced by its February 26, 1970 re-printing of an American Legion Post resolution that condemned newspapers and television commentators for tearing down "America and our Armed Forces" during the Vietnam War. The resolution objected to the continued "spread of gossip, rumor, and hearsay directed against officers and men of the United States Army." *The Florence Herald* editorial conceded that some newspapers and commentators played up the sensational side of the news, resulting in "a great disservice to the nation's morale, both at home and abroad." It concluded, "Until our fighting men are brought home we are with them one hundred percent."[57]

A 1970 editorial in *The Florence Herald*, published on March 26, responded to the presumed conservatism of its readers when it referred to an "assortment of bearded and banded" University of Alabama students. The students were criticized for heckling former Alabama Governor George Wallace at a campus event. The editorial referred to the students' behavior as "shameful." The editorial also speculated that some of the heckling students would look back on their behavior and feel ashamed, adding, "We sincerely hope so, but we have our DOUBTS. They are just NOT OUR KIND OF PEOPLE."[58]

The *Algona* (IA) *Kossuth County Advance*, on the other hand, acknowledged the independent thinking among its readers when an editorial referred to recent elections and how Kossuth Countians voted both Democrat and Republican in national and local races. The November 13, 1978 editorial, signed "R.B.W."—for publisher R.B. Waller—stated, "On the national level, the results should send a clear message to Washington that there is an underlying dissatisfaction with the way some things are going, chiefly excessive government spending and inflation."[59]

Although knowing one's audience was an important element to editorial writing, even more important was attracting readers to the editorial pages—according to a respected journalism educator and former publisher. University of Georgia professor Ernest C. Hynds wrote a two-part series for *The Publishers' Auxiliary* in September 1977 on the importance of editorial writing. To encourage editorial readership, he said that editorials should take stands on important issues, especially local concerns. Also, he emphasized clarity in thinking and writing and the use of letters to the editor—which usually resulted in more calls and letters and subsequent editorial columns.[60] The second part of his series focused on tactics to increase reader participation in local concerns. For example, he recommended that papers offer coupons for readers who replied to editorials. Another suggestion included the use of question-and-answer columns. Readers were requested to respond to a particular question and their responses were published as a group of letters.[61]

Consolidations and Ownership: Larger Chains and Circulations, Fewer Family-Owned Papers

Consolidations continued into the 1970s—most aggressively in the area of group and chain ownership. A major incentive for consolidation was to increase group circulation to boost blanket coverage numbers and attract more national advertising. In fact, the decade opened with the announced formation of a national weekly newspaper group—Newspaper Corporation of America. Financier Cliff Hooper headed the Nashville-based company that indicated plans to offer weekly newspapers in all 50 states.[62] Another successful weekly chain was Newspapers Incorporated of Shelbyville, Kentucky. In 1970, it was only two years old but already claimed ownership of nearly 15 percent of the state's weekly newspapers. It also had printing contracts for 30 percent of the state's weeklies. A November 14, 1970 *Editor & Publisher* article indicated that demands from publishers to be absorbed by the company were outstripping its capacity to print more publications.[63]

The continued consolidation of printing operations of weeklies to a central plant—begun in the 1960s—resulted in savings of as much as 40 percent of operating costs, according to a December 24, 1976 article in *The Publishers' Auxiliary*. Three kinds of central printing were described that were often regional in popularity. For example, cooperative central printing originated in Wisconsin and remained the most widespread form. A cooperative plant was jointly owned by several newspaper publishers. Operating costs and revenues were shared among the owners. In another central plant operation, one newspaper might own a central plant that printed other publications for a fee. Other central printing plants were stand-alone commercial enterprises not owned by a newspaper or newspaper group. The appeal of centralized printing—in addition to saving equipment and labor costs—was the potential for profit and growth.[64]

Centralized printing plants also led to a reduction in the number of weeklies that maintained a commercial printing operation. Traditionally, revenues from a job shop enabled small-town weeklies to remain in business. However, as advertising revenue grew and central presses became an option, many weeklies abandoned their retail print operations. Generally, the larger-circulation non-dailies with higher average advertising-line rates and a higher percentage of national advertisements were less likely to have a commercial printing operation.[65]

But, a May 23, 1977 article in *The Publishers' Auxiliary* advised publishers to consider the profitability of their job shops before shutting them down. The article stated that commercial printing accounted for 34 percent of overall revenues for small-town newspapers with job shops. A survey of 128 publishers found that 98 had some form of commercial publishing income, derived mostly from the printing of stationery, business cards, and forms.[66] While solely commercial press operations were expanding in metropolitan areas, the combination newspaper-print business was the more likely type of printing operation to be found in rural communities.

Some weeklies found it beneficial to consolidate their newsroom operations—in addition to advertising. A University of Wisconsin study reviewed the merged operations of 26 community weeklies within the state. Given that most of the publishers owned two or more papers, their individual newspapers were often produced at one central editorial office. According to the study—reported in the October 3, 1977 issue of *The Publishers' Auxiliary*—advantages of the consolidations were lower operating costs, better printing arrangements, and increased advertising. A disadvantage was loss of contact with each community. But the reality was that many of the smaller papers could not make a profit as a stand-alone operation.[67]

Another concern about the growth of chains and consolidations was that chain-owned and consolidated newspapers would become homogenized editorial voices. In the 1970s, University of Minnesota professors Daniel Wackman, Donald Gillmor, and Everette Dennis looked at the homogeneity of chain-owned daily newspapers. They considered chain newspaper autonomy in relation to presidential endorsements and found that chain papers were more likely to endorse candidates, and that there was a degree of homogeneity within chains. But, they ascertained that as the number of chain newspapers and independent voters—often susceptible to endorsements—grew, the press could play an important role in maintaining a two-party system. Their argument was based on the "enormous Democratic Party registration edge and Republican-biased newspaper endorsements," which resulted in "adjusting the balance in partisan politics." While their study did not consider weeklies, similar observations could be drawn given the weeklies' history of strong endorsements for Republican presidential candidates.[68]

The rise in group and chain ownership—especially in suburban weeklies—also gave rise to concern about the loss of family-owned newspapers and potential members for weekly professional organizations. In fact, more growth was seen in suburban weeklies, as part of a corporate group or chain, than the traditional independent, family-owned weekly—although some publishing families did expand their ownership to multiple weeklies. Responding to this change in growth patterns, the Suburban Section of the National Newspaper Association merged with the Suburban Press Foundation and the Accredited Home Newspapers of America in 1971 to form the Suburban Newspapers of America. Three years later, the N.N.A. voted to change its bylaws to allow a place on its board for an S.N.A. representative.[69] Finally, in 1977, the N.N.A. determined that suburban papers were eligible for membership if at least 25 percent of their content was news.

The loss of family-owned weeklies also meant a loss in membership numbers for the National Newspaper Association—the oldest press association in the U.S., founded in 1885. Newspaper scholar Hiley Ward interviewed N.N.A. Executive Vice President William G. Mullen at the 1977 annual meeting of the Kansas Press Association, at which Mullen stated that N.N.A. would promote legislation to keep family newspapers from being sold. Much of the problem, Mullen explained, was in family newspapers being sold to pay estate taxes.[70] By 1980, N.N.A. faced fiscal challenges stemming from deficits in the late 1970s with moves to a new Washington, D.C. headquarters and retention of an outside attorney for postal lobbying efforts. Profitability questions arose about publishing its weekly tabloid—*The Publishers' Auxiliary*. In 1970, N.N.A. stopped publication of a monthly magazine—*National Publisher*. Other membership challenges came from the American Newspaper Publishers Association, which, in the mid-1970s, changed its membership restriction from dailies only to include weeklies. Some weekly and small daily publishers opted to reduce operation costs by maintaining membership in A.N.P.A. only. Also, Suburban Newspapers of America—formed by N.N.A. to conduct advertising research and other services for suburban papers—became its own entity in 1976, decreasing N.N.A.'s membership.[71]

To address concerns about high estate taxes for independently owned newspapers, Arizona U.S. congressman Morris K. Udall proposed legislation in 1977 designed to encourage independent local newspaper ownership by authorizing trusts to finance future estate tax liabilities from current newspaper profits. The proposed legislation was for weekly or daily papers not owned by chains or public corporations.[72] Udall urged the government to examine ownership concentration in the newspaper industry. In an August 3, 1977 article in *The Washington Post* on independent newspapers, he referred to letters he received in support of newspapers remaining in local hands. The congressman said that inheritance and business tax laws forced "papers to merge and chains to buy, often at twice what the paper is worth."[73] Two years later, there still was no legislative relief. At a 1979 hearing of the U.S. Senate Small Business Committee, a business analyst explained that newspaper operations were selling at about 50 times their earnings. For estate tax purposes, the Internal Revenue Service placed the valuation of the newspaper on what a buyer was willing to pay. Thus, an owner's heirs were often forced to sell the paper to pay taxes.[74] But the administration of U.S. President Jimmy Carter voiced its disapproval of proposed estate tax law changes aimed at keeping locally owned newspapers from being purchased by chains. A treasury department official admitted the proposal would "at best, make it less expensive to pass newspapers from generation to generation," but said it did not address the "market situation" of the "ability and willingness" of big companies to pay high prices for newspapers. The prime sponsor of the legislation, North Carolina U.S. Senator Robert Morgan, said, "Faced with the enormous amount of tax, with large cash offers from chains, and with little financial incentive to hold on to this important community service, the owners have sold out. They are selling out at a rate of one a week to chains." Like Senator Mo Udall's earlier proposal, the 1979 estate tax legislation included a provision to allow a local newspaper owner to set up a tax-exempt trust to pay estate taxes. Opponents voiced concerns of "special relief for only one group of small businessmen."[75] The estate tax issue remained unresolved at the end of the decade.

But weekly newspaper purchases were not exclusive to traditional business groups and newspaper chains. By the 1970s, some weeklies (total number unknown) became community-controlled publications as citizens combined their investments to maintain or revitalize financially troubled papers. The citizens often formed community foundations or independent trusts to maintain or establish an independent, locally focused news organization. A benefit—in addition to group capital—was an established advertising base that could guarantee a small paper's survival. A September 10, 1976 issue of *The Publishers' Auxiliary* featured an article on a community-controlled paper that was established in Lake City, Michigan. A former school superintendent was designated the publisher because he was the only retired member among the eight-man purchasing team. The article observed, "In this and other small communities, the business experience of local residents and the genuine community spirit have meant the survival of their newspapers."[76]

A group of citizens in Greenburgh, New York, tried to save the town's weekly after its publisher announced the January 1970 shutting down of *The Greenburgh (NY) Independent* due to financial difficulties. Greenburgh citizens formed a "Save the Paper Committee" and quickly raised $4,000, which was enough to publish another issue. A page-one banner on the issue read, "People Plead for Papers." A full-page advertisement on the front page proclaimed, "This Paper is About to Die." The advertisement solicited donations, and $6,000 was raised the following week.[77]

Another factor that impacted the loss of overall membership in the N.N.A. was an increase in the number of small-town newspapers that published more than once a week. As in the 1960s, it was not uncommon for weeklies located in rapid-growth areas to convert to daily or bi-weekly and tri-weekly publication. However, some communities gained a new weekly after an established weekly converted to a non-daily publication. So, after weekly numbers shifted between startups and conversions to non-dailies, N.N.A. was able to claim a membership of about 5,000 weeklies and 700 small-town dailies in 1977. Throughout its history, N.N.A. failed to gain a majority of weekly newspaper membership largely due to financial and time constraints for publishers. Most weeklies, however, were members of their state press associations. The number of weeklies and small-town dailies totaled nearly 9,000 by the end of the decade.[78]

Some weeklies were not successful in their conversion to daily publication. A 1976 article in a December 10, 1976 issue of *The Publishers' Auxiliary* pointed out that some weeklies struggled financially and physically in the conversion to a daily. Challenges included an initial drop in circulation, loss of advertising accounts to competing publications, weak advertising support for multiple issues, and an insufficient population base to support circulation and advertising demands. The article also inferred that some papers failed in their efforts to increase frequency simply because they were not given enough time to succeed.[79]

In other instances, newspaper entrepreneurs viewed a weekly's conversion to a daily as an opportunity to start another weekly in that same community. For example, *The Saline County (AR) Pacesetter*—a weekly that started in Benton, Arkansas, in 1972—benefited from the success of Benton's other weekly that transitioned to a daily. Its 22-year-old publisher Whitney Jones speculated that because the people of the county were accustomed to a strong weekly, they would support the *The Saline County Pacesetter*.[80]

Another major consolidation concern related to the issue of free versus paid circulation. Of course, most "free" weeklies began as shoppers—with little or no news content. The blanket circulation offered by free shoppers enticed some advertisers away from the traditional subscriber-paid weekly. Thus, weeklies often found it financially beneficial to consolidate with a shopper, or to start their own. The shopper was the focus of a July 11, 1977 article in *The Publishers' Auxiliary* pointing out that since shoppers arrived on the scene in the early 1950s, rural weeklies were still being advised to publish their own shopper before a competing one could be established. In 1977, it was estimated that 27 percent of small newspapers published shoppers. The article stated that weekly newspapers putting out a shopper did better financially than those that did not.[81]

A number of publishers converted their papers from paid circulation to free circulation in response to pressure from the free shoppers' blanket circulation, the dailies' zoned editions, and advertisers. Zoned editions refer to changes in advertising and content to reflect the particular region, outlying community, or suburb, to which the newspaper is delivered. The advantage of free circulation—also known as controlled circulation—was that a newspaper was delivered free of charge to areas of desirable demographics for advertising solicitation purposes. Despite the conversion to free circulation, news content was not always compromised. For example, even though the Toms River (NJ) *Shopper Reporter* began as a "throwaway," it transitioned to the *Reporter* in 1968, when news content was added to the weekly. Following the conversion from a shopper, more than 9,000 subscribers voluntarily paid for delivery of the *Reporter* under a controlled-payment plan. Founders and publishers Gilbert M. Seiznick and Leonard Lipitz emphasized that the free-circulation aspect of the operation gave advertisers the benefit of mass circulation (46,874) while enhanced editorial content gave the paper its readership.[82]

Father and son publisher and editor Edward B. Wright, Sr. and Edward B. Wright, Jr. converted their newspapers from paid to free circulation because they anticipated that free distribution from their competitors was inevitable. The Wrights owned the *Forest Hill* (OH) *Journal* and *Forest Hill* (OH) *Community Weekly*. Then, they started a new free weekly, the *Community Journal*, to compete with paid weeklies in adjoining Cincinnati-area counties. The Wrights increased their circulation from 7,200 paid to 40,000 controlled. They maintained the editorial integrity of the papers and their original broadsheet size to avoid being labeled tabloid-sized shoppers.[83]

Like the Wrights' papers, the *Westport* (CT) *News* emphasized local news content since it began publishing in 1964 as a free-circulation newspaper. It later converted to controlled circulation, but its contents always reflected that of a traditional newspaper. Publisher B.V. Brooks, Jr. observed, "A free paper can buy circulation but must earn readership." He said that in a town like upscale Westport, the average free newspaper could not survive. "There are too many bright people and you can't feed them anything but quality."[84]

A mid-1970s recession and the changeovers to free circulation, shoppers, group ownership, and multi-weekly publication resulted in a modest decline in weekly circulation for the first time in more than a decade. On the positive side, the N.N.A.'s 25th Weekly Newspaper Cost Study revealed that advertising revenue for weeklies climbed to $1.1 billion in 1975. Despite a two-year recession, total revenues from advertising, commercial printing, circulation, and miscellaneous income brought the total to $1.8 billion.[85] In 1975, weekly circulation dropped 616,279 to 35.1 million—according to figures released by the N.N.A. Also, the total number of weeklies dropped, from 7,612 in 1974 to 7,482 in 1975. Among reasons cited for the circulation losses were recession-led shutdowns of newspapers and a shift to shopper-type publications whose circulation figures were not included in N.N.A. reports. Other reasons given were the conversion of weeklies to dailies, and rising postage prices. Higher postage rates brought a decrease in the number of, or amount of, free-circulation newspapers.[86]

A 20-year analysis of weekly circulation from 1960 until 1980 showed that overall circulation increased 102 percent—mostly derived from an increase in free circulation. Since 1960, paid circulation increased by 65.5 percent, while free circulation increased by 172 percent. Paid circulation was highest among rural weeklies (47.3 percent) as compared to only 39.7 percent of suburban weeklies, and 13 percent of weeklies in resort communities. The study used a proportion random sample of papers from New Jersey, Georgia, Michigan, and

Washington. The study also revealed that 60 percent of group-owned papers had more free than paid circulation.[87]

Computerization Takes Over

The 1970s saw a near complete transition in the weekly newspaper field from "hot metal" to "cold type" printing—in which the images of a newspaper page were created through photocomposition rather than in metal type. In his 1980 work, *Goodbye Gutenberg*, Anthony Smith provided a detailed description of new printing technologies that were available by the end of the 1970s. As he explained, a central processing unit (C.P.U.)—which served as a memory storage unit—replaced trays of molten lead, and web-fed offset presses replaced antiquated sheet-fed letterpress equipment. Reporters and editors used video display terminals (V.D.T.s) to type their copy on a standard typewriter-type Q.W.E.R.T.Y. keyboard. The V.D.T.s had a cathode ray tube on which text appeared as keys were struck. Completed text was then sent to the C.P.U. for editing. Another means to send copy to the C.P.U. was through an O.C.R.— or optical character reader—which was often referred to as a "scanner." The O.C.R.-read copy was typed on an electric typewriter and created an electronic signal that passed into the C.P.U. for memory storage. The O.C.R. could also create a punched paper tape that was fed into the C.P.U.'s memory. The C.P.U. automatically made corrections in hyphenation and justification of copy that was fed into the unit. Editors also used V.D.T.s for more complex editing—such as selection and arrangement of wire service and local copy, and designating the placement of photographs within the copy. The C.P.U. produced paper strips of columned copy that was cut and pasted onto a life-size copy of each newspaper page, with spaces left for photographs. The pages were then sent to the camera room where they were photographed to produce a negative, from which a printing plate was made.[88]

A 1975 National Newspaper Association equipment survey revealed that most of the newspapers surveyed planned to spend the largest part of their equipment budget on composition equipment in the coming two years. The survey revealed that 91 percent of the country's weeklies were printed on an offset press, 20 percent planned to purchase O.C.R. equipment, and 10 percent used a computerized V.D.T. system. Also, photocomposition was the composition method of choice by 77 percent of the N.N.A. survey respondents.[89]

Bruce Turvold—of the award-winning, 4,000-circulation *Cresco* (IA) *Times-Plain Dealer*—was one of the many small-town editors who embraced new technologies for typesetting and design. He also encouraged the use of a picture page as often as possible—given the advances in photocomposition that made it much easier to incorporate and produce high-quality photographs. Offset production and camera-ready copy was prepared at the *Cresco Times-Plain Dealer* office and delivered to a central plant at Calmar, Iowa, for printing.[90]

Despite the advances in technology, costs remained a major concern for weeklies. It was not uncommon for a print shop to use equipment several decades old. But replacements had to come much more quickly with the development of computerized equipment. And despite cost savings on production and staff due to advanced technologies, newspapers were still printed on paper. Throughout the decade, the newspaper industry faced newsprint prices that had doubled since 1970 amid allegations of price-fixing among newsprint producers.[91] In addition, the industry faced newsprint shortages—particularly in the latter half of the decade—that reached record levels.[92] A major contributing factor was a mid-decade strike by the Canadian Paperworkers Union against four Quebec newsprint companies—which hampered newsprint production for six months.[93] Newsprint shortages proved to be another factor forcing small, independent publications to shut down or to be sold to a chain.[94]

While computer technology brought production costs down, it also raised concern among employees that their positions would be eliminated or shifted to other responsibilities. Anthony Smith, the *Goodbye Gutenberg* author, described the dire newspaper-production-staff employment situation as follows: "Between the newsroom and the loading dock very few employees remain."[95] National Newspaper Association Executive Vice President Theodore A. Serrill pointed out that weeklies and small dailies avoided some potential unionization problems because they were quick to embrace offset printing and computerized typesetting—resulting in publishers being "freed from the printer's apron."[96] The result of real or presumed staff downsizing, however, made the prospect of unionization among weekly newspaper employees a concern for publishers. Attendees at the 1977 N.N.A. Convention were advised to listen to employees' complaints and remedy legitimate concerns in an effort to thwart union organization attempts. Media labor consultant Robert Ballow suggested that management meet with employees to explain business trends and production figures—thus giving employees a sense of involvement in the company.[97] Ultimately, the move to offset meant fewer workers were required in the press operations, so weeklies did not have to deal with as many union organization efforts and the threat of strikes as the metropolitan dailies.

Reporters and editors were not as concerned about being replaced by a computer as they were about using a computer for everyday job functions. The use of a V.D.T. required more skill than a regular typewriter. Some veteran journalists decided to retire rather than learn the new technology. Training of newsroom staff became a key component of successfully making the transition to computerization. And it was not a certainty that recent college graduates would be well trained on the technology since much of their classroom training was on older, often outdated equipment.[98]

So, as computers reduced many production-efficiency problems, they also increased human resource problems. Most of these employee problems, according to author Anthony Smith, related to "the tension and anxiety of a staff about to undergo a major shift in work habits—even if direct loss of employment has been eliminated through negotiation." He asserted that the motivational system of the staff was thus altered as departments disappeared and others were merged. As a result, Smith said that trust and dependence between supervisors and employers were often "drastically altered."[99]

Weekly Newspaper Industry Faces Hard Realities: Make a Dollar or Make a Difference

The 1970s brought attention to some hard realities for the weekly newspaper industry. While new business models and chain ownership provided financial models for success, proud traditions such as family ownership and independent editorial voices were dying. Publishers—once revered as community leaders and outspoken critics—were becoming more concerned about making a dollar than making a difference. More weekly publishers no longer lived in their newspapers' communities—thus lacking a personal investment in the overall prosperity of the towns their publications served. Also, newsprint shortages and unionization threats made it difficult for small operations to survive. Estate tax laws forced a number of publishing families to relinquish not only their livelihoods, but a defining part of their lives.

Maine weekly publisher Alexander Brook echoed concerns about the loss of strong, independently owned weekly newspapers. In his 1993 book about his years in weekly journalism, Brook boasted that before he left the *York County* (ME) *Star* in 1977, it averaged between 60 and 84 broadsheet pages a week devoted exclusively to news about 50,000 residents in 15 communities. In comparison, he observed that *The New York Times* devoted roughly 40 pages a week on crime and government activities of the roughly 12 million residents of its city and surrounding communities. "A moderately active Kennebunker could expect to find his name repeated hundreds, even thousands, of times in the *Star* during his lifetime and the community events that shaped it," he said. "The average Brooklyn resident never, all his life long, finds himself mentioned in the *Times*."[100]

Notes

1 Paul V. Peterson, "U.S. J-Enrollments Jump Nearly 16 Per Cent," *Journalism Educator* 28:4 (January 1974): 3.
2 Robert O. Blanchard, "Rising J-Enrollments Caused by More than Watergate Glamor," *Journalism Educator* 30:3 (October 1975): 56–58.
3 Mark Mehler, "The Weekly Editor: More Work than Play," *Editor & Publisher* 106:23 (June 9, 1973): 19. Clemson, in South Carolina's Pickens County had a population of 5,561 in 1970. *Nineteenth Census of the United States*, "Population," volume 1, part 42, section 1, 42–07, Table 2. http://www.census.gov/.
4 In 2022, according to the latest government figures based on the Consumer Price Index, $148.50 from 1974 was worth $892, $7,722 was worth $46,383, $187.50 was worth $1,126, and $9,750 was worth $58,565. http://www.measuringworth.com/.
5 George Speers and Richard W. Davis, "Salaries of Community Newspapers in New England for 1974," *Journalism Quarterly* 52:2 (Summer 1975): 346. In 2022, according to the latest government figures based on the Consumer Price Index, $200 from 1974 was worth $1,200, $10,400 was worth $62,469, $282.50 was worth $1,696, and $14,690 was worth $88,238. http://www.measuringworth.com/.
6 "N.N.A. Cost Study Shows What Weekly Publishers Pay Themselves," *The Publishers' Auxiliary*, August 10, 1976, 1. In 2022, according to the latest government figures based on the Consumer Price Index, $200,000-$400,000 from 1975 was worth $1.1-$2.2 million, $19,211 was worth $105,728, $26,909 was worth $148,094, and $286,090 was worth $1,574,509. http://www.measuringworth.com/.
7 "1975 Grads Found Jobs, Newspaper Fund Reports," *Journalism Educator* 31:3 (October 1976): 24. In 2022, according to the latest government figures based on the Consumer Price Index, $140 from 1975 was worth $770 and $7,280 was worth $40,065. http://www.measuringworth.com/.
8 Theodore Serrill, "Weeklies Attract More Graduates," *The Publishers' Auxiliary*, April 25, 1975, 1.
9 Quintus C. Wilson, "Community Journalism Makes Curriculum Gains," *Journalism Educator* 33:4 (January 1979): 9.

10 Bruce M. Kennedy, *Community Journalism, A Way of Life* (Ames, IA: Iowa State University Press, 1974).
11 John McKinney, *How to Start Your Own Community Newspaper*, 3rd ed. (Port Jefferson, NY: Meadow Press, 1977).
12 Edward Miller, Kathleen Cushman, and Larry Anderson, *How to Produce a Small Newspaper* (Harvard, MA: The Harvard Common Press, 1978).
13 Clifton O. Lawhorne, "Editors of Smaller Newspapers See Weaknesses in J-Education," *Journalism Educator* 31:1 (April 1976): 3–5. Elsinore, in California's Riverside County had a population of 3,530 in 1970. *Nineteenth Census of the United States*, "Population," volume 1, part 6, section 1, 6–30, Table 6. http://www.census.gov/.
14 John M. Inglish and David L. Martinson, "Cures Suggested by Editors Might Be Worse than Disease," *Journalism Educator* 31:3 (October 1976): 48–49.
15 Craig Tomkinson, "The Weekly Editor: Youth Takes Over," *Editor & Publisher* 103:3 (January 17, 1970): 309. Millersburg, in Pennsylvania's Dauphin County had a population of 3,074 in 1970. *Nineteenth Census of the United States*, "Population," volume 1, part 40, section 1, 40–10, Table 2. http://www.census.gov/.
16 D. Earl Newsome, Curtis MacDougall, et al., "A Crisis on the Campus—Is the Emphasis on Theory Undermining Journalism Education—and Ruining Tomorrow's Journalists?" *The Publishers' Auxiliary*, May 23, 1977, 18.
17 "Students Take Over Tombstone 'Epitaph,'" *Journalism Educator* 30:1 (April 1975): 33. Tombstone, in Arizona's Cochise County had a population of 1,241 in 1970. *Nineteenth Census of the United States*, "Population," volume 1, part 4, section 1, 4–10, Table 6. http://www.census.gov/.
18 "N.E.F. Plans Community Journalism Program," *Journalism Educator* 31:1 (April 1976): 41.
19 In 2022, according to the latest government figures based on the Consumer Price Index, $15,000 from 1977 was worth $74,700. http://www.measuringworth.com/.
20 Susan Holly, "Women in Management of Weeklies," *Journalism Quarterly* 56:4 (Winter 1979): 811–814.
21 Craig Tomkinson, "The Weekly Editor: Young at Heart," *Editor & Publisher* 103:43 (October 24, 1970): 40. Duncannon, in Pennsylvania's Perry County had a population of 1,739 in 1970. *Nineteenth Census of the United States*, "Population," volume 1, part 40, section 1, 40–16, Table 2. http://www.census.gov/.
22 Mike Masterson, "The Weekly Editor: Former Teacher Gets On-the-Job Education," *Editor & Publisher* 106:29 (July 21, 1973): 22. Manila, in Arkansas' Mississippi County had a population of 1,961 in 1970. *Nineteenth Census of the United States*, "Population," volume 1, part 5, section 1, 5–12, Table 6. http://www.census.gov/.
23 Craig Tomkinson, "The Weekly Editor: Classified Success," *Editor & Publisher* 103:42 (October 17, 1970): 40.
24 Gerald C. Stone and Janet Morrison, "Content as a Key to the Purpose of Community Newspapers," *Journalism Quarterly* 53:3 (Autumn 1976): 494, 497–498.
25 Bradley Greenberg, "Community Press as Perceived by Its Editors and Readers," *Journalism Quarterly* 41 (Summer 1964): 437, 440.
26 Gerald C. Stone and Patrick Mazza, "Impact of Consensus Theory on Community Newspaper Organization," *Journalism Quarterly* 54:2 (Summer 1977): 314, 319.

27 "Progress Will Be Community's Voice," *The Deer Park* (TX) *Progress*, January 1, 1970, 1. Deer Park, in Harris County, is located in southeast Texas, just east of Houston. Deer Park had a population of 12,773 in 1970. *Nineteenth Census of the United States*, "Population," volume 1, part 45, section 1, 45–12, Table 6. http://newspaperarchive.com/, http://www.census.gov/.

28 Ernest C. Hynds and Charles H. Martin, "How Non-Daily Editors Describe Status and Function of Editorial Pages," *Journalism Quarterly* 56:2 (Summer 1979): 318.

29 Craig Tomkinson, "The Weekly Editor: Editor Attacked Again," *Editor & Publisher* 103:4 (January 24, 1970): 38. Madisonville, in Tennessee's Monroe County had a population of 2,614 in 1970. *Nineteenth Census of the United States*, "Population," volume 1, section 44, part 1, 44–08, Table 2. http://www.census.gov/.

30 Craig Tomkinson, "The Weekly Editor: Politicos Start Rival Paper," *Editor & Publisher* 103:8 (February 21, 1970): 43. Newport, in Tennessee's Cocke County had a population of 7,328 in 1970. *Nineteenth Census of the United States*, "Population," volume 1, section 44, part 1, 44–05, Table 2. http://www.census.gov/.

31 Margaret Fisk, "The Weekly Editor: Truth Draws Fire in Georgia," *Editor & Publisher* 106:11 (March 17, 1973): 39. Ludowici, in Georgia's Long County had a population of 1,419 in 1970. *Nineteenth Census of the United States*, "Population," volume 1, part 12, section 1, 12–13, Table 6. http://www.census.gov/.

32 Mark Mehler, "The Weekly Editor: New Publisher Rouses Yankee Town," *Editor & Publisher* 106:21 (May 26, 1973): 24. Marblehead, in Massachusetts' Essex County had a population of 21,295 in 1970. *Nineteenth Census of the United States*, "Population," volume 1, section 23, part 1, 23–04, Table 2. http://www.census.gov/.

33 Margaret Fisk, "The Weekly Editor: Arkansas Editor Faces Trial," *Editor & Publisher* 106:6 (February 10, 1973): 12. Cave City, in Arkansas' Sharp/Independence Counties had a population of 807 in 1970. *Nineteenth Census of the United States*, "Population," volume 1, part 5, section 1, 5–11, Table 6. http://www.census.gov/.

34 Alexander B. Brook, *The Hard Way: The Odyssey of a Weekly Newspaper Editor* (Bridgehampton, NY: Bridge Works Publishing Co., 1993), 257. Kennebunk, in Maine's York County had a population of 5,646 in 1970. *Nineteenth Census of the United States*, "Population," volume 1, section 21, part 1, 21–09, Table 3. http://www.census.gov/.

35 Sharon Mikutowicz, "Battle for Suburbs—Washington 'Davids' Face 'Goliath' Post," *The Publishers' Auxiliary*, August 25, 1975, 1.

36 "Zoned Editions Aren't Eligible for Legal Notices, Court Rules in Illinois," *The Publishers' Auxiliary*, December 10, 1976, 1.

37 Margaret Fisk, "The Weekly Editor: Father, Son Team Expose Pa. Prison," *Editor & Publisher* 106:39 (September 29, 1973): 14. Collegeville, in Pennsylvania's Pickens County had a population of 3,191 in 1970. *Nineteenth Census of the United States*, "Population," volume 1, section 40, part 1, 40–15, Table 2. http://www.census.gov/.

38 Margaret Fisk, "The Weekly Editor: Realtors Pressure on Arkansas Paper Fails," *Editor & Publisher* 106:40 (October 6, 1973): 15. Mountain Home, in Arkansas' Baxter County had a population of 3,936 in 1970. *Nineteenth Census of the United States*, "Population," volume 1, part 5, section 1, 5–12, Table 6. http://www.census.gov/.

39 "The Weekly Editor: Merchants' Attitudes," *Editor & Publisher* 103 (March 14, 1970): 27.

40 "Newspapers Are No. 1 in Local Information Readers Say in Survey," *The Publisher's Auxiliary*, September 10, 1975, 1.
41 Steve Stewart, "E-mail Interview with Author," June 25, 2009. Monroeville, in Monroe County, is located in south-central Alabama. Monroeville had a population of 4,846 in 1970. *Nineteenth Census of the United States*, "Population," volume 1, part 2, 2–11, Table 6. http://www.census.gov/.
42 *Santa Rosa* (NM) *News*, October 20, 1977, 6. Santa Rosa, in Guadalupe County, is located in east-central New Mexico. Santa Rosa had a population of 2,485 in 1970. *Nineteenth Census of the United States*, "Population," volume 1, part 33, 33–11, Table 6. http://newspaperarchive.com/, http://www.census.gov/.
43 *The Hamburg* (IA) *Reporter*, April 27, 1972, 3, 7. Hamburg, in Fremont County, is located in the southwest corner of Iowa. Hamburg had a population of 1,649 in 1970. *Nineteenth Census of the United States*, "Population," volume 1, part 17, 17–13, Table 6. http://www.newspaperarchive.com/, http://www.census.gov/.
44 Viola Roadcap Groce, "The Weekly Editor: Little Chronicler," *Editor & Publisher* 103:17 (April 25, 1970): 38. Richmond, the largest town in Missouri's Ray County, had a population of 7,951 in 1970. The county population stood at 17,599. *Nineteenth Census of the United States*, "Population," volume 1, section 27, part 1, 27–15, Table 2. http://www.census.gov/.
45 *The Democrat*, December 6, 1979, 5. Emmetsburg, in Palo Alto County, is located in the northwest part of Iowa. Emmetsburg had a population of 4,150 in 1970. *Nineteenth Census of the United States*, "Population," volume 1, part 17, 17–12, Table 6. http://newspaperarchive.com/, http://www.census.gov/.
46 "The Proverbial Stag Line," *The Hamburg* (IA) *Reporter*, April 27, 1972, 6.
47 "Rabbit Suppers Served This Friday Night," *The Greene* (IA) *Recorder*, May 9, 1973, 10. Greene, in Butler County, is located in the northeast part of Iowa. Greene had a population of 1,363 in 1970. *Nineteenth Census of the United States*, "Population," volume 1, part 17, 17–13, Table 6. http://newspaperarchive.com/, http://www.census.gov/.
48 Leslie D. Polk, John Eddy, and Ann Andre, "Use of Congressional Publicity in Wisconsin District," *Journalism Quarterly* 52:3 (Autumn 1975): 544–545.
49 Al Hester and Sharron Smith Millwood, "How Georgia Weeklies Utilize Extension Service News," *Journalism Quarterly* 53:2 (Summer 1976): 330–331, 333.
50 "Publisher Hits Weekly Tobacco 'News' Service," *Editor & Publisher* 106:50 (December 15, 1973): 15. Gibson City, in Illinois' Ford County had a population of 3,454 in 1970. *Nineteenth Census of the United States*, "Population," volume 1, section 15, part 1, 15–09, Table 2. http://www.census.gov/.
51 Bruce Gregory Temple, "The Weekly Editor: Readers Like New-Old Look," *Editor & Publisher* 106:19 (May 12, 1973): 15. Nashville, in Indiana's Brown County had a population of 527 in 1970. *Nineteenth Census of the United States*, "Population," volume 1, section 16, part 1, 16–05, Table 2. http://www.census.gov/.
52 Ann Geracimos, "The Weekly Editor: Weekly for Sale," *Editor & Publisher* 106:43 (October 27, 1973): 34. Columbia Falls, in Montana's Flathead County had a population of 2,652 in 1970. *Nineteenth Census of the United States*, "Population," volume 1, section 28, part 1, 28–04, Table 2. http://www.census.gov/.

53 "One of Three People Read Community Newspapers, Readership Report Says," *The Publishers' Auxiliary*, November 28, 1977, 4.
54 Michael W. Singletary and Marianne Cowling, "Letters to the Editor of the Non-Daily Press," *Journalism Quarterly* 56:4 (Winter 1979): 165–166.
55 Clarice N. Olien, George A. Donohue, and Phillip J. Tichenor, "Community Structure and Media Use," *Journalism Quarterly* 55:3 (Autumn 1978): 445, 447–449.
56 George M. Winford, "Newspaper Versus 'Newspaper': A Statewide Study of the Weekly," *Journalism Quarterly* 55:1 (Spring 1978): 136–137.
57 "A Resolution," *The Florence* (AL) *Herald*, February 26, 1970, 2. Florence, in Lauderdale County, is located in northwestern Alabama. Florence had a population of 34,031 in 1970. *Nineteenth Census of the United States*, "Population," volume 1, part 2, section 2, 2–11, Table 8. http://www.census.gov/.
58 "A Shameful Episode," *The Florence* (AL) *Herald*, March 26, 1970, 2.
59 "Independent Thinkers," *The Algona* (IA) *Kossuth County Advance*, November 13, 1978, 10. Algona, in Kossuth County, is located in north-central Iowa. Algona had a population of 6,032 in 1970. *Nineteenth Census of the United States*, "Population," volume 1, part 17, 17–11, Table 6. http://www.newspaperarchive.com/, http://www.census.gov/.
60 Ernest C. Hynds, "The Newspaper Editorial Page—Is it Heading for Oblivion, or Does it Remain an Important Vehicle for Service to the Public?, Part 1," *The Publishers' Auxiliary*, September 12, 1977, 6.
61 Ernest C. Hynds, "The Newspaper Editorial Page—Is it Heading for Oblivion, or Does it Remain an Important Vehicle for Service to the Public?, Part 2," *The Publishers' Auxiliary*, September 19, 1977, 7.
62 "Network of Weeklies Planned by New Firm," *Editor & Publisher* 103:2 (January 10, 1970): 24.
63 Craig Tomkinson, "The Weekly Editor: One More and Growing," *Editor & Publisher* 103:46 (November 14, 1970): 70. Shelbyville, in Kentucky's Shelby County had a population of 4,182 in 1970. *Nineteenth Census of the United States*, "Population," volume 1, section 19, part 1, 19–10, Table 2. http://www.census.gov/.
64 "Central Printing, Once a Trend, Is Now the Norm," *The Publishers' Auxiliary*, December 24, 1976, 4.
65 Gerald C. Stone, "Financial Statement Will Determine Job Shop Value," *The Publishers' Auxiliary*, May 30, 1977, 5.
66 Gerald C. Stone, "Considering Dropping Your Job Shop Business—Study the Figures Closely," *The Publishers' Auxiliary*, May 23, 1977, 20.
67 Janet Rodekohr, "Merged Editorial Offices Have Given Wisconsin Weeklies Upper Hand on Costs," The *Publishers' Auxiliary*, October 3, 1977, 1.
68 Daniel B. Wackman, et al, "Chain Newspaper Autonomy as Reflected in Presidential Campaign Endorsements," *Journalism Quarterly* 52:3 (Autumn 1975): 420.
69 "N.N.A. Members Approve Several By-Law Changes," *The Publishers' Auxiliary*, October 10, 1974, 3.
70 Hiley Henry Ward, "Ninety Years of the National Newspaper Association: The Mind and Dynamics of Grassroots Journalism in Shaping America," (dissertation, University of Minnesota, 1977), 313.

71 "Dark Cloud Hangs Over National Newspaper Association," *Editor & Publisher* 113:39 (September 27, 1980): 14.
72 William H. Jones, "Udall's Newspaper Bill Gets Industry Support," *The Washington Post*, October 7, 1977, E3.
73 William H. Jones and Laird Anderson, "Endangered Independents," *The Washington Post*, August 3, 1977, D9.
74 Nancy L. Ross, "U.S. Cautious on Media Concentration," *The Washington Post*, May 30, 1979, E3.
75 "Change in Estate Tax Law Opposed," *The Washington Post*, November 11, 1979, F12.
76 "Community Ownership—Good Idea," *The Publishers' Auxiliary*, September 10, 1976, 1. Lake City, in Michigan's Missaukee County had a population of 704 in 1970. *Nineteenth Census of the United States*, "Population," volume 1, section 24, part 1, 24–11, Table 2. http://www.census.gov/.
77 Craig Tomkinson, "The Weekly Editor: Never-Say-Die," *Editor & Publisher* 103:7 (February 14, 1970): 50. In 2022, according to the latest government figures based on the Consumer Price Index, $4,000 from 1970 was worth $30,516 and $6,000 was worth $45,774. http://measuringworth.com/. Greenburgh, in New York's Westchester County had a population of 85,746 in 1970. *Nineteenth Census of the United States*, "Population," volume 1, section 34, part 1, 34–14, Table 2. http://www.census.gov/.
78 Ward, "Ninety Years of the National Newspaper Association," 309.
79 Bill White, "Not All Papers Succeed at Increasing Their Frequency," *The Publishers' Auxiliary*, December 10, 1976, 3.
80 Heber Taylor, "The Weekly Editor: Doctor's Son Makes Success of Arkansas Weekly," *Editor & Publisher* 106:17 (April 28, 1973): 50. Benton, in Arkansas' Saline County had a population of 16,499 in 1970. *Nineteenth Census of the United States*, "Population," volume 1, part 5, section 1, 5–11, Table 6. http://www.census.gov/.
81 Edgar Trotter and Gerald Stone, "Shoppers Are Permanent Fixtures—But What Else?" *The Publishers' Auxiliary*, July 11, 1977, 11.
82 "The Weekly Editor: From Free to Paid," *Editor & Publisher* 103:24 (June 13, 1970): 56. Toms River, in New Jersey's Ocean County had a population of 7,303 in 1970. *Nineteenth Census of the United States*, "Population," volume 1, section 32, part 1, 32–06, Table 2. http://www.census.gov/.
83 Craig Tomkinson, "The Weekly Editor: Converts to Free," *Editor & Publisher* 103:50 (December 12, 1970): 53. Forest Hill is a neighborhood in the Cleveland Heights and East Cleveland sections of Cleveland in Ohio's Cuyahoga County. The two sections had a combined population of 100,367 in 1970. *Nineteenth Census of the United States*, "Population," volume 1, section 37, part 1, 37–06, Table 2. http://www.census.gov/.
84 Craig Tomkinson, "The Weekly Editor: No Longer Free," *Editor & Publisher* 103:44 (October 31, 1970): 15. Westport, in Connecticut's Fairfield County had a population of 27,414 in 1970. *Nineteenth Census of the United States*, "Population," volume 1, part 8, section 1, 8–12, Table 6. http://www.census.gov/.
85 Theodore Serrill, "Total Weekly Revenues Increase $75 Million to $1.8 Billion During '75," *The Publishers' Auxiliary*, July 24, 1976, 1. In 2022, according to the latest government

figures based on the Consumer Price Index, $1.1 billion from 1975 was worth $6.16 billion and $1.8 billion was worth $10.09 billion. http://measuringworth.com/.
86 "Weeklies' Circulation Takes Modest Dip During 1975," *The Publishers' Auxiliary*, March 10, 1976, 1.
87 Eugenia Zerbinos, "Analysis of the Increase in Weekly Circulation, 1960–1980," *Journalism Quarterly* 59:3 (Autumn 1982): 467, 469–470.
88 Anthony Smith, *Goodbye Gutenberg: The Newspaper Revolution of the 1980s* (New York: Oxford University Press, 1980), 86–87, 89–91.
89 "Conversion to Offset of Weeklies, Dailies Is Nearing Completion," *The Publishers' Auxiliary*, November 10, 1975, 1.
90 Gerald B. Healey, "The Weekly Editor: Imagination at Central Plant," *Editor & Publisher* 106:47 (November 24, 1973): 42. The *Times-Plain Dealer* was named Iowa's Newspaper of the Year for two consecutive years and won numerous state and national awards. Cresco, in Iowa's Howard County had a population of 3,927 in 1970. *Nineteenth Census of the United States*, "Population," volume 1, section 17, part 1, 17–12, Table 2. http://www.census.gov/.
91 Bill White, "Antitrust Investigation of Domestic Newsprint Producers Is Under Way," *The Publishers' Auxiliary*, July 25, 1977, 1.
92 "Supplies of Newsprint Averaged 30 Days for October, Lowest Level in Seven Years," *The Wall Street Journal*, December 4, 1979, 10.
93 "Paperworkers, 4 Quebec Mills Reach Settlement on New Wage Package," *The Publishers' Auxiliary*, January 24, 1976, 1.
94 Jones and Anderson, "Endangered Independents," D9.
95 Smith, *Goodbye Gutenberg: The Newspaper Revolution of the 1980s*, 86.
96 Jeffrey Colin Van, "The Community Press: Health Is Good," *The Publishers' Auxiliary*, January 24, 1976, 1, 3.
97 "Threat of Union Organizational Moves for Smaller Newspapers Held Greater," *The Publishers' Auxiliary*, November 7, 1977, 2.
98 Smith, *Goodbye Gutenberg: The Newspaper Revolution of the 1980s*, 97.
99 Ibid., 106–107.
100 Brook, *The Hard Way: The Odyssey of a Weekly Newspaper Editor*, 255.

References

1970 Census of Population. edited by United States Bureau of the Census: Washington, DC: Government Printing Office, 1972.

"1975 Grads Found Jobs, Newspaper Fund Reports." *Journalism Educator* 31:3 (October 1976): 24.

Blanchard, Robert O. "Rising J-Enrollments Caused by More than Watergate Glamor." *Journalism Educator* 30:3 (October 1975): 56–58.

Brook, Alexander B. *The Hard Way: The Odyssey of a Weekly Newspaper Editor*. Bridgehampton, NY: Bridge Works Publishing Co., 1993.

"Central Printing, Once a Trend, Is Now the Norm." *The Publishers' Auxiliary*, December 24, 1976, 4.

"Change in Estate Tax Law Opposed." *The Washington Post*, November 11, 1979, F12.

"Community Ownership–Good Idea." *The Publishers' Auxiliary*, September 10, 1976, 1.

"Conversion to Offset of Weeklies, Dailies Is Nearing Completion." *The Publishers' Auxiliary*, November 10, 1975, 1.

"Dark Cloud Hangs Over National Newspaper Association." *Editor & Publisher* 113:39 (September 27, 1980): 14.

The (Emmetsburg, IA) *Democrat*, December 6, 1979.

Fisk, Margaret. "The Weekly Editor: Arkansas Editor Faces Trial." *Editor & Publisher* 106:6 (February 10, 1973): 12.

Fisk, Margaret. "The Weekly Editor: Father, Son Team Expose Pa. Prison." *Editor & Publisher* 106:39 (September, 29, 1973): 14.

Fisk, Margaret. "The Weekly Editor: Realtors Pressure on Arkansas Paper Fails." *Editor & Publisher* 106:40 (October 6, 1973): 15.

Fisk, Margaret. "The Weekly Editor: Truth Draws Fire in Georgia." *Editor & Publisher* 106:11 (March 17, 1973): 39.

Geracimos, Ann. "The Weekly Editor: Weekly For Sale." *Editor & Publisher* 106:43 (October 27, 1973): 34–35.

Greenberg, Bradley. "Community Press as Perceived by Its Editors and Readers." *Journalism Quarterly* 41 (Summer 1964): 437–440.

Groce, Viola Roadcap. "The Weekly Editor: Little Chronicler." *Editor & Publisher* 103:17 (April 25, 1970): 38.

The Hamburg (IA) *Reporter*, April 27, 1972.

Healey, Gerald B. "The Weekly Editor: Imagination at Central Plant." *Editor & Publisher* 106:47 (November 24, 1973): 42.

Hester, Al, and Sharron Smith Millwood. "How Georgia Weeklies Utilize Extension Service News." *Journalism Quarterly* 53:2 (Summer 1976): 330–334.

Holly, Susan. "Women in Management of Weeklies." *Journalism Quarterly* 56:4 (Winter 1979): 810–815.

Hynds, Ernest C. "The Newspaper Editorial Page—Is It Heading for Oblivion, or Does it Remain an Important Vehicle for Service to the Public, part 1." *The Publishers' Auxiliary*, September 12, 1977, 6.

Hynds, Ernest C. "The Newspaper Editorial Page—Is It Heading for Oblivion, or Does it Remain an Important Vehicle for Service to the Public, part 2" *The Publishers' Auxiliary*, September 19, 1977, 7.

Hynds, Ernest C., and Charles H. Martin. "How Non-Daily Editors Describe Status and Function of Editorial Pages." *Journalism Quarterly* 56:2 (Summer 1979): 318–323.

"Independent Thinkers." *The Algona* (IA) *Kossuth County Advance*, November 13, 1978, 10.

Inglish, John M., and David L. Martinson. "Cures Suggested by Editors Might Be Worse than Disease." *Journalism Educator* 31:3 (October 1976): 48–49.

Jones, William H. "Udall's Newspaper Bill Gets Industry Support." *The Washington Post*, October 7, 1977, E3.

Jones, William H., and Laird Anderson. "Endangered Independents." *The Washington Post*, August 3, 1977, D9.

Kennedy, Bruce M. *Community Journalism, A Way of Life*. Ames, Iowa: Iowa State University Press, 1974.

Lawhorne, Clifton O. "Editors of Smaller Newspapers See Weaknesses in J-Education." *Journalism Educator* 31:1 (April 1976): 3–6, 60.

Masterson, Mike. "The Weekly Editor: Former Teacher Gets On-the-Job Education." *Editor & Publisher* 106:29 (July 21, 1973): 22.

McKinney, John. *How to Start Your Own Community Newspaper*. 3rd ed. Port Jefferson, NY: Meadow Press, 1977.

Mehler, Mark. "The Weekly Editor: More Work than Play." *Editor & Publisher* 106:23 (June 9, 1973): 19.

Mehler, Mark. "The Weekly Editor: New Publisher Rouses Yankee Town." *Editor & Publisher* 106:21 (May 26, 1973): 24.

Mikutowicz, Sharon. "Battle for Suburbs—Washington 'Davids' Face 'Goliath' Post." *The Publishers' Auxiliary*, August 25, 1975, 1.

Miller, Edward, Kathleen Cushman, and Larry Anderson. *How to Produce a Small Newspaper*. Harvard, Mass.: The Harvard Common Press, 1978.

"N.E.F. Plans Community Journalism Program." *Journalism Educator* 31:1 (April 1976): 41.

"Network of Weeklies Planned by New Firm." *Editor & Publisher* 103:2 (January 10, 1970): 24.

Newsome, D. Earl, Curtis MacDougall, et al. "A Crisis on the Campus—Is the Emphasis on Theory Undermining Journalism Education—And Ruining Tomorrow's Journalists?" *The Publishers' Auxiliary*, May 23, 1977, 18.

"Newspapers Are No. 1 in Local Information Readers Say in Survey." *The Publishers' Auxiliary*, September 10, 1975, 1.

"N.N.A. Cost Study Shows What Weekly Publishers Pay Themselves." *The Publishers' Auxiliary*, August 10, 1976, 1.

"N.N.A. Members Approve Several By-Law Changes." *The Publishers' Auxiliary*, October 10, 1974, 3.

Olien, Clarice N., George A. Donohue, and Phillip J. Tichenor. "Community Structure and Media Use." *Journalism Quarterly* 55:3 (Autumn 1978): 445–455.

"One of Three People Read Community Newspapers, Readership Report Says." *The Publishers' Auxiliary*, November 28, 1977, 4.

"Paperworkers, 4 Quebec Mills Reach Settlement on New Wage Package." *The Publishers' Auxiliary*, January 24, 1976, 1.

Peterson, Paul V. "U.S. J-Enrollments Jump Nearly 16 Per Cent." *Journalism Educator* 28:4 (January 1974): 3–5.

Polk, Leslie D., John Eddy, and Ann Andre. "Use of Congressional Publicity in Wisconsin District." *Journalism Quarterly* 52:3 (Autumn 1975): 543–546.

"Progress Will Be Community's Voice." *The Deer Park* (TX) *Progress*, January 1, 1970, 1.

"The Proverbial Stag Line." *The Hamburg* (IA) *Reporter*, April 27, 1972, 6.

"Publisher Hits Weekly Tobacco 'News' Service." *Editor & Publisher* 106:50 (December 15, 1973): 15.

"Rabbit Suppers Served This Friday Night." *The Greene* (IA) *Recorder*, May 9, 1973, 10.

"A Resolution." *The Florence* (AL) *Herald*, February 26, 1970, 2.

Rodekohr, Janet. "Merged Editorial Offices Have Given Wisconsin Weeklies Upper Hand on Costs." *The Publishers' Auxiliary*, October 3, 1977, 1.

Ross, Nancy L. "U.S. Cautious on Media Concentration." *The Washington Post*, May 30, 1979, E3.

Santa Rosa (NM) *News*, October 20, 1977.

Serrill, Theodore. "Total Weekly Revenues Increase $75 Million to $1.8 Billion During '75." *The Publishers' Auxiliary*, July 24, 1976, 1.

Serrill, Theodore. "Weeklies Attract More Graduates." *The Publishers' Auxiliary*, April 25, 1975, 1.

"A Shameful Episode." *The Florence* (AL) *Herald*, March 26, 1970, 2.

Singletary, Michael W., and Marianne Cowling. "Letters to the Editor of the Non-Daily Press." *Journalism Quarterly* 56:4 (Winter 1979): 165–167.

Smith, Anthony. *Goodbye Gutenberg: The Newspaper Revolution of the 1980s*. New York: Oxford University Press, 1980.

Speers, George, and Richard W. Davis. "Salaries of Community Newspapers in New England for 1974." *Journalism Quarterly* 52:2 (Summer 1975): 346–348.

Stewart, Steve. "E-mail Interview with Author." June 25, 2009.

Stone, Gerald C. "Considering Dropping Your Job Shop Business—Study the Figures Closely."*The Publishers' Auxiliary*, May 23, 1977, 20.

Stone, Gerald C. "Financial Statement Will Determine Job Shop Value." *The Publishers' Auxiliary*, May 30, 1977, 5.

Stone, Gerald C., and Patrick Mazza. "Impact of Consensus Theory on Community Newspaper Organization." *Journalism Quarterly* 54:2 (Summer 1977): 313–319, 356.

Stone, Gerald C., and Janet Morrison. "Content as a Key to the Purpose of Community Newspapers." *Journalism Quarterly* 53:3 (Autumn 1976): 494–498.

"Students Take Over Tombstone 'Epitaph.'" *Journalism Educator* 30:1 (April 1975): 33.

"Supplies of Newsprint Averaged 30 Days for October, Lowest Level in Seven Years." *The Wall Street Journal*, December 4, 1979, 10.

Taylor, Heber. "The Weekly Editor: Doctor's Son Makes Success of Arkansas Weekly." *Editor & Publisher* 106:17 (April 28, 1973): 50.

Temple, Bruce Gregory. "The Weekly Editor: Readers Like New-Old Look." *Editor & Publisher* 106:19 (May 12, 1973): 15.

"Threat of Union Organizational Moves for Smaller Newspapers Held Greater." *The Publishers' Auxiliary*, November 7, 1977, 2.

Tomkinson, Craig. "The Weekly Editor: Classified Success." *Editor & Publisher* 103:42 (October 17, 1970): 40–41.

Tomkinson, Craig. "The Weekly Editor: Converts to Free." *Editor & Publisher* 103:50 (December 12, 1970): 53.

Tomkinson, Craig. "The Weekly Editor: Editor Attacked Again." *Editor & Publisher* 103:4 (January 24, 1970): 38.

Tomkinson, Craig. "The Weekly Editor: Never-Say-Die." *Editor & Publisher* 103:7 (February 14, 1970): 50.

Tomkinson, Craig. "The Weekly Editor: No Longer Free." *Editor & Publisher* 103:44 (October 31, 1970): 15, 38.

Tomkinson, Craig. "The Weekly Editor: One More and Growing." *Editor & Publisher* 103:46 (November 14, 1970): 70.

Tomkinson, Craig. "The Weekly Editor: Politicos Start Rival Paper." *Editor & Publisher* 103:8 (February 21, 1970): 43.

Tomkinson, Craig. "The Weekly Editor: Young at Heart." *Editor & Publisher* 103:43 (October 24, 1970): 40–41.

Tomkinson, Craig. "The Weekly Editor: Youth Takes Over." *Editor & Publisher* 103:3 (January 17, 1970): 46, 309.

Trotter, Edgar, and Gerald Stone. "Shoppers Are Permanent Fixtures—But What Else?" *The Publishers' Auxiliary*, July 11, 1977, 11.

Van, Jeffrey Colin. "The Community Press: Health Is Good." *The Publishers' Auxiliary*, January 24, 1976, 1, 3.

Wackman, Daniel B., Donald M. Gillmor, Cecilie Gaziano, and Everette E. Dennis. "Chain Newspaper Autonomy as Reflected in Presidential Campaign Endorsements." *Journalism Quarterly* 52:3 (Autumn 1975): 411–420.

Ward, Hiley Henry. "Ninety Years of the National Newspaper Association: The Mind and Dynamics of Grassroots Journalism in Shaping America." Dissertation, University of Minnesota, 1977.

"Weeklies' Circulation Takes Modest Dip During 1975." *The Publishers' Auxiliary*, March 10, 1976, 1.

"The Weekly Editor: From Free to Paid." *Editor & Publisher* 103:24 (June 13, 1970): 56.

"The Weekly Editor: Merchants' Attitudes." *Editor & Publisher* 103:11 (March 14, 1970): 27.

White, Bill. "Antitrust Investigation of Domestic Newsprint Producers Is Under Way." *The Publishers' Auxiliary*, July 25, 1977, 1.

White, Bill. "Not All Papers Succeed at Increasing Their Frequency." *The Publishers' Auxiliary*, December 10, 1976, 3.

Wilson, Quintus C. "Community Journalism Makes Curriculum Gains." *Journalism Educator* 33:4 (January 1979): 9–13.

Winford, George M. "Newspaper Versus 'Newspaper': A Statewide Study of the Weekly." *Journalism Quarterly* 55:1 (Spring 1978): 135–139.

www.measuringworth.com.

Zerbinos, Eugenia. "Analysis of the Increase in Weekly Circulation, 1960–1980." *Journalism Quarterly* 59:3 (Autumn 1982): 467–471.

"Zoned Editions Aren't Eligible for Legal Notices, Court Rules in Illinois." *The Publishers' Auxiliary*, December 10, 1976, 1.

· 9 ·

THE 1980S: TECHNOLOGY VS. TECHNIQUE; CORPORATE-OWNED VS. COMMUNITY-OWNED; AND ECONOMICS VS. ENTERPRISE

The 1980s brought Republican party conservatism to the country, along with its leader, U.S. President Ronald Reagan. The introduction of personal, desktop computers and advanced computing options took over the education and business world. Atlanta-based CNN (Cable News Network) was founded in 1980 by Ted Turner as the first 24-hour television news channel. In addition, the tearing down of the Berlin War, an AIDS health crisis, N.A.S.A.'s Challenger spacecraft explosion, the Russian Chernobyl nuclear disaster, the Alaskan Exxon Valdez oil spill, U.S. intervention in the Iran-Iraq War; these were among the national and international events that grabbed headlines and attracted news consumers to their preferred news sources. But while continuing their weekly information-gathering and newspaper production/distribution duties, direct threats to the community weekly industry throughout the decade included the following: technological advancement that changed the work environment, hiring practices, and preprofessional training—resulting in less attention to quality content and writing; daily and free-circulation competitor expansions and consolidations in the weekly field that threatened their community leadership and standing; and an economic downturn that challenged local weekly newspaper operations to pursue new means of revenue streams to keep their businesses afloat.

On the weekly newspaper production side, technology advancements made headlines with output taking precedence over input—resulting in cost efficiency at the cost of staffing time and talent. Industry publications reported a dizzying display of technological advancements throughout the decade. A June 13, 1981 issue of *Editor & Publisher* printed excerpts from a speech that Katharine Graham—chairman of the board of the Washington Post Company and American Newspaper Publishers Association chairman and president—gave at the A.N.P.A. Production Management Conference. She remarked, "Just as our 1960 conference is remembered as the start of the offset era, and the conferences of the 1970s marked the introduction of electronic editing technology, this conference may well be remembered as the beginning of the full-page pagination era." She observed that in just 25 years, the arrival of offset presses challenged newspapers to look for ways to convert their existing letterpress to lithographic printing, and new competitive challenges required newspapers to search for ways to modify the relatively new offset presses.[1]

With national newspaper chain consolidations, and voluntary pay newspapers and weekly shoppers increasing, locally or regionally owned weekly newspapers faced decreased community influence, paid subscribers, and advertisers. Publishers and editors fought back with editorials and promotional advertisements supporting their localized content from locally based reporters and editors. The July 17, 1982 issue of *Editor & Publisher* reprinted an editorial written by Jack Moseley, editor of the *Fort Smith* (AR) *Southwest Times Record*, that discussed the importance of a community newspaper and describing it as far more than a publication serving only as a means to distribute advertising messages. "A good community newspaper cares, worries, alerts, alarms, grieves, praises, recognizes, exposes and alarms. It's there for all, rich and poor, the business executive and the little guy who got a raw deal or accomplished something no one ever believed possible." He emphasized, however, that advertising revenue made it possible to pay personnel, production, and delivery costs, noting, "… thanks to advertisers who also care about this town and the people in it, the quality of life and opportunities they enjoy, where they are and where they're going, we're not just another shopper. We're a newspaper and very proud of it."[2]

The Technology Takeover Emphasizes Output over Input

The 96th Annual National Newspaper Association Convention and Trade Show in Boston in 1981 focused on the burgeoning possibilities for electronic publishing. One speaker observed the true dawning of an information age would occur only when a "critical mass of available information services" was reached. Thus, he said, the builders of databases—including local newspapers—must assure that potential customers have enough computer terminals available to access the databases and be willing to pay for such services. A new electronic network offered by Radio Shack centered on a microcomputer that allowed a retrieval system to be activated by eight or 16 telephone callers simultaneously.[3]

An April 10, 1982 *Editor & Publisher* article focused on technology advancements that allowed weekly newspapers to automate text processing, invoicing, and mailing list management using the same micro-based system with Interlink Inc.'s software programs. The article explained that Publish-ER 7 used the Commodore microcomputer hardware, and was said to be the first general purpose system designed exclusively for weekly newspapers at a cost of $7,950. Among its features, the program allowed sending copy directly to a phototypesetter and processing it without rekeyboarding.[4]

An October 23, 1982 *Editor & Publisher* article featured a low-cost computer software system for handling all aspects of advertising in weekly and small daily papers—made available by Sunlight Software, Inc., of Mill Valley, California. The software—ADmaster—was developed by two former newspaper publishers who claimed it contained features formerly only available on big computer systems. These features included advertising scheduling, a reminder system to prevent papers from leaving advertisements out of their intended issues, a system to provide automatically generated reminder notices for slow-paying accounts, and billing and sales reports.[5]

By late 1982, residents in Cody and Powell, Wyoming, could watch a 24-hour news, weather, and classified advertising channel programmed by *The Cody* (WY) *Enterprise* weekly newspaper on a Mycro-Tek character generator that was broadcast on a low-power television channel. According to a December 25, 1982 *Editor & Publisher* article, "The News Channel" was a joint venture between *The Cody Enterprise* owner, Sage Publishing, and Telecrafter Corp.—the cable industry's largest service organization. The 6,000-circulation *The Cody Enterprise* entered the television programming partnership to increase its community service, according to publisher Carl Bechtold.[6]

Printing technology advancements were a boon for print shop startups, threatening those weekly newspapers that traditionally included a print shop to counteract newspaper printing and circulation costs. An October 24, 1981 article in *Editor & Publisher*—acknowledging that the influx of fast-print shops had a negative impact on the commercial printing business operations of many weekly newspapers—reported that many publisher-printers had moved to more aggressive promotion of their services, including expansion of their services to include design and layout. The article highlighted the *Bayshore Independent*—a weekly newspaper in Keyport, New Jersey—that purchased a duplicator and a second-color unit to allow for the efficient and high-demand printing of short-run jobs in black and white, plus two-color jobs, with maximum cost efficiency. The article stated, the new equipment permitted the weekly "to be well-positioned to meet whatever competition for printing jobs that are sold in its area."[7]

In an April 23, 1988 *Editor & Publisher* feature, Miles, Texas, printer-publisher Lonnie M. Rankin discussed the ease of offset printing operations, as opposed to the linotype days when he entered the industry in 1946, after serving in the U.S. Navy during World War II. "I think young people are missing a lot by not getting into the printing industry. Now, there's not as much to learn—for the Compugraphic, you can take a good typist from high school and in two hours you can have a top-notch typesetter who can turn out type by the mile, while on the Linotype, it would take several years to learn to turn it out." Rankin and his wife, daughter, and son, worked in the family business—which owned-operated a press in Miles and three weekly newspapers published since the 1950s. The 600-circulation *Miles* (TX) *Messenger* was the largest of the three, serving the city northeast of San Angelo—with a population of 720 at that time. The 200-circulation *Rowena* (TX) *Press* served Rowena—located eight miles northeast of Miles. The 200-circulation *Concho Herald* served the Paint Rock community—located 21 miles southeast of Miles.[8]

Personal computers and new software programs emerged at a fast pace—changing the composition of the composing room, from work tables and handheld tools, to clean desktops and finger strokes on a computer keyboard. During a panel discussion on personal computer applications for smaller newspapers at the California Newspaper Publishers Association's 98th annual convention in Coronado, publishers were advised that circulation profits could improve with the "right" computer system. The key was in the software—not the hardware—said computer consultant Dana Sohr, stressing that a productive software system could provide reports on sales, sales analysis, aging accounts, run sheets and end-of-month statements, and place orders. Steve McNamara—publisher of the weekly *Pacific Sun* in Mill Valley, California—advised other weekly publishers to keep affordability in mind. "Remember, you can't get a $35,000 [system] out of a $3,500 system." In the same article, William Burleson—publisher of the weekly *Gridly (CA) Herald*—praised the Macintosh desktop computer, utilizing its desktop publishing software for full-page ads, his column, and other tasks, and said that it took from 20 minutes to two hours to teach someone to use the "Mac.[9]"

A February 4, 1984 *Editor & Publisher* article featured the Citizen Publishing Company of Beaver Dam, Wisconsin, and its development of an in-house software program that enabled the newsroom to write, edit, store and typeset copy, capture and edit wire news, and telecommunicate, using Apple IIE microcomputers. The in-house software was developed because "off-the-shelf stuff (software) was never designed to handle the volume of writing and editing that goes on in a newsroom," said Steve Samer—editor of the *Beaver Dam (WI) Daily Citizen*—adding, "and it had no provision for special characters or handling wire news." Cost savings were a big factor in the newspaper's entry into microcomputing, and replacement equipment and new parts could be bought at a local Apple dealer store. The Apple microcomputers also allowed for other uses, such as direct advertising data entry and tracking, typesetting, and telecommunications via locally available telephone modems so that remote bureaus at the company's weekly papers could send stories, memos, and other data to the main plant.[10] Reporters passed their stories on discs to editors for checking. The discs were then fed into another Apple—which interfaced with the newsroom typesetter to set type. In further developments, the company began working with the authors of an 80,000-word, spell-check dictionary. Work on networking Apples together to common databases while retaining their stand-alone reliability was also underway.[11]

A Pennsylvania software company developed a personal computer-based system for creating mockup newspapers, as described in a February 1, 1986 *Editor & Publisher* article. Software Consulting Services of Nazareth, Pennsylvania, installed the system at the Tab newspapers of Newton, Massachusetts—a group of five weeklies totaling 100,000 circulations. The system had applications for small newspapers that placed advertisements manually on paper dummies, according to Richard Cichelli, president of S.C.S.

He said the affordable system also communicated with various computerized editorial, classified, and business systems to provide a base for pagination.[12]

All of these innovations were part of a new generation of software that was behind a new trend to use off-the-shelf personal computers as the front-end of electronics newsrooms—replacing the traditional powerful mainframes. This trend led to a boom in new text, editing, graphics, and composing software packages, and increased availability of local area networks—which allowed newspapers to join various electronic workstations with printers and typesetters, creating a unified publishing system.[13]

However, there remained the holdouts—the traditionalists, who began their weekly newspapering careers on typewriters, Linotype machines, and manual presses, and were determined to end their careers using equipment and methods from years past. Among them was highly respected and awarded former weekly editor and Colorado State University journalism professor Edward DeCourcy. A Spring 1988 *Grassroots Editor* article featured the retired editor of the *Newport* (RI) *Argus-Champion* and former president of the International Society of Weekly Newspaper Editors—who maintained a strong following of readers even after his retirement from newspapering and move into academia. Among the 150 honors he received were awards presented by the I.S.W.N.E.—including the 1971 Golden Quill Award for writing the top two editorials in the nation (a tie for first place), and the Eugene Cervi Award in 1981 for public service through journalism. The article mentioned his continued use of a manual Olympia typewriter to write columns for eight New England publications. He offered many reasons why he had not purchased a word processor, noting, "The real reason is that I don't really need it. I use press room scrap for copy paper, and I can type lots of carbons; I think I can get more carbons on copy paper than on regular bond paper."[14]

For some, it was not so much a preference of older equipment, but a cost-saving measure. In 1987, Jack Douthit—publisher-editor of the weekly *Sterling City* (TX) *News-Record*—was still using a Linotype machine he bought in 1946. In a September 19, 1987 *Editor & Publisher* feature, Douthit recalled, "I ordered the Linotype in 1945. The war was over, but just barely, and the Office of Price Administration still had a ceiling price on Linotypes." However, by the time he ordered the Linotype, the ceiling price had been lifted, with the price raised an additional $1,000. "Even then, it was still under $5,000," he said. Douthit used a Campbell press to print his paper and for job printing.

Douthit learned the printing trade in the 1930s in San Angelo, Texas, later working for the *San Angelo News*. In 1937, he leased the *Mertzon* (TX)

Star and edited it for seven years. He bought the *Sterling City News-Record* in 1944—only the second owner of the merged paper that first published in 1902 after consolidating two Sterling City papers that began publishing in the 1890s. The small town had a population of roughly 800 in the 1940s.[15]

On-the-Job and in-the-Classroom Training Response to Technology Trends

Hiring standards for community weeklies evolved with technology advancements. The pressing question: was it more difficult to train new hires on writing, or computer-based writing and editing skills? Ideally, job candidates were proficient in both areas, but the challenge remained in attracting college graduates to small-town journalism. A journalism professor at the University of Tennessee told members gathered at the 1981 winter meeting of the Tennessee Press Association that too much emphasis had been placed on computer technology and not enough on quality of writing. Professor Kelly Leiter said a "helluva lot" of what readers were getting in newspapers was more "typing" than "writing."[16]

A series of surveys of magazine and newspaper executives—the first administered in 1979—demonstrated a high level of dissatisfaction with the quality of journalism graduates being sent out into the job market. Richard L. Rath—editor of *Boating* magazine—said, "We're better off taking English majors." The editor of a small Kentucky daily observed, "They [journalism graduates] come to us with plenty of theory and experience covering fraternity parties. They are not prepared to cover day-to-day government and/or political activities. An apprenticeship should be mandatory. By and large, they can't spell worth a damn. Worse yet, they either can't or won't open the dictionary." But despite the findings that journalism students wanted to take more journalism classes and their prospective employers encouraged more practical training, the Association of Educators in Journalism continued to insist that only 25–30 percent of a student coursework be in journalism.[17]

An April 19, 1986 *Editor & Publisher* article featured the 1986 formation of a committee by the Arizona Newspaper Association to bring together academic and professional journalists to identify and suggest solutions for issues of mutual concern. A.N.A. board member Gerald Garcia—publisher of the *Tucson Citizen*—said, "A committee of this type can help all of us in journalism define issues and establish goals and objectives which will result in stronger and more effective journalism in the state."[18]

Philip Mangelsdorf—a former journalist and journalism professor—defended current teaching practices, but distinguished between teaching and learning. A University of Arizona journalism professor since 1964 and former newspaperman—having worked for three newspapers and as an Associated Press correspondent—he observed in a May 23, 1987 *Editor & Publisher* article that journalism students were equal in abilities with their predecessors, but that hiring practices led to dissatisfaction with more recent journalism school hires. Professor Mangelsdorf said, "Editors inquire persistently, 'Why don't you teach students to spell, or write a lead, or ask questions?'" His response: "We do teach them those things, but we can't force them to learn." After 23 years as a journalism professor, he said the mechanics of reporting—i.e., spelling, grammar, lead sentences, etc.—could be easily taught, but, "I learned that creativity comes from challenging the rules and breaking them when it seems appropriate. I developed a respect for much of the mass communications research that gave another dimension to classroom lectures." He said the job of a journalism teacher was not to train students to be journalists, but to help them gain an education. If he were an editor reviewing recent graduates to hire, Mangelsdorf said he would choose a "straight-A graduate with a classics degree rather than a journalism graduate from a program that focused on technical training." But, he added, "I would prefer a first-rate journalism graduate who knows the classics."[19]

Hiring difficulties in a fast-paced technology period were compounded by the historic problem of attracting college graduates to supposed lackluster weeklies as opposed to talk-of-the-town, big-city dailies, according to a November 15, 1986 *Editor & Publisher* article that highlighted a Kentucky editor's response to that concern. Rob Schorman—managing editor of the *Owensboro* (KY) *Messenger-Inquirer* who spoke at a panel session of the Associated Press Managing Editors convention—said that recruiting should take place among editors of small-town community newspapers to attract more journalism graduates. Among his recruiting tips were to: increase internship programs; give guest lectures at colleges and universities and network with their faculty and students; make their paper available to journalism program libraries and reading rooms; and create opportunities for growth within their organizations.[20]

But, a weekly newspaper report cited the academic community for its failure to attract new journalism graduates to small-town papers. Journalism graduates tended to shun community newspapers for potential employment, not only because of lower pay, but because most university journalism programs taught little or nothing about community journalism, according to the general findings of the National Newspaper Association's journalism education committee. The committee met at the N.N.A.'s 102nd annual convention and its findings were reported in an October 24, 1987 *Editor & Publisher* feature. Committee member Ed Arnold—a newspaper design consultant who formerly taught journalism at Syracuse University—said there was a need for community journalism and newspaper management courses, adding that no current textbooks on the subjects were even available. The committee pointed out that this was especially challenging with the dwindling number of journalism graduates opting for print journalism.[21]

Even though technology replaced some traditional typesetting and production positions, editorial staff members were still needed to generate local articles for the community-minded weekly. But, more journalism schools were finding students choosing specialty areas—such as public relations—and turning away from the traditional news-editorial field of study. In the early 1980s, public relations and advertising were the primary employment interests of one-third of all students enrolled as majors in schools and departments of journalism in the United States. A 1981 national survey of 15,000 journalism students—conducted by Professor Paul V. Peterson of the School of Journalism of the Ohio State University—found that only 14 percent of journalism majors expected to work for daily newspapers, the wire services, or community newspapers. The students represented one-fifth of all students majoring in journalism at the time of the survey.[22]

During a panel discussion on journalism education at the 1986 National Newspaper Association Convention in Nashville, Donald Smith—publisher of the *Monticello* (MN) *Times*—said that while enrollment in journalism programs across the country was increasing, the number of those majoring in news-editorial was declining. He observed that newspapers were not attracting the "best and the brightest" among students because of low pay and lack of glamour. He suggested state newspaper associations establish internship programs and allow students to attend professional conferences at reduced rates. He also suggested that instructors emphasize community newspapers as a "great starting place" for a journalism career.[23]

As continued growth of student enrollment in public relations and advertising programs fostered debate on whether these programs should be housed in communications or business colleges, a bitter divide was building between journalism practitioners and journalism professors. In a January 23, 1988 *Editor & Publisher* article, officials of the Association for Education in Journalism and Mass Communication repudiated a remark attributed to its president that public relations and advertising courses belonged in business schools. The comment by A.E.J.M.C.'s David Weaver appeared in a *Chronicle of Higher Education* article about changes in journalism education largely attributed to students wanting to study public relations, and advertising and marketing, rather than traditional reporting and editing subjects. Ohio State journalism professor Paul V. Peterson—who compiled annual statistics on journalism enrollment—reported that public relations and advertising students made up 44 percent of the total undergraduates in the nation's journalism and mass communications programs in 1986.[24]

Because of the growing competitiveness between journalism and public relations in numbers of undergraduates, some public relations professors felt their programs were shortchanged within their academic departments. Judy VanSlyke Turk—a member of the A.E.J.M.C. executive committee and an assistant director of the University of Oklahoma's School of Journalism and Mass Communication—claimed that many public relations and advertising faculty felt like "second-class citizens within journalism schools compared to print journalists. They have the greatest number of students and are getting the smallest portion of the resource pie."[25]

Community Newspapering Requires Community Involvement, a Spine, and a Sense of Humor

In general, the local-news-focused weekly newspaper industry continued to argue that it better served its communities through local—or at least regional—ownership, strong community involvement, and civic leadership. One study to back that claim was a 1982 survey of 148 newspaper editors by the American Society of Newspaper Editors. It showed editors in smaller cities were more active in civic affairs than their bigger-city counterparts. One-fourth of the 91 respondents from smaller cities listed membership on a charity board. Other common affiliations included cultural groups, and college and hospital boards. Most editors indicated they did not feel that serving on these boards related to a conflict of interest."[26]

In community weeklies, it was not uncommon to see free-of-charge display advertisements promoting local charitable organizations. The January 1, 1981 edition of *The Bladen Journal*, of Elizabethtown, North Carolina, contained a multi-columned, page two United Way logo, and a similarly sized logo on page three supporting The American Cancer Society. The 24-page, bi-weekly publication featured two sections, an eight-column format, and cost 25 cents for a single issue. The paper's forerunner was *The Bladen Express*, founded in 1898, later becoming *The Bladen Journal* in 1908.[27]

Community newspapers play a vital role in supporting charitable works, University of Tennessee College of Communications Dean Kelly Leiter told those gathered in March 1988 at Southern Illinois University for the 11th Howard R. Long Honor Lecture—honoring the founder of the International Society of Weekly Newspaper Editors. Leiter's lecture—reprinted in the Winter 1989 issue of *Grassroots Editor*—included the following: "In that one area alone, charitable work, the newspapers of this country are unsurpassed. If you measured the amount of free space given to charities alone in most newspapers, you would see that it is staggering. In fact, few community charities ... could survive without the kindness of newspapers to carry their message to the public."[28]

In fact, local small-town newspapers were so valued that, by the mid-1980s, the *SV Hornet Buzz*—a weekly newspaper published by students at Surprise Valley (CA) High School—became the only local newspaper serving the Medoc County communities of Cedarville, Fort Bidwell, Lake City, and Eagleville, in a remote area of the state. Residents received free mailed copies of the newspaper—converted from a school to community publication. Faculty adviser Jake Merritt said, "They [students] decided the paper could serve a more useful purpose by reporting local news than items on who's dating who." He and 20 students—a third of the school's enrollment—published 600 weekly copies of the 16-page paper on two office copiers.[29]

In *Newspapers of Maryland's Eastern Shore*, by Dickson J. Preston, data was reported from the August 18, 1982 edition of the 7,700-circulation *The Kent County News* in Chestertown, Maryland, as "to contain the names of 1,394 persons, nearly all of them Kent Countians. This is more than 8% of the county's entire population." Their names appeared in articles, briefs, and announcements related to weddings, funerals, births, hospitalizations, anniversaries, amateur sports, horse shows, church meetings, social visits, vacations, crab feasts, business news, turkey shoots, and court cases. Publisher-editor Hurtt Deringer explained in a September 20, 1986 *Editor & Publisher* feature that almost everyone in Kent County could expect to see his or her name in the paper at least once a year. "Reading about themselves and their friends is one thing that a county weekly can give people that they can't get anywhere else."[30]

Humansville, Missouri, weekly newspaper editor Gary Sosniecki—who had also worked as a weekly community editor in Kansas, and as a daily reporter—emphasized the close relationship a small-town weekly newspaper has with its local readers. A Fall 1987 *Grassroots Editor* article contained his excerpted comments to the May 1, 1987 meeting of the Southern Illinois Editorial Association, which included the following letter he received while at the *Humansville Star-Leader*. It read:

> Dear Editor,
> Since the last edition of your paper came into my home I have been unable to get any sleep or rest. You see, my husband got so excited after reading about the town meeting and the lady reported having seen an orgy, he spends his days on the phone trying to locate the lady or someone who might know where the orgy is to be held that night.
> Since we live just over the zone line for the telephone system, this is getting awfully expensive. Then my nights have to be spent pushing his wheelchair around looking for the action. So if the lady or anyone else knows the location of the next orgy, it would be a great help to me if they would let me know.
> It would ensure me of collecting his insurance and let him leave this world happy, and also give *me* somewhere to go instead of spending lonely evenings by myself after his departure.
> A concerned wife.

After reading the letter out loud, Sosniecki said, "Let's face it, folks. You don't get material like this sitting around the office of a daily newspaper."[31] His talk covered the transition from being a daily newspaper reporter—covering national and local issues—to co-editing a small weekly in the Missouri Ozarks with his wife, Helen Sosniecki, from the late 1970s until their 1987 purchase of the *Hillsboro (KS) Star-Journal* weekly.[32]

Advocating for community growth and improvements was a key role for longtime Thompson Falls, Montana, weekly editor K.A. "Doc" Eggensperger. His philosophy of newspapering held that "[a] country editor is placed in a leadership role. That's whether you accept it or not. But you're in the first seat on the front row of community activities," the then-67-year-old publisher-editor recalled from his 33-year newspapering career, in a March 21, 1987 *Editor & Publisher* feature. Eggensperger strongly supported presenting the news fairly and unbiased, as much as possible, but also standing for a strong editorial voice. "I've gotten the most satisfaction from improvements and achievements this community has made with the backing and support—and often at the instigation—of the *Sanders County Ledger*." For example, he mentioned editorial campaigns waged in support of building a new high school, a golf course, a Lions Club-backed 28-unit complex for elderly Lions Club members, converting the old jail to a town museum (with barred windows), and a day park and overnight campground.[33]

Newspapers are institutions in their communities and are in a unique position to serve as a catalyst for economic growth. This was the message of Jack Fisher—publisher of the *Morristown* (TN) *Tribune*—who moderated a panel at the 1986 National Newspaper Association convention and trade show in Nashville. The panel was titled, "Hometown Newspapers Need Hometowns." He said, "Communities will die without something to keep the economic wheels going," adding, "The newspaper's survival may depend on how committed to development you are."[34]

The Blair (WI) *Press* reminded its readers on its page-one nameplate that the *Blair Press* was "The Only Paper in the World That Cares Two Whoops for Blair, Wisconsin!" The weekly, founded in 1896, featured six pages of local news and a 16-page insert tab containing display and classified advertisements and television viewing listings.[35]

A Moab, Utah, community weekly couple—who served as co-publishers and co-editors of the 3,500-circulation *The Times-Independent*—were such strong supporters of community involvement in their publication, they reserved the first two pages of their weekly for staff-reported local news and editorials/opinions, and the remaining dozen or so pages were stories submitted by their readers. Featured in a June 20, 1987 *Editor & Publisher* article, Sam Taylor—53 at the time the article was published—had inherited the reins of the paper in 1956 from his father, Loren "Bish" Taylor, who arrived in Moab in 1909 to hand-set type for his attorney brother-in-law who had purchased the paper. A year later, Bish Taylor became editor and publisher. Sam's wife, Adrien Taylor, was named co-publisher-editor in 1977. Sam Taylor said, "Both Adrien and I have journalism degrees from the University of Utah and we're very proud about that. We work hard to produce a journalistically proper newspaper, but we also feel that the community itself has a great stake in the content of the paper." He explained that when stories were submitted by readers, "We correct simple spelling and grammatical errors, but we try not to destroy the writer's own sense of accomplishment by rewriting it."[36]

On being the editor of a weekly in a small community, Cary Stiff—former reporter at *The Denver Post* and co-publisher/editor with his wife, Carol Wilcox, of the then-2,005-circulation *Clear Creek Courant* in Idaho Springs, Colorado—explained in a February 7, 1987 *Editor & Publisher* feature one challenge of being part of a close-knit community. "You know everybody, but you can't have close friends. Sooner or later you're going to have to write a story that's uncomplimentary to people you know." He continued, "You can't let your friendships stop you from printing the story. If you do, you've lost your credibility and, if you damage it by pulling your punches, it takes you a long time to restore that credibility."[37]

Endorsing local candidates for office could invite controversy and criticism for the community newspaper. Former *Humansville* (MO) *Star-Leader* publisher-editor Gary Sosniecki had the following to say about economic pressure to give positive coverage to advertisers' pet projects or omit "bad news" as a result of local candidate endorsements. In a reprint of his Nov. 15, 1984 editorial in the Spring 1985 issue of *Grassroots Editor*, he wrote, "Our advertisers seem to realize that if the *Star-Leader* produces a lively, honest, and well-read edition every week, their ads have a better chance of being seen by the public." He added that the same theory should hold true for political candidates, whether they were eventually endorsed by the newspaper or not. "Should endorsements be determined by who spends the most money—maybe put endorsements out for bids? We might make more money than we do now, but we prefer to endorse the best candidate, not the richest."[38]

An April 4, 1987 feature in *Editor & Publisher*—a reprint of an article that first appeared in the *Roanoke* (VA) *Times & World-News*—focused on 79-year-old editor-publisher Preston Moses, who had announced his retirement after 51 years in community weekly newspapering at the *Chatham* (VA) *Star-Tribune*, formerly the *Pittsylvania Tribune*. Moses had intended to retire in 1969 when he sold the paper, but decided to stay on as editor for another 18 years. His feet were firmly planted in what a former newspaper competitor called "participatory journalism." Like editor-publishers of yesteryear, Preston held several public offices throughout his journalism career, including serving as a longtime member of the School, Trustee Electoral Board (which selected county school board members), as a member of the Virginia House of Delegates, and as commissioner of revenue for Pittsylvania County. Not surprisingly, he faced on and off criticisms for conflict of interest, but was viewed generally as looking out for the best interests of the community. A Chatham native—who went on to become a national writer—said of Moses that he "has been skilled in making absolutely everybody mad at him at the same time." But, he added that Moses blunted the collective anger by "jumping on everybody's enemies once in a while."[39]

A fellow weekly newspaper publisher-editor shared an opposing opinion on whether or not the community newspaper editor should hold public office. In a May 21, 1987 *Editor & Publisher* feature, then-66-year-old John U. Pavlik, publisher of the 2,335-circulation [in 1987] *Ritzville (WA) Adams County Journal*, said of holding public office that he tried it once during his 46-year newspapering career. "I served on the school board. It's difficult to have an opinion during meetings and one in the paper. These may coincide, but it's still tough to serve while running a community newspaper."[40]

In 1987, National Newspaper Association President Dick Nafsinger—publisher of the 5,600-circulation *Hood River (OR) News* and president of Eagle Newspaper, Inc., a chain of 15 community weeklies in Washington and Oregon—discussed the role of community leadership, among other topics, in a June 6, 1987 *Editor & Publisher* feature. While publisher of the *Hood River News*, he served on a local school board considering consolidation between the city and county school systems. The paper and its editor—who was not Nafsinger—pushed for the consolidation, which was eventually approved. Nafsinger recalled, "I don't buy the argument that local editors and publishers should stay above the fray to maintain objectivity." He added, "In a small town there are not that many people who can and will be leaders. You can't preclude yourself from serving. The editor should be in a leadership role."[41]

A vast increase in consolidations and chain ownership of community weeklies during the 1980s often led to a decrease in community buy-in and leadership for the newspaper reporters/editors who were not longtime residents of the community. Bob Hammes—owner of one of only 14 remaining family-owned weeklies in Idaho (of a total of 48 weeklies within the state in 1987)—was critical of the lack of community ties among chain-ownership weeklies. The then-76-year-old owner since 1958 of the 20-page, 3,300-circulation [in 1987] *St. Marie's (ID) Gazette Record* was interviewed for an April 18, 1987 feature in *Editor & Publisher*, in which he discussed the problems with chain employees. "If they [the chains] have a good man, they start him low on the ladder. When he shows promise, they move him from town A to town B. He keeps improving. He goes to town C. Then town D. He is not really a citizen of any of these places ... This reflects in the newspaper's attitude toward the community, and the community toward the paper. It's a detriment to both."[42]

Weeklies Offer Less Pay, but More Job Opportunities for Women, Agricultural Reporters

Low pay for journalists continued to be a concern in the 1980s as far as attracting college graduates to the field. Journalists' pay was equal to or lower than teachers. With an oversupply of journalism majors, it became easy for newspapers to underpay reporters and editors. But with entry-level jobs that barely paid more than minimum wage, top talent in college shied away from journalism because of its pay scale, and young journalists soon left to take better-paying jobs. An article in the November 5, 1983 edition of *Editor & Publisher* addressed the issue of merit pay—which was often argued for teachers—but noted that print journalists were dependent on the financial status of newspapers that "frequently run on a shoestring."[43]

However, concerns of making a comfortable living did not detract many from pursuing their dreams of making a difference in their hometown or small towns through community journalism. Edith Hunter—editor of *The Weathersfield* (VT) *Weekly,* one of New England's smallest newspapers—received the New England Press Association's prestigious Horace Greeley Award in 1983 for her work as editor, photographer, and circulation manager of the then-600-circulation paper. The award committee complimented the publication for carrying the latest news in a "homey style with no sacrifice of journalistic integrity." Hunter—a graduate of Wellesley College and the mother of four—is the author of several books, including one on the subject of Horace Greeley.[44]

By age 32, Suzanne Kennedy—two-time editor of *The Highlander*, a Marble Falls, Texas, weekly—met her teenage goals of becoming the paper's editor and making it the best newspaper in the state. An April 30, 1988 feature in *Editor & Publisher* observed that she had reached both goals. After having worked in the print shop while a teen, and taking on some reporting assignments, she later put her college journalism studies on hold to return to the paper to serve as temporary editor. On her drive home for that job, she was greeted with a Dairy Queen outdoor sign that read: "Welcome Back Suzanne, the Highlander Needs You." After graduation and living in New York City, she and her husband returned to Marble Falls to work at a graphics agency. It wasn't long before she returned for a third time to *The Highlander*—this time in the permanent editor's position. The paper was full of invited local opinions and guest columns. Controversial issues were not avoided. Soon after becoming editor, Kennedy filed a lawsuit against the city council and mayor for violating the state's open meetings law. Her hard work and dedication to community journalism was rewarded in 1988 when the Headliners Foundation of Texas—an organization of Texas journalists representing daily and weekly newspapers—awarded *The Highlander* its Outstanding Community Journalism Award.[45]

In the 1980s, a turndown in the agricultural economy put farm news on the front pages at the same time the number of farm reporters had decreased. The newspaper farm editor's job was broadened to write about how agricultural issues affected farmers and city dwellers. While traditional farm editors grew up on farms—but wanted to do something besides farming—new writers in the field had an interest in or were assigned to the topic. And women—once a rarity in farm coverage—comprised 50 percent of the 140 members in the Newspaper Farm Editors of America. Ann Toner—farm editor of *The Kansas City Times* and president of N.F.E.A.—said small newspapers continued to do a better job of farm reporting than the larger dailies.[46]

Defining Economic Threats, Searching for Cost-saving and Cost-creating Solutions

In 1980, 10 managers and publishers of Ohio weekly newspapers served as panelists at a seminar of the Buckeye Press Association to address whether the paid weekly was in danger of extinction with the threat of competition from free or voluntary pay newspapers and aggressive shoppers—containing mostly advertising, coupons, and shopping guides. It was generally agreed that the paid weekly in a rural area was less threatened than weeklies in a suburban market vying for advertising and circulation dollars in a saturated market. A publishing company executive noted that while advertising contract rates per column inch were typically higher in free newspapers, advertisers were attracted to their larger circulation numbers. Increased fuel and second-class postage rates were also mentioned as economic threats to paid newspapers. Some suggestions to combat these financial concerns included supplementing circulations of paid weeklies with zoned shoppers, and implementing a voluntary pay system. The panelists concluded that the editorial content of the paid weekly determined its success in terms of building circulation and advertising.[47]

A 1980 survey of advertisers in Utah weeklies—conducted by University of Utah journalism students—found advertising rates "about right" to "high" and "moderately" effective. Respondents also rated readership of weeklies as "heavy" compared to the state's metropolitan dailies. The 19-part questionnaire was titled, "The Space Buyer Looks at the Community Press." It was sent to the six heaviest advertisers in 12 Utah weekly newspapers. The survey also pointed out that advertisers were calling on more help from the weekly advertising representatives in planning advertising programs and campaigns.[48]

An Ohio weekly operating for more than 100 years fell victim to the shopper when *The Elizabethtown* (PA) *Chronicle*—a 112-year-old weekly with a 1981 circulation of 5,300—closed its doors in August 1981, after losing a battle for advertising revenues from a saturation distribution shopper, *The Merchandiser*—with an unpaid circulation of 30,000. *The Elizabethtown Chronicle* was owned by wealthy businessman Richard Scaife.[49] Fortunately, the paper reopened two months later, in October 1981, after owner Richard Scaife sold the publication to William S. Jackson and Rosemary K. Jackson, publishers of *The Sun* in Hummelstown, Pennsylvania—a weekly newspaper east of Harrisburg. More than 50 area merchants had previously met with representatives of two area newspapers who were asked to cover Elizabethtown after *The Elizabethtown Chronicle* ceased publishing. At the meeting was William Jackson of *The Sun*—who subsequently purchased *The Elizabethtown Chronicle*.[50] In its January 2, 1982 issue, *Editor & Publisher* published a list of the 136 non-dailies and shoppers that changed ownership in 1981.[51]

Concerning competition from free-circulation weeklies and shoppers, the July 9, 1983 edition of *Editor & Publisher* reprinted excerpts of a speech made at the Suburban Newspapers of America convention on June 24, 1983 in Toronto, Canada. The speech was given by David Asper Johnson—editor and publisher of the Argonaut Newspapers, Hermosa Beach, California. He said for years he practiced the daily routine of a small weekly newspaper—surrounding oneself with chamber of commerce members and friends of the arts, attending cocktail parties and mixers, and ribbon cuttings, and engaging in small talk with mayors, city councilmen, and other "big frogs in our little community ponds." But, he noticed the competition—about a dozen free-circulation and shoppers—was not attending weekly community breakfasts and luncheons or covering five- and six-hour city hall meetings. Instead, they were "putting out a newspaper the new demographics in our town could relate to." In response, his paper's news department was reorganized and staff laid off—opting instead to purchase news stories and features. "Out" were city halls, schools, churches,

Rotary, Kiwanis and Lions clubs—which continued to be covered by the area daily newspaper. The new "ins" were 10-k runs, health, beauty, and Nautilus exercise and aerobics, patio gardening, home computers, restaurants, and free outdoor concerts in the park. But, he told the group, they should consider demographics before making any content changes. "We have to know who's out there. Who's picking up our paper. And, who's reading it." Cutbacks were made in home delivery, with placements in local businesses "reaching a new market—tourists and visitors."[52]

A page three advertisement in the January 3, 1980 edition of *The Malakoff* (TX) *News*—an eight-page weekly published on Thursdays—encouraged its readers to subscribe to both the local weekly and metropolitan Dallas newspaper. The advertisement stated, "Read both your hometown newspaper and The Dallas Morning News. With The News you'll get Dallas, state, national and world news. Stimulating editorials and columns ... Wednesday focus on fashion. Thursday offers recipes, meal planning, wine tips. Sunday, TV listings." The Malakoff weekly was established in 1930 and, in 1980, sold for 15 cents an issue.[53]

In a column on the future of community newspapers, Conrad Fink—former executive of Associated Press and Park Newspapers and University of Georgia journalism faculty member—talked about the challenges of large metropolitan dailies, including inner-city deterioration, flight of the affluent reader to the suburb, slipping penetration figures, and rising costs. He suggested community newspapers could respond to daily strategies such as metro zoning, direct mail, shoppers, and electronic home delivery by improving journalistic quality with an emphasis on local news. He also recommended promoting the better product in an integrated marketing thrust, and, finally, make it easier and cheaper for major advertisers, particularly national advertisers, to do business with them.[54]

At its annual convention and trade show in Louisville, Kentucky, in September 1983, members of the National Newspaper Association were told that although they did not derive much of their revenue from national advertising, they would benefit from a new Standard Advertising Unit system to be introduced by the daily newspaper industry in July 1984. The reason for the change was regional retail advertising that was not prepared locally, explained Walter Mattson—president of the New York Times Company and chairman of the American Newspaper Publishers' Association Standard Advertising Unit committee. The key to strategy success for the S.A.U. was standardization across the newspaper industry, he explained.[55]

At the October 1986 N.N.A. convention and trade show in Nashville, regional sales managers for American Newspaper Representatives discussed the challenges facing sales representatives for weekly newspapers to convince advertising agencies of the benefits of advertising in weeklies, as compared to dailies. A.N.R.—owned by N.N.A. member publishers, and an N.N.A. affiliate—was a national sales organization representing more than 7,000 community newspapers at that time. Diane Johnson—New York City-based Northeast sales manager—said many advertisers viewed weekly newspapers only as shoppers. She described how she took sample newspapers to agency media people and said many were astonished to see weeklies with as many as four sections. A.N.R. research comparatives between weeklies and dailies showed that "weeklies are just as strong, if not stronger" when referring to penetration figures, Johnson noted.[56]

In the January 10, 1987 *Editor & Publisher* feature, "Weekly Editor," Dave Bonner—publisher and editor of the then-4,200-circulation *Powell* (WY) *Tribune*—explained how loss of advertising in a tough economy necessitated editorial staff layoffs from an already thinly spread staff. As a young reporter, Bonner joined the Powell paper in 1964 with options to buy stock and eventually gain control—which he accomplished 22 years later. In his 23 years at the helm of the *Powell Tribune*, it grew in subscriptions from 2,300 to 4,200, leading to an annual gross from $84,000 to $600,000. But in 1987, economic hits on the local agricultural industry hurt local businesses, leading to decreased advertising revenue for his paper. Bonner was optimistic, however, that continued modernization within the industry would increase productivity at reduced operating costs. "I'm intrigued like so many others, about laser technology. If we can deliver the same quality through it, then there's going to be savings. That's going to mean a lot to us."[57]

Concern over loss of potential advertising dollars—coupled with increased operating costs—prompted a variety of cost-creating and cost-saving measures. For example, a New Mexico weekly benefited from the purchase of 5,300 subscriptions by the Public Service Company of New Mexico. This action was in response to an article by the weekly—Albuquerque's *New Mexico Independent*—which was critical of a six-part series by the *Albuquerque Journal*. The *Albuquerque Journal* had run the six-part series on the electric utility industry in New Mexico. The utility company denounced the series and bought ads in the daily to present its side of the story. The utility then purchased 5,300 *New Mexico Independent* subscriptions and sent issues of the article criticizing the *Albuquerque Journal's* six-part series to its stockholders.[58]

Another example of fighting for revenue streams resulted from the Georgia Supreme Court upholding a local superior court judge's ruling designating the Savannah, Georgia, weekly—*Georgia Gazette and Journal Record*—as the official legal organ of Chatham County. The *Savannah Evening Press* had held the legal advertising designation for more than 40 years. Southeastern Newspapers Corporation—owner of the *Savannah Evening Press*—argued that the weekly did not comply with state law requiring that a legal organ have 85 percent paid circulation. A second complaint was that the weekly was printed outside of the county, eliminating it from designation as a Chatham County official legal organ. Georgia law allowed newspapers to use either an accrual method or a cash method of accounting to determine paid-circulation percentages. The *Georgia Gazette and Journal Record* used the accrual method.[59]

Another cost-saving measure called for weeklies to combine their resources to purchase operating materials in bulk. A consultant and former publisher-owner of an independent Pennsylvania newspaper proposed establishing a cooperative purchasing network for independent newspapers and small, privately owned groups for centralized large-volume buying of materials, such as newsprint and services.[60]

One of the more interesting means of saving circulation costs and involving the community was enacted by *The Weekly Gazette* in Greenwood, Indiana. The weekly was delivered exclusively by residents of the Greenwood Senior Center, according to an article in the February 21, 1987 edition of *Editor & Publisher*. This change from out-of-town contracted delivery services allowed for later editorial and advertising deadlines. The new carriers worked for and were paid by the senior center. Brian Kelly—president of Kelly Publications, Inc., the paper's publisher—was quoted in an article in *The Weekly Gazette* about the new circulation agreement. He said, "They [seniors] have a work ethic matched by none. And we are among the first to preach to people about keeping money in the Greater Greenwood area and helping our neighbors." Greenwood Senior Center Director Betty Davis said of identifying potential carriers, "I'm going to look for seniors who spend too much time at home. We will provide transportation and a good free lunch at the center for them. It will provide them [with] an activity and fellowship."[61]

Consolidations/Chain Ownership Keeps Many Weeklies Operating

Sometimes, newspaper consolidations and/or chain ownership were the only answers in maintaining a small-town newspaper. Townspeople were thankful their local publication could survive, whatever the ownership status. Early in the decade, the sale of 200 non-daily papers—including paid and voluntary pay circulation weeklies, semi-weeklies and shoppers—was announced. Of the 130 paid-circulation weeklies sold, 68 became affiliated with dailies. Among the sales, Media General Inc. of Richmond, Virginia, bought three community newspaper companies, representing 24 papers, at a cost of $20 million.[62]

A feature article in an October 24, 1987 *Editor & Publisher* issue described then-60-year-old Rhode Island weekly newspaper publisher Roswell Bosworth Jr. as having the characteristics of a media giant—having built his business from a long-run family weekly to four weeklies, a total-market-coverage paper, and a full-run classified section. He began his career under the tutelage of his parents, who bought the *Bristol* (RI) *Phoenix* in 1928. The weekly was founded in 1837. After serving in the Air Force during World War II and working on the college paper at the University of Rhode Island, Bosworth enrolled in a 1947 summer course in newspaper management at Northwestern University. A visit to a Chicago-area press operation—which published a dozen large weeklies in suburban Chicago—inspired him to branch out and develop a newspaper group within the Bristol region. After getting out of job printing in the 1950s, he branched out in 1958 and founded and edited the [4,602-circulation as of 1987] *Barrington* (RI) *Times*. In 1961, he started the [3,025-circulation as of 1987] *Warren* (RI) *Times-Gazette*, serving as its first editor. In 1966, he started the [5,895-circulation as of 1987] *Sakonnet* (RI) *Times*. In 1970, he created the *East Bay Window*—a feature section for his four weeklies. He also increased printings of the *East Bay Window* to 19,000 free circulations for total market coverage. His biggest and final addition to the group was in 1983 with the 25,000-run *East Bay Classifieds*, printed on yellow stock. This vastly expanded classifieds issue was stuffed into the five other publications, and allowed him to increase auto, real estate, and employment listings. In 1987, his staff had grown to 50, with gross profits of $1.5 million.[63]

A January 2, 1988 *Editor & Publisher* article reviewing newspaper chain activity in 1987, described the movements in ownership as "never so striking." Westward Communications—founded by two former *Dallas Times*

Herald editors—purchased 10 weeklies in 1987.[64] A number of these new press barons were in their mid-30s. For example, then-35-year-old William Dean Singleton and his partners built their chain with smaller and faltering family-owned papers, gaining a reputation for deep cost-cutting that sent reporters streaming out the door. "It gave us a little bit of a reputation at first as a 'slash-and-burn' operation," Singleton said, speaking to the Newspaper Personnel Relation Association in July 1987. "Some of that reputation was unfair. Some of it was very fair."[65]

A publicly owned weekly was established and thriving in Pigeon Forge, Tennessee, at the start of the decade when the *Smoky Mountain Star* began publishing on August 4, 1980—after capital was raised by selling stock to local citizens, which raised $100,000. General Manager Delmar Dennis reported first-year earnings at $150,000 and second-year advertising revenues exceeding $300,000. The paper competed with a 100-year-old, thrice-weekly, chain-owned paper. "The success of this paper is proof that the 'little guys' do have a chance even in today's economy and even with chain-owned competition," said James H. Dumas, *Smoky Mountain Star* editor-publisher.[66]

Notes

1 "Hello Pagination, Goodbye Stereotype," *Editor & Publisher* 114 (June 13, 1981): 9.

2 "Shop Talk at Thirty: What Is a Newspaper?," *Editor & Publisher* 115 (July 17, 1982): 48. Fort Smith, along the Arkansas River in northwest Arkansas's Sebastian County, had a population of 71,626 in 1980. *1980 Census of Population*, "Characteristics of the Population, Chapter A, Number of Inhabitants, United States Summary," part 1, 1–117, Table 25. http://www.census.gov/.

3 "Electronic News Systems Dominate N.N.A. Meeting," *Editor & Publisher* 114 (October 10, 1981): 62.

4 "Publisher-ER 7 Designed for Weeklies Has Micro Hardware/Special Software," *Editor & Publisher* 115 (April 10, 1982): 26. In 2022, according to the latest government figures based on the Consumer Price Index, $7,950 from 1982 was worth $24,411. http://www.measuringworth.com/.

5 "Calif. Publisher Markets Ad Software for Small Dailies and Weeklies," *Editor & Publisher* 115 (October 23, 1982): 26.

6 "Wyoming Weekly Programs Teletext News on Low Power TV Channel," *Editor & Publisher* 115 (December 25, 1982): 21. Cody, in northwest Wyoming's Park County, had a population of 6,790 in 1980. Powell, also in Park County, had a population of 5,310 in 1980. *1980 Census of Population*, "Characteristics of the Population, Chapter A, Number of Inhabitants, United States Summary," part 1, 1–160, Table 25. http://www.census.gov/.

7. "Two-Color Work Helps Weekly Stay Competitive," *Editor & Publisher* 114 (October 24, 1981): 36.
8. "Weekly Editor: Lonnie M. Rankin, Miles Messenger, Rowena Press, Concho Herald, Miles, Texas," *Editor & Publisher* 121:17 (April 23, 1988): 72,139. Miles, in central Texas's Runnels County, had a population of 720 in 1980. Rowena, also in Runnels County, had a population of 884 in 1980. Paint Rock, in central Texas's Concho County, had a population of 256 in 1980. *1990 Census of Population,* "Population and Housing Units 1970 to 1990," Texas, 38, 62, Table 8. http://www.census.gov/.
9. "PCs—Where Do They Fit in at Your Newspaper?" *Editor & Publisher* 119:21 (May 24, 1986): 52–53E. Mill Valley, just north of San Francisco in California's Marin County, had a population of 23,967 in 1980, and Gridley, north of Sacramento in California's Butte County, had a population of 3,982. *1980 Census of Population,* "Characteristics of the Population, Chapter A, Number of Inhabitants, United States Summary," part 1, 1–119, Table 25. http://www.census.gov/. In 2022, according to the latest government figures based on the Consumer Price Index, $35,000 from 1986 was worth $94,624 and #3,500 was worth $9,462. http://www.measuringworth.com/.
10. "News/Tech: Micros Invade the Newsroom." *Editor & Publisher* 117 (February 4, 1984): 32. Beaver Dam, in central-east Wisconsin along Beaver Dam Lake and Beaver Dam River in Dodge County, had a population of 14,149 in 1980. *1980 Census of Population,* "Characteristics of the Population, Chapter A, Number of Inhabitants, United States Summary," part 1, 1–159, Table 25. http://www.census.gov/.
11. Ibid., 35.
12. "New Software Allows Page Dummying with PC's," *Editor & Publisher* 119:5 (February 1, 1986): 27.
13. "Personal Computers Come Up Front in Newsrooms," *Editor & Publisher* 119:39 (September 27, 1986): 36.
14. "Where Are They Now?, New England Newsman," *Grassroots Editor* 29:1 (Spring 1988): 4. Little Compton, a coastal town in Rhode Island's Newport County, had a population of 3,085 in 1980. *1980 Census of Population,* "Characteristics of the Population, Chapter A, Number of Inhabitants, United States Summary," part 1, 1–175, Table 26. http://www.census.gov/.
15. "Weekly Editor: Jack Douthit, Sterling City News-Record, Sterling City, Texas," *Editor & Publisher* 120:38 (September 19, 1987): 20. Sterling City, in central Texas's Sterling County, had a population of 915 in 1980. *1990 Census of Population,* "Population and Housing Units 1970 to 1990," Texas, 64, Table 8. http://www.census.gov/. In 2022, according to the latest government figures based on the Consumer Price Index, $1,000 from 1945 was worth $16,459 and $5,000 was worth $82,308. http://measuringworth.com/.
16. "J-Prof Raps Sad State of Newspaper Writing," *Editor & Publisher* 114 (February 7, 1981): 16.
17. "News Execs Urge Major Overhaul of Journalism Training Program," *Editor & Publisher* 115 (March 6, 1982): 10, 30.
18. "Improving Journalism Education Programs," *Editor & Publisher* 119:16 (April 19, 1986): 46.

19 "Shop Talk at Thirty: Have J-School Students Changed? Or Have the Professors?," *Editor & Publisher* 120:21 (May 23, 1987): 48, 38.
20 "Recruiting Talent for Small-Town Papers," *Editor & Publisher* 119:46 (November 15, 1986): 26. Owensboro, in in northwest Kentucky's Daviess County, had a population of 54,450 in 1980. *1980 Census of Population*, "Characteristics of the Population, Chapter A, Number of Inhabitants, United States Summary," part 1, 1–131, Table 25. http://www.census.gov/.
21 "J-School Grads Shun Community Papers," *Editor & Publisher* 120:43 (October 24, 1987): 24.
22 "Students Eye Ad and PR Jobs," *Editor & Publisher* 114 (December 19, 1981): 36.
23 "Journalism Education Under the Microscope," *Editor & Publisher* 119:44 (November 1, 1986): 19. Monticello, in east-central Minnesota's Wright County, had a population of 2,830 in 1980. *1990 Census of Population*, "Population and Housing Units 1970 to 1990," Minnesota, 54, Table 8. http://www.census.gov/.
24 "Journalism School Debate: Should Advertising and Public Relations Courses Remain Part of the J-School Curriculum or Should They Be Taught in Business Schools?," *Editor & Publisher* 121:4 (January 23, 1988): 16.
25 Ibid., 45.
26 "Smaller Town Editors Are 'Joiners,'" *Editor & Publisher* 115 (May 1, 1982): 51.
27 *The Bladen Journal*, January 1, 1981, 2, 3. Elizabethtown, in Bladen County, part of North Carolina's southernmost region, had a population of 3,551 in 1980. *1980 Census of Population*, "Characteristics of the Population, Chapter A, Number of Inhabitants, United States Summary," part 1, 1–144, Table 25. http://www.census.gov/.
28 "We Need Community Papers," *Grassroots Editor* 30:4 (Winter 1989): 10.
29 "High School Students Publish Community Weekly," *Editor & Publisher* 119:12 (March 22, 1986): 17. Cedarville, Eagleville, Fort Bidwell, Lake City and Surprise Valley are located in California's Modoc County, located in the far northeast corner of California, The county had a total population of 8,610 in 1980. *1980 Census of Population*, "Characteristics of the Population, Chapter A, Number of Inhabitants, United States Summary," part 1, 1–165, Table 17. http://www.census.gov/.
30 "Weekly Editor: Hurtt Deringer, The Kent County News, Chestertown, Maryland," *Editor & Publisher* 119:38 (September 20, 1986): 50. Chestertown in northeast Maryland's Kent County, had a population of 3,300 in 1980. *1980 Census of Population*, "Characteristics of the Population, Chapter A, Number of Inhabitants, United States Summary," part 1, 1–133, Table 25. http://www.census.gov/.
31 "From Daily to Weekly," *Grassroots Editor* 28:3 (Fall 1987): 5–8,15. Humansville, in west-central Missouri's Polk County, had a population of 907 in 1980. *1990 Census of Population*, "Population and Housing Units 1970 to 1990," Missouri, 43, Table 8. http://www.census.gov/.
32 Ibid. *1980 Census of Population*, "Characteristics of the Population, Chapter A, Number of Inhabitants, United States Summary," part 1, 1–117, Table 25. Hillsboro, in central-east Kansas's Marion County, had a population of 2,717 in 1980. *1980 Census of Population*, "Characteristics of the Population, Chapter A, Number of Inhabitants, United States Summary," part 1, 1–130, Table 25. http://www.census.gov/.

33 "Weekly Editor: K.A. (Doc) Eggensperger, Sanders County Ledger, Thompson Falls, Mont.," *Editor & Publisher* 120:12 (March 21, 1987): 22, 56. Thompson Falls, in northwest Montana's Sanders County, had a population of 1,478 in 1980. *1990 Census of Population, "Population and Housing Units 1970 to 1990,"* Montana, 14, Table 8. http://www.census.gov/.

34 "Newspapers and the Community," *Editor & Publisher* 119:40 (October 4, 1986): 36. Morristown, in upper northeast Tennessee's Hamblen County, had a population of 19,683 in 1980. *1980 Census of Population, "Characteristics of the Population, Chapter A, Number of Inhabitants, United States Summary,"* part 1, 1–153, Table 25. http://www.census.gov/.

35 *The Blair Press,* January 29, 1987, 1. Blair, in Trempealeau County, is located along the central-eastern border of Wisconsin. Blair had a population of 1,142 in 1980. *1990 Census of Population and Housing, "Population and Housing Unit Counts, Wisconsin,"* 45, Table 9. http://www.newspaperarchive.com/, http://www.census.gov/.

36 "Weekly Editor: Sam & Adrien Taylor, The Times-Independent, Moab, Utah," *Editor & Publisher* 120:25 (June 20, 1987): 22. Moab, in central-eastern Utah's Grand County, had a population of 5,333 in 1980. *1980 Census of Population, "Characteristics of the Population, Chapter A, Number of Inhabitants, United States Summary,"* part 1, 1–156, Table 25. http://www.census.gov/.

37 "Weekly Editor: Carol Wilcox and Cary Stiff, Clear Creek Courant, Idaho Springs, Colo.," *Editor & Publisher* 120:6 (February 7, 1987): 18–19. Idaho Springs, in Colorado's Clear Creek County and part of the Denver metropolitan area, had a population of 2,077 in 1980. *1990 Census of Population, "Population and Housing Units 1970 to 1990,"* Colorado, 12, Table 8. http://www.census.gov/.

38 "Why Endorse Candidates?," *Grassroots Editor* 26:1 (Spring 1985): 3.

39 "Weekly Editor: Preston Moses, Chatham Star-Tribune, Chatham, Va.," *Editor & Publisher* 120:14 (April 4, 1987): 19, 38. Chatham, in south-central Virginia's Pittsylvania County, had a population of 1,390 in 1980. *1980 Census of Population, "General Population Characteristics, Places of 1,000 or More,"* Virginia, 48–8, Table 14. http://www.census.gov/.

40 "Weekly Editor: John U. Pavlik, Ritzville Adams County Journal, Ritzville, Wash.," *Editor & Publisher* 120:18 (May 2, 1987): 90, 150. Ritzville, in central-eastern Washington's Adams County, had a population of 1,800 in 1980. *1980 Census of Population, Vol. 1, "Characteristics of the Population,Chapter 1, Number of Inhabitants, Part 49, Washington,"* 49–10, Table 4. http://www.census.gov/.

41 "Weekly Editor: Dick Nafsinger, Hood River News, Hood River, Oregon," *Editor & Publisher* 120:23 (June 6, 1987): 98, 135. Hood River, a port on the Columbia River in northeast Oregon's Hood River County, had a population of 4,329 in 1980. *1980 Census of Population, "Characteristics of the Population, Chapter A, Number of Inhabitants, United States Summary,"* part 1, 1–148, Table 25. http://www.census.gov/.

42 "Weekly Editor: Robert Hammes, Gazette Record, St. Marie's, Idaho," *Editor & Publisher* 120:16 (April 18, 1987): 42. St. Marie's, in northwest Idaho's Benewah County, had a population of 2,794 in 1980. *1980 Census of Population, "Characteristics of the Population, Chapter A, Number of Inhabitants, United States Summary,"* part 1, 1–126, Table 25. http://www.census.gov/.

43 "Shop Talk at Thirty: Low Pay Imperils Newspapers," *Editor & Publisher* 116 (November 5, 1983): 52.

44 "Notes on People: 'We Were Impressed,' Committee Says," *Editor & Publisher* 116 (October 1, 1983): 27. Weathersfield, in central-eastern Vermont's Windsor County, had a population of 2,534 in 1980. *1980 Census of Population*, "Characteristics of the Population, Chapter A, Number of Inhabitants, United States Summary," part 1, 1–175, Table 26. http://www.census.gov/.

45 "Weekly Editor: Suzanne Kennedy, The Highlander, Marble Falls, Texas," *Editor & Publisher* 121:18 (April 30, 1988): 32, 51. Marble Falls, northwest of Austin in central Texas's Burnet County, had a population of 3,252 in 1980. *1980 Census of Population*, "Characteristics of the Population, Chapter A, Number of Inhabitants, United States Summary," part 1, 1–155, Table 25. http://www.census.gov/.

46 "The Changing Role of the Farm Editor," *Editor & Publisher* 119:25 (June 21, 1986): 84.

47 "Is the Second Class Weekly a 'Dead Duck'?," *Editor & Publisher* 113 (August 16, 1980): 32.

48 "Weekly Paper Satisfies Most Local Ad Buyers," *Editor & Publisher* 113 (August 2, 1980): 27.

49 "Shopper Drives Scaife Weekly Out of Business," *Editor & Publisher* 114 (August 15, 1981): 21.

50 "Weekly in Penna. Resumes Publication," *Editor & Publisher* 114 (December 5, 1981): 39. Elizabethtown, southeast of Harrisburg in southern-central Pennsylvania's Lancaster County, had a population of 8,233 in 1980. *1980 Census of Population*, "Characteristics of the Population, Chapter A, Number of Inhabitants, United States Summary," part 1, 1–149, Table 25. Hummelstown, near Harrisburg in Pennsylvania's Dauphin County, had a population of 4,267 in 1980. *1980 Census of Population*, "Characteristics of the Population, Chapter A, Number of Inhabitants, United States Summary," part 1, 1–150, Table 25. http://www.census.gov/.

51 "136 Non-Dailies and Shoppers Changed Ownership During '81," *Editor & Publisher* 115 (January 2, 1982): 38–41.

52 David Asper Johnson, "Adapting to Changing Local Demographics," *Editor & Publisher* 116 (July 9, 1983): 13–14.

53 *The Malakoff News*, January 3, 1980, 3. Malakoff, in central-east Texas's Henderson County, had a population of 2,082 in 1980. *1990 Census of Population*, "Population and Housing Units 1970 to 1990," Texas, 49, Table 8. http://www.census.gov/. In 2022, according to the latest government figures based on the Consumer Price Index, 15 cents from 1980 was worth 54 cents. http://measuringworth.com/.

54 "Bright Future Predicted for Community Newspapers," *Editor & Publisher* 116 (March 12, 1983): 9.

55 "S.A.U.s and the Small Newspaper: Is the Change Worth the Trouble?," *Editor & Publisher* 116 (October 1, 1983): 8.

56 "Selling Weeklies Nationally to Advertisers," *Editor & Publisher* 119:42 (October 18, 1986): 28.

57 "Weekly Editor: Dave Bonner, Powell Tribune, Powell, Wyo.," *Editor & Publisher* 120:2 (January 10, 1987): 13. In 2022, according to the latest government figures based on the

58. "Weekly Reaps Benefits in Energy Coverage Feud," *Editor & Publisher* 113 (July 12, 1980): 13.
59. "Georgia Weekly Ruled Entitled to Legal Ads," *Editor & Publisher* 113 (July 12, 1980): 22.
60. "Ex-Publisher Proposes Purchasing Co-op for Independent Newspapers," *Editor & Publisher* 116 (March 5, 1983): 27.
61. "Weekly Paper Is Delivered Exclusively by Senior Citizens," *Editor & Publisher* 120:8 (February 21, 1987): 19, 50. Greenwood, in central Indiana's Johnson County, had a population of 19,327 in 1980. *1980 Census of Population*, "Characteristics of the Population, Chapter A, Number of Inhabitants, United States Summary," part 1, 1–129, Table 25. http://www.census.gov/.
62. "200 Non-Dailies, Shopper Groups in '80 Purchase," *Editor & Publisher* 114 (January 3, 1981): 35. In 2022, according to the latest government figures based on the Consumer Price Index, $20 million from 1981 was worth $65.173 million. http://measuringworth.com/.
63. Weekly Editor: Roswell Bosworth Jr., East Bay Newspapers, Bristol, R.I." *Editor & Publisher* 120:43 (October 24, 1987): 18, 38. Barrington, southeast of Providence in Rhode Island's Bristol County, had a population of 16,174 in 1980. *1980 Census of Population*, "Characteristics of the Population, Chapter A, Number of Inhabitants, United States Summary," part 1, 1–151, Table 25. Warren, also in Rhode Island's Bristol County, had a population of 10,640 in 1980. *1980 Census of Population*, "Characteristics of the Population, Chapter A, Number of Inhabitants, United States Summary," part 1, 1–175, Table 26. Sakonnet-Little Compton, in Rhode Island's Newport County, had a population of 3,085 in 1980. *1980 Census of Population*, "Characteristics of the Population, Chapter A, Number of Inhabitants, United States Summary," part 1, 1–175, Table 26. http://www.census.gov/. In 2022, according to the latest government figures based on the Consumer Price Index, $1.5 million from 1987 was worth $3.91 million. http://measuringworth.com/.
64. "1987 in Review: The Year of the Newspaper Chain," *Editor & Publisher* 121:1 (January 2, 1988): 11.
65. Ibid., 13.
66. "Public-Owned Weekly Thriving," *Editor & Publisher* 115 (April 17, 1982): 33. Pigeon Forge, in northeast Tennessee's Sevier County, had a population of 10 in 1980. *1990 Census of Population*, "Population and Housing Units 1970 to 1990," Tennessee, 28, Table 8. http://www.census.gov/. In 2022, according to the latest government figures based on the Consumer Price Index, $100,000 from 1982 was worth $307,000, $150,000 was worth $460,000, and $300,000 was worth $921,000. http://measuringworth.com/.

References

"136 Non-dailies and Shoppers Changed Ownership During '81." *Editor & Publisher* 115:1 (January 2, 1982): 38–41.

"200 Non-dailies, Shopper Groups in '80 Purchase." *Editor & Publisher* 114:1 (January 3, 1981): 35–37, 42–43, 45.

1980 Census of Population. edited by United States Bureau of the Census: Washington, DC: Government Printing Office, 1983.

"1987 in Review: The Year of the Newspaper Chain." *Editor & Publisher* 121:1 (January 2, 1988): 11, 13, 68–69.

The Bladen (Elizabethtown, NC) *Journal*, January 1, 1981.

The Blair (WI) *Press*, January 29, 1987.

"Bright Future Predicted for Community Newspapers." *Editor & Publisher* 116:11 (March 12, 1983): 9.

"Calif. Publisher Markets Ad Software for Small Dailies and Weeklies." *Editor & Publisher* 115:43 (October 23, 1982): 26.

"The Changing Role of the Farm Editor." *Editor & Publisher* 119:25 (June 21, 1986): 84.

"Electronic News Systems Dominate N.N.A. Meeting." *Editor & Publisher* 114 (October 10, 1981): 62.

"Ex-Publisher Proposes Purchasing Co-op for Independent Newspapers." *Editor & Publisher* 116:10 (March 5, 1983): 27.

"From Daily to Weekly." *Grassroots Editor* 28:3 (Fall 1987): 5–8,15.

"Georgia Weekly Ruled Entitled to Legal Ads," *Editor & Publisher* 113 (July 12, 1980): 22.

"Hello Pagination, Goodbye Stereotype," *Editor & Publisher* 114:24 (June 13, 1981): 9.

"High School Students Publish Community Weekly." *Editor & Publisher* 119:12 (March 22, 1986): 17.

"Improving Journalism Education Programs," *Editor & Publisher* 119:16 (April 19, 1986): 46.

"Is the Second Class Weekly a 'Dead Duck'?" *Editor & Publisher* 113:33 (August 16, 1980): 32.

Johnson, David Asper. "Adapting to Changing Local Demographics." *Editor & Publisher* 116:28 (July 9, 1983): 13–14.

"Journalism Education Under the Microscope." *Editor & Publisher* 119:44 (November 1, 1986): 19, 38.

"Journalism School Debate: Should Advertising and Public Relations Courses Remain Part of the J-School Curriculum or Should They Be Taught in Business Schools?" *Editor & Publisher* 121:4 (January 23, 1988): 16, 45.

"J-Prof Raps Sad State of Newspaper Writing," *Editor & Publisher* 114:6 (February 7, 1981): 16, 26.

"J-School Grads Shun Community Papers." *Editor & Publisher* 120:43 (October 24, 1987): 24, 38.

The Malakoff (TX) *News*, January 3, 1980.

"New Software Allows Page Dummying with PC's." *Editor & Publisher* 119:5 (February 1, 1986): 27.

"News Execs Urge Major Overhaul of Journalism Training Program." *Editor & Publisher* 115:10 (March 6, 1982): 10, 30.

"News/Tech: Micros Invade the Newsroom." *Editor & Publisher* 117:5 (February 4, 1984): 32, 35.

"Newspapers and the Community." *Editor & Publisher* 119:40 (October 4, 1986): 36, 40.

"Notes on People: 'We Were Impressed,' Committee Says." *Editor & Publisher* 116:40 (October 1, 1983): 27.

"PCs—Where Do They Fit in at Your Newspaper?" *Editor & Publisher* 119:21 (May 24, 1986): 52–53E.

"Personal Computers Come Up Front in Newsrooms." *Editor & Publisher* 119:39 (September 27, 1986): 36, 38.

"Public-owned Weekly Thriving." *Editor & Publisher* 115:16 (April 17, 1982): 33.

"Publisher-ER 7 Designed for Weeklies Has Micro Hardware/Special Software." *Editor & Publisher* 115:15 (April 10, 1982): 26, 29.

"Recruiting Talent for Small-Town Papers." *Editor & Publisher* 119:46 (November 15, 1986): 26, 46.

"S.A.U.s and the Small Newspaper: Is the Change Worth the Trouble?" *Editor & Publisher* 116:40 (October 1, 1983): 8.

"Selling Weeklies Nationally to Advertisers." *Editor & Publisher* 119:42 (October 18, 1986): 28–29.

"Shop Talk at Thirty: Have J-school Students Changed? Or Have the Professors?" *Editor & Publisher* 120:21 (May 23, 1987): 48, 38.

"Shop Talk at Thirty: Low Pay Imperils Newspaper." *Editor & Publisher* 116:45 (November 5, 1983): 52.

"Shop Talk at Thirty: What is a Newspaper?" *Editor & Publisher* 115:29 (July 17, 1982): 48.

"Shopper Drives Scaife Weekly Out of Business," *Editor & Publisher* 114:33 (August 15, 1981): 21.

"Smaller Town Editors Are 'Joiners.'" *Editor & Publisher* 115:18 (May 1, 1982): 51.

"Students Eye Ad and PR Jobs." *Editor & Publisher* 114:51 (December 19, 1981): 36.

"Two-Color Work Helps Weekly Stay Competitive." *Editor & Publisher* 114:43 (October 24, 1981): 56.

"Weekly Editor: Carol Wilcox and Cary Stiff, Clear Creek Courant, Idaho Springs, Colo." *Editor & Publisher* 120:6 (February 7, 1987): 18–19.

"Weekly Editor: Dave Bonner, Powell Tribune, Powell, Wyo." *Editor & Publisher* 120:2 (January 10, 1987): 13, 37–38.

"Weekly Editor: Dick Nafsinger, Hood River News, Hood River, Oregon." *Editor & Publisher* 120:23 (June 6, 1987): 98,135.

"Weekly Editor: Hurtt Deringer, The Kent County News, Chestertown, Maryland." *Editor & Publisher* 119:38 (September 20, 1986): 19, 50.

"Weekly Editor: Jack Douthit, Sterling City News-Record, Sterling City, Texas." *Editor & Publisher* 120:38 (September 19, 1987): 20, 57.

"Weekly Editor: John U. Pavlik, Ritzville Adams County Journal, Ritzville, Wash." *Editor & Publisher* 120:18 (May 2, 1987): 90,150.

"Weekly Editor: K.A. (Doc) Eggensperger, Sanders County Ledger, Thompson Falls, Mont." *Editor & Publisher* 120:12 (March 21, 1987): 22, 56.

"Weekly Editor: Lonnie M. Rankin, Miles Messenger, Rowena Press, Concho Herald, Miles, Texas." *Editor & Publisher* 121:17 (April 23, 1988): 72, 139.

"Weekly Editor: Preston Moses, Chatham Star-Tribune, Chatham, Va." *Editor & Publisher* 120:14 (April 4, 1987): 19, 38.

"Weekly Editor: Robert Hammes, Gazette Record, St. Marie's, Idaho." *Editor & Publisher* 120:16 (April 18, 1987): 18, 42–43.

"Weekly Editor: Roswell Bosworth Jr., East Bay Newspapers, Bristol, R.I." *Editor & Publisher* 120:43 (October 24, 1987): 18, 38.

"Weekly Editor: Sam & Adrien Taylor, The Times-Independent, Moab, Utah." *Editor & Publisher* 120:25 (June 20, 1987): 20, 22, 34.

"Weekly Editor: Suzanne Kennedy, The Highlander, Marble Falls, Texas." *Editor & Publisher* 121:18 (April 30, 1988): 32, 51.

"Weekly in Penna. Resumes Publication." *Editor & Publisher* 114:49 (December 5, 1981): 39.

"Weekly Paper Is Delivered Exclusively by Senior Citizen." *Editor & Publisher* 120:8 (February 21, 1987): 19, 50.

"Weekly Paper Satisfies Most Local Ad Buyers." *Editor & Publisher* 113 (August 2, 1980): 27.

"Weekly Reaps Benefits in Energy Coverage Feud." *Editor & Publisher* 113 (July 12, 1980): 13.

"We Need Community Papers." *Grassroots Editor* 30:4 (Winter 1989): 8–10, 15.

"Where are They Now?, New England Newsman." *Grassroots Editor* 29:1 (Spring 1988): 3–5.

"Why Endorse Candidates?" *Grassroots Editor* 26:1 (Spring 1985): 3–4, 14–15.

www.measuringworth.com.

"Wyoming Weekly Programs Teletext News on Low Power TV Channel," *Editor & Publisher* 115:52 (December 25, 1982): 21.

· 1 0 ·

THE 1990S: LOCALISM IN OWNERSHIP AND CONTENT; THE WAL-MART FACTOR; WEEKLY/WORKER COMPETITION; AND A 24-HOUR NEWS CYCLE

The 1990s ushered in new technologies such as the World Wide Web and the Hubble Space Telescope, and political strife through the waging of a Gulf War in the Middle East, the end of the Cold War with the dissolution of the U.S.S.R., terrorist bombings carried out against U.S. citizens locally and abroad, urban riots and standoffs, a mass school shooting, and a presidential sex scandal. But while incorporating wire copy on these national and international stories, most community weeklies focused on localism and their important role in providing the information that impacted their local readers. In doing so, a familiar set of challenges faced community weeklies, but at enhanced levels in relation to losing local ownership, responding to advertising threats from national big-box stores, attracting and retaining employees, and competing against free-circulation papers/metropolitan daily zoned editions, all amid a 24-hour cable television/Internet news cycle.

During the storied history of community weeklies, the importance of local content was worn as a badge of honor by its editor-publishers throughout the United States. By the final decade of the twentieth century, the emphasis on "local" took on a double meaning in terms of not only content, but ownership. More and more weeklies were being bought by non-local newspaper chains or wealthy investors, raising fears in community subscribers that their hometown weekly no longer reflected the personalities, whims, and desires of its readers. Like English ivy clinging to a brick wall—where the deeper the roots and longer the ivy strand, the harder to pull it away from the wall—such was a locally owned weekly newspaper with long, established roots in a community.

The big-box stores—most notably Bentonville, Arkansas-based Wal-Mart—began buying multiple-page advertisements in weeklies, spurring increased advertising space purchases from locally owned competitors. But after driving out its local competitors that couldn't compete with Wal-Mart's larger variety, volumes, and lower prices, the weeklies lost these advertisers and eventually a reduction in Wal-Mart-generated advertising revenue. As a result, they were often scrambling for new revenue sources to keep the local weekly "local."

Entering the 1990s with a mild recession and sluggish employment recovery—which lasted into 1991—newspaper shoppers fared better than their paid-weekly counterparts as advertisers jumped to the higher-circulation free publications. In contrast to the paid weeklies' relentless battle with the U.S. postal service over mailing costs, some shoppers abandoned mail delivery altogether to cut costs, and boosted advertising recovery through joint advertising agreements with local cable television stations. Metropolitan dailies introduced zoned editions as a "part of your community" campaign, incorporating surrounding-rural-community or suburb-specific inserts within their larger publications. In spite of their competitors' tactics, anxious community weekly editors-publishers were advised to keep their readers' needs and interests at the forefront to survive the competitive onslaught.

"Transient journalist" became a recognizable expression during the decade as small-town weeklies struggled to retain reporters/editors with no local ties to their communities, who were always looking for bigger dollars and headlines at larger-circulation publications. It became even more challenging to recruit newspaper staffers, especially in smaller operations, as more and more college journalism students were turning to bigger salaries and the supposed "glamour" of the advertising, public relations, and television industries. In response, some weeklies established scholarship and internship programs to attract collegiate journalists, while the National Newspaper Association invited college newspapers to join their ranks.

A burgeoning 24-hour cable television news business forced newspapers to readjust their priorities and focus on a "news hole" crying out for more investigative reporting on local issues largely ignored by regionally owned weeklies and small dailies whose eyes were turned to national and international headlines. This required a reporting staff familiar with the community—even better—employees who sought solutions to improve the quality of life not only for their readers, but for their own families.

Keeping It Local: With an Emphasis on "O" for Ownership and "C" for Content

Early in the decade, journalism academics and weekly industry executives recognized that despite the many competitors and challenges facing community and suburban weeklies, the key was to emphasize localism. At the Suburban Newspapers of America 1990 summer management conference in San Antonio, Texas, S.N.A. President Chuck Lyons—president of DCI Publishing in Virginia, which published 21 weeklies representing a circulation of 500,000—said suburban papers that were traditionally weekly, had come into their own. Quality was improving, readership was growing, but so was competition in a flooded market from shoppers, advertisers, direct mail pieces, the emerging electronic information systems, suburban dailies, and zoned editions issued weekly by metropolitan dailies. Jim Buckley, communications professor at the University of Michigan, said the best strategy for suburban weeklies to combat these challengers was to stay close to their readers and advertisers.[1]

An investment banker predicted that community newspapers would emerge from the industry recession with higher growth rates than dailies. Lawrence Crutcher, with investment banking firm Veronis, Suhler & Associates, said the recession should continue through 1992, or into early 1993, after which he said weeklies could expect a growth rate of 8 percent or higher, compared to 6 percent for dailies. The reason, Crutcher said, "has to do with getting local." But he warned the growth would not relate to higher sales values for weeklies. Broker Richard Briggs—whose brokerage firm Richard Briggs and Associates of Landrum, South Carolina, specialized in small papers—said those publications would attract more owner-operator buyers as opposed to absentee owners "because the owner-operator will be identified personally with the paper in a way larger groups are not, chemistry is very important. It's a lot like falling in love," he said.[2] Other components of the 1990 Veronis, Suhler & Associates newspaper annual forecast that focused on weeklies included the following:

* advertising in weeklies will continue to grow faster than in dailies, but weeklies remain a small fraction of newspaper advertising.
* spending for weeklies will rise from $3.3 billion last year, at a rate of 7.9 percent a year, to $4.8 billion in 1994.
* paid weeklies will cost 39.3 cents in 1994, up from 33.3 cents last year, and will increase circulation 3.1 percent a year. Paid-weekly circulation will grow from 17 million last year to 18 million in 1994, while their share of the weekly market slips to 30 percent, from 33 percent.[3]

Editor & Publisher, on an April 14, 1990 front commentary titled, "Newspapers of the Future"—which referred to many task forces set up during the previous two years to study future opportunities and problems facing newspapers, culminating in a 98-page report—observed, "The biggest challenge for small newspapers in the '90s ... is to maintain and nurture their valuable local franchise. For people with local ties, local newspapers are a 'must read' on a daily basis."[4]

One of the key definitions in reference to keeping a community weekly "local" had to do with ownership and a growing concern about the loss of locally owned family or chain operations. But, in many cases, a family had no choice but to sell due to hefty taxes. A May 2, 1998 *Editor & Publisher* article on testimony before a congressional small business subcommittee pointed out that many family-owned newspapers were forced to sell to big media companies because of big estate tax bills when an owner died. David Lord—president of Seattle-based Pioneer Newspapers, Inc.—said family-owned newspapers were having to explore extensive financial planning, create large cash reserves, and establish expensive trusts in an effort to sell a newspaper due to what he termed "the inevitable death tax."[5]

Rapidly decreasing in numbers were those family-owned weeklies operating for more than 100 years, such as the *Milford Cabinet and Wilton Journal* in Milford, New Hampshire. The paper had been serving the readers of Souhegan Valley since 1802 and was purchased by Albert A. Rotch in 1869. His great-great-great-grandson William B. Rotch, was the publisher in the 1990s and wrote a letter in the May 27, 1992 edition concerning Memorial Day. His "letter from the publisher" was titled, "Memorial Day. It is both holiday and holy day." The 32-page paper featured four sections and two supplements and was published on Wednesdays. It contained community news from Amherst, Brookline, Hollis, Lyndeborough, Mason, Milford, Mont Vernon, and Wilton. A single issue sold for 50 cents.[6]

Into the 1990s, another longtime, family-owned weekly was the *Gowrie News* of Gowrie, Iowa. In 1991, it was being published by the fourth generation of the Patton family, with publishing duties taken over by new owners Robert Patton and Nancy Vogt from his parents, James and Annice Patton. The paper had been published by a Patton since 1899, when it was bought by Armanis F. Patton. His son, Lorimer, took over in 1943, and when he retired in 1963, Lorimer's sons Jerry and James became publishers. Jerry retired in 1984, and James continued as publisher until selling to his son, Robert, in 1991.[7]

Maintaining locally owned papers sometimes called for combining a few to become one publication, enhancing readership and revenues. Such was the case in Wellsburg, West Virginia, in 1994 when *The Brooke County Review* was established, resulting from the merging of *The Brooke News* and *The Follansbee Review*. The inaugural April 28, 1994 eight-page edition had these words placed over the masthead: "It's Here! Introducing the New The Brooke County Review, Vol. 1, Issue 1, published on Thursday. The NEW Review." Editor-Publisher George Wallace wrote, "We're pleased and proud to announce the merger of Brooke County's only home newspapers into the Brooke County Review, an independent Democratic newspaper ... As the only general circulation newspaper published in Brooke County, we have the opportunity to become a real force in the country." *The Brooke News* had served the area since 1937. *The Follansbee Review* was established in 1911.[8]

In contrast, more and more weeklies and small dailies were being snatched up by regional and national chains with no local ownership ties. The purchase of more Maine community and weekly newspapers by out-of-state companies concerned many locals who believed that distant owners were less likely to act in their community's best interest. A December 4, 1999 *Editor & Publisher* article reported on the purchase of Dallas-based American Consolidated Media, Inc.'s ninth coastal Maine newspaper. With the purchase of the then-4,500-circulation *York Weekly*, the total paid circulation of the Maine group—called Courier Publications—grew to about 62,000. Courier's Maine papers, in addition to the *York Weekly*, included the Rockland *Courier-Gazette*, the *Lincoln County Weekly*, *The Camden Herald*, *Capital Weekly* in Augusta, *York County Coast Star*, *The Republican Journal* in Belfast, *The Bar Harbor Times*, and the *Ellsworth Weekly*. In 1992, 20 percent of the ads ran in more than one of the group's papers, tripling to 60 percent in duplication among the group's papers by 1999. Alan L. Baker, publisher of the weekly *Ellsworth American*—which competed with two Courier papers for advertising customers—said, "It would probably be ill-advised to say we're not worried. We don't have deep resources to fall back on." The independent publications would count on their legacy, continued improvement, and specialty publications to stay viable, according to Baker.[9]

Across the country, a Los Angeles-based takeover specialist, Leonard Green & Partners—known for purchasing money-losing newspaper chains—changed directions and spent $310 million to buy 167 community newspapers from Hollinger International Inc., in 1996. The papers reported revenues of about $100 million the previous year and earnings exceeding $30 million. Among the 176 papers from 11 states were 56 dailies, 34 paid weeklies and 77 free papers, with a combined circulation of 900,000, many from southern Illinois, Missouri, western New York, Pennsylvania, and California.[10]

In its December 5, 1998 issue, *Editor & Publisher* reported on the Community Newspaper Holdings, Inc. $475 million purchase of 45 papers—28 dailies and 17 weeklies concentrated in the South—from Conrad Black's Hollinger International. The purchase gave 18-month-old, Birmingham, Alabama-based C.N.H.I. a total of 175 papers, making it the largest U.S. newspaper group in number of titles, mostly in small markets. C.N.H.I. was largely supported by the Retirement Systems of Alabama, which provided $600 million for its initial newspaper purchase.[11]

Even top leaders in professional associations promoting community weeklies were not immune to the takeover trend. Arkansas legislator Charlotte Shexnayder—the first woman to serve as president of the National Newspaper Association (1991)—and husband Melvin sold the *Dumas* (AR) *Clarion* after 44 years of ownership. The then-4,000-circulation weekly was sold to Emmerich Newspapers of Jackson, Mississippi, owner of three dailies and nine weeklies in Mississippi.[12]

At the end of the decade, Geneva Overholser—a syndicated writer for *The Washington Post* Writers Group, former editorial writer for *The New York Times*, and former editor of *The Des Moines Register*—wrote a column in the November/December 1999 issue of the *Columbia Journalism Review* bemoaning the loss of independent and locally owned newspapers and a move away from local-centric news. She said that a result of non-local ownership was that "precious few of today's newspapers read or feel as if they are put together by people who know well, and love deeply, their community." Despite the newspaper industry's touting of the importance of local news and promoting public journalism, she said the results, all too often, were "brittle and lifeless." She stressed, "We survey our readers and coordinate our staffers and plot our projects. But no amount of planning, no level of market research, can make up for 10 years of living in a town—not to mention growing up there, putting your kids through school there, watching your folks grow old there..."[13]

The former owner of two Minnesota weeklies and a large regional weekly shopper, wrote a letter to the editor, published in the March 7, 1998 edition of *Editor & Publisher*, that expressed his regret for having sold his company to a larger in-state newspaper/printing operation. Duane A. Rasmussen, former owner of Sell Publishing Company of Forest Lake, Minnesota, began by addressing the "age-old" question of whether chain ownership was good for a newspaper, its employees, and community. He wrote: "I have lived through two generations who have lost at the hands of chains." His parents, Harry and Geraldine Rasmussen sold the *Austin* (MN) *Daily Herald* to Thomson Newspapers in 1962. According to their son, the paper went from a circulation of 13,000 to just more than half that number 25 years later, and two owners since the Thomson purchase in 1962. Duane Rasmussen sold his weekly papers, the *Forest Lake* (MN) *Times* and *Post-Review* in North Branch, Minnesota, along with a large regional weekly shopper, community booklets and convention newspapers for the Twin Cities area, and a printing plant and commercial printing business to ECM Publishers, Inc. in 1993. In his letter, he said after growing the company from 12 to 65 employees, the new owner, only four years in, reduced the staff by two-thirds and closed some of the facilities. He concluded, "I still get my checks monthly and I have moved away. But the soul of newspapering is gone when a new owner can ignore the often expressed concerns of the seller and rip apart a company."[14]

Even into the 1990s, the perceived image of community weeklies as "boilerplate" publications persisted. An editorial in the August 24, 1991 edition of *Editor & Publisher* titled, "Boiler Plate," advised newspapers to prohibit the use of computer-generated materials prepared by advertisers, advertising agencies, or public relations people for their clients. It referred to the days when weeklies and small dailies filled many pages with "filler" material prepared by syndicate services, saving the costs of setting the type and hiring reporters to write the equivalent amount of copy. It called on "honest" editors to weigh the value of publishing computerized boilerplate instead of hiring an active newsperson, concluding, "In the long run, more readers will be attracted by live news report than by filler material."[15]

In contrast to those criticisms, and continuing to defend the localized content of small dailies and the traditional weekly community press, the Fall 1991 issue of *Grassroots Editor* reprinted an article by weekly editor Jack

Authelet from the April 1991 issue of the New England Press Association's *NEPA Bulletin*. Authelet wrote, "They [small dailies and weeklies] remain the single source of information that readers can get nowhere else. They are also papers that are keenly aware that if they don't print the information, it will never appear anywhere as a public record."[16]

For example, where else could senior citizens in Bagley, Minnesota, read and reminisce about life in Bagley throughout the decades than on the Seniors Page of the *Farmers Independent*? The March 3, 1993, 16-page edition included the following Seniors Page articles and columns: a local column, "The Good Old Days ..." by Mrs. Larry (Jeanne) Brustad; an article, "Sick and Tired of Being Sick and Tired?"; and standing features, "Turning Back the Pages" and "A Review of Local History from the Archives of the Farmers Independent" by Pearl Highberg.[17]

However, in a second article in the Fall 1991 issue of *Grassroots Editor*, Authelet bemoaned the fact that some community newspapers were charging fees for the publication of obituaries, weddings, and engagement announcements. On fees based on the length of an obituary, he observed, "The more survivors, the greater the haul. And don't forget to include all the clubs and affiliations and everything else you can think of, because the paper doesn't care anymore." He then questioned, "When did the wedding of some local kids stop being news? How long has it been since the death of a resident wasn't worthy of a story by the local newspaper?" Not only were obituaries and social news the sections in which the newspaper took great pride, he explained, but they also served as "great equalizers." He concluded, "If engagements, weddings, and funerals are no longer news, the downturn in the economy has been more costly than we imagined. Recessions come and recessions go, and while our bank balances may rise and fall, our integrity must be a constant."[18]

Despite criticisms for trying to monetize every means possible to stay afloat, local-centric weeklies remained much beloved by their readers. For example, Rick Friedman—past president of the International Society of Weekly Newspaper Editors—wrote a Summer 1992 *Grassroots Editor* article about the success of a new weekly begun only 13 weeks prior. The *Woburn Advocate*, was founded in 36,000-resident Woburn, Massachusetts—just 10 miles outside of Boston—by the largest local industrial developer, William Cummings. After 15 years working in community journalism—and 10 more writing about weekly newspapers for *Editor & Publisher*—Friedman began working for the *Woburn Advocate* as a freelance writer and consultant. He was interviewing a retired banker from the community for a feature about a popular local variety store owner. The banker said of the *Woburn Advocate*, "The thing is, you're Woburn oriented; you're writing about Woburn happenings, Woburn people. We don't want to know what's going on in Russia, Boston, Wakefield, and Winchester. We can read about those places in the Boston papers. The *Advocate* has done a hell of a job. I think you have a great purpose and a great future."

The then-16,774-circulation *Woburn Advocate* contained more than 90 percent of local content and competed against the Woburn-based *Daily Times Chronicle*—which covered Woburn and four other nearby towns, five days a week. But the daily rarely ran local editorials, and staff-written columns were frequently on non-local topics. Its "Lifestyle" section included mostly syndicated content. The *Woburn Advocate* was mailed to almost every residence and 2,000 businesses in Woburn. The paper regularly published between 40 and 48 tabloid pages, with advertising between 40 and 50 percent of the advertising/editorial split.[19]

A 1996 survey conducted by *The Washington Post* revealed that readers were much more interested in local news than national or international news. The survey results were released at the May, 1996 convention of the Newspaper Association of America. Findings showed that 70 percent of regular newspaper readers were very interested in local news, whereas only 56 percent were equally concerned with national news. Only 23 percent had an interest in news from abroad. That same year, an N.A.A. survey of newspaper editors and publishers found Americans considered local news the most valued element of a newspaper, followed by obituaries, classified and display advertising, and sports coverage.[20]

Edgar Crisler Jr.—publisher-editor of *The Port Gibson (MS) Reveille*—probably summed it up best in describing the role of a locally operated, locally sourced paper. In a September 24, 1994 *Editor & Publisher* feature, Crisler said that he saw himself and his newspaper in several ways. "I'm the local historian and the bulletin board. I have another function, the Irish idea of the *seanachie*, the oral historian. I'm contacted by people doing research on families or some aspect of local history." The then-59-year-old newspaperman came from a long family line of *The Port Gibson Reveille* owners, beginning with his grandfather, Henry Crisler, who bought the paper in 1898. Henry worked at the paper until his death in 1954. Edgar Crisler Jr.'s father, Edgar Crisler Sr., ran the paper until his retirement in 1970, and his mother, Sarah Crisler, was the bookkeeper from 1945 until 1992.[21]

Competing with the Big-Box Stores for Advertisers, Finding New Revenue Sources

The National Cost and Revenue Study for Weekly Newspapers—released in 1993 and sponsored by the Inland Press Association and 45 co-sponsoring state newspaper associations—found that smaller-circulation weeklies financially outperformed their larger counterparts. Comparing 1991 to 1992, single-flag weekly newspapers with circulations of less than 4,000 increased their percentage of revenue for payroll from 31.4 percent to 35.7 percent. During the same period, these publications increased their average total operating profit from 9.11 percent of total revenue to 11.5 percent. In addition, smaller weeklies increased their average advertising rate from $3.21 per Standard Advertising Unit column inch to $3.77. In comparison, papers with circulations of more than 20,000 showed a percentage decrease in operating profits during that period from 8.9 percent in 1991 to 8.5 percent in 1992. Payroll at these larger publications only improved slightly, from 34.6 percent in 1991 to 34.9 percent in 1992. The study involved 86 newspapers with more than 330 names, or flags.[22]

So, while the financial outlook was promising for weeklies, the proliferation of Wal-Mart stores in smaller communities was a mixed blessing for the local newspaper, according to Iowa State University economist Kenneth Stone. Although the mass merchandiser attracted more area buyers to a town, their opening ultimately led to the closing of smaller competitors—who were reliable advertisers in the local newspaper. Also, Wal-Mart could substantially add to a paper's advertising revenue in its first year of operation with printed inserts, but the more successful Wal-Mart stores usually turned to television advertising in the second and succeeding years of operation, he explained.[23]

The theme of a November 1993 conference of the Board of Visitors of the University of North Carolina's School of Journalism and Mass Communications tried to answer this question in its conference title: "Megastores: Threat or Bonanza for Small Town Newspapers?"

Walter Hussman Jr.—publisher and editor of the *Arkansas Democrat-Gazette* in Little Rock—argued that large discount stores, such as Wal-Mart, headquartered in Bentonville, Arkansas, had an adverse effect on small-town newspapers. For comparisons, Hussman—who also published the *Camden (AR) News*—said before Wal-Mart came to Camden (population 15,000) one local discount store regularly placed 15 pages of advertising in his newspaper. A competing discount store opened in 1972, and bumped up the advertising pages to 40 between the competing stores. Wal-Mart arrived in 1977, which drove up the number of advertising pages to 75 pages a month between the three stores. The two smaller stores went out of business in 1986 and 1987, and Wal-Mart incrementally dropped its advertising pages from 25 a month to eight.[24]

Joe Sink, publisher of *The Dispatch* in Lexington, North Carolina, said the opening of a Wal-Mart in his town brought more advertising to his newspaper, from new businesses opening up around the Wal-Mart. He said Wal-Mart advertising in *The Dispatch* totaled $102,000 in its first three years. He said Wal-Mart attracted other businesses and the additional advertising revenue from those stores continued to add 30 percent "to the bottom line." He admitted, however, that Wal-Mart's advertising in his newspaper had declined. The consensus of the conference was that while megastores do pose a challenge to small-town newspapers, publishers should be prepared to meet those challenges, both in editorial content and advertising strategies.[25]

A print advertising chief from national retailer, Sears Roebuck & Co., advised community publishers on how to attract more national advertising to their newspapers at the October, 1998 National Newspaper Association convention in Reno, Nevada. Sharon Stewart pointed out that "The Big Store"—as Sears was sometimes called—bought ads in 2,500 papers, of which 900 were regular customers. Also, Sears distributed 50 million preprinted inserts in Sunday papers and another 40 million in midweek buys. Advising conference attendees to better market the concept of community newspapers, she said, "You've got to develop initiatives at the national level that tell the facts about your readership and demographics." She said too many national advertisers erroneously believed that buying ads in metropolitan dailies was the most effective means of reaching their customer base. "Your papers are a truly local medium, and you have an advantage most other media do not, and that's the ability to interact with the local community." She called on community paper associations to develop standard research formats in consultation with big national advertisers.[26]

Making it easier for advertisers—especially those representing regional and national clients—to place ads in multiple papers within a targeted region or smaller weekly chain became a priority among weekly owners throughout the country. A November 4, 1995 *Editor & Publisher* articled reported on the formation of the Sonoma County Community Newspaper Network—a coalition of seven community papers in the northern California county designed to serve as a one-order, one-bill service for advertisers. The seven community newspapers in the then-400,000-population county included: the *Sonoma County Independent*; the *Petaluma Argus Courier*; the *Sonoma West Times & News*; the *Healdsburg Tribune & Window*; the *Community Voice*; and the *Sonoma Index-Tribune*. The idea for the consolidated advertising network came at the request of one local business owner to the general manager of the Sonoma Index-Tribune, Corp., "to make buying into all seven papers easier."[27]

Further evidence of this strategy was reported in a February 24, 1996 *Editor & Publisher* article about Community Newspaper Company of eastern Massachusetts nearing the one-year mark of offering a one-order, one-bill program for advertisers to most of its 117 newspapers. The program was introduced during the second quarter of 1995 and since that time, the company experienced a 4–5 percent gain in revenue, according to William R. Effers, chairman and C.E.O. of C.N.C. "The whole issue is that all reps, no matter where they are, no matter what newspaper, can sell into any papers," said Effers. The newspaper group—headquartered in Needham, Massachusetts—had 31 editorial locations, but sales representatives operated out of eight "hub" sites.[28]

Some weekly chains provided special training for their sales staff and advertisers. Others offered group-buying incentives for clients to boost advertising revenues. For example, Lesher Communications, Inc. (L.C.I.)—owner of around 30 newspaper dailies and weeklies in northern California—provided seminars for current and prospective advertisers entitled, "How to Produce Effective Ads." Seminar instructor Terry Donahoe explained, "It's important that the salesperson, the artist and the customer all learn to work as a team to produce a good ad." The $50 seminar charge was applied to each participant's next advertisement.[29]

In addition to strategies to increase traditional advertising revenues, many weeklies found other ways to increase their revenue streams. In 1993, the National Newspaper Association announced the start of a new service to assist its members in generating more revenues by delivering magazines, advertising, or product samples to their subscribers. Tonda Rush—named N.N.A. chief executive officer in 1992, and later serving as its director of public policy and general counsel—said the idea came from the previous year's N.N.A. convention session on the topic of alternate or private delivery. Mike Parta—publisher of the *New York Mills* (MN) *Herald*—spoke at that session. His paper joined seven neighboring papers to establish a cooperative delivery system for total-market-coverage and shopper publications. He said, "It's a question of survival. It also allows us to control our own destiny. It allows us to control our expenses." The system consisted of six separate routes, delivering one shopper and total-market-coverage products of paid newspapers. Since newspapers were usually mailed, the combined delivery routes cut mailing costs. Parta said mailing costs for his third-class publication were reduced from 30 to 40 cents per piece to eight or nine cents. "It saves me about $50,000 a year, which to a lot of papers is the difference between being profitable and unprofitable." He added, "We paid for our system in six months." The N.N.A. service provided a monthly newsletter of helpful tips and a report on the operation of alternate delivery systems throughout the country. The association also offered training programs and seminars, and established one hotline to answer questions and another to focus on legal issues.[30]

Ken Blum—weekly division manager of Spectrum Publications of Orrville, Ohio—told attendees at the Cincinnati-based September 1993 National Newspaper Association convention that niche publications, such as real estate guides, telephone directories, and entertainment tabloids, could bring successful new revenue streams to community newspapers. For example, his company—publisher of the then-2,388-circulation *The Courier-Crescent* in Orrville, Ohio—produced eight community guides, which brought an average gross profit of $26,000. Two of the company's most successful niche publications were monthlies: the *North Central Business Journal*, and *Horizons*, for senior citizens. Blum explained that circulation for the company's publications varied from 9,000 to 16,000 and advertisement rates varied from $200 to $300 for a quarter-page advertisement.[31]

California publishers shared revenue-enhancing innovations—from printing community phone books to an Easter coloring contest—at the July 1998 California Newspaper Publishers Association annual convention in Coronado. In a session titled, "Bringing in the Bucks—Bottom Line Ideas that Work," Randy Goldberg—publisher and C.E.O. of the weekly *Paradise (CA) Post*—said his company printed phone books not only for his community but for other small newspapers as well. Along with traditional advertising revenue, Goldberg said in its first year, the *Paradise Post*-generated phone book took in $202,000 in advertising revenue.[32]

After abandoning their commercial printing operations to focus fully on the weekly newspaper with its supplementary special editions, inserts, and magazines, some weeklies returned to a print shop-newspaper business model to build revenues back to a "stay-in-business" status. In 1991, it was loss of advertising revenue—due to aggressive reporting that questioned the activities of local officials—that led Keith Stickley, editor of the *Shenandoah Free*

Press in Woodstock, Virginia, to pool his savings, borrow money, and purchase a printing press to financially support his journalistic endeavors. His strategy worked, and the then-4,000-circulation weekly began to turn a profit while continuing to publish stories that "raised the ire of the community." He lost advertising from the lone local movie theatre, owned by the mayor, and a car dealership, owned by the brother of a developer, both caught in a sewage payment scheme covered by the *Shenandoah Free Press*. Stickley commented, "This is a small, rural community. Everyone knows everyone. At least once a month we run something in the paper that offends someone."

Stickley worked at Florida and Virginia newspapers before returning to his hometown to become managing editor of the *Shenandoah Valley Herald* and then launched the *Shenandoah Free Press* in 1985 to cover stories overlooked by the area's two other papers.[33]

The topic of a November 4, 1995 *Editor & Publisher* article reported that press capacity gained new meaning at many small newspaper press operations across the country. Whereas capacity traditionally referred to the number of pages a printer could produce, a new challenge was to see how many different newspapers could be printed in one or two shifts. Proponents of this cost-cutting tactic called it "clustering." Neighboring weeklies and small dailies began sharing press facilities, sometimes with added press units and inserting equipment.[34]

Another revenue-generating strategy was outlined in a March 1, 1997 *Editor & Publisher* article about Charles K. Cooper—founder of *The Penn-Franklin News*, which served several western Pennsylvania neighborhoods 30 miles from Pittsburgh—and daughter Charlene, who eventually became a co-publisher. They devised a subscription marketing strategy that remained popular as the family publishing operation grew to include the *Penn Trafford News* and the *Delmont Salem News*. In the article, Cooper's other daughter and then-editor Georgia recalled the marketing strategy of giving every subscriber one free, 16-word classified ad each week. She said the readers became so creative with those 16 words that it became "popular to buy our paper just to see the classifieds." In addition, it prompted the selling of paid classifieds and became a driving force in creation of the *Market Place*, a then-13,000-circulation shopper mailed Saturdays to nonsubscriber homes. The weekly shopper contained that week's classifieds and select display ads.[35]

If these revenue-generating means failed, many Nebraska editors, responding to a 1993 survey, indicated they'd accept government financial assistance—either through a government grant, or publish revenue-generating government advertisements—before they'd be forced to close. The survey results were reported in a February 6, 1993 Editor & Publisher article in which it was emphasized that the Small Business Administration bylaws did not allow loans to newspapers, because they editorialized. Francis Bachmann, deputy district director for the S.B.A. stated, "You can't use [S.B.A.] funds to push an agenda." One Nebraska publisher said a federal grant would make the newspaper dependent on the government, much like the government-supported agriculture industry. While some publishers would accept government assistance in the form of grants or revenue-generating advertisements, Leonard Warneke—publisher of the then-1,900-circulation The Plainview News—said he'd prefer federal relief in the form of revised postal rates.[36]

Recruiting and Retaining Employees in a Competitive Field

In a 1990 talk delivered by James Batten—chairman and chief executive officer of Knight-Ridder, Inc., after accepting the William Allen White Foundation National Citation at the University of Kansas—the newspaper industrialist said newsrooms were too "over-stocked with journalistic transients who care little about the town of the moment." He said they were more concerned about the next job in a bigger town and the "next rung of the ladder." These reporters knew little about the community's past and there was the "temptation to make their byline files a little more glittering at the expense of people and institutions they will never see again." He said his company did not want its newspapers to be seen as "branch offices of a distant, impersonal corporation. Strangers can't be leaders—or community builders," he concluded.[37] But in recessionary times of the early 1990s, weekly newspapers offered better employment opportunities for recent journalism school graduates, according to an Illinois State University survey. The survey found 83 percent of responding weekly editors hired journalists right out of school, and 70 percent had recent college graduates on staff. But the average starting weekly salary of $13,778 was nearly $4,000 less than $17,524 for large dailies.[38]

Celia McDonald—publisher-editor of the LaRue County Herald News of Hodgenville, Kentucky—wrote an article for the Summer 1990 issue of Grassroots Editor while spending three weeks as an editor-in-residence at Colorado State University. She posed this question: How do you tell journalism students what it's like to work at a community weekly newspaper?

She answered her question by responding, "They'll never have to watch soap operas again." She explained that a daily diet of drama—with the ups and downs shared with community members—is "surely enough to satisfy anyone's urge for secondhand thrills." She continued, "In a small community, the issues may not be as earthshaking, but they are every bit as important to the individuals who make up a newspaper's readership and they may affect them more directly." She went on to write, "It's not easy to treat everyone the same when you go to church with them, live next door to them, shop in their stores, when their advertising is your financial life and death." But, she added, "It can be done, but it's risky and difficult and sometimes you pay a price in friendship or advertising, at least temporarily."[39]

Responding to a change in college journalism programs that focused less on news-editorial and more on a broad liberal arts education, community newspaper editors turned to spouses of professional people tied to their towns as potential staff writers. Will Norton, dean of the College of Journalism, and Michael Stricklin, journalism professor, at the University of Nebraska in Lincoln, wrote, "Some of the best writing we have seen in Nebraska community newspapers is done by the spouses of lawyers, doctors, and/or other business and professional leaders." While most didn't have journalism training, "they are bright, articulate people who need a little bit of guidance, but that is often difficult because you don't have the time to devote to teaching." The university responded by designing the "Wonderworkshop," jointly sponsored with the Nebraska Press Association, which offered sessions on writing/editing, advertising, interviewing, and photography. University faculty taught the sessions for the two and a half day event.[40]

Discussions on the challenges of attracting employees to the weekly field inevitably led to an evaluation of the relevance, practical value, and future mission of college journalism education. This topic was the focus of a panel discussion at the August, 1993 convention of the Association for Education in Journalism and Mass Communication in Kansas City. National Newspaper Association Chief Executive Officer Tonda Rush accused journalism educators of "ignoring industry needs." She made a plea for effective teaching, resulting in a graduate "with some idea of how the world works, who can turn on a computer, find area codes in the phone book, hail a cab, ask delicate questions without offending someone, and comb his hair before he stands in front of 500 people with a Nikon in his hand." An October 2, 1993 *Editor & Publisher* article about the panel discussions and N.N.A. convention, described scholarly papers at the convention presented by journalism educators that rarely focused on improving student journalistic skills, but instead, addressed such topics as improving information recall, and the number of female characters in Saturday morning television cartoons.[41]

A California weekly newspaper publisher took on the challenge of attracting more journalism students to community weeklies by investing $335,000 in a journalism student intern program. Rowland Rebele—a Stanford University graduate, co-publisher of the twice-weekly *Paradise Post*, and past president of the California Newspaper Publishers Association—donated the funds in 1990 for Stanford University journalism majors who qualified, to obtain three- to six-month internships at weekly newspapers at salaries ranging from $250 to $300 a week. The publisher paid $125 to $150 of this amount, with the rest paid by the internship fund. After three years, 15 newspapers had accepted Stanford interns. Rebele said participants turned in positive reports of their internships. "They said they hadn't realized weeklies could be so much fun, or that there was such a variety of stories to cover. They also were impressed by the quality of the writing on weeklies."[42]

In a further move to reach out to college journalists as potential employees, the National Newspaper Association invited college newspapers to join its ranks, beginning in 1994. The first college newspaper to join the 4,200-member, Arlington, Virginia-based organization was the University of North Carolina *Daily Tar Heel*. The dues were $300 a year for college dailies and $200 for weeklies. Opening membership to school publications was part of an ongoing effort by the N.N.A. to build a bridge between newspapers and academia.[43] That same year, the headquarters of the National Newspaper Association was moved to suburban Arlington, Virginia, after 16 years in downtown Washington, D.C.[44]

While it seemed the obvious approach to journalism education in the 1990s was to train future journalists for a mix of skills and abilities tailored to a transformed technology of interactive media, instead, the rethinking of journalism school curricula prompted the teaching of a variety of "entrepreneurial" skills. "Obviously, people will have to be more computer literate than they are today, but my feeling is that training [in computer-based skills] is not something that should be part of the journalism school course work," said publisher Jack Fuller of *The Chicago Tribune* in a February 16, 1996 *Editor & Publisher* article. Fuller also served on the board of the Robert R. McCormick Tribune Foundation, which gave Northwestern University's Medill School of Journalism a $150,000 grant to examine what the school should teach.[45]

The continuing debate about training future journalists fell on deaf ears of "old-school" editors-publishers such as Jack McCloskey—publisher-editor of the *Mineral County Independent News* in Hawthorne, Nevada. In an April 23, 1994 *Editor & Publisher* feature, the then-82-year-old McCloskey—who had been at the *Mineral County Independent News* since 1933—said he preferred to be called a newspaperman, and not a journalist. "When the journalists, now they call themselves professionally trained journalists, get their tit in a wringer, they hide behind the First Amendment. This so-called racket we have will never be a profession. That's because it's the only business, line of work, or industry where you do not have to be admitted to practice it. Journalist is just a fancy word, and I don't want any part of it." McCloskey's weekly was a 16-page broadsheet with a 1994 circulation of 2,800—half of which were sold on press day. He enlisted dozens of "newsboys and girls working town streets" to sell his papers. They earned a 15-cent commission on the 35-cent cover price, plus tips. "Jasper" was McCloskey's page-one column—named in the 1930s after a reader presented him a sample of jasper ore. According to McCloskey, the reader explained, "It's one of the hardest metallic rocks around, Jack, just like your head."[46]

Nearing the end of the decade, journalists—print and broadcast—faced public scrutiny for their coverage of the President Bill Clinton-White House intern Monica Lewinsky sex scandal. In a May 21, 1998 *Editor & Publisher* article, Dave Bakke—editor of the *Catholic Times* in Springfield, Illinois—addressed the media's tarnished image and pointed out that his publication and the other small newspapers and radio stations across the country should not draw the ire of public dissent to the "circus sideshow" reporting from the mainstream media. He wrote, "To improve the image of our profession we must get the American public's attention refocused on the center ring: their local newspapers and stations." The problem, according to Bakke, was that the public didn't view smaller media outlets as "the media." He encouraged these outlets to make themselves known and appreciated. He encouraged fellow small-town reporters to defend their profession and remind readers, viewers, and listeners that local media reported on county fair winners, benefit concerts for local firefighters with terminal illnesses, the school lunch menu, local weather, and corn prices. He concluded, "If those of us in 'the sticks' don't stand up and start taking back our profession, then we can expect more media bashing… But remember this, when someone takes a poke at the national media, we're the ones who get our noses bloodied."[47]

Competing with Free-Circulation/Zoned Daily Papers

Despite their heavy readership, newspaper shoppers were not recession-proof, but they were faring better than their paid counterparts in the early 1990s. While members of the American Newspaper Publishers Association addressed ways to restructure newspapers for a more prosperous future, the Association of Free Community Papers—meeting in Kansas City in May 1991—heard that shoppers tended to do better in recessions and that many shoppers got their first boost during hard times because advertisers were attracted to their high circulation numbers. Shoppers found different means to make money through the 900-telephone-based Audiotex system, joint advertising agreements with local cable television stations, printing special sections, and zoned classifieds. They were also cutting costs by abandoning mail delivery.

In addition to cutting into paid-weekly advertising, shoppers were also increasing editorial content, as outlined in a June 1, 1991 *Editor & Publisher* article. Bruce Gotts, A.F.C.P. president, stated, "There's no question that the free paper industry is thriving and growing, gaining credibility among advertisers. The article also quoted J.J. Blonien—an outspoken advocate of adding editorial content to shoppers—who noted that about a third of A.F.C.P. papers ran editorial content. "There's a changing of the guard in free papers," he said. "The dad was the die-hard entrepreneur, very bottom line-oriented. The kids come in and now they have the dollars to work with that their father never did." However, the shopper industry reported declines in classified advertising, particularly real estate and auto, and a fall-off in retail display advertisements.[48]

By the middle of the decade, the growing number of shoppers assisted in the boost of total circulation of community newspapers and shoppers to nearly 100 million, according to a debut edition of an annual directory, the 1996 *Editor & Publisher/Free Paper Publisher Community, Specialty & Free Publications Year Book*. This marked the first time these data had been gathered and displayed in a comprehensive form, according to a November 9, 1996 *Editor & Publisher* article. The book listed 6,580 community weeklies, including 4,106 paid and 931 free, plus 1,257 shoppers. The community weeklies had a paid circulation of $20.4 million and free circulation of $25.4 million. The shoppers included $54.3 million in free circulation and paid circulation totaling $119,819. Illinois had the most community weeklies, 455, and Hawaii had the fewest, with five.[49]

Some paid weeklies were experimenting with an Internet version of their publication, while continuing to print issues. The August 8, 1995 printed edition of the *Death Valley Gateway Gazette* in Pahrump, Nevada, included a page two advertisement promoting the paper's Gazette Online, stating: "You can now contact the *Death Valley Gateway Gazette* via America Online or via the Internet. Our address for AOL is: DthVlyGaz. To E-mail us on the Internet: DthVlyGaz@AOL.com." The 32-page weekly located in Nye County and serving the counties of Nye and Esmerelda, and parts of Death Valley, was established in 1983.[50]

Printing special themed sections, inserts and magazines was another means incorporated by the paid weekly to compete with shoppers and zoned editions. For example, page three of the September 4, 1991 issue of the *Fort Oglethorpe Press*, in Oglethorpe, Georgia, promoted the sale of the 1991 edition of *PastTimes Magazine*, describing it as a "World War II: A Homefront Scrapbook," featuring a 120-page issue "with a detailed look back 50 years at the World War II home front in this region." The magazine sold for $5.95 and was published by the in-house printing company, News Printing Company.[51]

Responding to 24-Hour Cable TV/ Internet News

A growing challenge for all mainstream media forms, whether print, radio, or television, was adjusting to a 24-hour news cycle introduced in the 1980s with CNN (Cable News Network), and multiplying with more cable news outlets and expanded news programming on network radio and television stations. Newspapers had to respond with more in-depth coverage, and websites that posted breaking news. Community weeklies were inclined to review the local vs. non-local balance within their publications in terms of staying competitive with their daily counterparts. Northeastern University professor and former publisher-editor of the *Marblehead (MA) Messenger* William Kirtz wrote in a Fall 1991 *Grassroots Editor* article about the need for small newspapers to engage in investigative reporting. "Investigative reporting doesn't have to mean large staffs, huge risks, and high costs." For example, he encouraged staffers to check no-bid contracts and specifications for a building, or large-ticket city and county purchases tailored to fit one supplier. And what about ambulance response times? He observed, "A small paper lets young reporters showcase their wares, and puts its prestige on the line to run an in-depth series."[52]

However, weekly and community newspaper representatives were ultimately told they should not feel threatened by the expansion of news coverage through 24-hour cable services and the Internet, as long as they continued to focus on their local communities and the needs of local readers. Speaking at the Boston-based 1999 National Newspaper Association's annual conference, Tim Waltner—publisher of the *Freeman* (SD) *Courier* and vice president of the International Society of Weekly Newspaper Editors—said, "Those of us in the weekly field rarely break stories, even in our own community, but that's a good thing. It reminds us of our mission. Because of our relaxed deadlines, we can take more time to get more perspective—at least we should." During a lengthy speech that drew a standing ovation, he added, "As community newspapers, we should use that connectedness to write more human stories, more insightful stories, and more accountable stories ... It provides us with insight, understanding, and perspective that is unrivaled in major media."[53]

Notes

1 Suzanne Donovan, "Holding Their Own: Suburban Papers, Facing Increasing Number of Zoned Editions from the Metros, Continue to Battle for Their Share of the Market," *Editor & Publisher* 123:27 (July 7, 1990): 16.
2 Mark Fitzgerald, "Weathering the Recession: Community Newspapers Will Come Out in Good Shape, Analyst Says," *Editor & Publisher* 123:40 (October 6, 1990): 17.
3 George Garneau, "No Extinction for Newspapers: Annual Forecast by Veronis, Suhler & Associates Predicts Newspapers Will Again Exceed U.S. Economic Growth by 1992," *Editor & Publisher* 123:31 (August 4, 1990): 18. In 2022, according to the latest government figures based on the Consumer Price Index $3.3 billion from 1989 was worth $7.88 billion, $4.8 billion from 1994 was worth $9.59 billion, and 39 cents was worth 78 cents. http://measuringworth.com/.
4 "Newspapers of the Future," *Editor & Publisher* 123:15 (April 14, 1990): 6.
5 "Tax Lethal for Family Papers," *Editor & Publisher* 131:18 (May 2, 1998): 41.
6 *Milford Cabinet and Wilton Journal*, May 27, 1992, 9. In 2022, according to the latest government figures based on the Consumer Price Index 50 cents from 1992 was worth $1.06. http://measuringworth.com/. Milford, along the Souhegan River in New Hampshire's Hillsborough County, had a population of 11,795 and Hillsborough County 336,073 in 1990. *1990 Census of Population, General Population Characteristics, United States*, Table 1. http://www.census.gov/.
7 "Ownership Changes," *Editor & Publisher* 124:49 (December 7, 1991): 25. Gowrie, in central Iowa's Webster County, had a population of 1,028 and Webster County 40,342 in 1990.

8   *The Brooke County Review*, April 28, 1994, 1. Wellsburg, in northernmost West Virginia's Brooke County, had a population of 3,385 and Brooke County 26,992 in 1990. *1990 Census of Population, General Population Characteristics, United States*, Table 1. http://www.census.gov/.
9   Lucia Moses, "Fourth Estate: A Substantial Foothold on the Maine Coast," *Editor & Publisher* 132:23 (December 4, 1999): 16. York, in southern Maine's York County, had a population of 9,818 and York County 164,587 in 1990. *1990 Census of Population, General Population Characteristics, United States*, Table 1. http://www.census.gov/.
10 "Instant Newspaper Chain," *Editor & Publisher* 130:49 (December 6, 1997): 10–11. In 2022, according to the latest government figures based on the Consumer Price Index, $310 million from 1996 was worth $596 million, $100 million from 1995 was worth $198 million, and $30 million from 1995 was worth $59.4 million. http://measuringworth.com/.
11 "Hot. Type: Community in Huge Acquisition," *Editor & Publisher* 131:49 (December 5, 1998): 6. In 2022, according to the latest government figures based on the Consumer Price Index, $475 million from 1997 was worth $893.2 million and $600 million was worth $1.12 billion. http://measuringworth.com/.
12 "In Brief: Schexnayders Sell Arkansas Weekly," *Editor & Publisher* 131:18 (May 2, 1998): 18. Dumas, in southeast Arkansas's Desha County, had a population of 5,520 and Desha County 16,798 in 1990. *1990 Census of Population, General Population Characteristics, United States*, Table 1. http://www.census.gov/.
13 Geneva Overholser, "Voices, Newspapers: In the Age of Public Ownership, the Importance of Being Local," *Columbia Journalism Review* 38:4 (November/December 1999): 64.
14 "Letters to the Editor: Regrets Sale," *Editor & Publisher* 131:10 (March 7, 1998): 7. North Branch, in east-central Minnesota's Chisago County, had a population of 1,867 and Chisago County 30,521 in 1990. *1990 Census of Population, General Population Characteristics, United States*, Table 1. http://www.census.gov/.
15 "Boiler Plate," *Editor & Publisher* 124:34 (August, 24, 1991): 6.
16 Jack Authelet, "Local Coverage Succeeds," *Grassroots Editor* 32:3 (Fall 1991): 5.
17 *Farmers Independent*, March 3, 1993, 10. Bagley, in northwest Minnesota's Clearwater County, had a population of 1,388 and Clearwater County 8,309 in 1990. *1990 Census of Population, General Population Characteristics, United States*, Table 1. http://www.census.gov/.
18 Jack Authelet, "Should Readers Buy News?," *Grassroots Editor* 32:3 (Fall 1991): 12.
19 Rick Friedman, "Local Approach Pays Off," *Grassroots Editor* 33:2 (Summer 1992): 9, 11. Woburn, in northeast Massachusetts's Middlesex County, had a population of 35,943 and Middlesex County 1,396,468 in 1990. *1990 Census of Population, General Population Characteristics, United States*, Table 1. http://www.census.gov/.
20 Tony Case, "Local News Attracts Readers," *Editor & Publisher* 129:18 (May 4, 1996): 12.
21 Tom Riordin, "Weekly Editor: Edgar Crisler Jr., Port Gibson Reveille, Port Gibson, Miss.," *Editor & Publisher* 127:39 (September 24, 1994): 16–17. Port Gibson, in southeastern Mississippi's Claiborne County, had a population of 1,810 and Claiborne County 11,370 in 1990. *1990 Census of Population, General Population Characteristics, United States*, Table 1. http://www.census.gov/.

22 "Survey: Smaller Weeklies Outperform Bigger Dailies," *Editor & Publisher* 126:45 (November 6, 1993): 34. In 2022, according to the latest government figures based on the Consumer Price Index, $3.21 from 1992 was worth $6.91 and $3.77 from 1992 was worth $8.11. http://measuringworth.com/.
23 Mark Fitzgerald, "Mixed Blessing: Wal-Mart Proliferation Is Getting the Attention of Newspapers," *Editor & Publisher* 123:44 (November 3, 1990): 18.
24 Sarah McBride, "Advertising/Promotion: Wal-Mart and Newspapers," *Editor & Publisher* 126:47 (November 20, 1993): 30.
25 Ibid., 30–31. In 2022, according to the latest government figures based on the Consumer Price Index, $102,000 from 1993 was worth $206,326 http://measuringworth.com/.
26 Mark Fitzgerald, "E&P Marketing/Sales Advertising: How Community Papers Can Attract National Ads," *Editor & Publisher* 131:40 (October 3, 1998): 31–32.
27 Laura Riena, "Calif. Community Papers Form Advertising Network," *Editor & Publisher* 128:44 (November 4, 1995): 25. Northwest California's Sonoma County, had a population of 388,222 in 1990. *1990 Census of Population, General Population Characteristics, United States*, Table 1. http://www.census.gov/.
28 Laura Reina, "Weekly Group Offers One-Order, One-Bill," *Editor & Publisher* 129:8 (February 24, 1996): 22.
29 M.L. Stein, "Advertising: Helping the Smaller Advertiser Design More Effective Ads," *Editor & Publisher* 123:14 (April 7, 1990): 28. In 2022, according to the latest government figures based on the Consumer Price Index, $50 from 1990 was worth $113. http://measuringworth.com/.
30 Ann Marie Kerwin, "Advertising/Promotion: Alternate Delivery Help Offered to Community Papers," *Editor & Publisher* 126:37 (September 11, 1993): 36–37. In 2022, according to the latest government figures based on the Consumer Price Index, $50,000 from 1993 was worth $102,517 http://measuringworth.com/. New York Mills, in west-central Minnesota's Otter Tail County, had a population of 940 and Otter Tail County 50,714 in 1990. *1990 Census of Population, General Population Characteristics, United States*, Table 1. http://www.census.gov/.
31 Tony Case, "Niche Publications Can Be Profitable to Newspapers," *Editor & Publisher* 126:42 (October 16, 1993): 16. In 2022, according to the latest government figures based on the Consumer Price Index, $26,000 from 1993 was worth $53,309, $200 from 1993 was worth $410, and $300 from 1993 was worth $625. http://measuringworth.com/. Orrville, in northeast Ohio's Wayne County, had a population of 7,712 and Wayne County 101,461 in 1990. *1990 Census of Population, General Population Characteristics, United States*, Table 1. http://www.census.gov/.
32 M.L. Stein, "Conference: Small Papers Mine New Revenue in Golden State," *Editor & Publisher* 131:31 (August 1, 1998): 12. In 2022, according to the latest government figures based on the Consumer Price Index, $202,000 from 1998 was worth $367,000. http://measuringworth.com/. Paradise, in north-central California's Butte County, had a population of 25,408 and Butte County 182,120 in 1990. *1990 Census of Population, General Population Characteristics, United States*, Table 1. http://www.census.gov/.
33 Cathy Gedvilas, "Weekly Editor: Keith Stickley, Shenandoah Free Press, Woodstock, Va.," *Editor & Publisher* 124:25 (June 22, 1991): 24. Woodstock, in northeast Virginia's

Shenandoah County, had a population of 3,182 and Shenandoah County 31,636 in 1990. *1990 Census of Population, General Population Characteristics, United States*, Table 1. http://www.census.gov/.
34. Robert J. Salgado, "Clustering: One Plant Serves Multiple Papers," *Editor & Publisher* 128:44 (November 4, 1995): 10P.
35. Tom Riordan, "Weekly Editor: From School Teacher to Editor," *Editor & Publisher* 130:9 (March 1, 1997): 16–17.
36. R. Douglas Kappel, "Shop Talk at Thirty: Should Government Help Small Weeklies?," *Editor & Publisher* 126:6 (February 6, 1993): 52.
37. James K. Batten, "Linked to the Community," *Grassroots Editor*, 31:3 (Fall 1990): 3–5,13.
38. Mark Fitzgerald, "Weeklies Offer Grads Best Job Hopes, but Lower Pay," *Editor & Publisher* 124:31 (August 3, 1991): 31. In 2022, according to the latest government figures based on the Consumer Price Index, $13,778 from 1991 was worth $29,974 and $17,524 was worth $38,124. http://www.measuringworth.com/
39. Celia Creal McDonald, "Weeklies Are Daily Soaps," *Grassroots Editor* 31:2 (Summer 1990) 10. Hodgenville, in central Kentucky's LaRue County, had a population of 2,721 and LaRue County 11,679 in 1990. *1990 Census of Population, General Population Characteristics, United States*, Table 1. http://www.census.gov/.
40. Will Norton and Michael Stricklin, "The Heartbeat of America," *Grassroots Editor* 33:3 (Fall 1992): 9.
41. Don Corrigan, "Shop Talk at Thirty: Journalism Academia Out of Touch," *Editor & Publisher* 126:40 (October 2, 1993): 44, 34.
42. M.L. Stein, "Weekly Publisher Sets Up Intern Program," *Editor & Publisher* 123:13 (March 31, 1990): 36. In 2022, according to the latest government figures based on the Consumer Price Index, $335,000 from 1990 was worth $773,000, $250 was worth $577, and $300 was worth $692. http://measuringworth.com/.
43. "In Brief: N.N.A. Opens Door to College Papers," *Editor & Publisher* 127:44 (October 29, 1994): 5. In 2022, according to the latest government figures based on the Consumer Price Index, $300 from 1994 was worth $600 and $200 was worth $400. http://measuringworth.com/.
44. "N.N.A. Moves," *Editor & Publisher* 127:1 (January 1, 1994): 14.
45. B.G. Yovovich, "J-Schools in Transition," *Editor & Publisher* 129:7 (February 17, 1996): 201. In 2022, according to the latest government figures based on the Consumer Price Index, $150,000 from 1996 was worth $283,280. http://www.measuringworth.com/.
46. Tom Riordan, "Weekly Editor: Jack McCloskey, Mineral County Independent News, Hawthorne, Nev.," *Editor & Publisher* 127:17 (April 23, 1994): 70–71. Hawthorne, in east-central Nevada's Mineral County, had a population of 4,162 and Mineral County 6,475 in 1990. *1990 Census of Population, General Population Characteristics, United States*, Table 1. http://www.census.gov/.
47. Dave Bakke, "Shop Talk: Let Us Now Praise Unfamous Local Journalists," *Editor & Publisher* 131:18 (May 2, 1998): 56, 42.
48. Mark Fitzgerald, "Free Papers Less Hurt by Recession," *Editor & Publisher* 124:22 (June 1, 1991): 8–9, 124.

49 "New Directory Shows Prolific Community Press," *Editor & Publisher* 129:45 (November 9, 1996): 3. In 2022, according to the latest government figures based on the Consumer Price Index, $20.4 million from 1996 was worth $38,52 million, $25.4 million from 1996 was worth $47.96 million, $54.3 million from 1996 was worth $102.5 million, and $119,819 from 1996 was worth $226,255. http://measuringworth.com/.
50 *Death Valley Gateway Gazette*, August 8, 1995, 2. Pahrump, in southwest Nevada's Nye County, had a population of 7,424 and Nye County 17,781 in 1990. *1990 Census of Population*, United States Bureau of the Census, Washington, D.C.
51 *Fort Oglethorpe Press*, September 4, 1991, 3. In 2022, according to the latest government figures based on the Consumer Price Index, $5.95 from 1991 was worth $12.94. http://measuringworth.com/. Fort Oglethorpe, in northeast Georgia's Catoosa County, had a population of 5,880 and Catoosa County 42,464 in 1990. *1990 Census of Population, General Population Characteristics, United States*, Table 1. http://www.census.gov/.
52 William Kirtz, "Even Weeklies Can Invest in Investigations," *Grassroots Editor* 32:3 (Fall 1991): 10–11, 14. Marblehead, in north-coastal Massachusetts's Essex County, had a population of 19,971 and Essex County 670,080 in 1990. *1990 Census of Population, General Population Characteristics, United States*, Table 1. http://www.census.gov/.
53 Joe Strupp, "Stay Connected with the Locals: Finding Your Weekly's Niche in the News Biz," *Editor & Publisher* 132:40 (October 2, 1999): 17. Freeman, in southeastern South Dakota's Hutchinson County, had a population of 1,293 and Hutchinson County 8,262 in 1990. *1990 Census of Population, General Population Characteristics, United States*, Table 1. http://www.census.gov/.

References

1990 Census of Population. Edited by United States Bureau of the Census: Washington, DC: Government Printing Office, 1992.
Authelet, Jack. "Local Coverage Succeeds." *Grassroots Editor* 32:3 (Fall 1991): 5.
Authelet, Jack. "Should Readers Buy News?" *Grassroots Editor* 32:3 (Fall 1991): 12.
Bakke, Dave. "Shop Talk: Let Us Now Praise Unfamous Local Journalists." *Editor & Publisher* 131:18 (May 2, 1998): 56, 42.
Batten, James K. "Linked to the Community." *Grassroots Editor* 31:3 (Fall 1990): 3–5, 15.
"Boiler Plate." *Editor & Publisher* 124:34 (August 24, 1991): 6.
The Brooke County (Wellsburg, West Virginia) *Review*, April 28, 1994.
Case, Tony. "Local News Attracts Readers." *Editor & Publisher* 129:18 (May 4, 1996): 12, 44.
Case, Tony. "Niche Publications Can Be Profitable to Newspapers." *Editor & Publisher* 126:42 (October 16, 1993): 16.
Corrigan, Don. "Shop Talk at Thirty: Journalism Academia Out of Touch." *Editor & Publisher* 126:40 (October 2, 1993): 44, 34.
Death Valley Gateway Gazette (Pahrump, Nevada), August 8, 1995.
Donovan, Suzanne. "Holding Their Own: Suburban Papers, Facing Increasing Number of Zoned Editions from the Metros, Continue to Battle for Their Share of the Market." *Editor & Publisher* 123:27 (July 7, 1990): 16.

Farmers Independent (Bagley, Minnesota), March 3, 1993.

Fitzgerald, Mark. "E&P Marketing/Sales Advertising: How Community Papers Can Attract National Ads." *Editor & Publisher* 131:40 (October 3, 1998): 31–32.

Fitzgerald, Mark. "Free Papers Less Hurt by Recession." *Editor & Publisher* 124:22 (June 1, 1991): 8–9, 124.

Fitzgerald, Mark. "Mixed Blessing: Wal-Mart Proliferation Is Getting the Attention of Newspapers." *Editor & Publisher* 123:44 (November 3, 1990): 18.

Fitzgerald, Mark. "Weathering the Recession: Community Newspapers Will Come Out in Good Shape, Analyst Says." *Editor & Publisher* 123:40 (October 6, 1990): 17.

Fitzgerald, Mark. "Weeklies Offer Grads Best Job Hopes, But Lower Pay." *Editor & Publisher* 124:31 (August 3, 1991): 31–32, 40.

Fort Oglethorpe (GA) Press, September 4, 1991.

Friedman, Rick. "Local Approach Pays Off." *Grassroots Editor* 33:2 (Summer 1992): 9–11.

Garneau, George. "No Extinction for Newspapers: Annual Forecast by Veronis, Suhler & Associates Predicts Newspapers Will Again Exceed U.S. Economic Growth by 1992." *Editor & Publisher* 123:31 (August 4, 1990): 18.

Gedvilas, Cathy. "Weekly Editor: Keith Stickley, Shenandoah Free Press, Woodstock, Va." *Editor & Publisher* 124:25 (June 22, 1991): 24.

"Hot. Type: Community in Huge Acquisition." *Editor & Publisher* 131:49 (December 5, 1998): 6.

"In Brief: N.N.A. Opens Door to College Papers." *Editor & Publisher* 127:44 (October 29, 1994): 5.

"In Brief: Schexnayders Sell Arkansas Weekly." *Editor & Publisher* 131:18 (May 2, 1998): 18.

"Instant Newspaper Chain." *Editor & Publisher* 130:49 (December 6, 1997): 10–11.

Kappel, R. Douglas. "Shop Talk at Thirty: Should Government Help Small Weeklies?" *Editor & Publisher* 126:6 (February 6, 1993): 52.

Kerwin, Ann Marie. "Advertising/Promotion: Alternate Delivery Help Offered to Community Papers." *Editor & Publisher* 126:37 (September 11, 1993): 36–37.

Kirtz, William. "Even Weeklies Can Invest in Investigations." *Grassroots Editor* 32:3 (Fall 1991): 10–11, 14.

"Letters to the Editor: Regrets Sale." *Editor & Publisher* 131:10 (March 7, 1998): 7.

McBride, Sarah. "Advertising/Promotion: Wal-Mart and Newspapers." *Editor & Publisher* 126:47 (November 20, 1993): 30.

McDonald, Celia Creal. "Weeklies Are Daily Soaps," *Grassroots Editor* 31:2 (Summer 1990) 10–11.

Milford (NH) Cabinet and Wilton (NH) Journal, May 27, 1992.

Moses, Lucia. "Fourth Estate: A Substantial Foothold on the Maine Coast." *Editor & Publisher* 132:23 (December 4, 1999): 16–17.

"New Directory Shows Prolific Community Press." *Editor & Publisher* 129:45 (November 9, 1996): 3.

"Newspapers of the Future." *Editor & Publisher* 123:15 (April 14, 1990): 6.

"N.N.A. Moves." *Editor & Publisher* 127:1 (January 1, 1994): 14.

Norton, Will, and Michael Stricklin. "The Heartbeat of America." *Grassroots Editor* 33:3 (Fall 1992): 9.

Overholser, Geneva. "Voices, Newspapers: In the Age of Public Ownership, the Importance of Being Local." *Columbia Journalism Review* 38:4 (November/December 1999): 64–65.

"Ownership Changes." *Editor & Publisher* 124:49 (December 7, 1991): 25.

Riena, Laura. "Calif. Community Papers Form Advertising Network." *Editor & Publisher* 128:44 (November 4, 1995): 25.

Reina, Laura. "Weekly Group Offers One-Order, One-Bill." *Editor & Publisher* 129:8 (February 24, 1996): 22.

Riordin, Tom. "Weekly Editor: Edgar Crisler Jr., Port Gibson Reveille, Port Gibson, Miss." *Editor & Publisher* 127:39 (September 24, 1994): 16–17.

Riordan, Tom. "Weekly Editor: From School Teacher to Editor." *Editor & Publisher* 130:9 (March 1, 1997): 16–17.

Riordan, Tom. "Weekly Editor: Jack McCloskey, Mineral County Independent News, Hawthorne, Nev." *Editor & Publisher* 127:17 (April 23, 1994): 70–71.

Salgado, Robert J. "Clustering: One Plant Serves Multiple Papers." *Editor & Publisher* 128:44 (November 4, 1995): 10P, 12P, 23P.

Stein, M.L. "Advertising: Helping the Smaller Advertiser Design More Effective Ads." *Editor & Publisher* 123:14 (April 7, 1990): 28.

Stein, M.L. "Conference: Small Papers Mine New Revenue in Golden State." *Editor & Publisher* 131:31 (August 1, 1998): 12–13, 32.

Stein, M.L. "Weekly Publisher Sets Up Intern Program." *Editor & Publisher* 123:13 (March 31, 1990): 36.

Strupp, Joe. "Stay Connected with the Locals: Finding Your Weekly's Niche in the News Biz." *Editor & Publisher* 132:40 (October 2, 1999): 17.

"Survey: Smaller Weeklies Outperform Bigger Dailies." *Editor & Publisher* 126:45 (November 6, 1993): 34.

"Tax Lethal for Family Papers." *Editor & Publisher* 131:18 (May 2, 1998): 41.

www.measuringworth.com.

Yovovich, B.G. "J-Schools in Transition." *Editor & Publisher* 129:7 (February 17, 1996): 201.

· 11 ·

A CENTURY OF CHANGES AND CHALLENGES: COMMUNITY WEEKLIES COME FULL CIRCLE

The community weekly newspaper in the United States came full circle in the twentieth century. It began with printer-editors, who viewed their newspaper publishing as an aside to their job-printing, bookselling, and stationery businesses. In the coming decades, many weekly newspaper operations turned to a sole focus on their newspaper and soliciting advertisement revenues for financial stability and growth. But, by the end of the century, and after abandoning their commercial printing operations to focus fully on the weekly newspaper with its supplementary special editions, inserts, and magazines, some weeklies returned to a print shop-newspaper business model to build revenues back to a "stay-in-business" status.

In the early 1900s, the editor of a weekly—who also served as postmaster or official county printer—had an outlet to enhance his political aspirations and/or gain financial reward through lucrative government printing contracts. Unfortunately, many of the earliest printer-editors proved to be inept businessmen, consistently undercharging on printing jobs. But a majority of country editors were tied to their job-printing services as the only revenue-producing aspect of their publishing operations. While some viewed job printing as a burden that kept them from pursuing their newspaper interests, others recognized the print shop as providing the financial foothold that allowed them to continue in the newspaper publishing business.

Several decades later as more college-trained journalists entered the weekly field, there began a transition to the editor-publisher role. The printing of the newspaper and print shop duties were turned over to hired staff. As a result, the editor-publisher was able to focus more on journalism than job printing. Editors were encouraged to take on leadership roles and become the "voice" of their community by writing editorials and personal columns. Some editors found that emancipation from their job-printing duties actually made them better business people. They spent more time on main street gathering news and developing relationships with potential advertisers and subscribers.

But, by the latter half of the twentieth century, weekly publishers again turned their attention to the job-printing business for the purpose of joining with other publishers to operate centralized printing plants. The typical central plant owners were cooperative newspaper groups whose publishers were more likely to be business school graduates than journalism majors. Except for the smallest of newspapers, the publisher and editor positions were usually separate, with the editor managing the news operation while the publisher oversaw business and printing concerns.

There were even predictions of the death of the weekly newspaper when it faced direct competition from nearby metropolitan dailies that attempted to lure away subscribers, advertising dollars, and staff. The weaker small-town publications struggled to survive. Certainly there were weeklies throughout the period of examination that seemed to be nothing more than vehicles for advertisements and free publicity, but the overall image was that of an industry [the weekly newspaper field] aspiring to a genuine mission of public service.

As more weeklies survived, and even thrived, editors turned the heads of politicians and businessmen alike who recognized fully the benefit of advertising in their papers and winning the political backing of their readers. So, whatever the content of the weekly, whether it was awash in syndicate material or chock-full of local opinion and news items, the rural press was recognized for its influential role because of the economic potential of its readers and the editorial guidance it provided to a large portion of the country's populace.

Despite Charges of Inferiority, Weeklies Embraced the Concept of Professionalism

Starting in the early years of the twentieth century, weekly newspapers began to diverge from dailies as a clearly different type of publication. Some weekly editors and publishers resented the comparisons to the metropolitan press because they believed that weeklies were viewed as inferior journalistic endeavors. The weekly had a more personal and less objective tone than the metropolitan daily. Also, as a result of the extensive use of ready-print and boilerplate in weeklies and a decrease in locally written editorials and opinion columns, the image of the crusading editor of the nineteenth century was giving way to the newspaper businessman. Newspaper syndicates became the "silent partner" of the country press, writing and influencing the opinion of thousands of rural newspaper readers who were unaware of the source of much of their news. The businessman-editor was seen as being more concerned about advertising revenue and not offending the business community than stirring up controversy and increasing subscriptions.

But, soon into the twentieth century, community weeklies embraced the concept of professionalism through the establishment of national organizations, greater participation in state press associations, and growing support for college journalism programs. For the most part, weekly publishers and editors supported college journalism programs as a means to recruit more skilled workers to their publications. Eventually, a growing number of journalism programs offered specialized courses in community journalism. Training and sharing "best practices" at meetings and workshops—and through professional publications—proved extremely helpful as weeklies transitioned through business models and technological advancements that changed staffing and organizational needs. For example, weeklies had to adjust as fewer workers were needed in the business, production, and newsroom departments because computerization allowed for the consolidation or elimination of certain tasks. Recruitment also became an important issue for professional associations that catered to the weekly newspaper field because of an increased focus on member services—such as publications and advertising services, and political lobbying on behalf of the industry.

"Localism" Distinguished Community Weeklies from Metropolitan Dailies

While community weekly newspapers were not familiar to those who lived outside their geographical circulation boundaries, they were like an extended member of the family who tirelessly recorded the life happenings of relatives—as if in the pages of a cherished family album. Some weekly publishers and editors did gain recognition and readership well beyond their town's borders, but mostly from former residents who wanted to stay connected to "home."

The main purpose of the weekly editor was to produce a publication that provided a common link and, in some cases, a lifeline to local residents. Some weekly editors felt inferior to their metropolitan counterparts because they lacked the fame and acclaim that larger newspapers enjoyed. But for most weekly editors, the goal was not to produce a smaller version of a daily with the same type of content. They viewed their mission as being different from that of the large dailies, which explains why many readers of weeklies also purchased a nearby daily. Eventually many weekly editors embraced their niche as community boosters and took pride in bolstering the morale of their readers and business climate of their communities.

A 1920s rural newspaper publisher and scholar described the small-town newspaper as a "community institution" like the church, school, public library, and farm and home bureaus. However, he said many failed to recognize the country newspaper as such because, unlike traditional institutions, it was an enterprise in which the publisher had money invested.

Despite a persistent criticism of weeklies—which came mostly from metropolitan journalists, that a large percentage of their space contained propaganda and free publicity material—"localism" propelled weeklies from financial straits to monetary strength. In fact, dailies eventually became the prominent users of syndicate materials even though previous generations of daily publishers and editors turned up their noses at weeklies for heavy syndicate content. Longtime Maine weekly publisher Alexander Brook described syndicate materials as "risk-free and inexpensive" and admitted that a substantial amount of publicity and promotional materials became "filler" material. But he acknowledged a "glamour handicap" that weeklies had to overcome because they could not afford the same level of "spicy national and international items, titillating bits about celebrities and beautiful people, sensational crime, war, sports, and features" material available to dailies through syndicate services. Therefore, weeklies were challenged, he argued, to do a better job in presenting local news.[1]

A common criticism of community weeklies by social and political scientists and metropolitan journalists was in labeling them "boosterism" publications. However, the weekly newspaper field was proud of its role in bolstering community businesses and the role of the editor in providing much-needed local leadership during times of economic strife and war. Community weekly boosterism not only helped to establish communities along important transportation lines, rail and roadway, but it also forged an important relationship with the business community that enabled small-town commerce to thrive, especially during economic depressions. Weeklies served as lifelines to news about job availability and government relief programs. The weeklies served as morale boosters by encouraging local citizens to keep the faith and keep their money in the banks. But they also kept other businesses alive through advertising trade outs, promotional campaigns, and reinforcement of positive economic news. In wartime, the federal government found a willing partner in weeklies to promote all manner of civilian support. Community newspapers also served as a powerful recruiting tool to aid in the buildup of military forces.

Into the 1960s and a newly defined, though traditional, practice of "community journalism" that emphasized the impact of news on its readers, the challenge of small-town newspapers grew to include localizing larger issues and explaining their significance to local residents by fellow-citizen reporters and editors who had personal knowledge, experience, and devotion to their shared communities.

A Distinction between the Small-Town and Suburban Weekly Grew by Mid-Century

By mid-century, the traditional weekly mirrored the interests of rural and small-town residents while suburban weeklies addressed issues more in concert with those of a large urban area. Some suburban weekly publishers cited a sharp line of distinction between the suburban paper and the typical hometown weekly. Eventually, most suburban newspapers broke away from the National Editorial Association and joined the Suburban Press Foundation, claiming it to be an organization that better addressed their problems of labor, competition, and distribution.

Small-town editors were accused of being provincial and ignorant of global concerns. Their provincialism was sometimes reflected in their editorials or lack thereof. But, traditional weeklies did respond to a readership that became more interested in global issues following military deployments overseas and increased travel beyond regional borders. After receiving war news from abroad, even readers of weeklies who were not deployed developed a keen interest in news from beyond their town and surrounding communities. As "war brides" began to populate many smaller towns, weeklies began to feature more news from their native countries. In addition, improved roadways and affordable travel abroad exposed rural residents to interesting places and unusual customs that they could read about in syndicate features and news wire stories.

Traditional weeklies were charged with protecting the establishment elite—of which the editor was often a prominent member. Urban sprawl transformed once-rural areas into developed neighborhoods whose residents wanted a community newspaper that focused on local issues. The traditional weekly continued to serve residents of small towns situated miles from mid- to large-size metropolitan communities. It focused on keeping shoppers at home while the suburban weekly reaped the benefits of running advertisements for retailers from the large shopping centers and downtown shopping districts that permeated larger cities.

Threats to the traditional community weekly became much more aggressive from the 1950s and beyond as suburban weeklies multiplied and expanded their circulation areas. Also, shoppers, or free-circulation weeklies—whose content was mostly advertising—lured away advertising revenue and readers because they were cost-free and mailed to large geographic areas. Even dailies added zoned community news editions. In response to these threats, weeklies embraced a renewed focus on in-depth local reporting and a new approach to journalism. This new approach—often referred to as "community journalism"—emphasized a more activist role for the journalist in shaping the news.

Changing Business Models Kept Weeklies in Business

By mid-century, the introduction of group and chain ownership and central printing operations brought a new business model to the weekly newspaper field that enabled many communities to retain a newspaper, albeit under new or corporate ownership. Centralized printing was a key factor from which two conflicting trends were emerging. One was the growth of chain or group ownership, which would bring new newspapers and the revival of competition in one-newspaper communities. A downside to chain ownership was the loss of an independent editorial voice, as newspapers within a chain often reflected the political leanings of its owner(s). But, as weeklies declined in number they increased in financial well-being as consolidations and mergers closed down the weeklies that were unable to remain as stand-alone operations.

In response to the struggles that publishers had in deriving profits from single newspaper ownership, a number of weekly publishers looked to group ownership for financial stability. Group ownership proved to be risky initially—especially for family-owned operations because of the heavy financial borrowing often required to purchase another newspaper. But it often paid off in increased subscribers and local and national advertising accounts. In fact, a number of business concerns with no background in community journalism also viewed weekly newspaper group ownership as a profit-making venture and hired trained journalists to run their news operations.

Although chain ownership provided weeklies with a financial model for success, proud traditions such as family ownership and independent editorial voices were dying. As a result, more weekly publishers no longer lived in their newspapers' communities, thus lacking a personal investment in the overall prosperity of the towns their publications served. The viability of weeklies owned, managed, and edited by the same individual was a concern for publisher Alexander Brook at the end of his 20-year career in small-town journalism in the late 1970s. He described these individuals as an "obsolescing breed that became one fewer when I left." He predicted that few would remain, with the exception of one-person or husband-and-wife rural operations that printed their publication at an off-site central plant. "The individual sparkle of the weeklies will dim," he asserted, "as their owners cease to manufacture their products and lose control of makeup and design, which were once parts of their personal statement."[2] His prediction held true as more small-town family-owned weeklies sold out to chains because of burdensome estate taxes and lucrative buyout offers.

Another business trend was the impact that centralized printing of weeklies could have in a mass society—especially at the grassroots level—because it permitted anyone with little capital to start a newspaper. By the end of the century, press capacity gained new meaning at many small newspaper press operations across the country with the practice of "clustering," where the challenge was to see how many different newspapers could be printed in one or two shifts as neighboring weeklies and small dailies began sharing press facilities. In other cost-saving measures, computerization allowed for reducing production staff and decreasing overall operating costs.

Weeklies Joined Former Foes to Encourage Newspaper Readership

The once-competitive daily and weekly newspaper industries found it necessary to unite efforts to combat an overall drop in newspaper readership. After decades of infighting, daily and non-daily publishers and editors from the major newspaper industry associations set rivalries aside to join a Newspaper Readership Council project designed to keep readers interested in newspapers.[3] Rather than combating each other, they were called upon to fight a new battle: declining newspaper readership, especially among young people. A 1977 article in *The Publishers' Auxiliary* pointed out that illiteracy was another problem resulting in a growing number of young people who simply were incapable of reading a newspaper. If illiteracy rates and newspaper interest did not improve, the article speculated, the newspaper industry faced a steady decline in overall circulation.[4]

A 1979 study on newspaper readership among young adults found that small-town newspaper editors were more in agreement with young adults than metropolitan editors on the importance of civic-mindedness over individuality of character in news content. But young adults also expressed a preference for national and international news—which had a heavier emphasis in dailies—over local news. The study concluded that despite agreement among newspaper editors and young adults as to what newspapers' attributes should be, young readers were not "excited over the end product." Thus, the entire newspaper industry rushed to develop design layouts and content criteria that would appeal to a younger reading audience.[5]

Survival of the Weeklies: Resonating with Audiences, Responding to a Religious-like Calling

Despite all of the problems that faced the weekly newspaper industry throughout its long and proud history, the constants that remained were survival tactics in terms of reactive versus proactive responses to content, commercial, and professional concerns. Several times throughout the decades an obituary had been written for community weeklies. But they always found a way to fight back and happen upon a means, a method, or a message that resonated with audiences and advertisers enough so as to allow them to keep their doors open for another business day. Certainly a number of weeklies failed—whether because of poor business management or ill-advised political posturing—but many more survived and even thrived.

There was devotion among a majority of weekly publishers and editors. Some might even liken it to a religious calling to their chosen vocation. Even if their equipment was outdated and hard to manipulate, the survivalists were persistent in finding the right news-business formula to keep readers reading and advertisers advertising. From the preprinted pages of ready-print to the computerization of page paste-up, weeklies redesigned themselves and their pages to remain relevant. At times weekly content was accused of being: too commercial—as in "shopper" publications; too controversial—as in crusading editors who were more intent on bringing down political elites than propping up community morale; or too self-serving—as in the editor who used his paper as a partisan platform for personal political aspirations.

However, as emphasized in the introduction, community weeklies told the story of average American daily lives more thoroughly and in a more personal manner than the big-city dailies. In essence, the weekly publisher-editor served as author of his community's life story through birth, marriage, and death announcements, the comings and goings of the social elite, the accomplishments of local students, and the gatherings of community clubs, business and professional organizations, and church groups. One weekly editor described his role as being "in the first seat on the front row of community activities."[6] Even the introduction of radio, television, the Internet and mega-merged metropolitan dailies with "community news" inserts could not supplant the weekly as the main source for local news. Community newspapers were also full of primary sources because they contained the personal correspondence, journal entries, and political thought through "letters to the editor," editorials, and guest columns of everyday citizens. "Citizen journalists" thrived in weekly newspapers before they were designated as such.

In summarizing his lifelong journalism career, Claude V. Campbell—owner-editor of *The Jewell* (IA) *Record*—spoke for many weekly editors when he talked about living and working in a small town. He was the topic of a 1949 "Editor of the Week" feature in *The Publishers' Auxiliary* in which he recalled his 40-year journalism career. Campbell observed that despite their size, small communities offered an opportunity to "live decently and give part of one's time to service instead of trying to serve personal interests only." He added, "Best of all, when you get out near the end of the road, there is the feeling that the publisher of a small town paper has, and that nobody can take from him, that he has contributed something to his community in the years during which he has travelled [sic] that road."[7]

Notes

1 Alexander B. Brook, *The Hard Way: The Odyssey of a Weekly Newspaper Editor* (Bridgehampton, NY: Bridge Works Publishing Co., 1993), 256.
2 Ibid., 302.
3 Bill White, "Readership Project Brings Newspaper Groups Closer," *The Publishers' Auxiliary*, March 10, 1977, 13.
4 George Joplin, "Newspapers Will Face Many Old—and New—Problems," *The Publishers' Auxiliary*, January 25, 1977, 12.
5 Elden Rawlings, "What Editors and Young People Think of Newspapers: Testing a Method for Measuring Reader Expectations," *Newspaper Readership Journal*: Prototype Edition (April 1979): 27, 28.
6 "Weekly Editor: K.A. (Doc) Eggensperger, Sanders County Ledger, Thompson Falls, Mont.," *Editor & Publisher* 120:12 (March 21, 1987): 22, 56.
7 "Small Town Jams Come Easy, Claude V. Campbell Declares," *The Publishers' Auxiliary*, February 19, 1949, 4.

References

Brook, Alexander B. *The Hard Way: The Odyssey of a Weekly Newspaper Editor*. Bridgehampton, NY: Bridge Works Publishing Co., 1993.
Joplin, George. "Newspapers Will Face Many Old—and New—Problems." *The Publishers' Auxiliary*, January 25, 1977, 12.
Rawlings, Elden. "What Editors and Young People Think of Newspapers: Testing a Method for Measuring Reader Expectations." *Newspaper Readership Journal*, no. Prototype Edition (1979): 23–19.
"Small Town Jams Come Easy, Claude V. Campbell Declares." *The Publishers' Auxiliary*, February 19, 1949, 4.
"Weekly Editor: K.A. (Doc) Eggensperger, Sanders County Ledger, Thompson Falls, Mont." *Editor & Publisher* 120:12 (March 21, 1987): 22, 56.
White, Bill. "Readership Project Brings Newspaper Groups Closer." *The Publishers' Auxiliary*, March 10, 1977, 13.

INDEX

A

Ackley Inter County Journal 80
Ackley Phonograph 80
Ackley Tribune 80
Ackley World 80
Adams, Frederick Upham 29
advertising/advertisement 164, 170
    boosterism and 64–5
    budgeting, bartering and battling for 110
    cost per reader for advertisements 144
    daily *vs.* weekly newspapers 34–7
    free publicity and 54–5
    local merchants advertising 115–18
    of monopoly corporations 82
    one-order, one-bill program for advertisers 320
    pressures of domesticity through 149
    revenues 2, 122n47, 189, 220–1
    1940s 143–7
    small-town press *vs.* radio 74–7
    television ads 148–9
    thematic advertising promotions and special sections 116
advertising pamphlets 53–4
advocacy by newspapers 204–8
Agriculture Extension Department 83
Albuquerque Journal 296
All-American Country Weekly Newspaper 92
Allen, Charles 35, 76, 81, 83–4
all-home-print publications 30, 32, 43, 45, 49
The Alton Democrat 116
American Association of Teachers of Journalism 132
American Country Life Association 78
American History Puzzles 27
American immigration to Canada 47–9
American journalism 1
The American Journal of Sociology 75
The American Magazine 26
The American Mercury 88
American Newspaper Publishers Association 59

The American Political Science Review 77
The American Press 9
American Press Association 45, 118, 143, 165
  ready-print business 46
American Telegraph and Telephone Company 82
An Alabama Newspaper Tradition: Grover C. Hall and the Hall Family (Hollis, III) 8
Anderson, Sherwood 9, 85–6
antitrust laws 55
Associated Advertising Clubs of the World 50
Association of Free Community Papers 327
The Atlantic Monthly 134
Atwood, Millard V. 78, 89
Audit Bureau of Circulations 50

B

Bagdikian, Ben H. 207
Barnhart, Thomas 102, 129, 145
  journalism career 141
  textbooks for journalism students 141
  Weekly Newspaper Management 141, 172–3
bartering with subscribers 112–13
Bedford Gazette 137
Ben Franklin Club 54
Bernstein, Carl 240
Big Piney Examiner 80
Bittinger, Paul 116
Black Tuesday 93
Blanchard, Robert 241
Bleyer, Willard 33
Blonien, J. J. 327
Bloom, J. H. 56–7
boilerplate material 18, 24–5, 27, 35, 37, 43, 45, 169
Bond, Charles 119
boosterism 64–5
Bourne Newspaper Publicity law 50

Bowers, George E. 116
Bowker, R. R. 33
Boyles, Kate 29
Boyles, Virgil 29
Branned, William E. 203
The Brass Check 64
Brook, Alexander 9, 179–81, 205, 265–6, 340
Brooks, Jr., B. V. 262
The Brookshire (TX) Times 74–5
Bryan, William Jennings 51
The Bully Pulpit (Goodwin) 9
Burlington Standard Press 203
business boom-or-bust cycle 73
The Butts County Progress 64–5

C

The Caledonia Argus 85
Callahan, Lt. North 131
The Cambridge City Tribune 120n3
Campbell, Claude V. 345–6
Carter, Hodding 9, 182–3
Casa Grande Dispatch 134, 136
Casey, John H. 91
Cash, W. J. 87
Cavin, Lee 187
censorship regulations 59
Centralia (WA) Weekly Chronicle 51
Cervi, Gene 182
Ceylon Herald 227
Chapin, Earl V. 9
Cherokee Advocate 8
Cheshire, H. D. 47
Chicago Chronicle 24
child labor 77
Chillicothe (MO) Constitution 28
Clarion Democrat 227
Clarion Republican 227
Clark, Carroll D. 82
Clark, Edward B. 26
Clark, James "Champ" 47
Clark, Neil M. 26, 28

Clark, Thomas D. 88
college journalism 18, 240–3
  enrollment growth in 241, 243–4
college journalism programs 30
commercial printing 19
Committee on Public Information (Creel Committee) 129
community bulletin board 176–80
Community Conflict and the Press (Tichenor, Donohue, and Olien) 8
community editor 8
  editor-publisher role 338
community editors 204
community journalism 163, 201–2, 243–4, 341
community newspaper 166
  accountability 142
  editor's role 84–6
  as a social instrument 142
The Community Newspaper 201
community newspapers
  business and government lobbyists, influence of 44–5
  business of 18–23
  categories of topics 24
  competition between dailies and 34–7
  endorsements for formal journalism education 33–4
  importance of 77–9
  influential role 83–4
  national and world event coverage 25
  newspaper syndicate services, impact of 19, 23–4
  paper costs and postal rates, impact of 55–7
  political voice and profit margin 37
  profit margin 37
  as propaganda tools 44–50, 128–31
  war propaganda 58–63
The Community Press in an Urban Setting (Janowitz) 8
Contris, Joseph J. 204
correspondent reports 109
Cotton, Joseph S. 132

country correspondents 109–10
country editors 84–6, 92, 187–8, 337
  charitable drives and campaigns for relief funds 103–4
  formal education *vs.* traditional apprenticeship 86–7
  merchant-*versus*-editor relationship 117
Country Home 109
country journalism 44, 91, 93, 102
  back-to-the-country movement 104–8, 110
  community leadership roles 102–4
  fairness and favoritism 110
  free publicity 53
The Country Newspaper 9, 78
The Crane Chronicle 86
Crawford, Bruce 113
Creel, George 58
Cresco Plain Dealer 49
Crowell, Merle 84
crusading editor 2
Cuban missile crisis 202
The Cucamonga Times 212
Cummins, Albert 46
Cutler, John H. 9

D

daily and non- daily publishing communities 2
Deal, Charles 204
Debs, Eugene V. 51
The Deming Headlight 120n4
Democratic newspapers 91
Deseret (UT) News 7
desktop publishing 2
Dispatch Democrat 135
Door-for-Gore campaign 186
Dow Jones Newspaper Fund 242
Dragon, Peter 220–1
Dumas, James H. 299
Duncan, Charles T. 145, 179–80
Dunn, Arthur 56

E

The Eagle 88
Early Utah Journalism (Alter) 7
East, P.D. 9, 184–5
East Bay Classifieds 298
economic status of small-town journalism 88–90
Edelstein, Alex 203–4
Editor & Publisher International Yearbook 9
Eisenhower, Dwight D. 180, 186
The Elizabethtown Chronicle 294
Empey, Arthur Guy 49
Emporia Gazette 30–1, 133–4
Espionage Act of 1917 61
The Evening Sun 167

F

Federal Communications Commission 76
Fink, Conrad 295
Fish, H.H. 46
Fitzwater, Rev. P.B. 49
The Florence Herald 178–9, 206, 212, 221
Forbes, Malcolm 146
foreign advertising 90
formal journalism education, impacts of 33–4
free advertising 81
Freehold Transcript 92
free-in-county circulation privilege 57
Freeman, J.R. 213–14
free publicity 43–4, 50–4, 144–5, 214–16
  anti-liquor and pro-Prohibition editorials 52
  business opportunities and losses 54–5
  of pharmaceutical products 53
  presidential publicity campaigns 51
Friedman, Rick 205–6

G

Georgia Journalism 1763-1950 (Griffith and Talmadge) 7
Georgia Press Association 7
German war propaganda 62
Glass, Frank 59
Gore, Leroy 186
government printing contracts 20
Graduate School at the University of Georgia 7
Grassroots Editor 9
grassroots journalism 1
Greater Kentucky Publishing, Inc. 226
The Greenburgh Independent 260
The Guthrian 206–7
Gwin, Frank 36

H

Harding, Warren G. 85
Hardy, Albert 137
Harger, Charles 32, 36–7, 81
Harris, Emerson 89, 92
Harter, Eugene 170, 178
Hearst, William C. 227
The Hendricks (MN) Pioneer 19–20, 24
Henry W. Grady School of Journalism 7
Herbert, Benjamin Briggs 35
Highland Mills (NY) Star 75
The History and Development of Advertising (Presbrey) 6
Home Town News: William Allen White and the Emporia Gazette (Griffith) 9
Hooke, Elizabeth 89, 92
The Hopewell Herald 116, 123n58
Hotaling, H. C. 57, 114
Hough, Henry Beetle 9, 115, 130
"Household Affairs" column 27
Hubbard News and Reporter 223–4
Hussman Jr., Walter 318

I

The Indiana (PA) Democrat 27, 32
International Harvest Company 83
International Paper & Power Company 87
International Press Institute 226

J

Jackson Herald 221
job opportunities at weeklies 111–12
job-printing services 19, 116–17, 169–70
Joslyn, George 25, 46, 48, 50
Journalism Quarterly 9
Junkin, John E. 20

K

Kansas Editorial Association 62
KDKA radio station 76
Kellogg, Ansel Nash 6, 19, 80
Kellogg Company 19, 23, 25–9, 36
Kelly, Brian 297
Kennebunk Star 179
Kennedy, Bruce M. 243
Kerrville Mountain Sun 134, 136
Kettlitz, H.F. 62
Key West Citizen 179
King Features Syndicate of New York 129
Kocher, Ben 243
Ku Klux Klan 88

L

labor publications 1
Lake Elsinore Valley Sun 243
Lake Grove Press 167
Lanston, Tolbert 21
Larson, Cedric 58
Laurel (MS) Ledger 28
Lee, Robert E. 33

leisure reading 150
Lesher Communications, Inc. 320
The Lexington Advertiser 212
Liberty Loan Drive 60
Life 150
Lindsey, Betterman 29
Little, Luther B. 51
local news *vs.* syndicated material 29–32
The Logansport (IN) Chronicle 59–60
Lovejoy, Elijah Parish 184
Lynd, Helen 77
Lynd, Robert 77

M

The Malakoff News 295
Marshall Plan 153
Martin, John D. "Jack" 178, 221
McCormick, Medill 51
McCoy, Bruce 110
McKean County Democrat 133–4
McKinney, John 243
McMillan, M.H. 46
Meredith Jr., C.M. 102
Mergenthaler, Ottmar 21
Meter, John Van 206
metropolitan dailies 249–50
metropolitan newspapers 34–5
Middletown: A Study in American Culture (R. S. Lynd and H. M. Lynd) 8
Milam, J. 113
Miller, Douglass W. 132
Millford Chronicle 92
The Milwaukee Leader 61
Mock, James 58
Monticello (IA) Express 62
Montross, Lynn 81
Moreau, D. Howard 142
Morelock, T.C. 92
Mount Pleasant Journal 117
multi- week publication schedule 17
Munsey's Magazine 23 51

N

"names make news" approach 24
National Blue Ribbon Newspaper "accreditation" program 243
National Editorial Association 57
National Editorial Journalist and Printer and Publisher (National Printer- Journalist) 35
National Newspaper Association 225–6, 258–62, 296
National Press Club 85
National Printer- Journalist 9
National Publisher 9
National Road Traveler 177
national theme weeks 116
National Weekly Newspaper Service 129
New Albany (IN) Public Press 36
New Mexico Independent 296
The New Republic 82, 113
newsgathering 18
newspaper business, 1930s 99–100
    advertising accounts 114–15
    bartering with subscribers 112–13
    charitable drives and campaigns for relief funds 103–4
    consolidations and closings of weeklies 110
    effects of Depression 100, 110
    golden rule approach to business 100–2
    strategy for business survival 114–15
    surviving and thriving of weeklies 110, 118–20
newspaper business, 1940s
    advertisement management 143–7, 149
    advertisements of soldier recruiting methods 131
    community pricing on foods and other items 135
    coverage on racism 151–2
    features on farm wives 149
    first-person accounts of battlefronts and foreign travels 129
    focus on women's wartime homemaking roles 134–6
    free publicity 144–5
    gender makeup of college journalism 131–2
    informational columns and articles 129
    internment camp newspapers 132–3
    newspaper syndicates 129
    news wire services 129–30
    number of weekly newspapers 132
    postwar changes in news preferences 147–8
    postwar recovery efforts 137
    production problems related to wartime 127–8
    professionalism 141–3
    public relations program 144
    reports on polio cases 151–3
    use of community correspondent 129
    use of press wire and photographs 137–41
    war bonds campaigns 133–4
    Warsaw bombings 130
    war-support campaigns 136–7
newspaper business, 1950s
    advertisements 168
    advertising revenue 189
    average newspaper income per subscriber 188
    campaigns against Ku Klux Klan 183, 185
    community bulletin board 176–80
    conservatism of country editors 187–8
    coverage on racism 183–5
    defending unpopular causes and civil liberties 183–5
    distinction between rural and suburban weeklies 167–8
    importance of local news 180–2
    job-printing service 169–70
    locally written editorial opinion and assertions 187
    new "pioneer printers" 167
    newspaper ownership 172–4
    offset and rotary printing 170–2

opportunities for community
  newspapers 166
press-operating times 170
profitability plan of group
  ownership 174–6
promotional advertisements 170
ready-print service 168–9
reliance on syndicated opinions 186–7
shift of population and decrease in
  weeklies 165–8
suburban market 166–7
suspensions of weeklies 165–6
syndicated opinion columns 186–9
turnover in reporter staffs 180–1
weekly newspapers editorial
  comments 181–3
newspaper business, 1960s
  advertisement management 200
  advertisement revenues 220–1
  average income per subscriber 228
  average subscription rates 223
  business outlook for weeklies 228
  circulation among weeklies 224–5
  community advocacy 204–8
  community journalism 201–2
  community leadership role 199
  competition for subscriptions 222–6
  editorial, opinion column and personal
    column 199
  free publicity 214–16
  offset services 219
  operating by regional concept 226–8
  "paid" and "free" weeklies 222–3
  photocomposition technology 228
  politically conservative and progressive
    newspapers 208–10
  printing of supplements 221
  printing quality 222
  recruitment of reporters 216–22
  regional concept 200
  self-congratulatory reporting 210–12
  sponsorship of special events 222
  "unpleasant happenings"
    headlines 212–14

weeklies' role in leadership,
  decision-making 202–4
newspaper business, 1970s
  computer technology and changes in
    operations 240, 263–5
  content of weeklies 240, 246–51
  free and paid circulation 261–2
  group and chain ownership 240,
    256–63, 265
  job market 239
  journalism enrollment 241, 243–4
  management opportunities for
    women 244–6
  newsprint shortages and unionization
    threats 265
  product promotion or political
    posturing 251–3
  readers of weeklies 253–6
  salaries of newsroom employees 242
  tax laws and 259
newspaper business, 1980s 277
  advertisements 278
  advertising revenues 293–5
  changes in operating costs 293–7
  community involvement and leadership
    of newspaper editors 286–91
  consolidations and chain
    ownership 298–9
  editorial content of paid weekly 293
  editorial staff layoffs 296
  hiring standards for community
    weeklies 283–6
  national newspaper chain
    consolidations 278
  opportunities for women and agricultural
    reporters 292–3
  reporting of national and international
    events 277
  slash-and-burn operation 299
  technological advancements, impact
    of 277–83
newspaper business, 1990s
  advertising space purchases 310
  cost-cutting measures 310

focus on localism 309–17
   free circulation *vs.* community
      weeklies 327–8
   percentage of revenue 318
   recruitment and retainment of
      employees 323–6
   revenue-enhancing strategies 318–23
   Wal-Mart stores and 318–19
newspaper chains 119
Newspaper Enterprise Association of
   Cleveland 129
newspaper readership 344
newspaper syndicates
   audience of 43
   federal government intervention in
      affairs 46
   locally generated news and editorials
      vs. 29–32
   power and influence of 25–9
   prominent users of syndicate
      materials 340
   propaganda distribution 45–50
   1940s 129
   services, impact of 19, 23–5
   as silent partner 25
   syndicated advertising services 116
   trade war between W.N.U. and
      A.P.A. 45–50
   use in propaganda campaigns 46–7
Newspaper Union 45
New York Call 61, 64
The New York Times 56, 58, 62, 87, 132
The New York Tribune 80
Nieman Reports analysis of weeklies 180
N.W. Ayer & Son's American Newspaper
   Annual and Directory 91
N.W. Ayer & Son's Directory of Newspapers
   and Periodicals 9

O

Obert, John C. 187, 207
Official Bulletin 58

offset printing 117, 164, 219, 278
Oklahoma Heritage Association 7
Oklahoma Newspaper Foundation 7
Oklahoma Press Association 7
one-order, one-bill program for
   advertisers 320
The Outlook 81–2
ownership of a country newspaper 93

P

Padgett, George 241–2
paper costs 55–7
patriotism 58–63
patriot press 127
Patterson, Wright A. "Pat" 26, 28, 31, 52,
   53, 60, 64, 146
Pearl Harbor bombing 127, 129
Perry, John H. 84, 118
photo-offset 170–1
poliomyelitis epidemics 151
political organs 32
political propaganda 83
Porte, Roy T. 54
Porte Publishing Company 54
postal rates 55–7
postmaster-publisher 18
printer- publisher 18
printing jobs 54
Procter, Colonel William Cooper 119
product publicity 81
professional associations 225–6
profitability of newspapers 92
profit margin of community weeklies 37
publication industry 2
Publick Occurrences Both Forreign and
   Domestick 18
Public Opinion Quarterly 9
The Publishers' Auxiliary 9, 19, 21, 25, 131,
   152, 225
   advantages of consolidations 257
   barter with subscribers 113
   boxed advertisements 171

college journalism 217
community-controlled paper 260
financial struggle of weeklies 140, 260
free-in-county privilege of country newspapers 57
government printing services 20
illiteracy problem 344
importance of editorial writing 256
literary serials 29
metropolitan dailies 250
postal zone system 56
power of weekly newspaper editorials 145
price of an annual weekly subscription, 1920s 90
printing operations of weeklies 256–7
profitability of job shops 257
publicity opportunities 61
staff recruitment 131, 217
staff reduction 242
"stellar" weeklies 92
study of Missouri weekly newspapers 214–15
support for journalism students 141
pure advertising 76

Q

Quaife, Milton M. 80

R

radio 73–4
  advertising revenues 74–7
  advertising through program sponsorship 114
  coverage of local issues of importance 188
  programming 76
  1940s 130–1
  stations 76–7
Rae, Walter 171
railroads 76
Rand, Clayton 9

The Readers' Digest 150
readership satisfaction surveys 142
Reading Times 118
ready-printed pages 6
  subscribers 79–80
  in weeklies 79
ready-print industry 45
ready-print service 168–9
Red Cross advertisements 59
regional concept 226–8
religious publications 1
Republican newspapers 91
The Richwood Gazette 113, 120n2
The Rio Grande Republican of Las Cruces, New Mexico 19–20
Rochester Times-Union 78
The Rocky Mount (NC) Weekly News 75
Rogers, Charles E. 142
Roosevelt, President Theodore 26
Rural Free Delivery 54–5
rural journalism 9

S

Safley, James Clifford 92
The Saturday Evening Post 89, 119, 150
Savannah Evening Press 297
school library 150
Schulz, J. Blaine 203
Scripps, James G. 118
Sears-Roebuck Agriculture Foundation 83
Sears Roebuck & Co. 319
Sedition Act of 1918 61
The Seguin Gazette 201
Seitz, D.C. 87
The Selinsgrove Times 117–18
sensationalism 2
The Sheffield Standard 93, 116
Shurtleff III, W.H. 224
The Sikeston Herald 177
Sim, John Cameron 166
Sinclair, Upton 51, 64
  The Brass Check 51–2

single-sponsor programs 73
Small Town in Mass Society (Vidich and Bensman) 8
Smith, Alfred E. 87
Smith, Courtland 47
Smith, Hazel Brannon 212–13
Smith, O. E. 53
Smoky Mountain Star 299
soft news 24–6
Sorrells, John H. 136
Southern Indiana Press Association 36
special- interest weeklies 1
Spencer Times- Record 119
Standard Oil Company 82
Standard Oil Corporation 76
Stanford, Al 227
Steiner, Jesse Frederick 75, 79–80, 82
Stevens Point (WI) Gazette 53
Stewart, Sharon 319
stock market crash of 1929 74
Stone, Park F. 184
The Story of Advertising (Wood) 6
Story of Oklahoma Newspapers 1844 to 1984 (Carter) 7
suburban communities 1
survival of newspaper business 74, 338, 344–6
  1930s 110, 114–15, 118–20
  1950s 165, 183
  1970s 260
  1980s 289
  1990s 320
"survival of the fittest" factor 146
Switzler, William 33
syndicate material 18

T

Taft, William H. 50
The Taney County Republican 109
Taylor, Carl C. 78
television viewing 148–50
  commercials for time-saving products 148
  coverage of local issues of importance 188
  24-hour television news channel 277, 310, 328–9
  as a new entertainment option 148–9
Temby, Mabel 178
Thomas, T. H. 134
Thompson, Thomas E. 62
Time magazine 118, 207
The Titonka Topic 201
Town-Country Agency 78
Trading-with-the-Enemy Act of 1917 61
transient journalist 310
Trimont Progress 227
The Troy (IL) Weekly Call 27, 29
Truman, Harry 137, 186
Turner, George Kibbe 50
The Turners Falls Herald 132
The Tuscumbia Times 120n6

U

Underwood, Oscar 47
University of Georgia Press 7
University of Oklahoma School of Journalism 7
The Upland News 212
urban neighborhoods 1
U.S. Bureau of Education 83
Utica Observer-Dispatch 78

V

veiled propaganda 82–3
video display terminals (V.D.T.s) 263
The Vineyard Gazette 115, 130
Volk, Harry 166–7

W

The Wakefield Advocate 83
war bonds campaigns 133–4

war news 58–63, 128–31
　addressing personnel problems 63–4
　German war propaganda 62
　as informational 60
　publicity agents and 61
　tone of reporting 62–3
　Warsaw bombings 130
War Production Board 135
Warren, Robert L. 141
War Revenue bill 56
war-support campaigns 136–7
The Washington Post 47–8, 85, 134
Watson, Elmo Scott 79, 86, 146
The Wayne Herald 92
Weaver, Kenneth 221
weekly community newspapers 1
　accountability 142
　advertising rates 90
　advertising threat of radio 114
　annual weekly subscription charges 90
　boosterism 341
　business model 342–4
　community categories 1
　controversy related to patent medicine advertisements 6
　distinction between small-town and suburban weekly 341–2
　financial stability 88–90
　formal journalism education impacts 33–4
　impact of radio and television 3
　importance of 77–9
　investments 20
　in journalism histories 4–10
　localism 3, 340–1
　national and world event coverage 25
　newspaper syndicate services, impact of 19, 23–4
　numbers and distribution, 1900 to 1930 91
　political voice and profit margin 37
　professionalism 339
　role in information dissemination 3
　role in leadership, decision-making 202–4
　small-town 3
　as a social instrument 142
　subscribers 90
　survival of 338, 344–6
　threat of government intervention 3–4
　tonal writing 2
　twentieth-century 2–3, 10
　war propaganda 4
Wells, Jr., Horace V. 184
Western Newspaper Union 25, 45, 129, 143
　anti-liquor and pro-Prohibition editorials 52
　investigation of Canada's immigration 47–9
　non-controversial editorials 81
　ready-print business 46
　ready-print or stereotype plate services 52
　"Sunday School Lessons" column 49
　trade war between W.N.U. and A.P.A. 45–50
White, Horace 33
White, William Allen 9, 30–1, 133
Willey, Malcolm M. 79, 90–1
Williams, Walter 33
Wilson, Woodrow 50
Wirges, Gene 213
Women's Army Corps 135
"women's" columns 27
women's wartime homemaking roles 134–6
Wood, James Playsted 75
Woodward, Bob 240
Woodyard, Ted 119
Woodyard Associates, Inc. 119
Wright, Don C. 86
The Wright County Monitor 181

Y

York County Star 179

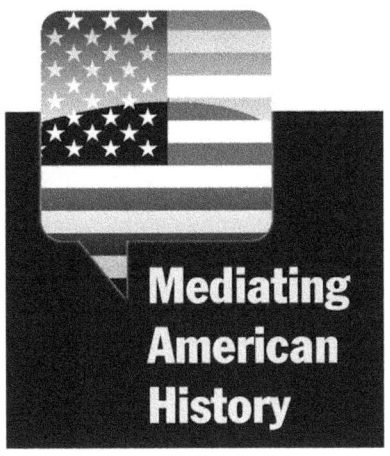

SERIES EDITOR: KIMBERLY WILMONT VOSS

Realizing the important role that the media have played in American history, this series provides a venue for a diverse range of works that deal with the mass media and its relationship to society. The new series is aimed at both scholars and students. New book proposals are welcomed.

For additional information about this series or for the submission of manuscripts, please contact:

      editorial@peterlang.com

To order other books in this series, please contact our Customer Service Department:

      peterlang@presswarehouse.com (within the U.S.)
      orders@peterlang.com (outside the U.S.)

Or browse by series:

      WWW.PETERLANG.COM

www.ingramcontent.com/pod-product-compliance
Ingram Content Group UK Ltd.
Pitfield, Milton Keynes, MK11 3LW, UK
UKHW022229230426
12048UKWH00016BA/1144